Goals for Mankind

Ervin Laszlo *et al.*

Goals for Mankind

A Report to the Club of Rome
on the
New Horizons of Global Community

E. P. Dutton
New York

Library of Congress Cataloging in Publication Data

Main entry under title:
Goals for mankind.

   Includes bibliographical references.
   1. Civilization, Modern—1950- I. Laszlo,
Ervin, 1932- II. Club of Rome.
CB430.G6 1977   909.82   76-30471
ISBN: 0-525-11430-0 (cloth)
       0-525-03455-2 (paper)

Published simultaneously in Canada by Clarke, Irwin & Company
Limited, Toronto and Vancouver

10 9 8 7 6 5 4 3 2 1

First Edition

Contents

Foreword

by Aurelio Peccei and Alexander King

If the ways of God are inscrutable, the path of man has become incomprehensible. Modern man, despite the wonderful body of knowledge and information that he has accumulated and the means to apply it, appears to be muddling ahead as if he were blind or drugged, staggering from one crisis to another. It is increasingly evident that he is unsure where he is going or where he wants to go beyond the next few tentative steps. Yet he has received all sorts of signals that he is treading fields that are heavily mined and require thorough exploration and mapping. Only by charting his further course intelligently has he a chance of advancing into new territories offering immense opportunities for his continued enterprise.

The Club of Rome, which is a body concerned with the well-being of mankind as a whole, is future-oriented in its thinking and must necessarily take into account the incongruities of the human condition, its values and goals, both actual and desirable, if the species is to survive. That is why this book is warmly recommended to the reader. It comes fifth among the "Reports to the Club of Rome," while logic would have demanded that it be the first. The series of these reports, labeled "The Predicament of Mankind," opened with *The Limits to Growth,* the heretical analysis directed by Dennis Meadows. It denounced the growth obsession of a society in which every individual, family, group, corporation, or nation was trying to become bigger, richer, and more powerful all the time, without considering the ultimate costs of exponential growth. Expounding this simple theme, it drew to authors and sponsors a deluge of anathema and criticism, but triggered off a debate that resounded throughout the world.

In the footsteps of reasoning on limits, a further project was elaborated by Mihajlo Mesarovic and Eduard Pestel, published as *Mankind at the Turning Point.* It provided a badly needed tool for the present generation to assess in a rational manner their policies and strategies. At the same time it showed incisively the kind of traps and pitfalls awaiting all peoples and nations if they were to continue to be mesmerized by the threat of incumbent problems and the gains of expediency, without scrutinizing as carefully as possible what may happen ten or fifteen years hence. It also indicated the immense costs in money and human suffering of the delay in making decisions on some of the fundamental and unavoidable issues. This new tool, indispensable to decision-makers for their long-term planning, is still in the prototype stage and is undergoing continuous refinement and development. It is an encouraging sign, however, that even at this stage it is being tested out in many countries that are beginning to be sensitive to the longer-term future. One can envisage a time, not too distant, when thanks to this technique, a world network of decision centers will be in operation in mutual communication.

Then came *RIO: Reshaping the International Order,* a project led by Jan Tinbergen. Taking sides essentially with the poor and deprived of the world, it makes a meticulous analysis of the principles and measures that must be adopted if a more just and equitable—and hopefully more peaceful—world society is to be evolved; if the orientation is to be at last the human community as a whole.

Finally, still another Club of Rome–sponsored study was recently completed and is being published on the use of science and technology in the solution of a number of basic world problems. The authors, Dennis Gabor, Umberto Colombo, Alexander King, and Riccardo Galli try to show in their book, *Beyond the Age of Waste,* what the options are if science and technology are used wisely and well to enable society to extricate itself from its self-imposed plight and move toward a higher level of civilization.

However, a basic perplexity clouds all these efforts. What are, in reality, the goals of mankind? Is it willing to give human development precedence over material growth, to make those radical changes in its structure and behavior, which will be necessary if it is to put its house in order? Will it be ready to forgo the satisfaction of immediate desires in favor of future stability and the possibility of decent conditions of life for generations to come? Will it be able to use its enormous techno-scientific power with a long view, for the benefit of humanity as a whole and without damage to the planet? The importance of such questions is so fundamental that rationally, at this stage of human evolution, the discourse on the goals should come first. After having conquered the whole planet, our species, now teeming with people to an unprecedented extent (there are now four billion of us and soon there will be five billion), bursting with power (thanks to hitherto undreamed-of technologies and the promise of more to come), and impetuous as never before (being the fountainhead of change in the world), must ask itself where it wants to go and what it wishes to accomplish. The inquiry into what we are up to, what we can or should do with ourselves and future generations, should undoubtedly come first, if for no other reason than because without an overall design our frenzied activities can but give rise to colossal disorder—which is precisely what is beginning to occur today.

However, logic can be applied only when people are culturally and emotionally prepared to accept its exacting prescriptions. This is the justification for the sequence of our projects following the inverse path, starting with a comparison of dimensions on the global scale, moving next to consider the means to rationalize the decision-making process, and then to suggest the kind of order that should reign internationally and the better ways to harness the techno-scientific processes—leaving for later the definition of the goals, which all this is supposed to serve. We believe that the moment for inquiring into and defining our goals has now come.

In fact, in a matter of a very few years, with great perception and in unexpectedly large numbers, ordinary men and women throughout the world have become conscious that enormous dangers are hanging over the heads of all peoples and nations, irrespective of their economy, geography, technological prowess or their ideology, and that the marvelous promise inherent in this age is being frittered away, because our generation has failed to develop the understanding, the vision, and the willpower required to live in consonance with it. All over the world concerned individuals and groups of citizens want to know more, and do more, and are prepared to strive and make sacrifices to ensure a more durable society and a future fit for succeeding generations. Many of them are willing to overcome the present fatal divisions that tear mankind apart, and to stretch out their hands to potential or erstwhile adversaries, but they are confused and have yet to detect what actually are the basic interests they have in common, what attainable objectives they should pursue jointly. The present book tries to open a dialogue with a view to clarifying these issues and facilitating the search for the reasons for, and ways and means of, a new global venture uniting all peoples. It attempts to formulate the goals of the different regions, ideologies, and religions of the world with a view to establishing the extent to which common objectives exist which might become the nuclei of solidarity for all the peoples. It attempts to identify the gaps between the focus on short-term national concerns and long-term global considerations. It distinguishes, too, between the goals of different elements of a single society such as governments, business corporations, religious groups, intellectuals, and the broad masses of the people. The difficulties of such a task are enormous, and the present volume must be seen as a pioneering attempt that opens up this subject of major human significance, but which will have to be followed by a continuing, and even deeper, study of the value systems of societies and their interactions. One can always question the extent to which expressed goals are followed in individual, group, and national behavior; and one can ask how far people in some cases are in fact free to express their personal credos. There may be three layers of goals in reality: first, the overt and explicit formulations; second, the unexpressed and covert motivations that find expression in national or individual behavior, not always in harmony with the formulated objectives; and third, the unconscious goals of individuals and societies, which may conflict with all formulated motivations and may lead to internal frictions.

The stress of this volume is on the gaps between goals that concentrate on short-term issues and those that manifest a sufficient appreciation of long-term objectives and needs, necessary to tackle global problems. These gaps are clearly illustrated by a series of national goals charts, which distinguish the distribution of goals in several major policy sectors. These analyses do not intend to suggest that short-term issues are unimportant; in the economic sector, for example, it is essential that immediate matters should be taken seriously, otherwise the result would be poverty and social disruption. Rather, this report calls attention to the need to reconcile short-term realities with long-term needs.

It will be readily appreciated that the area covered by Ervin Laszlo and his army of collaborators and correspondents is so vast and complex that it is impossible to condense it into a volume of less than 500 pages while at the same time doing justice to all the forms and trends of human expectation, imagination, fear, and purpose concerning the future. The reader will find in these pages a rich if somewhat uneven treasury of insights and thoughts, and will probably judge many of them to be enlightening and significant, while some others less impressive. The atlas of contemporary goals is itself a major achievement. It is a challenge to human imagination and enterprise, much as the early world maps drawn by the sixteenth-century cartographers were for our ancestors. For Renaissance man the breakthrough was the discovery of the global reality of the planet he was set to conquer, while the breakthrough now is to create a new Renaissance of humanistic understanding of the logic of global functioning.

The book points out that if our goals are unrealistic, narrow, and shortsighted, world problems will lead to catastrophes, while if they are realistic and farsighted, new horizons of need fulfillment and peace can open for the world community. We fully share this view, but wish to warn that this should not be interpreted to mean that mankind is living in a situation of fifty-fifty probabilities, that the road to salvation is as easy as the present downward course to the precipice. The possibility for mankind to emerge safe and even stronger from its current multiple predicaments does exist, but the possibility that mankind will do so is frighteningly slim. The situation can be turned around and human prospects made bright only by a supreme concerted effort by all peoples and nations, before it is too late.

The simplest truths are the surest ones. That the health of the parts of any organism, for instance the human body, contributes to the soundness of the whole, and that the state of this whole conditions the functioning of each part, is an accepted truth. We easily recognize such a truth, but are reluctant to apply it to the world system. And yet modern society is caught in a race in which its own survival is at stake —a race between the eruption of global problems and a world mobilization to meet them before they become altogether intractable.

Ervin Laszlo calls this movement of mobilization "the world solidarity revolution." Whatever name we give it, we submit that it should spread not only horizontally to all nations—or rather to all peoples and human groups—but also vertically, to penetrate all strata of society. Human evolution is reaching a point where a greater cleavage now exists than that between nation and nation: one that is often cutting across the very body of nations, pitting class against class, race against race, the rich against the poor, the majority against the minority, and the governing against the governed. As a prerequisite for survival and progress, solidarity has indeed to be established to an extent where it can permeate global society in all directions. A condition for survival and progress can only be achieved by creating a communality (or at least a harmonious complementarity) of goals—which is precisely the supreme goal we must pursue today.

Preface

All societies in the world today are in a process of transformation. Technologies and institutions, as well as values, beliefs, and goals are changing. In industrialized societies optimistic belief in the automatic continuation of rapid economic growth has waned and its benefits are questioned. In communist countries confidence in the rapid achievement of world communism has been replaced by a more pragmatic interest in management of present structures and movements. The developing world is questioning the desirability of following traditional Western or communist strategies of development, and in the least developed and resource-poor countries belief in adequate and speedy development itself has given way to desperate efforts to ensure day-to-day survival.

These transformations are signs of deep-seated trends and tensions that pose major threats to the future of the human community. The countries of the industrialized world represent but 30 percent of the world's population, and will represent no more than 10 percent in the next century. They will not be able to continue their economic growth and the prodigious rate at which they use up the world's natural resources, while the great majority of the international community is forced toward a subsistence level of existence and suffers from malnutrition, unemployment, and disease. Moreover, the resource-poor developing countries will not be able to attain anything like parity with the material standard of living of the industrialized world unless the international economic order is reshaped, technologies are made more appropriate, and the governments and peoples of the affluent nations voluntarily change their attitudes. Even the resource-rich developing countries will find it impossible to achieve sufficient growth in their industry, agriculture, and institutions to render them competitive with the developed nations before their present sources of wealth are depleted.

While the aspirations and dreams of nations and peoples falter and change, their interdependence increases. Networks of trade crisscross the globe. Multinational corporations and international organizations exert increasing influence on the economic and political processes of nation-states. Exponential increases in strategic nuclear weapon capabilities and in sophisticated conventional arms threaten peace and life itself. Nonrenewable natural resources flow from the poor to the rich parts of the world and return only in small part as expensive industrial, agricultural, and consumer imports.

In our world of interdependence, the goals on which nations and peoples act assume crucial importance. If these are unrealistic, narrow, and shortsighted, world problems will lead to catastrophes, and amid mounting tensions the arms of ultimate destruction could finally come into use. If, on the other hand, governments, peoples, corporations, and organizations adopt realistic and farsighted goals, new horizons of need fulfillment and peace can open for the world community as nations extricate themselves from the precarious ties of interdependence and cooperatively strive for collective self-reliance.

What can be done to establish goals that are appropriate to the present global situation of mankind? Every individual citizen of planet Earth should face this question, for each person can play a meaningful and important role in promoting the healthy transformation of values and goals. This report suggests three areas where concerned individuals can contribute to the creation of a safer and more humane world.

First, all people should inform themselves of the current operative goals and aspirations of the world community. As established values are questioned, as technologies change and international power and wealth patterns shift, new values evolve; fresh perceptions begin to cause new and more appropriate goals to be set. Because what one society aspires toward affects its neighbors and, ultimately, all segments of the human community, a knowledge of the goals of all societies must be had by each. *We provide an overview of goals in today's world in Part I of this report.*

Second, everyone should gain a fair knowledge of the kind of long-term international goals which, if achieved, could bring about a safer and more humane world. A number of world-level policies and goals are being advocated and debated today, and their importance is gaining recognition among forward-looking people in all parts of the world. The best of these goals and projects must be systematically discussed and expertly defined. Eventually they must gain recognition as compass points in the direction-setting of all long-term policies, whether on the local, national, regional, or corporate level. *We offer a basic assessment of a variety of global goals in Part II of our report.*

Third, all concerned persons should play an active part in forwarding the adoption of beneficial goals-change in their cultures and societies. Religion, ethics, world views, and ideologies need to focus on breaking through mankind's current "inner limits," which, even more than the outer limits of finite resources and environment, constrain our alternatives for the future. Inner limits in the form of narrow and short-term goals must be overcome; more adequate goals need to be pursued, inspired by a greater sense of human solidarity. *We review the relevance of the great religions, as well as of the modern world views, to the issue of inner limits vs. world solidarity in Part III.*

Concerned individuals could incite a wide-ranging transformation of values and goals if they joined together with full knowledge of the goals pursued today, of the nature of the required global goals, of the gap between them, and of the motivating forces that could close the gap. Such a transformation of values and goals may be more important at the present time than the specification of further models, plans, and strategies, however expertly it may be done. Without the will to create a global community of peace, human fulfillment and solidarity, the best-intentioned plans for reform will not be carried out.

The new horizons of a global community can still be opened for mankind. To make this possible, peoples and nations must cooperate to harmonize, for the benefit of all, the goals which guide public policies and behavior. A change from self-centered and short-term goals to mankind-centered and long-term ones is in the interest of all people. To work for such a change has become a moral imperative for all who are concerned with the future of humanity.

The Goals for Mankind Contributors

This Report is the work of some one hundred thirty individuals, from many disciplines and from all parts of the world. Some have contributed original studies, commissioned by the project director; they constitute the International Project Team. Others have reviewed materials and provided additional information; they make up the roster of Project Consultants. A further group of eminent scholars has been consulted from time to time—this group constitutes the Panel of Distinguished Advisors.

All who have contributed to *Goals for Mankind* express their own views, and these may or may not reflect, or coincide with, those of their governments, institutions, and organizations. Since in some countries distinctions between personal and official views are blurred, a few contributors, who believe that their personal views may not reflect those of the ruling governments, asked to have their names withheld. Thus their contributions have proved to be selfless and are all the more appreciated.

Those whose names are clearly associated with this Report must, however, be guarded from unjust censure. The material presented here is in part politically sensitive, and responsibility for it must rest solely with the project director. He assembled the final text, often from a variety of sources, including inputs from several contributors and consultants. Thus individual contributors may dissent from given formulations even in sections to which they have directly contributed. In a world of imperfect freedom of expression and sensitivity of national egos, such right to dissent needs to be stressed and will, it is hoped, be clearly respected.

The International Project Team (in alphabetical order)

Goals of the Soviet Union
V. G. Afanasiev
Soviet Academy of Sciences
Moscow, USSR

Goals in Poland
Ludwig Jerzy Baworowski
Technical University
Wrocław, Poland

Official goals in Eastern Europe
Mihail C. Botez
with Mariana Celac,
Paul Dimitriu,
Ileana Ionescu-Siseti, Ana-
Maria Sandi, and Adrian
Vasilescu
Center of Methodology of
Future and Development Studies
Bucharest, Romania

Goals in English-speaking West Africa
Kodwo Ewusi
University of Ghana
Legon, Ghana

Goals in the northwestern countries of Latin America
Juan Antonio Gomez
with Jaime Bustamante, Horatio
Godoy, and Alvaro Soto
University of Bogota
Bogota, Colombia

Global security goals
David C. Gompert
Council on Foreign Relations
New York, USA

Islam and world solidarity
Wadi Z. Haddad
MacDonald Center for the Study
of Islam and Christian-Muslim
Relations
Hartford, Connecticut, USA

Christianity and world solidarity
John Harwood-Jones
Ottawa, Canada

Goals of Japan
Shigeyuki Itow
with Teiich Aoyama,
Toshiaki Izeki, Churo Nobe,
Yoshihito Sumiyoshi,
Nobuo Tomita, and
Hisakazu Usui
Tokyo, Japan

Global socio-economic, energy, resource, and food goals
Thomas E. Jones
New School for Social Research
New York, USA

The Chinese tradition and world solidarity
Hwa-Yol Jung
with Petee Jung
Moravian College
Bethlehem, Pennsylvania, USA

Goals of the European alternative cultures
Robert Jungk
Salzburg, Austria

Goals of multinational corporations, case studies
Asterios G. Kefalas
University of Georgia
Athens, Georgia, USA

Goals of the United Nations
Donald F. Keys
Planetary Citizens
New York, USA

Goals in the Middle East and North Africa
Bijan Khorram
with Parviz Esmaelzadeh,
Jamshid Gharajedaghi,
Saeed Rahnema,
Daryush Ashouri, and
Cyrus Sakhalili
Industrial Management Institute
Teheran, Iran

Goals of the European Community
I. B. F. Kormoss
College of Europe
Bruges, Belgium

The African traditions and world solidarity
Issiaka-Prosper Lalèyê
Nouakchott, Mauretania

Marxism and world solidarity
Donald C. Lee
University of New Mexico
Albuquerque, New Mexico, USA

Goals in Sub-Sahara Africa
Aklilu Lemma with
Asefa Mehretu
University of Addis Ababa
Addis Ababa, Ethiopia

Goals of the People's Republic of China
Paul T. K. Lin
Montreal, Canada
with Han-sheng Lin
Sonoma, California, USA

Buddhism and world solidarity
Joanna Rogers Macy
Syracuse University
Syracuse, New York, USA

Goals in the United States
O. W. Markley
with David MacMichael, Ruth
Miller, and Peter Schwartz
Stanford Research Institute
Palo Alto, California, USA

Goals of the Italian Communist Party, the World Council of Churches, and the Roman Catholic Church
Eleonora Barbieri Masini
with Barbara Terenzi Baruchello,
Cristina Lombardini,
Luigi Pelizzoli, and
Carlo Virgilio
Rome, Italy

Goals in east central Africa
Kiwuto Ndeti
Center for African Family
Studies
Njoro, Kenya

Goals in Scandinavia, global energy and resource goals, analysis and integration of goals charts
Jørgen Nørgård
with Bente Christensen
Copenhagen, Denmark

Goals in Australia
Peter North
North Sidney, Australia

Goals in Canada
John O'Manique
Carleton University
Ottawa, Canada

Goals in Latin America, alternative cultures and world solidarity
Janis A. Roze
City University of New York
New York, USA

Goals in French-speaking West Africa
Seydou Madani Sy
University of Dakar
Dakar, Senegal

Goals of the International Labour Organisation
Albert Tévoèdjré
International Institute for
Labour Studies
Geneva, Switzerland

Goals in Southeast Asia
Robert O. Tilman
North Carolina State University
with Phan Thien Chau, R.
William Liddle, and Clark D.
Neher
Raleigh, North Carolina
Lawrenceville, New Jersey,
Columbus, Ohio, and DeKalb,
Illinois, USA

Goals in India
T. K. N. Unnithan
with Gerda Unnithan
University of Rajasthan
Jaipur, India

Goals in Hungary
Iván Vitányi
with Elemér Hankiss and
István Kiss
Institute for Culture
Budapest, Hungary

Liberal democracy and world solidarity
Edward Walter
University of Missouri
Kansas City, Missouri, USA

Hinduism and world solidarity
Charlotte Waterlow
Cambridge, Massachusetts, USA

Islam and world solidarity
James G. Williams
Syracuse University
Syracuse, New York, USA

Goals of multinational corporations
Ian H. Wilson
General Electric Company
Fairfield, Connecticut, USA

Project Consultants

Yoshio Abe, Tokyo, Japan
Paul Abrecht, Geneva, Switzerland
Radh Achuthan, Southampton, New York, USA
Aqueil Ahmad, Hyderabad, India
Ahmad Ashraf, Teheran, Iran
Kamal Azfar, Karachi, Pakistan
Archie J. Bahm, Albuquerque, New Mexico, USA
Joseph Barnea, United Nations (New York)
David Brooks, Ottawa, Canada
Carlos Manuel Castillo, San José, Costa Rica
John Coleman, Ottawa, Canada
Ian Connerty, Ottawa, Canada
J. J. N. Cooper, Bruges, Belgium
Arthur Cordell, Ottawa, Canada
Mohammed A. El-Badry, United Nations (New York)
Hamid Enayat, Teheran, Iran
T. L. de Fayer, Ottawa, Canada
Eckhard Festag, Chicago, Illinois, USA
Gerald Garvey, Princeton, New Jersey, USA
Harold Geltmann, Ottawa, Canada
Jan Geyer, Amsterdam, Holland
Walter A. Hahn, Washington, D.C., USA
Robert D. Hamrin, Washington, D.C., USA
Hiroshi Honda, Tokyo, Japan
Helio Jaguaribe-Mattos, Rio de Janeiro, Brazil
Douglas Jolley, Ottawa, Canada
Mohammed Kassas, Cairo, Egypt
Leopold Kohn, Portland, Oregon, USA
Paul A. LaViolette, Portland, Oregon, USA
Donald R. Lesh, Washington, D.C., USA
Harold A. Linstone, Portland, Oregon, USA

Dennis L. Little, Washington, D.C., USA
M.-J. Lory, Bruges, Belgium
Robert McKinnell, Ottawa, Canada
Robert H. Murray, Portland, Oregon, USA
James Moore, Ottawa, Canada
Michael Nagel, Los Angeles, California, USA
Kaoru Okano, Tokyo, Japan
M. P. Pandit, Sri Aurobindo Ashram, India
Geoffrey Pearson, Ottawa, Canada
Helveg Petersen, Copenhagen, Denmark
Carl Riskin, New York, USA
Dorothy Rosenberg, Ottawa, Canada
Devendra Sahal, Portland, Oregon, USA
Kjell Samuelson, Stockholm, Sweden
Clyde Sanger, Ottawa, Canada
W. H. C. Simmonds, Ottawa, Canada
Leon Tabah, United Nations (New York)
Nestor E. Terleckyj, Washington, D.C. USA
Hugo Thiemann, Vevey, Switzerland
Inga Thorsson, Stockholm, Sweden
Kemal Tosun, Istanbul, Turkey
Robert Triffin, New Haven, Connecticut, USA
William Watts, Washington, D.C., USA
Thomas W. Wilson, Jr., United Nations (New York)
S. H. Wittwer, East Lansing, Michigan, USA
Jong Y. Yoo, Seoul, Korea
Antoine Zahlan, Beirut, Lebanon

Panel of Distinguished Advisors

Ralph W. Burhoe
Philippe De Seynes
Karl W. Deutsch
Richard A. Falk
Gerald Feinberg
Charles Hartshorne
K. B. Madsen
Margaret Mead
Saul Mendlovitz
John Platt
Ilya Prigogine
Adam Schaff
Glenn T. Seaborg
Hans Selye
Albert Szent-Györgyi
Alastair M. Taylor
Paul A. Weiss

Project Offices and Staff

College of Arts and Science
State University of New York
Geneseo, New York, USA

Anthony J. Fedanzo, assistant to the project director
Mrs. Nancy Moran, secretary to the project director

United Nations Institute for Training and Research (UNITAR)
New York, USA

Thomas E. Jones and J. Arnold Roze, research associates

John Harwood-Jones (Ottawa) and Richard Coe (Boston), editorial consultants

Joel Katz (Haverford, Pennsylvania, USA), design and artwork

Ervin Laszlo, project director

Goals for Mankind

Part I:
A World Atlas
of Contemporary
Goals

Research on international and world issues has been increasing in recent years. World politics and security, energy, food, and resource issues have been researched and reported; computer models of the world have made their appearance, and international opinion surveys have been conducted. But the goals of the many societies and organizations of mankind have not been systematically and jointly investigated. Yet the survey and assessment of contemporary goals is feasible, and it is of great importance, even though goals are value-sensitive and values are notoriously difficult to express with precision, and notwithstanding the political and practical difficulties of canvassing all societies and organizations whose goals are of international significance.

The first world goal survey—although a preliminary and tentative one—is presented in Part I of this report. It brings together information on the goals and objectives pursued today by nations, regions, corporations, and international organizations.

Social, economic and political processes in this world are not governed by fate, but are sensitive to human decisions. These are made in the light of certain values and perceptions, and issue in goals and objectives. While the results are often different from expectations, many human decisions influence social and economic processes the world over. For example, when Arab leaders temporarily closed the valves of Mid-East oil fields, and subsequently quadrupled the price of oil, the effects went beyond the anticipated political pressure and higher income, and necessitated a complex range of international adjustments, not only in politics and finance, but also in industry, commerce, agriculture, and lifestyles. Similarly, the stockpiling of weapons by great and small nations is intended for national defense, but its ripple effects influence global power balances as well as economic and social processes. The self-centered economic growth ambitions of industrialized nations have a negative effect on the availability of fossil fuels and raw materials in world markets. On the other hand, the national resource policies of developing countries often drive up the price of such resources, and therewith put new constraints on the growth of industrialized nations. Pronatalist policies in high-fertility nations impact not only on balances of power in their region (often the prime consideration) but also on the level of pressure exerted on the international economic and monetary systems—and so on.

Our interdependent world is atomized in its pursuit of goals. Nations, corporations, and organizations set goals in the light of their own perceived immediate interests, and hope that by achieving them they will somehow benefit others. In truth, they often expose these others, and even themselves, to unpleasant surprises. The economist Adam Smith talked of an "invisible hand" that harmonizes the interests of people bent on achieving their own goals. Today it has been suggested that Smith's invisible hand has turned into an invisible foot which kicks back when and where one least expects it. Hence, both in the enlightened self-interest of individuals, organizations, and nations, and in the interest of the human community as a whole, the spectrum of current goals must become better known, and the need to orchestrate them to mutual benefit given more serious consideration.

The world atlas of contemporary goals presented here constitutes a first attempt to satisfy this requirement. It needs to be followed by more detailed studies, and by increasingly sophisticated computations of reciprocal effects. But the beginning is mutual awareness of intentions. It is this purpose that our world atlas is designed to serve, and it is here that, notwithstanding its preliminary and sketchy nature, it may render a service.

Section 1:
An Atlas of National and Regional Goals

In the first of the two sections of our world atlas of contemporary goals we survey and summarize the currently dominant as well as the emerging operational goals of the world's nations and multinational regions. These goals express the aspirations of governments, intellectuals, business groups, and the various urban and rural population strata concerning their own future in the local, regional, or world context. Goals and aspirations tell us what people and institutions expect of themselves, and of those with whom they interact, and thus what others, in turn, may expect of them. The descriptions provide a broad panorama, encompassing a wide range and variety of goals. Readers can nevertheless note recurring patterns and underlying similarities, and may recognize their own goals paralleled, with cultural variations, in other parts of the globe. Yet the fallacy of assuming that all people want the same thing everywhere will also become apparent. Beyond the goals of sheer physical survival, goals and ob-

5

jectives diversify and show that indeed, "It takes all kinds to make a world."

No value judgments are intended in the description of the various kinds of contemporary goals. The equal rights of human beings should surely include the right to express goals and expectations, and to be heard without prejudice. While this does not imply that all goals are ultimately equally humane, or universally beneficial in their consequences, it does mean that the right to express one's goals should be vouchsafed to everyone. Indeed, unless this right is guaranteed and actively exercised, the nature and the appropriateness of current goals cannot be ascertained. Hence, while in the subsequent parts of this report we shall compare current goals with universally desirable global goals, we first present national and regional goals on their own terms in an attempt to give them as fair and clear a presentation as the limited space available permits.

We cover the map of the world in two broad sweeps. The more northerly one begins in the west with Canada and the United States, crosses to Western Europe, then to the Soviet Union and Communist Eastern Europe. It moves on to the People's Republic of China and ends at the Far East with Japan.

The more southerly sweep begins in Mexico, moves down to South America, then crosses the Atlantic to Africa and the Middle East. It continues with India and Southeast Asia, and ends with Australia. Readers can, however, follow their own itineraries, or pick out such nations and regions as are of particular interest to them.

Chapter 1

Goals in Canada and in the United States

I. Goals in Canada

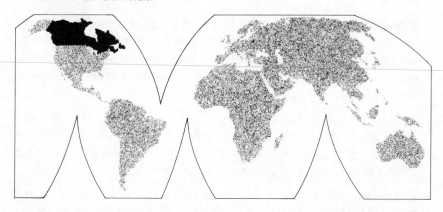

With its area of 9.4 million square kilometers (3.6 million square miles), Canada is one of the largest countries in the world, yet it has a population of only 23.6 million. The average density of 2.5 persons per square kilometer is about one-tenth the density of the United States of America, which has approximately the same area. But this comparison is misleading. Because of climate and terrain, much of Canada is not suitable for urban development or industrial activity.

Yet Canada is highly urbanized, in that three-quarters of its population live in cities and towns situated along a corridor bordering the
U.S.A. and comprising only about 1 percent of the nation's land area.
Two-thirds of the urban population cluster in twelve large cities and
six metropolitan areas. If the recent high rate of urbanization continues (4 percent a year), 90 percent of the population will be urbanized by the year 2000, and 75 percent will be concentrated in
twelve cities which, incidentally, can grow only at the expense of
some of Canada's best agricultural land.

The country has a number of other paradoxical features:

Canada fronts on three oceans and has perhaps the longest coastline of any country in the world. Yet Canada is not one of the major
shipping nations.

Canada has one of the largest and most productive continental
shelves in the world. Yet its annual harvest of fish is modest compared with that of many other nations that fish close to Canada's
coast.

Canada occupies some 6.3 percent of the world's total land area,
yet it has little more than one-half of 1 percent of the world's population.

Canada is responsible for the fragile ecology of vast Arctic areas.
Yet about 33 percent of its population is concentrated in the Great
Lakes–St. Lawrence basin, far from the Arctic, and only 20 percent
of its population lives more than 100 miles away from the United
States border.

Though the latest estimates of the reserves of coal, oil, gas, and
uranium are less optimistic than earlier estimates, Canada still has
considerable energy resources. Yet it has long had to depend on
capital from abroad to develop these resources.

Canadians generally have welcomed the foreign investments needed
to develop their country. Yet there is a growing concern for a
greater proportion of domestic capital in resource development.

Canada is a federal state with two official languages, English and
French, but a wide and varied multicultural base. The country
proudly celebrated its one-hundredth birthday in 1967. Canadians
have never been rabidly nationalistic, though there is a continuing
concern for national unity and identity.

Regionalism, based on physical and cultural factors, is evident, but Canada is striving to build a strong national consciousness which can harmonize regional differences. The cultures of its native peoples, the Indians and Eskimos, still exist along with those of the English and French, but there are also many communities of other ethnic origins, such as Germans, Italians, Norwegians, Icelanders, Slavs (represented by a large Ukranian population), and smaller groups of Japanese and Chinese origin.

As in many industrialized countries in the 1970s, there is concern in Canada with inflation and unemployment, a source of unease carried over from the still remembered days of the depression of the 1930s. By the test of GNP per capita Canada is one of the richest nations in the world, but in July 1976 roughly 7 percent of the Canadian work force was unemployed. The figures are somewhat higher in the Atlantic provinces and lower in the Prairies. Canada has not only political subunits (the provinces and territories) but also some economic subunits, which have evolved in relation to differing resources and physiography, and to certain historical factors. The existence of such regions with their different levels of employment, growth, inflation, and industrial base adds to the difficulties of formulating economic policy for the country as a whole.

Because of Canada's great size, it is sometimes more advantageous to deal with readily accessible markets outside Canada than to face the costs of transportation inside the country. For example, coal is exported from British Columbia and the Atlantic provinces, and imported into southern Ontario. Oil is exported in the west and imported in the east.

Canada's great size, natural wealth, and relative internal peace make it still today a good place in which to live. Canadians are well fed, warm, well educated. Yet in the midst of all this there is a growing recognition of the interdependency of the human community and the biosphere, of the limits to certain forms of growth, and the necessity for a global ethic.

The Publicly Formulated Goals

Canada is now in a time of transition, involved in a conflict between economic goals and objectives established at the end of World War II and the emerging new goals and objectives articulated by the few who are seriously addressing global issues. The traditional direction of Canadian society has been toward growth. Growth began long before 1945, but it has been largely unquestioned in the past, and its pace has been accelerating. In its growth orientation, Canada has been in line with the whole of the industrial world.

A brief review of some of the public Canadian policy statements since World War II will show the evolution of the traditional goals and the emergence of new ones. In a white paper presented to the Canadian Parliament and to the public in April 1945 by the Minister of Reconstruction under the title "Employment and Income," the government's primary goal was said to be "a smooth, orderly transition from the economic conditions of war to those of peace, and to maintain a high and stable level of employment and income." The goal of continuing economic growth was developed and accepted for more than twenty years, and Canada succeeded in achieving a steady increase in GNP.

The Economic Council of Canada was created nineteen years later by an act of Parliament, and was directed "to study and advise upon the medium and long-term development of the Canadian economy in relation to the attainment of five economic and social goals." These were full employment, a high rate of economic growth, reasonable stability of prices, a viable balance of payments, and an equitable distribution of rising incomes. The council anticipated 1,500,000 new members in the labor force from 1963 to 1970, and presented this as the prime factor requiring an expansion in the economy.

In the late 1960s, however, a different set of goals began to be articulated as public awareness of social and ecological issues increased. In 1971 the council recommended "the development of a comprehensive set of statistical measures to monitor the changing conditions of our society over a broad spectrum of concerns" (*Eighth Annual Review*). The traditional measures, such as growth, real output per person employed, and price indexes, were still seen as necessary, but no longer sufficient. In its *Eleventh Annual Review, 1974*, the council identified two basic goals: well-being (determined by the extent to which material, socio-cultural, psychological, and other needs of society are met) and equity (the distribution of well-being). To provide guidelines for policy formulation in relation to these goals, areas of concern were identified which include, along with economic matters such as employment, production and consumption, income and assets, such things as individual rights and responsibilities, social rights and national identity, health, information, training and education, and the natural and manmade environments. While it still regarded economic growth as a prior objective, in the wake of the 1973 oil crisis the council pointed to the need to restrain the growth of Canadian energy consumption.

The Science Council for Canada, which, like the Economic Council, is free to report directly to the public, argued in its first major science policy statement that policy for the use and development of science must be based on national goals. In 1968 it identified national prosperity as the first such goal. This included a high rate of economic growth, reasonable price stability, equitable distribution of rising income, viable balance of payments, full employment, and reduction of regional economic disparities. The council did, however, recognize the problems associated with growth and advocated the "development of sound programs for the use, conservation, and replenishing of resources." More recently, however, the council has been seriously questioning the established priorities, and has been studying the implications of a "conserver society." It stated:

> If there is one overriding concern which the Science Council of Canada would like to see dominate science policy thinking in the decade ahead, it would be that of seeing a major shift from today's consumer society, particularly as seen in the industrialized world, towards what we have called a Conserver Society. (*The Science Council of Canada Study on the Implications of a Conserver Society,* 1975)

The Science Council, like the prime minister, sees a conflict between the required goals and objectives and the existing system, that is, between a conserver and a consumer society. (It has recently begun to publish *Conserver Society Notes* to give information on the subject, and report on ideas and progress.)

In January 1974 the Task Force on Energy Research and Development, reporting to the minister of energy, mines, and resources, was established by the Cabinet. Among the objectives presented were energy conservation, the protection of the physical and social environment, and the improvement of the quality of life in all activities related to energy development and use. Between 1974 and 1977, recommended expenditures for research on renewable energy resources increased from 1.2 percent of the total energy research budget to 5.8 percent ($10 million). The proportion for nuclear energy research has been reduced from 76.9 percent of the total to 50.6 percent, but it still has the lion's share of the budget. The task force reports show a growing awareness of the costs, both economic and environmental, and the potential dangers involved in nuclear power development. The task force also expresses a concern about possible energy depletion in Canada, and the consequent need for conservation.

Canada has developed its own nuclear reactor system, based on heavy water and natural uranium. This CANDU reactor does not require an enrichment process and is a highly efficient user of uranium ore. Though there have been public protests about the disposal of nuclear waste material, Canada has in fact 6 nuclear power plants now in operation and one projection sees 115 operational in Canada across the country by the year 2000. In the export field Canada's sale of reactors to India and Pakistan, and the negotiations for sales to Argentina and South Korea have excited considerable public opposition.

An instance of the struggle in Canada between the traditional and the emerging goals is evident in a 1970 federal government foreign policy statement. In it, Canadian foreign policy was set forth as an extension of a national policy which seeks to achieve six goals: economic growth, sovereignty and independence, peace and security, social justice, quality of life, and a harmonious natural environment. These goals were seen to be interrelated at both the national and international levels. Notice is taken of "the most profound effects for the Canadian people which could be caused by the continued and widespread questioning of Western value systems—particularly the revolt against the mass-consumption society of North America with its lack of humanism." The dangers of continued economic growth to social justice, quality of life, and a harmonious natural environment are also noted. Yet in spite of the statements throughout the document that Canada consumes much more than her share of resources, and the warnings of the consequences of this, the report ends, somewhat surprisingly, with the assertion that "the Government is of the view that the foreign policy pattern for the 1970s should be based on a ranking of the six policy themes which gives highest priorities to economic growth, social justice and quality of life policies." (The original intent of those who drafted the document was to present the six goals on a hexagon which could rotate on its axis. It was their desire to have no order of priorities and present the goals as interrelated.)

In 1971 a new federal department, Environment Canada, was formed. It was believed that the department's paramount objective should be to provide leadership for a national undertaking in which special responsibilities fell on each level of government, national, provincial, and municipal. Federal responsibility lay in the areas of atmospheric research, water management, fisheries, forestry, wildlife, land use and inventory, and environmental protection. Several laws have been enacted by the Government of Canada to protect its natural resources, for example, the Canada Water Act, the Clean Air Act, amendments to the Fisheries Act, and, in 1975, the Environmental Contaminants Act. Emission and effluent standards have been set, air and water monitoring stations established, and pollutants have been identified and in many cases prohibited or reduced. Responsibility for environmental quality objectives is shared by other federal departments and agencies such as National Health and Welfare; Transport; Agriculture; Mines and Resources; and the National Research Council, as well as by appropriate governmental departments at the provincial level. A number of other federal departments and agencies have been stressing the objectives of environmental quality, energy conservation, the "conserver society," and quality of life in general.

Canada shares many air and water pollution problems with the United States, particularly in the eastern part of the country. Close cooperation between the two countries is becoming increasingly necessary. Detroit's air, for example, quickly becomes Windsor's air because of prevailing winds. In the matter of water quality in the Great Lakes, through which the international boundary line runs, a firm Canada–United States agreement was signed in 1973 by Prime Minister Trudeau and President Nixon. This agreement on water quality objectives in the greatest fresh water system in the world had to be thrashed out by the governments of both countries at the state and provincial as well as the federal levels, and is backed by a firm commitment to carry out specified programs of various kinds to achieve these objectives.

The most recent statement of Canadian goals and objectives in relation to developing countries was made by the Canadian International Development Agency (which comes under the authority of the secretary of state for external affairs). These include: greater foreign aid, the goal being the quota of .7 percent of GNP recommended by the U.N.; priority to the poorest countries; greater liquidity of transfers; untying of aid; and relief of Third World debt (noting that the service charges on this debt are greater than the total official aid from all developed countries). In fact, official Canadian development assistance (which in 1974 amounted to 42.5 percent of the total Canadian aid) rose from .28 percent of GNP in 1967–68 to an estimated .57 percent for 1975–76.

The Debate on the New Goals

Debate on the new goals has recently intensified. It is complicated, however, by the political structure of the country. Canada is a federal state, and in addition to the national government it has ten provincial governments. Although the British North America Act did not identify jurisdiction in environmental matters (it was not a problem in 1867), it did give the provinces primary responsibility in many key areas, including natural resources and education. The federal government must, therefore, tread carefully in these areas. Furthermore, the ten provinces do not have the same ecological or economic problems; they are at different levels of economic development, have varying cultural and national backgrounds, and are of somewhat diverse political persuasions. The federal government is Liberal. Both Liberals and Conservatives are traditionally free enterprise parties, both are "small l" liberal, and are considerably interested in social welfare within the capitalist context. The New Democrats are a moderate democratic socialist party. The total political spectrum does not contain elements so radically opposed to the status quo as to bring about significant change, but is varied enough to preclude easy consensus on change.

Yet on a number of occasions Prime Minister Trudeau has publicly called for a shift "from a society based on quantity to a society based on quality." He repeated this call in London, England, in March 1975 and went on to say:

> The human community is a complex organism linked again and again within itself as well as with the biosphere upon which it is totally dependent for life. This interdependency demands of us two functions: first, the maintenance of an equilibrium among all our activities, whatever their nature; second, an equitable distribution, worldwide, of resources and opportunities. . . . The process required must be global in scope and universal in application. . . . The role of leadership today is to encourage the embrace of a global ethic.

At Duke University, in May 1974, he said that there are limits to the rate at which the earth's resources can be exploited, that there are limits to the ability of our biosphere to absorb pollution, that there are limits to the capacity of the globe to support human life. For mankind to live harmoniously within these limits requires, according to Mr. Trudeau, an enlarged sense of responsibility, extending to all of nature and to all mankind, including future generations. The responsibility falls most heavily on the advanced industrial societies of which Canada is one. Mr. Trudeau endorsed the suggestion that, since the gross national product does not measure social progress or cultural attainment, it should be replaced by a new standard such as net human benefit. As far back as 1968 the Canadian federal Cabinet was seeking social indicators in addition to GNP, and the discussion continues in various government departments and agencies.

The democratic poltical system itself, however, could be allowed to impede the development of a new ethic by the government. Any solution to long-range problems—such as replacing GNP with "Net Human Benefit"—would require short-term sacrifices—at least, that is how a reduced material standard of living would be viewed by most Canadians at the present time. The ethic required would be one of sharing, concern for others, and self-control rather than one of consumption, egoism, and self-indulgence. All of this may sound wonderful, but its actual implementation by a government could make that government unpopular to the extent that it succeeds. In any case, four years in office is not sufficient time to carry out such a program. The continuity of effort required would necessitate a program understood by the public and accepted by all parties.

Realizing these constraints, Prime Minister Trudeau used the opportunity presented in an hour-long interview on Canadian television in December 1975 to repeat, once more, his view that the changing world required a return to the values of "sharing," "being good trustees of what we have," "tolerance," "brotherly love," "a new society . . . where net human benefit would be the important thing rather than gross national product, where the good life would replace the life of 'more,' where the value of people would be judged by not what they owned but what they are and what they do." He pointed also to the current problems of inflation and unemployment; the fact that energy shortages had not changed consumption patterns; and that, in spite of Third World rumblings and starvation, some Canadians still wanted to reduce foreign aid. Within this broad concept of local and global problems Mr. Trudeau said that the old habits, behavior, and institutions and, specifically, the free market system, were not working; and that if attitudes did not change during the present period of wage and price controls, some kind of government control of big business and big labor would have to continue.

A survey of subsequent news reports and editorials in forty editions of fifteen different Canadian newspapers showed an almost total lack of comment or discussion of the prime minister's remarks about the new society in the context of global threats. Almost all focused on his statements about the failure of the free market system and the possibility of continued government control, and put these in a narrow national economic context rather than in the original broad global context. Some branded his views as socialist, fascist, communist, dictatorial. Items in only three newspapers gave any evidence of an understanding of, or interest in, Mr. Trudeau's analysis of the Canadian situation in the world perspective. Whether or not the press in Canada agrees with the prime minister is, of course, not the issue. The point is the level of awareness of, or even interest in, the questions raised by Mr. Trudeau.

But there is another matter worthy of attention in the reactions to the prime minister's message. A major concern about government control was evident. Mr. Trudeau himself said, during the interview, that he would be worried if suddenly he felt that some government would have to impose these principles (those required for the "new society") on people. The furor was apparently caused by disagreements on the desirability of interventions in the operation of the free market system. Those Canadians who equate free enterprise with basic freedom saw any hint of controlling the free market system as a totalitarian threat. Some other Canadians believe, however, that global problems cannot be solved without some very specific controls on or directions for the market system.

Two points of view are presently discernible: an older point of view evincing the belief that a resumption of economic growth is primarily what is needed, and hence opposing both government intervention and direction; and a newer point of view showing awareness of the reality of serious human, social, environmental, and energy issues, but no certainty as to what to do about them. Since the furor over the prime minister's Christmas speech, the older point of view has regained strength and has led to an increasing questioning of the government's basic philosophy.

Perspectives and Constraints

The main issue in the Canadian context is the degree of change required in the existing economic system. The more conservative elements, such as the Economic Council, seem to propose relatively minor changes within the existing context; it is assumed that growth as now defined has continued priority, and that the free enterprise system can adjust sufficiently with minor government intervention. The prime minister, the Science Council, and some others appear to give priority to the idea of a *new* society—a conserver society. The required adjustments in the economy would follow. It has not yet been made clear by them how great these adjustments would have to be.

The Churches, or more precisely, certain significant groups within the Churches, are among the most aware and concerned regarding the problems, and also present some of the more radical solutions. Many Church statements point clearly to the incompatibility between the existing system and the required new society.

While the response of the Churches seems to be developing at the top and filtering down, the response of educational systems is essentially a grass-roots type, though with some support from above.

The media, which are of course very influential, show on the whole a lack of awareness of the global problems and tend in general to see everything in the narrow economic terms of the present system. In Canada, as elsewhere, it is immediate "gut" issues that sell newspapers, not discussions of global ethics.

The attitude of the masses on long-term issues and global concerns, however, is not clear. There is some evidence that many Canadians are not aware or concerned about them. Their concerns about getting "more," about keeping up with or ahead of inflation—essentially material and economic concerns—are those that feed the present system and help maintain the status quo. On the other hand, there is growing public involvement in activities related to certain global problems—contributions to conferences on development and security, membership in environmental groups, participation in church projects. There are some 500 volunteer groups in Canada expressing environmental concern at one level or another. Such groups, however, still represent a small minority of the total population.

As we have seen, a new set of goals and objectives is emerging in Canada. If Canadians actually moved toward these new goals there would be shifts away from wasteful modes of production and excessive consumption and toward new modes of distribution to overcome regional disparities, both national and global. But the forces behind these changes are still weak compared with the established ethic with its materialism and egoism, and its readiness to respond to the requirements of the Canadian and the world market system.

II. Goals in the United States of America

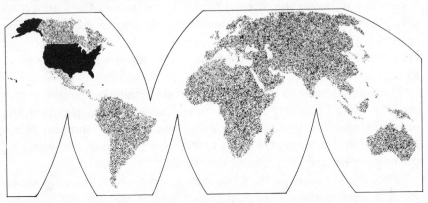

The goals the United States professes, and the degree to which the nation is united on and committed to those goals, are of both national and global importance. In a world growing ever more interdependent, the decisions of large, strong, and wealthy nations inevitably influence or constrain other nations in their choice of goals. Because the United States happens to be one of the world's largest, most powerful, and wealthiest nations, its national goals go far toward determining the fate and future of the global community, for better or worse.

In terms of physical size and population, the United States ranks fourth among all nations, with almost 9.4 million square kilometers of land (3.6 million square miles), 47 percent of which is actively farmed, and 217 million inhabitants that make up 5 percent of the world population. The population is a mixed one, with a wide variety of racial and cultural backgrounds. It is growing at an annual rate of approximately 1.1 percent and, until very recently, has been becoming increasingly urban.

With a gross national product of more than $14 trillion the United States is the wealthiest nation in the world. Although its nonwhite races have incomes that are on the average about 30 percent lower than those of whites, individual and family incomes are more equally distributed among its inhabitants (as indicated by the Gini coefficient) than in any other major nation except China.

The United States is one of the world's largest importers of raw materials and manufactured goods, importing considerably more than it exports. The country consumes annually about one-third of the world's total energy output and just under half of the world's basic resources. It also accounts for about 65 percent of the world's advertising which, at $115 per capita per year, makes advertising expenditures in the U.S.A. higher than the yearly per capita income of at least 800 million people in the world.

On the other hand, the United States is the largest of the very few food surplus countries in the world, and it now supplies almost half of the world's food exports. Access to the American marketplace is essential to the economies of many countries, and the American standard of living remains the virtual growth goal of many peoples of the world—however unrealistic this goal may prove to be even for the United States five to fifteen years hence.

Articulation of Goals in the United States

In the United States, authorized national goals are usually expressed and justified in terms of "canonical" writings (the Declaration of Independence, the Constitution, the Bill of Rights, the Federalist Papers, and other writings of the nation's founders), and in terms of some later documents that have achieved similar status (Washington's Farewell Address, the Monroe Doctrine, and the Emancipation Proclamation). The only recent declaration that might qualify as a canonical work is Franklin Roosevelt's 1944 State of the Union address —which became the American "Economic Bill of Rights"—in which full employment, adequate income, decent housing, medical care, education, and security in old age were put forward as specific national goals.

All formal U.S. goals, if they are to have legitimacy, must be based on these documents, which have been deliberately called canonical because the formal establishment and articulation of national goals is a quasi-religious exercise in the United States. This contention is strengthened when one looks at the role of the Supreme Court, whose function is to interpret these documents whenever the nation, in response to perceived new requirements, expresses new goals or seeks to achieve old ones through unfamiliar means. It is for the Supreme Court to say whether these new goals violate or are in accord with the national Constitution—the primary canonical document of the country.

The most often cited statement of the basic goals of the United States is found in the Preamble to the Constitution:

to form a more perfect union

to insure domestic tranquility

to provide for the common defense

to promote the blessings of liberty to Americans and their posterity.

The postrevolutionary constitutional government of the United States was formed in such a way that it was to pursue these goals by fulfilling the following objectives and no others:

to provide for the common defense

to make rules about trade

to fix a common currency

to collect taxes.

All other types of governance were to be exercised either by the several states (for example, in providing for public education) or by the people themselves (for example, in controlling religious customs and observances). No procedures for centralized planning or for the setting of national goals were laid down. Apparently the framers of the Constitution supposed that all necessary planning at the federal level would be done by the Congress in the making of appropriations, and that planning in other areas would be done by the states and other collectivities, or by individuals, in whatever manner should seem to make most sense. Although debated heatedly by the founding fathers, the belief prevailed that "He who governs least, governs best."

As a matter of historical fact, however, it turned out that the emergence of a vast technological and industrial free-enterprise system created problems which that system had no responsibility to solve. Consequently the federal government had to undertake roles not given it by the Constitution. Formal, comprehensive planning and goal setting, however, have not become added responsibilities taken on by the federal government—except for matters of foreign affairs and national defense, which became subject to future-oriented planning and goal setting when President Eisenhower established the National Security Council. By and large, the federal government has resisted any systematic program of comprehensive long-range planning, and usually it has resisted the formal setting of goals as well. The authors of the Employment Act of 1946 deleted the term "full employment" from the act precisely because it seemed to open the door to goal setting by the federal government. It remains to be seen whether currently proposed legislation to create a centralized planning mechanism for the Congress will become law.

A variety of mechanisms have been explored by which the federal government might set goals for the nation. Reports prepared for Presidents Hoover in 1933 and Roosevelt in 1937 reviewed social trends and their possible impacts as bases on which to formulate national policies. President Eisenhower created the President's Commission on National Goals, whose purpose was to articulate a broad and balanced set of goals for the nation. The recommendations of the commission, published in 1960, are summarized in Table 1-1. Table 1-2 compares the goals cited by the commission in 1960 with the 1933 report made to President Hoover on "Recent Social Trends."

More recently a professional National Goals Research Staff was created in the Nixon Administration. Unlike the one-shot Eisenhower Commission, this group was created to identify the most pressing and difficult issues of the present and the future. In part because its staff members insisted on tackling such future-oriented issues as limits-to-growth policy, the National Goals Research Staff survived only long enough to publish a much watered-down first report. Organized and visible efforts to think through future-oriented issues from a global perspective have found almost no support by the U.S. government, and generally very little support by nongovernmental agencies throughout the United States.

In contrast to efforts aimed at a centralized formulation of policy-related goals for the nation, are exercises that collect representative opinions of the people through either regional hearings or national opinion polls. The results of these hearings and polls are sometimes assumed to be the most direct and representative expressions of the beliefs and desires of the American public. Table 1-3 summarizes the concerns expressed in a series of hearings held by former Vice-President Rockefeller and key cabinet officials in six major U.S. cities. Tables 1-4 and 1-5 summarize a number of the hopes and fears expressed by U.S. citizens in the latest (1976) opinion poll. The relationship of these hopes and fears to the priorities honored in the national budget(s) can be seen by comparing Tables 1-4 and 1-5 with Tables 1-6 and 1-7.*

---

* In order to avoid confusion of the American with the Continental uses of "billion," we shall express all large sums in multiples of million.

Table 1-1
Fifteen Goals for Americans

Goals at Home

 1 *The Individual*
    "The status of the individual must remain our primary concern. All
    our institutions—political, social, and economic—must further en-
    hance the dignity of the citizen, promote the maximum development
    of his capabilities, stimulate their responsible exercise, and widen
    the range and effectiveness of opportunities for individual choice."

 2 *Equality* (should be strengthened)

 3 *The Democratic Process* (should be strengthened)

 4 *Education* (should be strengthened)

 5 *The Arts and Sciences* (emphasis should be on basic science for
    understanding and for health, economic growth, and military power)

 6 *The Democratic Economy* (should avoid high concentrations and
    imbalances of power . . . maximize individual freedom of choice in
    jobs, goods, and services)

 7 *Economic Growth* (should be maximum rate consistent with other
    goals)

 8 *Technological Change* (should be promoted, with concern for adverse
    impact on individuals)

 9 *Agriculture* (system has some problems that need to be solved)

10 *Living Conditions* (should be improved, with special emphasis on
    decaying slums in large cities and balanced development of suburban
    regions)

11 *Health and Welfare* (should be made more available at lower cost
    to the individual)

Goals Abroad

12 *Help to Build an Open and Peaceful World*
    "The healthiest world economy is attained when trade is at its freest.
    This should be our goal."

13 *The Defense of the Free World* (should contain communist aggression
    and subversion)

14 *Disarmament* (should be our ultimate goal)

15 *The United Nations* (should be supported and strengthened)

Source: President's Commission on National Goals, *Goals for Americans,* Prentice-Hall,
Inc., Englewood Cliffs, N.J., 1960.

Table 1-2
Goals Stated by President's Commission, 1960, that also Figure in
Recent Social Trends, **1933**

	Number of Goal Areas, 1960	Goal Areas also in 1933 Report
The individual	6	2
Equality	3	1
Democratic process	11	4
Education	5	0
Science	8	1
Democratic economy	9	6
Economic growth	9	5
Technological change	5	1
Agriculture	5	1
Living conditions	10	6
Health and welfare	10	10
Total	81	37

Source: Table 2.2, in Albert D. Biderman, "Social Indicators and Goals," in Raymond A. Bauer, *Social Indicators,* M.I.T. Press, Cambridge, Massachusetts, 1966.

Table 1-3
Concerns Expressed by the People of the United States during Hearings of the 1975 Public Forums on Domestic Policy

High unemployment and inflation, excessive government spending, and lagging economy

Lack of congressional action on a comprehensive energy policy

Need to achieve environmental protection along with economic growth and job opportunities

Inequities in social programs and the bureaucratic red tape of the federal government in administering such programs

Rising cost of health care and lack of a comprehensive health policy or system

Excessive and ever-changing federal regulations of business and of state and local governments

Source: "Report to the President on the White House Public Forums on Domestic Policy, Summary of Findings," (December 15, 1975).

Table 1-4
Hopes of the American People

	1959	1964	1971	1972	1974	1976
	(percentage of mentions)					
Personal Hopes						
Better or decent standard of living	38	40	27	29	29	31
Good health for self	40	29	29	27	28	29
Aspirations for children (opportunities, especially educational; success; happiness)	29	35	17	23	24	28
Happy family life	18	18	14	18	15	20
Peace in the world; no wars	9	17	19	32	16	15
Good health for family	16	25	13	12	11	13
Own a house or live in a better one	24	12	11	12	11	13
Good job; congenial work	7	9	6	10	11	13
Peace of mind; emotional stability and maturity	5	9	8	7	9	13
Economic stability in general; no inflation	*	*	6	7	15	11
Wealth	*	5	7	8	8	10
Better world; more international understanding and cooperation; relaxation of tensions; brotherhood	*	*	*	*	8	10
Happy old age	10	8	6	6	8	9
Leisure time; recreation; travel	11	5	6	8	9	8
Safety from crime, violence	*	*	*	7	6	8
Employment	5	8	6	6	6	7
Concern about, relationships with, or assistance to relatives	*	*	*	*	7	6

Hopes of the American People (continued)

	1959	1964	1971	1972	1974	1976
			(percentage of mentions)			
Better, more honest government or politics (including specific references to Watergate)	*	*	*	*	10	6
Social justice (greater equality; elimination of discrimination)	*	*	*	6	7	5
Resolution of personal religious, spiritual, or ethical problems; gaining admittance to heaven	*	*	*	*	5	5
Christian revival in general	*	*	*	5	5	5
Success in one's work; making a contribution to one's field	*	*	*	*	5	5
National Hopes						
Peace	48	51	51	56	27	31
Economic stability; no inflation	12	5	18	13	24	26
Employment; jobs for everyone	13	15	16	17	10	23
Improved standard of living in general; greater national prosperity	20	28	11	10	11	16
Integrity in government and politics	*	*	*	5	25	15
Efficient government; competent leadership	*	*	*	6	11	14
Law and order	*	*	11	14	11	14
National unity and political stability (internal peace and order; absence of unrest, tensions, antagonisms)	*	9	15	11	15	12

Continued on next page

Hopes of the American People (continued)

	1959	1964	1971	1972	1974	1976
	(percentage of mentions)						
Change of presidents; get a better president	*	*	*	*	12	10
Better public morality (ethical standards; religion)	7	10	8	5	10	10
National independence; economic self-sufficiency	*	*	*	*	6	9
Elimination of discrimination	*	*	*	*	*	9
Better world; brotherhood	*	*	*	*	*	9
Public health; improved medical care	*	*	*	*	5	6
More democratic or representative government	*	*	*	*	5	6
Improved ecology; reduced pollution; preservation of natural resources	*	*	*	*	5	6
Social justice; greater equality in treatment and opportunities	*	*	*	*	*	6
Balanced government; checks and balances	*	*	*	*	*	5
Welfare; smaller welfare rolls	*	*	*	*	*	5
Improvement in the public's sense of political and social responsibility; working for the common good	*	*	*	*	*	5

* mentioned by less than 5 percent

Source: William Watts and Lloyd A. Free, "America's Hopes and Fears," *Policy Perspectives 1976/1*, Potomac Associates, Washington, D.C.

Table 1-5
Fears of the American People

	1959	1964	1971	1972	1974	1976
	(percentage of mentions)					
Personal Fears						
Ill health for self	40	25	28	21	25	28
Lower standard of living	23	19	18	18	16	24
War	21	29	17	28	18	17
Economic instability in general; inflation	*	*	11	9	26	16
Ill health in family	25	27	16	12	12	16
Unemployment	10	14	13	10	12	16
Crime	*	*	5	8	9	10
Inadequate opportunities for or unhappiness of children	12	10	8	8	10	9
Social decay (spiritual, ethical, religious)	*	*	*	5	9	9
To be dependent on others; loneliness; old age	*	*	*	*	*	9
No or unhappy family life; separation from relatives	*	*	*	*	*	9
Lack of freedom (especially of speech)	*	*	*	*	6	6
Lack of integrity in politics or government; no improvement in government	*	*	*	*	5	6
National Fears						
War	64	50	30	35	24	37
Economic instability; inflation; recession	18	13	17	13	28	26
Lack of law and order	*	5	11	16	13	13
The threat of communism	12	29	12	8	8	12
Unemployment	7	6	7	5	*	12

Continued on next page

Fears of the American People (continued)

	1959	1964	1971	1972	1974	1976
	(percentage of mentions)					
National disunity or political instability (unrest, tensions, antagonisms, chaos)	*	8	26	13	12	10
Lack of public morality (ethically, religiously)	*	5	6	6	6	9
Dishonesty in government or politics	*	*	*	*	8	8
Inefficient government; poor leadership	*	*	*	*	5	8
Loss of democratic or representative government	*	5	5	5	7	7
Food shortages	*	*	*	*	6	7
No improvement in, or inadequate, standard of living; decreased national prosperity	*	*	*	*	6	6
Deterioration in our ecology; increased pollution	*	*	9	8	6	5
Threat, aggression, or domination by a communist power	*	*	*	5	5	5
Loss of freedom	*	*	*	*	*	5
Too powerful or centralized government	*	*	*	*	*	5

* mentioned by less than 5 percent

Source: William Watts and Lloyd A. Free, "America's Hopes and Fears," *Policy Perspectives 1976/1*, Potomac Associates, Washington, D.C.

Table 1-6
Federal Budget Outlays for Several Fiscal Years

Amounts in thousand millions of current dollars

Category[a]	1960, actual Amount	Percent[b]	1970, actual Amount	Percent[b]	1976, estimated Amount	Percent[b]
Defense and international affairs	48.2	51.6	82.8	41.6	100.3	27.8
National defense	45.2	—	79.3	—	94.0	—
International affairs	2.9	—	3.6	—	6.3	—
General science, space, and technology	0.7	0.7	4.6	2.3	4.6	1.3
Natural resources, environment, and energy	1.7	1.8	3.6	1.8	10.0	2.8
Aid to businesses, agriculture, and communities	8.8	9.5	17.7	8.9	21.5	5.9
Agriculture	2.6	—	5.2	—	1.8	—
Commerce and transportation	5.8	—	9.1	—	13.7	—
Community and regional development	0.4	—	3.5	—	5.9	—
Human resources	25.5	27.3	72.7	36.5	177.0	49.0
Education, manpower, and social services	1.0	—	7.9	—	14.6	—
Health	0.8	—	13.1	—	28.0	—
Income security	18.3	—	43.1	—	118.7	—
Veterans benefits and services	5.5	—	8.7	—	15.6	—
Law enforcement, justice, and general government	1.5	1.6	2.9	1.4	6.5	1.8
Law enforcement and justice	0.4	—	1.0	—	3.3	—
General government	1.1	—	1.9	—	3.2	—
Revenue sharing and general-purpose fiscal assistance	0.2	0.2	0.5	0.2	7.2	2.0
Net interest	6.9	7.4	14.4	7.2	26.1	7.2
Allowances [c]	0.0	0.0	0.0	0.0	8.1	2.2
Gross outlays	93.4	100.0	199.2	100.0	361.3	100.0

Continued on next page

Federal Budget Outlays for Several Fiscal Years (continued)

Details may not add to totals because of rounding; percentages are calculated from
unrounded data.

a These categories differ only in minor respects from those used in the 1976 *Budget,*
pt. 5. One difference is that offshore oil receipts and retirement fund contributions are
considered to be financial adjustments and are not deducted from gross outlays. Second,
interest received by federal trust funds is considered a deduction in computing net
interest outlays, not as an undistributed offsetting receipt as in the budget document.

b Only computed for major categories.

c Energy tax offset payments, pay raises for civilian agencies, and contingency allowances.

Source: Table 1-2, in B. Blechman, E. Gramlich, and R. Hartman, *Setting National Priorities,
the 1976 Budget,* Brookings Institution, Washington, D.C., 1975.

Table 1-7
Projected Outlays in the U.S. Budget by Function, 1977–1981

	1977	1978	1979	1980	1981
(in thousand millions of dollars)					
Outlays:					
National defense	101.1	112.9	121.5	132.3	142.8
International affairs	6.8	7.8	7.8	8.1	8.0
General science, space, and technology	4.5	4.6	4.5	4.4	4.1
Natural resources, environment, and energy	13.8	14.4	15.1	14.9	14.5
Agriculture	1.7	2.6	2.6	2.8	2.8
Commerce and transportation	16.5	19.4	19.1	18.7	18.7
Community and regional development	5.5	6.0	6.2	6.0	6.1
Education, training, employment and social services	16.6	15.3	15.3	15.3	15.3
Health	34.4	37.7	40.3	43.4	47.0
Income security	137.1	147.1	158.3	170.1	182.9
Veterans benefits and services	17.2	17.2	16.7	16.3	15.7
Law enforcement and justice	3.4	3.3	3.3	3.3	3.3
General government	3.4	3.9	3.6	3.6	3.7
Revenue sharing and general-purpose fiscal assistance	7.4	7.7	7.9	8.0	8.2
Interest	41.3	44.8	46.5	46.9	46.9
Allowances	2.3	5.6	8.1	10.5	12.8
Undistributed offsetting receipts	−18.8	−20.7	−21.4	−22.1	−22.9
Total	394.2	429.5	455.7	482.5	509.9

Source: The Budget of the United States Government: Fiscal Year, 1977, House Document No. 94–343, U.S. Government Printing Office, Washington, D.C., p. 35.

Inferred Operational Goals and Objectives of the United States

In the following section we describe the operational goals and objectives of the United States, which we characterize as inferred. First we state the basic enunciated goal that influences all others; then we cite ten specific operational goals and two or more instrumental objectives under each.

The Primary U.S. Goal: Health of the Democratic System *

There is a strong tendency in the United States to idealize such terms as "democracy" and "free enterprise," even though neither exists in pure form either in this country or elsewhere. These concepts are enshrined in the Constitution. While in older countries nationhood is felt in the culture, the common ethnic heritage, and history, nationhood in the 200-year-old United States is manifest in the consciously created constitutional system. In it, the American people have sanctified the free enterprise, representative democracy system itself. As a consequence, trade-offs among goals often occur which seem to make little sense in themselves, but which in fact minimize damage to idealized notions about this system. In this sense, system preservation has become a basic goal, and has priority over most other goals except perhaps national survival. In recent years this basic goal has also been extended to promote various "free world" alliances (for example, the North Atlantic Treaty Organization [NATO], the Southeast Asia Treaty Organization [SEATO], the Organization of African States [OAS]).

Related Goals and Objectives

The goals listed below are distinct from, yet closely related to the primary U.S. goal of assuring the health of the democratic system. Each goal has associated objectives through which it is pursued within the domestic context.

BASIC GOAL 1: PEACE AND THE PROTECTION OF NATIONAL INTERESTS

Instrumental Objectives:

Refrain from initiating any *overt* military actions abroad.

Participate in preventing or stopping any major wars that may break out anywhere in the world, especially where there is a potential confrontation with the U.S.S.R. such as in the Middle East.

Exercise a key role in maintaining the security of allied nations as

---

* The names and the order of most of the goals listed below are based on the "Hopes and Fears" poll data developed by the Potomac Associates. Thus both the conceptual organization and the substantive content of these goals are to a large extent based on an empirical assessment of individual goals for the nation. Where there were obvious gaps, we added additional goals and objectives. These goals do not refer to the U.S. government alone, but to the "established" or predominant position of the nation taken as a whole, as opposed to the position of various minorities.

well as of the United States, and hence maintain a strong military capability and provide arms aid to friendly or potentially friendly nations.

Encourage and participate in such limited forms of arms control as are believed not to endanger national security (e.g., the strategic arms limitation talks [SALT] and pursuit of "detente").

Achieve greatest feasible energy independence as a means of protecting domestic needs from foreign control, and freeing U.S. foreign options.

BASIC GOAL 2: PROSPERITY—FULL EMPLOYMENT AND ECONOMIC STABILITY

Instrumental Objectives:
Pursue policies that stimulate economic growth to allow rising per capita *real* income.

Provide for the basic welfare of those in the low income brackets through employment, if possible, and through subsidized income maintenance, if necessary.

Prevent unemployment from rising above 4 percent, if possible, without jeopardizing other economic goals; for the next five years, however, accept 6 percent unemployment, if necessary.

Minimize the rate of inflation as far as is possible without jeopardizing other economic goals; maintain high levels of per capita real income (relative to world standards).

BASIC GOAL 3: AN ORDERLY, JUST, AND FREE SOCIETY

Instrumental Objectives:
Reverse or at least slow the recent high rate (16 to 18 percent per year) of increase in crime.

Develop advanced surveillance and police systems to prevent and control terrorism and dissident organizations that promote change.

Preserve existing social institutions such as the family and a common system of public education.

Maintain a criminal and civil justice system whose professed ideal is to treat all people equally and not to discriminate on the basis of race, religion, and, to a lesser extent, sex and wealth.

Discourage dissent in order to produce a peaceful and internally unified nation.

Preserve basic civil liberties, such as freedom of the press, freedom of speech, freedom from invasion of privacy, and so on.

BASIC GOAL 4: A HEALTHY POPULACE

Instrumental Objectives:

Maintain and advance a technologically superior health care system of high quality for those who can pay.

Enhance the accessibility to general health care by various insurance and public support programs.

Maintain an education and enforcement program to reduce drug and alcohol abuse.

Support medical research in general and large-scale cancer research in particular.

Ensure safety of food products, drugs, and other medical and psychological devices and processes.

BASIC GOAL 5: AN AESTHETIC AND HEALTHY ENVIRONMENT

Instrumental Objectives:

Reduce the existing levels of air and water pollution to recently enacted minimum standards.

Control the use of hazardous substances, especially pesticides and radioactive materials.

Conserve at least some of the unique wilderness in a *relatively* pristine state.

Ensure compliance with reasonable aesthetic standards (e.g., housing density, size of advertising signs, etc.)

BASIC GOAL 6: A WELL-EDUCATED POPULACE

Instrumental Objectives:

Provide at least thirteen years of schooling for everyone.

Provide equal access to low-cost higher education for all who qualify.

Encourage creativity and problem-solving skills by programmatic support of educational institutions.

BASIC GOAL 7: A BETTER WORLD

Instrumental Objectives:
Improve the general climate of international trade and economic affairs, and foster supportive institutions.

Encourage economic and technical cooperation among all nations.

Provide significant financial support for and active participation in the United Nations.

Provide disaster relief as needed, especially food and medical supplies.

BASIC GOAL 8: GOOD HOUSING

Instrumental Objectives:
Enforce appropriate standards and provide limited forms of subsidy to ensure a minimum standard of housing for all.

Encourage tax policies and financing programs that ensure access to ownership of individual houses by middle-income families, and public housing for low-income families.

BASIC GOAL 9: LIVABLE CITIES

Instrumental Objectives:
Find new means for financing those major U.S. cities that are tending toward fiscal bankruptcy.

Improve the habitability of major cities, especially in relation to crime, poverty pockets, and delivery of services.

BASIC GOAL 10: ARTS AND CULTURE

Instrumental Objectives:
Maintain a strong and growing entertainment industry to provide popular culture to the general public.

Provide at least a minimal level of support for "high" culture.

Preserve and maintain historic buildings and other historical resources associated with the national heritage.

The degree of concern Congress feels for goals such as these (as well as for other instrumental objectives associated with science and technology, transportation, basic resources and energy, and management and communication infrastructures) is reflected in the *Major Issues System* of the Congressional Research Service. This system furnishes a series of issue briefs, which are produced on request and

Table 1-8
Number of Issue Briefs in the Major Issues System of the Congressional Research Service Related to Principal U.S. Goals and Objectives

Number of Related Issue Briefs	U.S. Goal/Objective
26	1. Peace and Protection of National Interests
19	2. Prosperity—Full Employment and Economic Stability
31	3. An Orderly, Just, and Free Society
26	4. A Healthy Populace
19	5. An Aesthetic and Healthy Environment
4	6. A Well-Educated Populace
7	7. A Better World
2	8. Good Housing
1	9. Livable Cities
0	10. Arts and Culture
	Instrumental Objectives
34	1. Basic Resources and Energy
28	2. Management and Communications
10	3. Science and Technology
7	4. Transportation

Note: Data are as of March 10, 1976.

are updated as needed, to inform members of Congress about emerging issues that may require legislative attention in the near future. As Table 1-8 indicates, basic resource and energy concerns figure most prominently in these briefs at the time this paper is written.

The Evolution of U.S. Goals

In contrast to the study of changing U.S. budgetary priorities (which deal primarily with instrumental objectives), there are studies of the evolution of basic goals. In a recent Congressional Research Service study entitled "The Evolution and Dynamics of National Goals in the United States," Franklin P. Huddle suggested that the five decades since the close of World War I are typified by six periods, in each of which a different national goal was predominant:

1. 1920–1929, to restore cultural and economic patterns that had prevailed before 1910; epitomized by President Harding's campaign slogan "Back to Normalcy."

2. 1930–1941, to overcome the profound economic depression with its attendant unemployment and loss of material values.

3. 1942–1945, to defeat the Axis powers in World War II.

4. 1946–1957, to contain communist expansion and stabilize the world political system; to offer aid to developing countries.

5. 1958–1967, to make appropriate responses to the technological surprise disclosed by the USSR, eventuating in such specifics as global communications satellites, weapons treaties, and Apollo flights.

6. As of 1968, to attend to the quality of the domestic physical environment vis-à-vis such threats as pollution, wastes, and hazards to health and safety.

Whereas the goals in the Preamble to the Constitution are related to abstract, though positive, concepts of political theory, those of the past half-century have been aimed at the alleviation of undesirable conditions. Similarly reactive goals seemed to be still pursued in 1976 when, despite the fanfare of the nation's bicentennial, no ennobling "central projects" were proposed to excite the commitment of the nation's citizens and enhance its prestige. Indeed, this lack of inspiring and prestigious national projects during the bicentennial may indicate that the United States is in a state of transition with regard to national goals.

Although it is not clear just what the future holds regarding national goals in the United States, it is instructive to compare a statement made in April 1976 to the Club of Rome by Nelson A. Rockefeller (then Vice-President of the United States) with new alternative views which are now emerging and are reflected in opinion surveys. Rockefeller said,

> More growth is essential if all of the millions of Americans are to have the opportunity to improve their quality of life. . . . It is naive, indeed dangerous to assert, as some do, that the industrialized nations of the world must support the underdeveloped nations of the globe through massive and long-term foreign aid in goods and services and massive grants of capital.

While such views are being expressed by high officials, many voluntary groups are continuing to work in the United States on behalf of goals of ecological balance, world order, peace, and human well-being. Increasingly, these groups appear to be asking whether it is consistent to express belief in, and to work toward these general goals, while at the same time personally consuming resources at the relatively high levels that typify the U.S. standard of living.

Recent data from national surveys conducted by Louis Harris and Associates indicate that this type of discrepancy has become the concern not just of a minority of dedicated persons, but of the majority of people in the United States. Harris' first indication of this trend stemmed from a survey taken September 9, 1975. As described in a speech the following month at the National Conference of State Legislators, he found that:

> An 85 to 90 percent majority felt that "most government leaders are afraid to tell it like it is—that is, to tell the public the hard truth about inflation, energy, and other subjects."

> By 67 to 22 percent, a three-to-one majority endorsed the statement that "the trouble with most leaders is that they don't understand people want better quality of almost everything they have rather than more quantity."

To probe these findings further, on September 16, 1975 Harris confronted the respondents with the much-cited statistic that Americans comprise 6 percent of the world's population (now 5 percent), but consume 40 percent of the world's production of energy and raw materials. The following responses were made to a number of questions asked in connection with this level of consumption:

74 percent said this uses up our own natural resources and those of others abroad.

74 percent said this makes products and raw materials scarce, thereby driving prices up.

By 50 percent to 31 percent, most thought that, sooner or later, this will turn the rest of the world's people against us.

By 55 percent to 30 percent, most believed that this hurts the well-being of the rest of the world.

By 61 percent to 23 percent, almost a three-to-one majority, most felt that this is "morally wrong."

In this same survey, more than two out of three people admitted that they themselves are "highly wasteful." Ninety percent thought that "we are going to have to find ways to cut back on the amount of things we consume and waste." Some 64 percent agreed that such a cutback will mean lowering the U.S. standard of living. When the alternative was posed between "changing our lifestyle" in order to consume fewer physical goods, and "enduring the risks of continuing inflation and unemployment due to raw material shortages," a 77 to 8 percent majority of the American people opted for a change in lifestyle (see Table 1-9 for the specific changes people were willing to make).

A number of additional viewpoints are being advocated in the United States as alternatives to the established view. Many of them embody the overall intent of the global goals described in Part II of this report. Some half-dozen groups in the United States have enunciated some type of "declaration of interdependence," hoping to create a new ethical standard for the nation. Which of these viewpoints—if any—will rise to predominance in the future is not clear. What is certain is that the decade-long series of poll data indicates a continuing erosion of confidence in the policies that govern the nation, especially when these policies are compared with other more stable social indicators.

Table 1-9
Responses to a Louis Harris and Associates Survey
Taken between August 30 and September 6, 1975

The following questions were put to a stratified sample of 1,497 persons, with this preamble: "Now let me ask you about certain specific areas which have been suggested for people to cut down on the amounts they consume. Would you personally be willing, or not, to . . ."

		Willing	Not Willing	Not Sure
1.	Have one meatless day a week?	91%	7%	2%
3.	Stop feeding all-beef products to pet animals?	78%	15%	7%
7.	Do away with changing clothing fashions every year?	90%	7%	3%
8.	Wear old clothes, even if they shine, until they wear out?	73%	22%	5%
9.	Prohibit the building of large houses with extra rooms that are seldom used?	73%	19%	8%
12.	Make it much cheaper to live in multiple-unit apartments than in single homes?	57%	34%	9%
16.	Eliminate annual model changes in automobiles?	92%	5%	3%
20.	Sharply reduce the amount of advertising urging people to buy more products?	82%	11%	7%

Source: Louis Harris & Associates, Inc. (personal communication).

Chapter 2

Goals in Western Europe

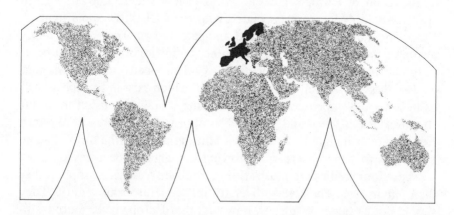

The countries of Western Europe are among the oldest and most diverse in the world. Their socio-economic development reflects not only the effects of modern technology but their long cultural heritage. The complexity and diversity of the national and cultural mentality of Western Europeans defy brief description. Rather than attempt a generalized statement of their goals, we offer four sample case studies to illustrate the nature as well as the breadth of European ambitions and aspirations.

In the first of these case studies, we examine the goals of the European Economic Community. These focus on increasing integration and cooperation on a broad scale of issues among the nine member nations. Although a European union is still in the realm of wishful thinking, the European Community boasts notable achievements, and its experience provides valuable insight into problems of integration and cooperation among diverse and sophisticated nations.

In the second study we describe the recent goals espoused by the countries of Scandinavia. These were traditionally in the vanguard of progressive social movements, and their current experiments with new forms of socialism are important both for what they can accomplish in Scandinavia and for what they can show by way of example and experience to the rest of the world.

In the third, we consider the goals proclaimed by the Italian Communist Party (*Partito Communista Italiano* [PCI]). Along with the Communist parties of France and Spain, the PCI represents a major socio-political force in Europe—the so-called "Euro-Communism." A specifically Western European variety, its independence from Soviet and Eastern European communism is well documented. But the nature of its vision of Europe and the world is less widely known. Recent speeches and documents associated with the PCI throw some light on Euro-Communist aspirations and indicate the alternatives currently available to Italy as well as several other countries of Western Europe.

In the fourth case study we describe European antiestablishment goals—those of the "alternative cultures," which exist in Europe as well as in other developed countries, and bring a new dimension to mainstream society's ideas and ideals. The alternative cultures of Western Europe are articulate in stating their aims, and herald the birth of some new ideas that may exercise a growing influence in decades to come.

These four studies are illustrative of goals in Western Europe, rather than exhaustive. Their very diversity reflects European reality. They should not be taken to suggest, however, that Europe lacks more traditional, materialistic, and middle-of-the-road goals and aspirations. Such are still adopted by the majority, though they are no longer likely to dominate Western Europe's social and political destiny.

I. Goals of the European Community

The European Community encompasses nine countries: Belgium, Denmark, France, Germany, Great Britain, Ireland, Italy, Luxembourg, and the Netherlands. They have a combined population of about 260 million people and constitute one of the greatest economic powers in the world.

The professed goal of the Community is to create a progressively closer union among the peoples of Europe and achieve economic and social progress through joint action. Internally, the countries strive for equitable and uniform standards in their economic and social policies. With respect to the outside world, they would like to "speak with a single voice," a goal which, so far at least, falls short of realization.

European union is prompted by multiple considerations associated with the interdependence of Western European countries in the areas of the economy, the environment, science and technology, political balance, and security. Although actual integration is still to be attained, the idea of an integrated European community is gaining strength in the thinking and behavior of Europeans. Increasingly they work with one another and rely on one another's products and services. They learn the major European tongues, ride on Trans-Europe Expresses, watch Eurovision TV broadcasts, work in neighboring lands, and visit one another's countries for business and pleasure.

That the "European idea" has penetrated the minds of the masses is shown in recent public opinion surveys. The 1973 survey of the Commission of European Communities covered these five major items:

attitudes concerning the Common Market and European unification

satisfaction with quality of life

systems of societal values and objectives

political and ideological currents

impact of various types of information upon the above-mentioned attitudes

The answers concerning the Common Market and European unification were of special interest. As Table 2-1 indicates, the six nations

Table 2-1
An Index of Pro-European Attitudes in European Community Member Countries

Country	Number of Persons Polled	Percentage of Pro-Europeans
Belgium	989	53.8
Denmark	1,062	47.6
France	1,776	58.6
Germany (Federal Republic)	1,626	82.0
Great Britain	1,703	34.6
Ireland	1,017	55.3
Italy	1,569	74.4
Luxembourg	264	79.9
Netherlands	1,203	68.2

longest associated with the Community came up with relatively high scores, with the German Federal Republic the highest and Belgium the lowest of the six. People in the three newly associated countries were less positive about the Common Market and unification, although Ireland scored higher than Belgium. The combined average was nevertheless significant: 63.2 percent manifested a pro-European attitude. A further breakdown of such attitudes among seventy subnational units confirmed the results; the seven highest-ranked regions were in Germany, while the lowest-ranked regions were British. The lowest score registered was for Wales, 22.6 percent.

People in member nations believe that a great many of the problems confronting them would be better handled by a European government than by a national one (see Table 2-2). Here too, the long-associated members lead the scores, and the United Kingdom and Ireland bring up the rear.

Table 2-2
Problems Better Handled by a European than by the National Government
Affirmative answers by a sample of the national populations

Ranking	Problems	Belgium	Denmark	France	Germany	Great Britain	Ireland	Italy	Luxembourg	Netherlands
1	Pollution	x	x	x	x			x	x	x
2	Inflation			x	x			x	x	x
3	Poverty and unemployment			x	x			x	x	x
4	Drugs	x	x	x	x			x	x	x
5	Economic growth	x		x	x			x	x	x
6	Scientific research	x	x	x	x	x	x	x	x	x
7	Development aid	x	x	x	x	x	x	x	x	x
8	Foreign investment	x								
9	International treaties	x	x	x	x	x	x	x	x	x
10	Military defense	x	x	x	x	x	x	x	x	x

The strength of the hold of the European idea upon the minds of Europeans was also indicated in the results of major referenda on the issue of entering the Common Market. Referenda held in 1971 showed 54 percent *against* in Norway, 63 percent *for* in Denmark, and 59 percent *for* in the United Kingdom, though at the same time public opinion polls scored 61 percent *against* entry. In the 1975 United Kingdom referendum, an affirmative vote of 67 percent indicated a changing trend.

A Brief History of the European Idea in Recent Years

The European idea had already been raised by Aristide Briand, France's Minister of Foreign Affairs, in a speech to the League of Nations in 1929. Briand spoke of a European commonwealth of independent and sovereign states, united through greater political and economic solidarity. But his idea was stillborn. There was opposition from Britain and Italy, and later from the triumphant national socialism of Germany.

After the cataclysm of World War II, Winston Churchill raised once more the question of European unity in Zurich, on September 17, 1946:

> What is this sovereign remedy? It is to recreate the European family, or as much of it as we can, and provide it with a structure under which it can dwell in peace, in safety and in freedom.
>
> Our constant aim must be to build and fortify the strength of the United Nations. Under and within that world concept we must recreate the European family in a regional structure called, it may be, the United States of Europe. If at first all the States of Europe are not willing or able to join the Union, we must nevertheless proceed to assemble and combine those who will and those who can. . . .

The idea and the name were launched. Two years later (May 1948), on Churchill's initiative, a "European Congress" was convened by the International Committee of the Movements for European Unity, bringing together the "Hertensteiner" federalists (European Union of Federalists), the British United Europe Movement for the United States of Europe, Les Nouvelles Equipes Internationales (Christian Democrats), and the European League for Economic Cooperation. A compromise resolution was adopted:

> That the Congress
> Recognizes that it is the urgent duty of the nations of Europe to create an economic and political union in order to assure security and social progress. . . .
>
> Declares that the time has come when the European nations must transfer and merge some portion of their sovereign rights so as to secure common political and economic action for the integration and proper development of their common resources. . . .
>
> Demands the convening, as a matter of real urgency, of a European Assembly chosen by the Parliaments of the participating nations, from among their members and others. . . .
>
> Considers that the resultant union or federation should be open to all European nations democratically governed and which undertake to respect a Charter of Human Rights. . . .
>
> Resolves that a Commission should be set up to undertake immediately the double task of drafting such a Charter and of laying down standards to which a State must conform if it is to deserve the name of democracy. . . .
>
> Declares that in no circumstances shall a State be entitled to be called a democracy unless it does, in fact as well as in law, guarantee to its citizens liberty of thought, assembly and expression, as well as the right to form a political opposition.

At the final plenary session, the delegates adopted this "Message to Europeans":

> We desire a united Europe, throughout whose area the free movement of persons, ideas and goods is restored;
>
> We desire a Charter of Human Rights guaranteeing liberty of thought, assembly and expression as well as the right to form a political opposition;
>
> We desire a Court of Justice with adequate sanctions for the implementation of this Charter;
>
> We desire a European Assembly where the live forces of all our nations shall be represented.

In September 1948 the Belgian and French governments submitted the proposals of the "European Congress" to the three other governments of the Brussels Treaty (the United Kingdom, the Netherlands, and Luxembourg). On May 5, 1949, ten states (Belgium, the Netherlands, Luxembourg, France, Great Britain, the Republic of Ireland,

Denmark, Norway, Sweden, and Italy) signed the Statute of the Council of Europe, a compromise between the French-Belgian and the British view. It embodied a Consultative Assembly, meeting in public (but without any real power, the decisions being taken by a Committee of Ministers meeting in private) to present "recommendations" to the governments of the member states.

The statutes of the organization constituted a weak basis for political union. Controversies characterized the debate of the Consultative Assembly, erupting between those who favored an intergovernmental approach (Britain and the Scandinavian countries) and those who advocated "political authority with limited but real powers" (France, Italy, and the Benelux countries). The council followed traditional methods of intergovernmental cooperation except in two areas: the field of human rights (the *European Convention for the Protection of Human Rights and Fundamental Freedoms* was signed in Rome in November of 1950 and entered into force in September of the following year), and the area of travel and cultural exchange, facilitated through the Council for Cultural Cooperation (1961).

On May 9, 1950, French Foreign Minister Robert Schuman proposed the first institution that was not intergovernmental but supranational in character: the European Coal and Steel Community (ECSC). According to many, this "leap in the dark" (which proved to be successful), opened the way toward European integration. It reconciled France and Germany six years after the ending of World War II, and created a common market for coal and steel for a population of over 170 million. Britain, however, refused to join it.

The Statute of the European Community was submitted to the foreign ministers of the six participating nations on March 10, 1953, by Paul Henry Spaak, President of the Ad Hoc Assembly. Spaak, like other "Eurocrats," was still not satisfied. The Statute constituted, he said, "a rather weak step." He went on to say,

> . . . after calling for a European government and a freely elected parliament endowed with fiscal powers, the organs of which were also given the tasks of assimilating the Coal and Steel Community and the proposed EDC [European Defense Community] and of legislating on matters pertaining to the common market, it placed at the side of these institutions a council of ministers from the member States who had to approve unanimously every act of the community. This free federal construction, restricted at every move by the ministers of national States, was the best that the parliamentarians of the *ad hoc* assembly could do.

After 1955 there was a renewal of interest in European integration through the activities of Spaak in Belgium, Beyen in the Netherlands, and Bech in Luxembourg. But the "Golden Year of Europe" (as Dehousse, Secretary General of the Study Group for a European Constitution, called the year 1952) was over. The French Parliament defeated the idea of a European Defense Community, and the attempt failed to find a common European solution to the problem of the Saar by giving it a new status in international law, with its administration supervised by the Council of Europe. The plan to concentrate all European organizations in the Saar, in a kind of "federal" European territory, had to be abandoned. The European organizations had to be distributed in seven cities—Brussels, Luxembourg, Strasbourg, Geneva, London, Paris, and, most recently, Florence. They now include the European Council, the Council of Ministers, the European Commission, and the Court of Justice, and jointly employ more than 10,000 persons.

Current Goals of the European Community

Although many of the great projects of the past had to be abandoned or exposed to compromise solutions, there continue to be numerous expressions of goals for the continuation of European integration not only in economic, but also in the political, social, cultural, and international domains.

The European organizations were never satisfied with their given achievements and have always aimed to forge closer ties among the peoples of member nations. When, for example, the Customs Union was established on July 1, 1968, the European Commission published a Declaration that began by calling that date a milestone in the history of Europe, and went on to assert the need not only for further economic harmonization and unification, but also for a political union, a unified approach to human problems, and systematic cooperation and association with the developing world.

The most recent expression of goals for the European Community was given by Leo Tindemans, Prime Minister of Belgium, in a report commissioned by and submitted to the members of the European Council, and made public on January 7, 1976.

Tindemans consulted well over 1,000 individuals, including several heads of state and of government, and about 200 influential organizations. His report to the Council is important both for what it says and for how it was received. We quote his principal recommendations.

As a result of my consultations in all our countries I propose that the European Council should define the different components of European Union as follows:

1. European Union implies that we present a *united front to the outside world*. We must tend to act in common in all the main fields of our external relations whether in foreign policy, security, economic relations or development aid. Our action is aimed at defending our interests but also at using our collective strength in support of law and justice in world discussions.

2. European Union recognizes the *interdependence of the economic prosperity* of our States and accepts the consequences of this: a common economic and monetary policy to manage this prosperity, common policies in the industrial and agricultural sectors and on energy and research to safeguard the future.

3. European Union requires the *solidarity of our peoples* to be effective and adequate. Regional policy will correct inequalities in development and counteract the centralizing effects of industrial societies. Social action will mitigate inequalities of income and encourage society to organize itself in a fairer and humane fashion.

4. European Union makes itself felt in *people's daily lives*. It helps to protect their rights and to improve their lifestyle.

5. In order to achieve these tasks European Union is given *institutions* with the necessary powers to determine a common, coherent and all-inclusive political view, the efficiency needed for action, the legitimacy needed for democratic control. The principle of the equality of all our States continues to be respected within the Union by each State's right to participate in political decision-making.

6. Like the Community whose objectives it pursues and whose attainments it protects *European Union will be built gradually*. So as to restart the construction of Europe straight away and increase its credibility its initial basis is the political commitment of the States to carry out in different fields specific actions selected according to their importance and the chances of success. . . .

Tindemans sees the precondition of the social well-being of Europeans to be economic prosperity. Sharing out the benefits of prosperity will remain essentially the responsibility of the member states, who can take into account the varying traditions and conditions of European peoples. The social policy of the Union must be to formulate projects which guide and supplement the action of individual states. Such projects are to include job security for the working strata, and their participation in economic and company decisions as well as in profits. The tendency of the market to concentrate capital and activity in the most competitive areas must be offset by a policy of net transfers of resources. A large proportion of these transfers are to be made through the budget of the Community, either directly by means of regional aid programs, or indirectly through the effects of agricultural and industrial policies on regional economies.

Tindemans came out in favor of direct elections of a European Parliament—a step approved by a meeting of the heads of state in the fall of 1976—and more authority and greater role for the European Council, the Council of Ministers, the European Commission, and the Court of Justice. According to him the delegation of executive power by member states is essential if European organizations are to work toward the creation of a European Union.

The current tasks of governments and European organizations, according to the Tindemans report, consist in

> arriving at a political consensus on the aims and main features of the Union in terms which give expression to the deep aspirations of our peoples;
>
> then, determining the consequences of this choice in the various areas of the Union's internal and external activities;
>
> setting in motion, by positive action in each of those fields, the dynamic process of attaining the Union under conditions which give new credibility to the European undertaking;
>
> strengthening the institutional machinery to enable it to cope with the tasks awaiting it.

The Tindemans report has been criticized for being too utopian, as well as for not being imaginative and demanding enough. The champions of European integration were disappointed above all else by the reticence of national leaders to discuss the report in public. One of the exceptions, Gaston Thorn, Prime Minister of Luxembourg and former Chairman of the Community's Council of Ministers, pointed out that those who reproached Tindemans with a lack of dar-ing are the very same persons who would preserve at the most one-tenth of his report. He continued,

> We have lost much time for little results, and even if the European Community exists, I have never seen so little European spirit.
>
> Europe presents a prestigious image to the outside world but, paradoxically, does not accomplish any progress toward gaining strength internally.
>
> The only hope that remains for Europe at this time is the organization of direct elections to the European Parliament. I don't expect miracles, but this is the last chance to individually mobilize the European citizen. (Interview in *Le Soir,* Brussels, July 2, 1976)

Although a "European spirit" may be at a low ebb, it is significant that there appears to be a minimum consensus among the democratic forces in Europe on the nature of the required changes. Tindemans found such consensus in a demand for a new type of economic growth that would display more respect for the quality of life and the physical and human environment, and be better able to reconcile various economic and social objectives.

The main force of European integration lies currently in the sphere of the economy. Although national governments have final say in the regulation of their economies, and tend to fall back on the "tested methods" of national policy when threatened by crises, the Community boasts a number of notable economic achievements. Between 1958 and 1973 the six original members increased their imports by 309 percent and their exports by 337 percent. In 1963 the Community concluded a convention with 18 African countries that laid the foundations for a zone of free exchange and launched an ambitious program of economic and technical assistance. After 1969, 3 additional African countries became affiliated, and in 1973, 1 more. At present 44 nations of Africa, the Caribbean, and the Pacific are trading with the Community. The Community is also associated with Greece, Morocco, Tunisia, Malta, and Cyprus, and has preferential trade agreements with Spain, Israel, Egypt, and Lebanon, and nonpreferential agreement with Yugoslavia. Since 1971 it entertains economic relations with Argentina, Uruguay, and Brazil. Agreements for economic cooperation were concluded with India in 1973 and with Canada in 1976. Further agreements, to take effect in 1977, have been signed with European countries that do not wish to join the Community as members: Austria, Finland, Iceland, Norway, Portugal, Sweden, and Switzerland. The Community is the first among the world's major economic powers to grant 104 developing nations "generalized preferences" constituting favorable terms for practically all its exports of manufactured goods.

Achievements outside the economic sphere include the reconciliation of conflicts that would threaten violence and war among member states; the agreement to protect human rights and freedoms through a convention signed by all member states of the European Council (but not ratified by France); and a gradual redistribution of wealth and equalization of levels of development through transfers from the Community's more prosperous to its less prosperous regions.

II. Goals in Scandinavia

The three Scandinavian countries considered here are Sweden, Norway, and Denmark. These three nations have a joint population of about seventeen million and, notwithstanding geographic differences, show considerable similarities in values and goals. Their cultural, religious, and ethnic backgrounds are related, and the national populations are highly homogeneous with but few and small minorities. Although they are bound by a feeling of mutual solidarity, each country pursues its own domestic and foreign policy. These diverge in a number of respects: Sweden has ventured furthest toward socialism, Norway and Denmark are members of NATO, and Denmark alone is a member of the European Community. Yet their typical goals and aspirations remain sufficiently similar to be described together.

Domestic Goals

National policies have been much influenced during the last half century by the Scandinavian Social Democratic parties; that of Sweden remained in power continuously from 1936 to 1976. As a result, all three countries have struck a balance between capitalism and socialism. Elements of a free market economy are combined with central planning and guidance. In this political framework Scandinavian nations have been particularly concerned with public welfare, the quality of working and private life, proper direction and ultimate limitation of economic growth, and their national roles in the international community.

These countries were among the first in the noncommunist world to expand their public sectors to provide free education at all levels, free health care and old-age pensions, as well as nurseries, kindergartens, and similar services. Not only the Social Democrats, but all parties have included in their programs various degrees of attention to public welfare. In recent years, however, a growing opposition has been felt toward the further expansion of centralized administration and institutionally operated services. It was most recently expressed in the defeat of the Social Democratic Party at the polls. There are three principal reasons for this opposition: first, the public sector should, it is believed, accept its fair share of the general cutback forced by the economic recession; second, the taxes required to maintain the welfare system are weighing excessively on the wage-earning segment of the population (Scandinavian taxes are already the highest in the world); and third, doubts have arisen concerning the human benefits to be derived from further reliance on public and private institutions to provide essential human and social services.

Scandinavians feel economically secure. They have a well-developed welfare system, and a high per capita GNP, more evenly distributed than in most free market societies. Indeed, a saturation point may soon be reached in the area of material goods and services. Such prospects are not officially acknowledged; nevertheless, there are steps being taken to raise the quality of life in other areas. The conditions of work are to be improved, not only regarding health and security. A recent Norwegian legislative proposal would require that work be personally stimulating and would ban further assembly-line production systems. In Sweden the Volvo automobile factory has already discontinued routine assembly-line work and in doing so has achieved greater efficiency and productivity. There are other programs designed to increase employee participation in the management of firms; employees are to share in company earnings so as to bring about a more equitable distribution of wealth. Working hours are to be further reduced; an inquiry by the Danish National Institute of Social Research reveals that 60 percent of those engaged in remunerative work would prefer an extra hour of leisure to an extra hour of pay. Proposals have been made to allow employees to decide how many hours a week they will work. They may choose, for example, between a twenty- and a thirty-hour work week. The Swedish Social Democrats proposed to give people sixty years and over the right to reduce their working hours as they wish, and to reach full retirement at their own pace. Maternity and paternity leaves for a full year were also suggested.

Reforms of this kind not only help to raise the quality of life today, but will also aid in solving future problems of unemployment by reducing the active work force and diminishing the per capita output.

The governments are beginning to pay increasing attention to areas of development which do not involve further increases in GNP and per capita income, although continued economic growth remains a goal. In addition, the people themselves are placing more value on quality of life, humanism, and human solidarity, both national and international. On the surface, however, Scandinavian lifestyles do not differ much from those elsewhere in the developed world. Except among the youth and the alternative cultures, the new values have yet to elicit major changes in social institutions and personal behavior. Negative reactions by many to certain aspects of modern technology have not yet reduced their own habitual dependence on that same technology.

A tradition of governmental interference with the management of private business and production processes provides the regimes with an opportunity to guide economic development. Individuals themselves can influence production and consumption patterns through an extended chain of cooperative enterprises. But such opportunities have not so far been fully seized either by the governments or by those individuals who have recently become quality conscious.

Resource and environmental conservation is a matter of concern, and questions are raised whether continued economic growth is either feasible or desirable. These relatively small but highly industrialized countries are keenly aware of their interdependence in energy and resources. Yet, the insights gained in debates on limits to growth have failed to influence the behavior of the public or the politicians, though some high-ranking statesmen have participated in these debates. Faced with today's economic problems, people tend to disregard long-term issues, and focus on restoring or increasing prosperity, leaving any action on limiting growth until after this has been achieved.

Energy, however, is a matter of deep concern to Scandinavians. Their overall dependence on imported oil is about 80 percent. But their future prospects are different; Norway is soon to become energy self-sufficient, with oil from the North Sea and hydropower; Sweden, too, has more hydropower potential, and has five nuclear reactors in operation. Denmark, at least in the immediate years ahead, will continue to depend almost entirely on foreign oil.

Energy conservation is a high priority in all Scandinavia. New standards for the thermal insulation of houses require three sheets of window pane. The public favors the development of nonnuclear renewable forms of energy, mainly windpower and solar water and space heating, although the governments have still not committed themselves to a full-scale support of the required research and development. Public opposition has delayed and reduced plans for the construction of nuclear power plants; and the future of those already operating in Sweden is uncertain.

International Goals

The 1975 Program of the Socialist Democratic Party of Sweden declares that its goal is to realize liberty, equality, democracy, and solidarity not only for the Swedish people but for all mankind. Achieving world solidarity, it believes, implies a genuine understanding of one another and a disposition toward mutual care and consideration. The program states:

> The destinies of nations and peoples have been linked together in mutual dependence. The problems on which the future of mankind hangs are of a global nature. National initiatives will not suffice to solve them. To secure the peace of the world, to economize on the resources of the earth and curb the destruction of the environment, to eliminate poverty and starvation—these tasks must be shared by all the peoples of the world.

These global sentiments, as well as the domestic goals of Swedish Socialists, may, however, be somewhat ahead of their times. The Socialist Democratic Party of Sweden was defeated in the elections of September 1976.

Scandinavian countries do not show much enthusiasm for membership in either NATO or the European Community, but they have a strong sense of affiliation with the United Nations. They also provide significantly high levels of economic aid to the developing world: between .6 and a full 1 percent of their GNP. Aid is channeled, in large part, through the United Nations Development Programme and is given without economic or political strings and conditions. The average Scandinavian citizen continues to be preoccupied with his own well-being; he shows sympathy but not much active concern for the plight of developing nations; at the same time he does not object to the relatively high levels of developmental aid offered by his government.

All three Scandinavian countries supported the proposal to use international funds to stabilize commodity prices at the Nairobi 1976 UNCTAD meeting (United Nations Committee on Trade and Development), and Sweden proposed to release developing countries from their obligations to repay their debts to developed nations.

III. Goals of the Communist Party of Italy (PCI)

Notwithstanding a generally high level of industrialization and the progressive coordination of economic policies, the nations of Western Europe find themselves at different stages of economic development and some are plagued by recurrent crises. The inequities and difficulties have led to various movements of social reform and revolution. The more radical movements gain strength especially in the poorer, less developed nations and regions of Europe. While various forms of social democracy and socialism emerge in such highly industrialized countries as Germany, Denmark, Norway, and Sweden, Communist forces gain strength in Italy, Spain, and France.

Euro-Communism, a complex phenomenon, is nourished in part by the objective economic and political problems of nations, and the consequent dissatisfaction of the average citizen, and in part by historical affinities with socialist and communist ideas. Levels of satisfaction vary widely in Europe, as the 1973 opinion survey conducted by the Commission of European Communities, cited earlier in this chapter, has found. This poll was limited to the nations of the European Community and thus, unfortunately, excluded countries such as Spain and Greece. It found that within the Community the eleven regions where people are most satisfied with their condition are all in Holland, Denmark, and the Flamand regions of Belgium. These satisfied regions have a combined population of nine million people. On the other hand of the eleven least-satisfied regions, five are in Italy and four in France (the remaining two are the Saar and the industrial areas of northwest England). About ninety-six million people live in these areas. Those least satisfied are not always the least developed economically—areas such as Wales, Scotland, and several of the poorer provinces of France professed higher levels of satisfaction—but they are predominantly those with a history of radical ideals. In Italy and France (and, one may presume, also in Spain), current dissatisfaction feeds the growing wave of Euro-Communism.

The fact of Euro-Communism does not signify the intrusion of outside economic or political interests into Western Europe. Euro-Communists typically seek to find culturally and historically fitting "national paths" to constructing socialism in their countries. They wish to overcome the limitations of their nations' social democracies which, they say, have failed to resolve the contradictions both of capitalism and of Eastern European socialism. The social ideals of the latter are inappropriate, Euro-Communists believe, to Western Europe.

The French Communist Party has openly broken with the basic tenet of Marxism-Leninism concerning the necessity of establishing a "dictatorship of the proletariat." The Italian Communists have likewise renounced this aim and have suggested instead a "historical compromise" for Italy. In the following section we examine in more detail the goals of the Italian Communist Party, both for Italy and for the international community.

Goals for Italy

"Historical compromise" (*compromesso storico*) means an agreement among the principal forces of Italian society—the Communist, the Socialist, and the Catholic—to pursue a single societal goal of overriding importance. This should embody a political direction, according to PCI Secretary Enrico Berlinguer, capable of guiding "the life of the country toward aims of collective interest with which the great majority of the Italian people can identify."

A new phase of democratic development is to be achieved in which "some specific elements of socialism" are introduced. Underlying the philosophy of the historical compromise is the belief that the solution to the problems of Italy calls for an exceptional effort in which all segments of the population must participate. Thus the Italian Communist Party works to create "a great majority which comprises all popular and democratic forces, and keeps account of the different ideological and traditional political matrices by which these forces recognize and organize themselves."

Among the concrete policy objectives of the Party are the moral cleansing of public life, the enhancement of the functioning of the state apparatus, and the achievement of a solution to the country's economic crises. The Party proposes tax reforms, a fight against economic parasitism, reform of the state bureaucracy, and similar measures. With respect to the economy, the Party aims to convert and enlarge the production system as well as that of investment and development, and to create more employment, making use of all human resources and progressively eliminating waste, special privileges, and parasitism. It suggests that Italy must reverse the trend whereby it has been becoming more and more peripheral in the European economy; it must aim at international economic policies, and not rely on loans and assistance from other countries.

In rebuilding the Italian economy, the PCI wishes to safeguard the interests of all socio-economic strata. As early as 1956 the Eighth Party Congress declared:

> The building of socialist society must foresee, given the Italian economic structure, the protection and development of handicraft as well as the cooperation of small and medium producers which, not having a monopolistic character, may find in a socialist regime conditions of prosperity for a long period to come. . . .

> It must be clear that for the decisive groups of the middle class the move to the new ways of socialism will only occur on the basis of their economic advantage and free consensus . . . their economic activity will be guaranteed.

Since that time, the Party has consistently sought economic reform through the so-called democratic programming in which the public interest prevails, and which gives ample scope for private enterprise and initiative. The drawbacks of further nationalization, in view of the already large size of the public sector, have been repeatedly emphasized. The 1976 electoral program reaffirmed that not only the social function of small and medium enterprises, but also that of free private initiative must be recognized. A democratic program of development must be initiated which does not ignore the market mechanism through which private enterprise operates for profit. But the capacity of such enterprise is to be used in the general public interest, and can no longer be permitted to serve private monopolies.

At the 1976 summit conference of Communist parties in Berlin, Berlinguer also affirmed guarantees of personal and collective freedom, practical rather than ideological principles of state policies, the plurality of political parties and the possibility of alternating majorities, the autonomy of trade unions, and freedom of expression, religion, culture, art, and the sciences.

In accordance with such ideals, the Italian Communist Party takes a nondogmatic line in cultural matters, permitting its intellectuals to engage in debates, but itself not pronouncing judgment on competing currents of thought and cultural movements. It deplores the deter-

ministic and mechanistic deformation from which the workers' movement has sometimes suffered and, although it emphasizes the need
for a "specific battle" to form the public's consciousness, it opposes
ideological indoctrination in the school and everywhere else. As the
report of a conference of Communist teachers and school workers
stated: "We do not ask for a school that educates to Marxism, we are
for a completely democratic public school that respects pluralism and
is open to the confrontation of Italy's diverse cultural and ideational
positions." The Party perceives, however, "an axis of cultural unity"
around which all curricula must rotate. This axis upholds antifascist
values, respect for the Constitution, education toward critical participation in public debates, and historical knowledge that is both
critical and scientific. Italian public education must especially counteract the tendency to devalue manual labor—"one of the basic vices
of the scholastic tradition" of the country.

International Goals

"Cooperation, peaceful coexistence and detente among nations are
the only ways," wrote Berlinguer, "that can enable us to avoid the
disaster of atomic war, to break the aggressive and catastrophic logic
of present-day imperialism, and to bring the conquests and possibilities of science and technology . . . to the service of peace and the
economic, social and personal development of all the world's peoples."
The envisaged system of international cooperation would involve all
nations and all problems, including energy, industrial and agricultural
production, social services, technologies, and scientific research.
Within such a system Europe is to affirm its own identity and occupy
an autonomous position with respect to the different power blocs.
Three levels of action are envisaged by the Italian Communist Party
in Europe: the pan-European level, where it is to contribute to international cooperation and detente; the Western European level, where
it is to promote the convergence of leftist and democratic forces; and
the community level, where the process of integration is to become
a democratic process, responsive to the interests of the working
people. These concerns are not to harden into a "Eurocentric" position, nor act as a limitation on internationalism, but to lead to a
broader and more active contribution toward the resolution of great
world problems. Open conflicts, like that in the Middle East, must be
peacefully resolved in accordance with U.N. decisions, and the superpowers are to pursue concrete negotiations toward the limitation of

strategic arms. These goals, aimed at international detente, are weighty enough for Italian Communists to refrain from requesting Italy's withdrawal from NATO for fear of upsetting the balance of power and thus creating new tensions.

The PCI offers support not only to other Communist parties but to all socialist, social democratic, and Christian forces who work toward these international goals.

IV. Goals of the European Alternative Cultures

The alternative cultures of Europe grew during the late 1960s in response to the counterculture and student movements in the United States. They have, however, their own historical roots in Europe. There were similar values among German youth between 1920 and 1933, suppressed by the rise of the Nazi regime. They enjoyed a renaissance in the 1960s in the form of a youth culture aimed at creating a nonauthoritarian school system. While this particular effort was for the most part unsuccessful, the values of youth, and of the discontented and protesting layers of European populations in general, are gaining influence.

The European alternative culture movements, like their counterparts elsewhere in the industrialized world, are impatient with the practices and projects of mainstream society. They are disappointed not only with the bourgeois, capitalist society, but also with some of the new forms of socialism that keep putting their promised reforms off for another day. The slogans on the walls of Paris during the student riots of 1968 were *l'Imagination au Pouvoir,* and *Vivre au Présent*.

Members of the European alternative cultures realize that modern industry, with its goals of production and profit, was first conceived in Europe. They now feel obligated to offer concrete examples of a return to more modest and responsible ways of life.

"Think Anew—Turn Around" was the title of a traveling exhibit created by students from two universities in Zurich. It displayed the many current projects undertaken by the alternative cultures in farming, the generation of power, the construction of houses, and the organization of health and social services, and thus demonstrated that man does not have to be a ruthless exploiter of nature and his fellow men but can function as a provider and partner. The influence of thinkers like Ivan Ilich (Mexico) and E. F. Schumacher (Great Britain), who both originated within the central European culture, has long spread to all Europe. Their warning to be "self-restraining," and that "small is beautiful" is understood not only as a summons to sacrifice, but also as a positive step toward release from excessive and harmful burdens.

The alternative cultures do not tire of showing that the advantage of self-restraint is to reduce the compulsive pressures of work—an essential condition for human self-realization. The positive results of self-restraint are a smaller demand for, and thus a reduced dependency upon, consumer goods, and better insight into community life, in working and living environments small enough to permit close human relationships.

Rural communes represent the most widespread attempts of the new cultures to find their proper lifestyle. Their distance from the centers of industrial civilization permits their members to experiment with attitudes and behaviors that deviate from the standard. They prefer less inhabited regions also because the land is cheaper. Here they can engage in manual labor, form close relationships with nature, adopt a simple lifestyle, and practice mutual dependence among themselves.

According to the latest findings, there are from 700 to 800 rural communes in Western Europe. They are growing in number. Since youth unemployment started spreading in Western Europe, several rural communes consciously try to attract the young unemployed. They experiment with simpler smaller-scale technologies (particularly in Holland, Wales, and southern France), and with less environmentally damaging methods of generating power. "Deko" houses, most of which are heated by solar energy, combine architectural and "soft" technology experiments.

There are also new "part-time" rural communes, whose members earn money for part of the year outside the commune and thus satisfy the dependence they still have on urban civilization. Some communes accept writers, painters, and others engaged in creative professions, but demand that they participate in argicultural or domestic work for a portion of their time.

Many members of rural communes have formerly done work in developing countries. After their return, the poverty they saw led them to refuse to participate in a lifestyle based on waste. Through their personal contacts, peasants from Africa, India, Latin America, or Indonesia are invited to teach in West European communes, a promising reversal of "development aid."

Members of rural communes—particularly in southern Germany and France—have often helped neighboring farmers in their battle against industrialization. The initial enmity the farmers felt for the communes has been replaced in most cases by friendly relations.

Urban communes have also sprung up, mainly in the aftermath of the student movement of 1968. Their popularity and numbers increased even after agitation at the universities abated. About ten to fifteen young people of both sexes (sometimes including young couples with children) rent an apartment, keep house jointly, and share their income, which they usually receive from outside employment. At the end of 1973, the estimated number of these communes in the Federal Republic of Germany alone, mostly in university towns, was well over 1,000.

Some residential cooperatives are set up for purely economic reasons. But most of them are based on aspirations for a better kind of life and for changes in society to make that possible. A typical "platform," published by the group *Humanes Wohnen* (Hamburg), a collective of different residential communes, stresses the following:

> A residential commune must be the counterforce to the obligatory family and must formulate alternative values to those suitable to the capitalist system.

> These values include:
> Abandoning irrational authority and analyzing its causes;
> Promoting the capacity for objective criticism and articulation of interests;
> Readiness to change one's own personality in association with others;
> Capacity to love, learning solidarity in behavior;
> Cessation of unreasonable distribution of sex roles;
> Readiness to resist all forms of repression.

In Western Europe today there is an extensive transnational network of residential communes, whose members grant each other hospitality and financial aid. Urban communes attract many people who took active part in resistance movements but were later cast out of the establishment. They also provide a haven for many who have "flipped out."

Some of the communes have a religious orientation, and their members strive for an expansion of consciousness by Western as well as Oriental methods of meditation and prayer. Most communes, however, would like to produce goods for sale. They aim at collective ownership within the commune, a new work style and ethic, and a nonhierarchical form of organization.

Few communes, if any, have reached the goal of economic independence. They cannot compete successfully on the open market, but remain dependent on subsidies from foundations and local, regional, and state authorities.

Some of the rural communes have been economically successful. When few or no investments in means of production are needed there is a greater chance of becoming self-sustaining. Among the more successful are the craft communes (e.g., "white operations" in Holland); art communes (painting, sculpture, music), like the art labs in Great Britain; music groups; actor collectives; TV and movie producers who collaborate artistically and live together; author-publishers managed by the authors themselves; architectural advocate groups (in Germany, England, France, Sweden); medical centers for low-income groups (e.g., in the Gropius Stadt, Berlin); and alternative schools.

Outside support for such communes often comes if they fill a gap in established society, for example by providing work for the hardcore unemployed, or offer medical and educational services to populations deprived of adequate facilities. Since an economic base of the new cultures is provided only when they fill a need in society, many communes have disbanded. Others have become politically active, joining various leftist groups. Still others, while not giving up their original aims, have decided to work inside the established system and attempt to change it. Thus many strands of direct and indirect cooperation have evolved between persons sharing the goals of the alternative cultures while accepting a role in society, and such "establishment" institutions as welfare offices, educational authorities, ministries of economic affairs, cultural institutions, scientific and humanistic foundations, the public media, and even progressive political parties.

Chapter 3

Goals in the Soviet Union
and Eastern Europe

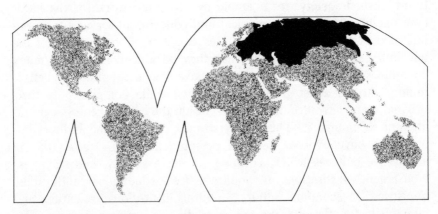

The publicly stated and collectively pursued goals in Eastern Europe and the Soviet Union are those of the Communist and Workers' parties. These official goals are set and reviewed at party congresses, and their thrust is incorporated into five-year plans. The plans are implemented by all administrative organs of the state and, given the centralization of the economy and social life, have considerable impact on all strata of society.

The goals espoused by the parties thus affect the lives of the people in their country and interact with grass-roots hopes and aspirations that are becoming more influential in the goal-setting process itself. The national Communist and Workers' parties are attempting to satisfy the increasingly vigorous demands of their people, even while they are trying to implement socialism and build the road to communism.

The domestic goals of the Eastern European Communist parties have begun to adapt to the simultaneous flattening of economic growth curves and rising of grass-roots demands and expectations. Emphasis is changing from extensive growth to intensive improvement of productivity, efficiency, and the ethics of work in general. Apparent throughout the formal, ideologically proper formulation of the goals is a real concern with maintaining social cohesion and satisfying popular demands, as well as continuing to make progress toward the long-term ideals of building socialism and communism.

The independence of European Communist parties from the Soviet Union has been progressively affirmed since the Berlin meeting of June 1976. Such independence, however, affects the setting of domestic goals and strategies more than the sphere of foreign policy. In the latter the Eastern European socialist countries by and large follow the Soviet example. Some, like Hungary and Poland, prefer not to "rock the boat," but use their good fraternal relations with the USSR to pursue their own paths to socialism.

All are aware of having limited individual leverage in world affairs, being integrated both militarily and economically with the Soviet–European socialist bloc, and attempt few innovations other than in their choice of some developing countries for closer trade and aid relations. However, Romania is increasingly insistent on the independence of her foreign policy from that of the Soviet Union; Yugoslavia, which has pursued an independent path in all policies since the late 1940s, continues to set forth an intermediate course between East and West, while Albania chooses to side with the People's Republic of China.

Statements of the official positions will be followed by case studies on the evolving goals and expectations of the people themselves. It is the interaction of these "top-down" and "bottom-up" influences that determines the actual course of events in the socialist world of Eastern Europe.

I. The Official Goals

The goals of the Communist Party are here stated by Soviet Academician V. G. Afanasiev, editor-in-chief of the newspaper Pravda. *This quasi-official statement is published slightly condensed and without alterations.*

The Communist Party of the Soviet Union (CPSU)

"The ruling party of the USSR is the Communist Party. Naturally, its main and ultimate goal is the creation of a communist society in the land of the Soviets. In programming this general aim, the Communist Party proceeds from the fact that its achievements in the conquest of the world for man by man make it mandatory to achieve a series of five intermediate goals:

> the achievement of a socialist revolution and the consolidation of a dictatorship of the proletariat
>
> the implementation of the transitional period from capitalism to socialism
>
> basically, the building of socialism
>
> the gradual development of socialism into communism
>
> the spontaneous construction of a communist society.

Led by the Communist Party, the Soviet People have accomplished the following: a developing socialist society has been built in the Soviet Union and a gradual transition to communism is being translated into reality. An economic structure (material-technical basis) was created with the capability of satisfying the material and spiritual needs of the people as fully as possible, and in the final result, of insuring the abundance which allows these needs to be satisfied. The Soviet Union is not concerned with satisfying some whims and fancies or superficial claims, but wise and healthy needs which permit the individual to maintain a condition of intellectual and physical fitness."

Domestic Policy Goals

"The CPSU has always placed satisfying the needs of the people as its main goal of domestic policy. But desire is one thing and realistic possibilities are another; and for a long time these possibilities were limited.

In the first place, during the almost sixty years of the Soviet government's existence it was obliged to devote about twenty years (one-third of its life) to defending its gains by force of arms, and had to make up human losses and restore the war-torn economy. Twenty million lives were lost, 1,710 cities destroyed, 70,000 towns and villages wiped off the face of the earth—such was the appalling price of victory for the Soviet people over German fascism.

In the second place, the Soviet government, quite frankly, received a lamentable economic inheritance from Tsarist Russia: the production of 4.2 million tons of steel (compared with 141 million in 1975); 29.1 million tons of coal (701 million in 1975); 18 million tons of oil (136 million in 1975); 1.9 billion kilowatt hours of electric energy (1038 billion kwh in 1975). This was an extremely poor showing for such an immense country as Russia. That is why there were years and years of strenuous labor; why there had to be the anonymity of the individual in the name of the growth of a powerful motherland; why there was asceticism, a giving up at times of some of the most essential things so that the Soviet Union could effectively answer the challenges of her imperialistic opponents.

At the present time, the economic possibilities have grown to an extraordinary degree in the Soviet Union, and as much as possible of the resources of the Party are turned to safeguarding the life and culture of the Soviet man—even though, to this very day, the nation spends large amounts on defense. It does not try to cover up this fact. The CPSU has learned that the weak are not taken into account, they are slaughtered. This, by the way, is one of the most important reasons for the persistent struggle of the Party for peace and peaceful coexistence with states having different social structures.

It should be understood that the Soviet Union has its problems, and they were discussed with complete frankness at the Twenty-Fifth Congress of the CPSU in 1976. The Soviets have not yet learned how to run their production effectively, how to build quickly and well, to market products of the highest quality, to overcome drought, to successfully run agricultural production, and so on. At the Twenty-Fifth Party Congress, the task of overcoming these shortcomings, mistakes, and difficulties were placed before the people.

But all the shortcomings, difficulties, and problems did not prevent the Party from following, firmly and with assurance, its chief aim: that of raising the standard of living of the people. For the period from 1971 to 1975 the average monthly earnings of blue-collar and white-collar workers rose 20 percent, and the wages of collective farm workers rose 25 percent. Considering the stability of prices (something which cannot be claimed by the West, where inflation has taken on the characteristic of a real national calamity), and the reduction of prices on several types of consumer goods, it can be said that the rise in salaries represents a real growth in the income of the people. For the past five years this growth has been 25 percent.

The CPSU has set before itself the main task of raising the material and cultural levels of the workers. In the tenth five-year plan the following programs were set forth: increasing the production of industrial manufacture by 35 to 39 percent; increasing agricultural production by 14 to 17 percent; increasing the average wages of blue- and white-collar workers by 16 to 18 percent; increasing the income of the workers on the collective farms by 24 to 27 percent.

The tenth five-year plan was declared to be a plan of quantity and effectiveness. The Party devoted its attention to such chief problems of economic development as acceleration of scientific and technical progress; the further development of agriculture (the investment of this five-year plan amounted to 172 billion rubles—an increase of 41 billion); an increase in the production of consumer goods; improvement of trade and everyday services; development of foreign trade; and perfection of the management of the economy in a mechanized society."

Foreign Policy Goals

"The foreign policy aims and goals of the CPSU are organically tied with its domestic policy goals. Safeguarding favorable peaceful conditions for the building of socialism and communism, and safeguarding universal peace and the safety of the nations on our planet—these are the general and unchanging aims.

This strategic foreign policy program has concrete content at every stage of development of Soviet society. It envisages elaboration and implementation of specific measures to insure peace on earth.

The Twenty-Fourth Congress of the CPSU suggested a program of peace. Its main thesis consists in this, to use the support of the might, solidarity, and activity of world socialism and its firm alliance with all progressive and peace-loving forces, to achieve a turning point in international relationships moving from "cold war" to peaceful co-existence with states of differing social structures; a turning point from war-threatening tensions to detente in normal, mutually beneficial co-operation.

To this end, the Soviet Union has introduced many peaceful initiatives, the enumeration of which would take a long time. We would only mention the convening of the General European Conference on Security and Cooperation in Helsinki (in which the U.S.A. and Canada also took part). This conference, by strengthening the positive outcomes of the Second World War, developed principles for the peaceful and progressive growth of Europe. The improvement of relationships between the USSR and the United States has great signifiance for the cause of peace, especially through an agreement on the limitation of strategic arms.

The tendency toward detente is gaining strength. In essence the policy of the CPSU in relation to the Western world is to do all it can to make detente irreversible, and to make universally triumphant the principle of peaceful coexistence and fruitful, mutual cooperation between states of differing social structures.

Yet even in the present time, in the camp of the opponents of detente, voices resound that the course that the USSR is following toward peaceful coexistence is an empty gesture, a result of the well-known balance of power in the world arena. They would suggest that precisely when the Soviet Union, the Eastern world, surpasses the Western world in economic and military fields, there will be an end to peaceful coexistence, and the bayonet will become the chief policy argumentation of the USSR. The present Chinese leadership heats up arguments of this type, trying to put the suggestion to Europe that a Russian sword is aiming its point at Western Europe.

The Soviet people, its Party, and its state completely reject fabrications of this type. They spoke with complete decisiveness, and now state and will repeat indefatigably in the future, that their peace-loving course of action is not a temporary empty gesture. This is a principled, consistent, and immutable course of the Soviet socialist state.

The Soviet state has followed this course of action since the first days of its existence. Literally, in the first hours of the Soviet state, Lenin stated: "We reject all political platforms based on plunder and coercion, but we cordially accept all political platforms which include good neighbor policies and economic agreements—these we cannot reject." (*Complete Works,* Vol. 35, p. 20)

The Soviet people have personally experienced all the horrors of war. And this is one of the reasons why peace is dear to them, perhaps more dear than to any other people.

Introducing, defending, and consistently following the principles of peaceful coexistence, the CPSU takes into consideration also the fact that in the contemporary world the accelerated internationalization of the world economy occurs under the influence of the scientific-technical revolution and the integration of economic contacts in the international division of labor. Even today, it is difficult for a large country to develop all branches of production effectively under its own power and to implement large-scale scientific and technical projects. This can only be done with the cooperative efforts of many countries. Only by close cooperation will the countries of the world be able to solve the global problems which concern all mankind—such as the protection of the natural environment, the distribution and use of energy, natural resources, and food reserves, the battle against the most dangerous and widespread diseases, and the research and conquest of the cosmos and the oceans.

The CPSU considers that in the present situation, when mankind has monstrous thermonuclear weapons available with unheard-of destructive power, together with the means to deliver them to any point on our planet, a new war on a worldwide scale would bring colossal suffering and destruction. It could wipe whole nations from the face of the earth. It follows, therefore, that the avoidance of thermonuclear war is imperative. And this is the common task of all the nations of the world, regardless of their social system.

The CPSU therefore proceeds from the fact that there are in the world right now forces capable of successfully struggling for peace and avoiding war. We are referring to the cooperation of socialist countries, for whom the safeguarding of peace on earth is a central goal. We are also referring to the peoples of all the countries of the world who are led by the working class. With their hands and minds the workers have created everything of value in the world; they are above all interested in protecting and increasing the fruits of their labors. Even thinking bourgeois personalities and leaders with an understanding of peace initiatives and of the peace-loving aspirations of people are realistically interested in protecting and increasing the products of their labor.

In carrying out a consistent policy of peace, the CPSU will not back down one step from its classical Marxist-Leninist principles; from the concept of class struggle and revolution. It is useless when some bourgeois individuals express amazement and incredulity at the solidarity of the Soviet communists and the Soviet people in the struggle to attain freedom, social progress, and socialism for other peoples. These individuals forget, or more likely ignore, the fact that detente and peaceful coexistence concern the relations between states and that this means that arguments and conflicts between countries ought not to be resolved by war, or resorting to threats of force, or force itself, but by peaceful means.

Detente does not, nor can it ever, rescind or change the laws of class struggle and socialist revolution, which are dictated by the clear illogicality of the development of capitalism, which proceeds from its inherent internal contradictions, and above all from the contradictions between labor and capital, which are impossible to reconcile. In actual fact, is it possible to say that when tensions are eased, the communists have reconciled themselves with capitalist exploiters, and that monopolists have become supporters of revolution? Quite clearly, no. In addition to this, one of the inherent conditions of detente is the strict observance of the principle of noninterference in the affairs of other states, and respect for their independence and sovereignty.

Therefore, the struggle for communism, waged by the Communist Party of the Soviet Union, is intrinsically bound up with the struggle for peace in the world. In other words, communism and world peace are inseparable."

(End of statement by V. G. Afanasiev)

The Bulgarian Communist Party

The historical goal of the Bulgarian Communist Party is to develop socialist society in Bulgaria and implement a gradual transition to communism. Immediate goals are stated in the seventh five-year plan, dedicated to "high efficiency and high quality."

Domestic Policy Goals

In the economic sphere, the main goals are an increase in production and in the material and spiritual standard of living. This is to be achieved through a dynamic and well-balanced development of the economy. First Party Secretary Zhivkov, at the 1976 Party Congress, declared, "The struggle to increase material well-being, the struggle for more and more complete satisfaction of the needs for goods and services, the struggle to improve the human environment—all these are by no means manifestations of a 'materialistic approach,' and do not mean that our people are becoming bourgeois." Specific objectives are: a rapid increase in efficiency and productivity; modernization and the application of the latest scientific-technical advancements; a rise in the working peoples' social consciousness; and consolidation of the socialist way of life in the country.

Bulgaria will achieve these things by adopting a regional principle of economic development, economizing with materials and energy to make the best use of scarce resources, and training more people for qualified leadership ("cadres"). Industrial and agricultural growth remain basic goals, to which is added protection of the environment.

In the social sphere, in addition to increased well-being and need-satisfaction, the goal is to promote the growth of the working class and its alliance with cooperative farmers and with intellectuals. The increased leadership role of the Party is a principal goal in the political sphere. "No matter how conditions change or technology develops, and regardless of the implementation of cybernetic principles, the Leninist tenet remains and will continue to remain true: the cadres are all-decisive." In the area of ideology, the major goals are to consolidate socialist values and the socialist way of life; to provide class-conscious, patriotic, and proletarian-international education; to increase the practice of criticism and self-criticism in the entire Bulgarian society; and to enhance the ideological role of the arts and the mass information media.

Foreign Policy Goals

In assessing the world situation and the international activities of the Bulgarian Communist Party, First Secretary Zhivkov observed, "One thing is beyond any doubt for all of us. The decisive contribution of the creation and consolidation of the new climate in the world is due first of all to the Soviet Union, to the CPSU." Hence the Bulgarian and Soviet Communist parties are to draw increasingly close together. The further development of society in all socialist countries is meant to lead, as Lenin prophesied, toward the creation of a unified cooperative of socialist nations. (Since the foreign policy goals of the Bulgarian Communist Party are fully aligned with those of the CPSU, they are not restated here.)

The Czechoslovak Communist Party

The basic long-range goal of the Czech Communist Party is the building of a developed socialist society in Czechoslovakia. Its immediate goals are stated in the sixth five-year plan for the country, 1976–1980.

Domestic Goals

The growth of Czechoslovak production is in response to the growing demands and needs of the Czech working people. As General Secretary Husak said at the Fifteenth Party Congress (April 12, 1976), "We have gained rich experiences, but what was enough yesterday will not be enough tomorrow. . . ."

The desired features of new economic growth correspond to the leadership's perception of new national and international conditions. Extensive growth is to be replaced by intensive growth: the resources for growth having been virtually exhausted, production must grow through a more effective functioning of the entire economy. This means a balanced development of the productive and nonproductive spheres, the protection of the living environment, better use of natural resources, improvement of the structure of production, greater productivity, and higher exports. In this way the long-term conditions of the world economy, relative to raw materials, energy supplies, foodstuffs, and prices, are to be taken into account in the Czech planning process.

Economic development is to be based on social, rather than natural, resources, that is, on the qualification and commitment of people, on labor initiatives, on the achievement of a scientific-technical revolution, on international socialist integration, and on assistance by the Soviet Union.

Concrete economic targets include a rise in the national income by 27 to 29 percent until 1980 (of which at least 90 percent is to be achieved by increased productivity); total increases in industrial production by roughly 34 percent; the use of nuclear energy to make possible an annual reduction of 2 to 2.5 percent in the use of conventional fuels in industry; overall growth of 14 to 15 percent in agricultural productivity; and the restructuring of the system of production to greater concentration and specialization.

No targets are set for consumption. The individual is to be able to satisfy his needs within the reach of his average monthly income, and therefore the stability of retail prices must be assured. Income policy is to be based on a differentiation of personal incomes according to performance, and the social significance of the work. Higher pay will encourage improved quality of performance and higher qualification. Quality of life is to be raised by improving the quality of social services; social consumption in the areas of education, health services, social care, culture, and physical training are to grow by 38 percent compared with the previous five-year plan. Housing is to be improved and more protection exercised over the environment, especially in the North Bohemian region. Planning management is to be improved, and investment in consumer-related fields is to grow by 38 percent.

In the political arena the role of the Party will be enhanced, together with the role of political organizations such as the National Front. At the same time the growing significance of subjective aspects, such as personal activity and consciousness, have to be recognized: "The creativity of people is the constant, recurrent, inexhaustible and innate source of socialist society." A greater role is to be assigned to culture and art, and there is to be more criticism and self-criticism.

Foreign Policy Goals
Better and more active use of latest science and technology is being sought in Czechoslovakia, through a vigorous program of manufacturing under foreign licenses and more effective integration within the Council for Mutual Economic Assistance (CMEA). On the ideological and political levels the alliance with the Soviet Union and other socialist countries is to be strengthened, and contributions made to the international communist and workers' movement. National liberation movements in developing countries are to be supported and the principles of peaceful coexistence applied in conjunction with the struggle against the forces of imperialism and the opponents of detente.

The Socialist Unity Party of Germany

The stated basic goal of the Socialist Unity Party of Germany is the further evolution of the German Democratic Republic's socialist society and the creation of basic conditions for a gradual transition to communism. Its immediate goals are stated in the five-year plan for the country, 1976–1980, as "the further raising of the effectiveness and quality of production."

Domestic Goals
The main task consists of the further improvement of the material and cultural living standard of the people of the German Democratic Republic, based on a high development rate of socialist production, the enhancement of the effectiveness of scientific-technical progress, and the growth of labor productivity.

Concrete economic targets include a rise in the national income of 27 to 30 percent by 1980, of which some 90 percent is to be achieved by increased labor productivity. In line with growing economic power, foreign trade has been assigned a high priority, to provide the basis for a further rise in imports of energy, raw materials, machinery, and equipment, as well as consumer goods. Import purchases are to be mainly from the USSR and other socialist countries. Net money income is to increase by 20 to 22 percent by 1980. The program outlined earlier by the Eighth Party Congress included promotion of retail stores, private restaurants, and cooperatives as well as private artisan workshops. Methods were sought to stimulate interest in better work performance, and improved consumer supplies and services.

The Economic Development Directives, discussed and approved by the Ninth Congress of the Socialist Unity Party (May 1976) sets high targets for agriculture, forestry, and the food industry. A stable, constantly growing agricultural production system is to be created. To strengthen the alliance of the working class with the cooperative peasants, commitments to the agrarian sector are to be completely and punctually met.

In the Congress Report, Erich Honecker, First Secretary of the Central Committee, termed scientific-technical progress "the key to a high level of economic dynamics." The economical use of materials is to play a decisive role in production processes and in project planning. An 80 percent level of savings is foreseen through improved use of science and technology. Domestic raw materials and secondary materials are to make a significant contribution to the long-term conservation effort.

In social policy, increasing expenditures are foreseen for education, health, recreation, culture, and sports. In health policy, efforts are to be particularly concentrated on sickness prevention, early diagnosis, and treatment.

Foreign Policy Goals

The foreign policy goals of the German Democratic Republic are fully aligned with the policy of the Soviet Union. As the Seventeenth Plenum of the Central Committee of the Socialist Unity Party of Germany declared, "The generally applicable knowledge and experience made evident by the 25th Congress of the CPSU will be of maximum use for the German Unity Party." The working principle is "Side by side with the Soviet Union for all times—this is our revolution!"

The Polish United Workers' Party

The stated basic goal of the Polish United Workers' Party is the well-being of Poland; its task is service to the nation through implementing the directions for socialist and communist construction.

Domestic Policy Goals

Two tasks of particular importance for the Polish economy are a considerable increase in the production of goods and services to maintain the rise in personal cash incomes; and further development of production for export in industries in which Poles have greatest experience (mining, iron and steel, smelting and processing of copper and aluminum, shipbuilding, sugar refineries, and so forth). No growth is foreseen for road construction and power generation, while the potentials of the electronic, chemical, housing, and household appliance industries, as well as medicine, cosmetics, and small-car production are to be exploited to the maximum. Agriculture is to continue its process of socialization through state farms, and it is to increase food production by 35 to 37 percent. To fulfill these tasks the investment cycle is to be shortened, and employment policy and work spirit improved.

The fundamental tenet of domestic policy is to improve the living standards of workers and families through a 16 to 18 percent growth in wages and other incomes. These are to be differentiated according to work performance. Even price stability is subordinated to creating conditions for increases in income, with special attention to raising the income of the lowest-paid strata. At the same time its is affirmed, "On the higher level of social development, social and cultural conditions become more and more important: awareness of the country's development, feeling for social justice and social security, social ties and participation in the life of the nation, access to knowledge and culture, the insuring of health care and good leisure facilities, the protection and shaping of the environment, and many, many other factors." (Report by Party Secretary E. Gierek, Seventh Congress, December 8, 1975)

In the political sphere, the United Workers' Party is said to "direct," and the government to "govern." Cooperation with the Socialist and Democratic parties, which acknowledge the leadership of the United Workers' Party, is to be assured in implementing the program of development.

Foreign Policy Goals

The principal stated goals of the Polish United Workers' Party are fraternal relations with the Soviet Union; cooperation with the CMEA and Warsaw Pact nations; solidarity with the international socialist movement; support of the struggle for liberation of developing nations; peace in Europe in the spirit of the Helsinki European Security Agreement; and peace in the world in general.

The Romanian Communist Party

The principal basic goal in Romania is to build a multilateral developed socialist society and create the conditions for building communism. The immediate goals are spelled out in the current five-year plan, 1976–1980, "The Five-Year Plan of the plenary assertion of the technical and scientific revolution in all the compartments of activity in Romania."

Domestic Policy Goals

The principal goal of the Romanian Communist Party is to promote the powerful growth of the productive forces, especially industry, which is to be oriented toward highly technical branches to ensure a high-grade use of raw materials and labor. To this end new raw material and energy resources are to be prospected and tapped, and the corresponding technologies developed. The country's hydroelectric potential is to be fully exploited and atomic energy added. Ferrous and nonferrous metallurgy, the chemical industry, electrical engineering (especially electronics and computers), the timber and building materials industry, as well as the consumer goods industry and the food industry are to be developed. Production is to be more concentrated and specialized, and better distributed over the country. The growth of productivity is emphasized through improvement in efficiency. More emphasis is placed on consumption, with 68 to 70 percent of the national income earmarked for the consumption fund and 30 to 32 percent for the development fund.

Personal incomes are to be significantly raised. Per capita income in 1990 is to be equivalent to approximately 2,500 to 3,000 U.S. dollars. Relations among the productive forces, and social relations are to be harmonized; the alliance between workers and peasants is to be strengthened. In contrast to other socialist countries, Romanian income differences are to be reduced. No essential difference is to be made between manual and intellectual labor, and differences between industrial and agricultural labor are to be lessened. Highest and lowest incomes for the period 1976–1980 are to be kept to a ratio of about six to one.

The population goal is to protect the family as the nucleus of society, and promote the growth of Romanian population to 25 million by 1990, and 30 million by the year 2000.

The leading role of the Party is to be placed in greater prominence, and there is to be an intensification of political, ideological, and educational activity in molding the new man, asserting the principles of socialist ethics and equity, and promoting criticism and self-criticism. The roles of women and youth are to be emphasized, and literature and art are to shape socialist awareness.

Foreign Policy Goals

Romania is to participate actively in the international division of labor, in the world exchange of material assets, and in the world network of scientific and technical information. Economic cooperation is to be further developed with all the socialist countries, whether or not they are members of CMEA. Trade and economic cooperation are also to be evolved with the countries of the developing world, as well as with the developed capitalist nations.

As a socialist and developing country, Romania belongs to the Group of 77 and supports the Manila Program, with the aim of intensifying both national and international efforts to eliminate economic development gaps, establish a new world economic order, and insure the free development of each nation in the spirit of equality.

II. The Evolution of Eastern European Values and Aspirations

As we have seen, the official goals of Eastern European socialist countries center on building socialism at home, advancing toward the higher stage of communism, and maintaining those relationships with other nations that generally advance the communist cause. Within this overall context, Eastern European regimes grapple with the problem of containing the aspirations of their peoples within the socialist mold and redirecting them if necessary. The main problem in this regard is the harmonization of the long-term goals of the leadership and the most immediate demands of the people.

The general goal of fully developed socialism and communism is accepted in principle and, according to official sources, is contested only by the remaining pockets of bourgeois mentality. While there is no widespread contestation of the principle itself, there is a definite tendency to put off its realization into a vague and distant future. The present aspirations of people tend to be different from their conception of socialism and communism for future generations. Yet the regimes insist on certain features of socialism to the extent that they prove to be implementable with the present mentality of their populations. Such features include the collective ownership of the means of production and of agricultural lands (with compromises in several countries in actual practice); an income distribution that corresponds not only to work performed but also to need (although the policy of homogenizing national incomes tends to be replaced by a policy of income differentiation to provide more incentives and improve the sagging work ethic); a high level of scientific and technical development (which is also a feature of free market societies, but is employed in Eastern Europe to promote state-owned production processes); and an advanced socialist and communist education, leading to the development of the all-round socialist personality having aspirations and demands fully aligned with the long-term official goals (processes which are made difficult by the independence of educators, scientists, writers, and artists—the "intelligentsia"—which represents a considerable source of social and cultural influence in these countries).

Thus there is an ongoing confrontation between the official long-term goals of the Communist and Workers' parties and the immediate aspirations of the people. This colors each country's actual policies and socio-economic behavior.

It is impossible to estimate what grass-roots aspirations might be in the absence of their constant interaction with the official goals. In contrast with such goals, they tend to be oriented toward material possessions, with the accent both on the quantity and on the quality of goods, and on the range of choice among them. Travel continues to be highly valued, and ambitions grow in geographic scope. In post-war years people in each country prized highly the opportunity to travel to their own country's vacation spots, then they coveted travel to other socialist countries when that became possible. Since the late 1960s many Eastern Europeans (outside the Soviet Union) have found it occasionally possible to travel to Western Europe, and for the urban strata this became a mark of accomplishment.

The Eastern Europeans' evaluation of the West is a complex matter. While they highly prize Western products and services because of their high level of technology and expertise, they feel the Western type of social order to be, for the most part, inhuman and aggressive. They have a genuine sympathy for recently decolonized peoples in their struggle for independent development, and they show empathy and understanding for the struggles and aspirations of the people of other socialist countries.

The following brief studies on Hungary, Poland, and Yugoslavia illuminate some further specifics of the evolution of values and aspirations in the socialist countries of Eastern Europe, and of the problems and opportunities they present to their leadership. (A firsthand study from the Soviet Union was not available.)

Hungary

Values and aspirations in Hungary are in a state of radical transformation, more intense than in all earlier decades and centuries. They evolve in three interconnected spheres: those related to basic needs and material production; those concerned with social needs related to social conditions; and those related to cultural conditions, higher consciousness, and knowledge.

In discussing material needs and goals, it is important to remember that Hungary is still in a state of relative underdevelopment. This condition has a historical background. Before World War II, the country was half feudal, with large land holdings, and a peasant population exceeding 50 percent of the total. Industry was concentrated mainly in Budapest, the capital city. The first task after the war was to solve problems typical of the first industrial revolution, rather than of the second. These problems were, by and large, solved. The agrarian population decreased to 24 percent, and workers increased to 44 percent of the workforce. New factories and industries were created; the volume of production showed a considerable rise, and the living standard of the whole population improved. Whereas prewar Hungary was sometimes called a country of three million beggars, today the economy ensures a substantially higher, essentially fair standard of living to all layers of the population, although they are still not as well supplied with consumer goods and services as people in the developed countries.

Economic growth has created large-scale internal transformations, affecting the entire society. Large numbers of the peasantry were turned into industrial workers, and the old working class and the peasantry jointly produced much of the new leadership of the country. These developments, nevertheless, lagged behind progress in the developed world in two major respects: level of technology, and development of the service sector.

Present economic growth is shifting from an extensive to an intensive mode. This involves a change of emphasis from quantity to quality, from growth in absolute numbers to growth in productivity.

The second dimension of needs and goals concerns the social sphere. The tasks achieved in the West, through a structure based on private ownership, have been undertaken in Hungary, as in other socialist countries, through the collective ownership principle. This was necessary also because the old feudal-capitalist leadership could not cope with the problems, and new social tensions surfaced that called for revolutionary changes. The transition from private to public ownership began to be put into effect during the postwar period. Numerous achievements resulted, of which one deserves special mention: social security. By the mid-1960s all strata of Hungarian society enjoyed the benefits of social security, ranging from wide-scale social insurance, free medical care, and the elimination of unemployment, to a humanistic treatment of personal problems.

However, the revolutionary transformations in the early postwar period (including land reform, the nationalization of factories, and the consequent disappearance of landowners and capitalists as socioeconomic classes) launched a process of social development in which the long-term goals were clear (the road to socialism), but the medium- and short-term objectives were not elaborated. It was not clear how the long-term goal was to be realized through the immediate tasks, that is, how socialism was actually to be created in Hungary. A lack of experience made for dogmatic and doctrinaire formulations, and for mistakes in implementation. Because of this, the new phase of development in the 1960s focused on establishing realistic plans and objectives. It attempted to bring together the goal of socialism with the objectives of day-to-day living.

Three dimensions of needs and goals are found among Hungarians today. One is concerned with maintaining life in a basically unchanged form; another with achieving quantitative improvements in the material conditions of life; the third with improvement in the quality of life. Recent sociological investigations show that the value and goal systems of the Hungaran people tend to shift from the static to the quantitative, and from the quantitative to the qualitative. The increasingly broad segment of society which seeks a qualitative improvement in conditions of life includes highly skilled workers as well as intellectuals. In fact, the cultural tastes, social behavior, leisure-time activities, and customs of these two groups tend to converge.

These characteristics of cultural aspirations derive from processes initiated shortly after World War II. Already at that early period, cultural development was extremely intense; the cultural monopoly of the old ruling classes was broken, and all strata of society acquired access to cultural facilities and services. Although not all strata of Hungarian society exploited cultural opportunities, especially in rural areas, comparative studies show that the level of cultural demand in Hungary matches that of economically advanced countries. This is demonstrated in statistics on book sales, theater and concert attendance, visits to museums and exhibits, attendance at scientific lectures, and similar activities.

Poland

The Polish nation has been in existence for some 800 years, but its history has been marked by frequent occupation and partitioning of the territory by powerful invaders. The most recent traumatic experience for Poles was the German occupation during World War II. According to official statistics, more than six million Poles were killed, mostly civilians. About 644,000 fell in military action.

The population, about thirty-four million in 1939, dropped to less than twenty-four million after the war. It is now again approaching its prewar level. While the Poles themselves comprised no more than 75 percent of the nation's population before the war, the national population now is almost entirely Polish.

Before the war, about 52 percent of the people were peasants. Almost half of them lived in poverty, farming small land holdings. The working class amounted to about 20 percent of the population. The traditional gentry numbered about 180,000 (around .5 percent). Most of the latter became assimilated into the intelligentsia and the bourgeoisie. These numbered 750,000 in the early 1930s and, together with the lower middle classes (about three million), were highly diverse in socio-economic status and culture. They had an influence, however, on the values and lifestyles of the working class and the peasantry.

World War II changed the demographic and socio-economic structure of the country. The gentry and the bourgeoisie lost their leadership role; the lower middle classes were partly destroyed in the Nazi slaughter of the Jews. The peasantry was less decimated, but the working class suffered severe losses.

The national culture was, and still is, strongly oriented toward Catholicism. This is partly a reaction to the terror suffered by the nation, and partly a protest against the persecution of Catholics by the Nazis, who killed one-fourth of the Catholic clergy in their concentration camps.

Three major population strata can be distinguished in Poland, according to their role in the socio-economic system:

the public sector of state-owned and cooperative enterprise and farms, where persons are co-owners as well as salaried employees. The bulk of the working class and the intelligentsia work in this sector;

the private agricultural sector of lands, individually owned and farmed by the traditional peasantry;

the private manufacturing, trade, and service sector, where the remaining members of the bourgeoisie are active as owners of small enterprises.

The interests and goals of each sector are represented by separate political parties: the public sector by the Polish United Workers' Party, the private agricultural sector by the United Peasants' Party, and the private manufacturing, trade, and service sector by the Democratic Party. About 70 percent of the total labor force is employed in the public sector, 25 percent comprise the private agricultural sector, and 5 percent the private manufacturing, trade, and service sector.

The general, long-term goal for Polish society as a whole is articulated by the Polish United Workers' Party, the primacy of which is acknowledged by the other parties. The party's goals were described in the previous section, but the basic and general goal it articulates can be stated as follows:

achievement of social and political stability in terms of national independence, peace, personal safety, full employment, social security, and the further development of society as well as of each individual, with *rapprochement* between the working classes and all other strata

achievement of a definite level of prosperity in terms of industrialization and the adequate provision of material and nonmaterial
goods and services.

Even if this general goal is shared by all strata of Polish society, the
manner of realizing it is perceived differently by the various strata. For
example, the development of socialist society and the achievement of
prosperity may necessitate a transition to more productive forms of
agriculture than small peasant holdings. This causes many difficulties
for the peasantry. Their future is also affected by the continuing migration from villages to cities, the desire to use improved farm equipment, the aging of the peasants and their practice of handing their
property over to the state in exchange for old-age pensions.

On the whole, the peasantry is oriented toward the status quo, while
the working class considers that its interests lie in the further development of a prosperous socialist economy. An analogous conflict occurs
with respect to the aspirations of the owners of small manufacturing,
trade, and service enterprises.

Differences occur also with respect to the objectives of the Roman
Catholic Church. While the overall goal is accepted, the Church's
more conservative elements have traditionally opposed state authority.
They still think the general goal can be realized with a continuation
of private ownership in agriculture, trade, and industry. An increasingly large number of the Church hierarchy, however, particularly on
its lower levels, now supports the Marxist program of social and
economic development.

There are differences concerning more immediate objectives among
the working class and the intelligentsia itself, though both are predominantly employed in the public sector. The working class emphasizes the material aspects of prosperity, while the intelligentsia
insists on higher levels of spiritual and cultural life and education.
Such divergences are understandable, especially in view of the well-
remembered past deprivation of the working class.

Polish society today consists of a *central management system,* which
includes the government agencies and organs; a *directly controlled
system,* including the public sector of the economy, the army, the
educational and cultural systems; an *indirectly controlled system,*
which embraces the private sector, and scientific and cultural produc-
tions and institutions; a *relatively independent system,* comprising
religious groups, ethnic minorities, and extended families; and an

almost independent system, which includes various informal groups and local communities. While their goals conform to the general long-term social goal, many immediate differences become apparent because of the imperfect way the goal is broken down into sectoral tasks and responsibilities. Such differences are expected to be temporary, to be overcome with the process of industrialization and the improvement of social planning methods.

Yugoslavia

Shortly after World II, Yugoslavia gave up the established pattern of goals and objectives of the Eastern European countries, and embarked on a search for a new road toward socialism. Today, while Yugoslavs refuse to be considered a part of Western Europe and its capitalist socio-economic order, they also reject being identified with the Eastern European socialist bloc. They do not uphold the most sacred tenets of the Eastern European socialist countries: a strong political bureaucracy, state monopoly of the economy, and central planning. Indeed, decentralization has progressed to a point in Yugoslavia where the federal government is in charge of few things other than foreign policy and running the postal, rail, and similar public services. Marxism is not a state doctrine, but merely a point of departure for the discussion of social issues.

Many Yugoslavs feel that a confrontation with the bloc of Eastern European socialist countries will sooner or later be unavoidable. They are anxious to preserve their identity and accomplishments and would rather risk tensions than join the Soviet and Eastern European fold. Since their differences serve as points of identity and matters of pride, Yugoslav intellectuals tend to exaggerate them. They are bent on appearing as democratic and free as Westerners, and yet being possessed of the superior wisdom of their own form of socialism.

The Yugoslav goal-setting effort since 1948 has been directed toward socio-economic *improvement* and only generally oriented toward the long-term ideal of a classless communist society. This change of attitude was definitively formulated in the new program of the League of Communists cf Yugoslavia (Communist Party of Yugoslavia until 1952) adopted at the Congress of 1958. The new attitude was expressed throughout the document and was most effectively stated in the last sentence: "Nothing that has been created must be so sacred for us that it cannot be surpassed and cede its place to what is still more progressive, more free, more human."

"Workers' management" is the key concept and goal. The basic idea is to "disalienate" the worker by replacing a relationship of wage earner and employer with a relationship between equal associates. First introduced in the sphere of industrial organizations, the system was later transferred to other spheres. In the 1960s it encompassed almost all areas of production, commerce, services, utilities, and administration and greatly influenced agricultural activity.

The long-term goal is to amplify the role of workers into that of managers and decision makers. It is realized, at the same time, that the structures of production and administration inherited from the past are unsuited for this. Hence the realization that workers' management requires a general overhauling of the establishments and structures of Yugoslav society.

Another concept introduced in the early postwar years was economic development without demanding undue sacrifices of the present generation. This, together with the workers' management concept, led to the decision to implement a market economy in which the role of the state is reduced to a minimum and the market mechanism is allowed to regulate relations among worker-governed enterprises.

A further consequence was the abolition of central planning. It was replaced by forecasts based on broad consultations and decisions reached through the confrontation of different interests and ambitions. This process now takes place partly in the assemblies of the member states and partly in the federation. The goal is to have the whole process occur within the system of cooperation and coordination that grows out of the self-management system in the enterprises. It is directed toward the building of a new organization for the totality of economic activities with as few chain-of-command features as possible.

The regime's insistence on decentralization, a controlled market mechanism, and worker management of enterprises, creates a climate in which individuals can increasingly participate in a wide spectrum of social roles and responsibilities. Yugoslav individuals now come into close contact with a great number of foreign visitors (more than five million annually) and can view films and television programs from many parts of the world. Through these contacts, and because of the decentralization and self-management principles of the state, the appearance of Yugoslav lifestyles has become very much the same as that of Western Europe. A similar convergence holds also for wants and needs. These vary with economic position and education, as well as with age group. Generally, there is a tendency to desire and acquire durable consumer goods (cars, first of all) and to want to travel abroad.

In the cities the influx of rural populations is visible and creates problems of adaptation. There is a strong trend toward acquiring higher education, as shown in rapidly increased enrollments at established universities and the opening of new universities. Beyond normal school age, this same trend is reflected in increasing numbers of adult training and education programs and institutions and in an increasing interest in foreign languages, especially English.

Goals and objectives in the sphere of lifestyles necessarily differ among individuals, but there is a strong insistence on individuality and personal dignity, as contrasted with the traditional dejected attitude of peasants. This change is probably a result of urbanization and the self-management system. Combined with it is the desire to affirm one's identity, evidenced by a strong desire to live in one's own apartment. Assisted by easy loans from the state, condominiums have become the dominant solution to the Yugoslav housing problem.

Chapter 4

Goals in China
and in Japan

I. Goals in the People's Republic of China

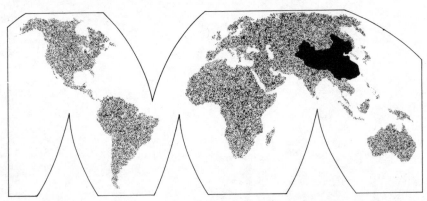

China is one of the largest countries in the world, and is certainly the most populated one. Its territory measures more than 9.5 million square kilometers, and its population is estimated at 800 million.

The People's Republic of China was established by Mao Tse-tung and his followers in 1949, and its policies and goals have elicited worldwide interest and speculation. Though it is a communist developing country, it has departed from the Soviet and Eastern European interpretation of Marxism-Leninism, and its goals and aims must be understood on their own terms.

The goals of the People's Republic of China center on development. They do not constitute a neatly conceived "model" drawn up by theorists and planners and implemented by government fiat. They need to be understood in the terms in which they are conceived—as the shared consciousness of millions of people resulting from their repeated, protracted struggles for their own emancipation. The history of the present Chinese revolution has, perhaps in a unique sense, been simultaneously the history of the growth and deepening of this consciousness. Thus China's goals, objectives, and strategies of development must be analyzed in the holistic perspective of a political, economic, and cultural revolution within a historical epoch. In the Chinese view, it is the conscious and direct action of many working, creating human beings, transforming society and nature, that provides the sound basis for evaluating development, as well as determining the best choice of goals and strategies.

Of course, leadership plays a crucial role in refining and articulating this consciousness, and spreading and deepening it. However, to form a theory about the dynamics of change and to base policies on such a theory is not enough, for such theories and policies can be effective only to the degree that they are understood, accepted, and tested time and again by millions of people in the course of everyday work and life. This approach is based on a half-century of success and failure in the Chinese revolution. In Yenan thirty years ago, Mao Tse-tung wrote:

> Twenty-four years of experience tell us that the right task, policy and style of work invariably conform with the demands of the masses at a given time and place, and invariably strengthen our ties with the masses; and the wrong task, policy and style of work invariably disagree with the demands of the masses at a given time and place, and invariably alienate us from the masses. ("On Coalition Government," April 24, 1945)

In many earlier statements, he tried to press home the method of leadership required by this perspective:

> . . . go to the masses and learn from them, synthesize their experience into better, articulated principles and methods, then do propaganda among the masses, and call upon them to put these principles and methods into prac-

tice so as to solve their problems and help them achieve
liberation and happiness. ("Get Organized!" November
29, 1943)

A remarkable characteristic of China's road is that the fashioning
of appropriate tasks and strategies is, as closely perhaps as one can
hope, the result of this kind of unending two-way interaction between
leadership and the rank-and-file.

In China's own experience, both before and after the 1949 revolution, the politics of development have consisted of: (a) penetrating
behind the facade of declared goals and objectives to the essential
reality—the differing interests and values of the social classes served
by differing strategies of development; and (b) struggling for strategies which favor the classes of the majority as against the minority.
(The underlying assumption would seem to be that there does not
exist any development strategy which serves *all* social groups and
classes equally, since it is almost the very essence of most of human
history up to this point that "development" for the few who live on
the labor of the many means inequitable development, or *anti*development.) The central problem of planning in the People's Republic of
China since its inception can be stated in these terms: How to influence the dynamics of development in such a way that it will not only
spur balanced growth, but increasingly serve the many, and curtail
and eliminate exploitation by the few.

In the light of this analysis, it becomes clear that the issue is far
larger than that encompassed by such technical criteria, or indicators,
as rates of investment, capital output ratios, GNP per capita, and so
on. In the Chinese approach, the indicators cannot be confined to
economic factors. Indeed, economic indicators must yield priority to
other normative criteria which test the basic direction in which the
whole society is going. In this respect, the superordinate "indicator" is
improvement in the character of human relations, judged by the values of the formerly most deprived majority of the population. The
priority issue is not the technical efficiency of growth (*high* or *low?*)
but its political strategy (*for* the people or *against?*).

Such an approach logically leads to a primary stress not on linear,
incremental growth in material production, but on the dialectical
process of reducing disparities as the dynamic which underlies healthy
growth. This means correcting the endemic tendency in the old society toward human exploitation and alienation, and toward a widening of key disparities such as those between agriculture and industry,

between city and countryside, and between mental and manual labor. The gradual reduction and elimination of such disparities, in turn, requires the restructuring of many institutions and values, since what is involved is no less than the revolutionary transformation of the whole pattern of human relations and attitudes.

If the Prometheus who transforms nature has been a Western obsession, the Chinese Prometheus can be said to be the Titan who transforms *himself* in the process of transforming nature or, to paraphrase the more Chinese metaphor, the "Old Man Who Moves the Mountains"—of social and economic backwardness.

The Lessons of Recent Chinese History

For today's leaders of China, her own modern history has offered the most telling lesson. In the late nineteenth century, the tottering Manchu dynasty sponsored eleventh-hour attempts to make China just modern enough to resist further Western aggression. The "self-strengtheners" pushed sporadic technological modernization, concentrating on arsenals, shipping, and a few other sectors for this purpose. At the same time, they jealously guarded the totally incompatible but sacrosanct traditional Confucian order. Kang Yu-wei's "100-Day Reform" of 1898 was an attempt to change the institutional infrastructure to fit "modernization," and was aborted for precisely this reason.

These attempts had a common characteristic—they sought a solution through imperial decrees, totally ignoring (as the mandarinate by its very nature must) the potential of enlisting popular understanding and action. Their failures were accentuated by the kind of economic dislocation that had been brought about by the predatory foreign powers following the first Opium War of 1839–1841. By the end of the century, these wars had reduced China's economy to a kind of half-life, first by the colossal indemnities imposed after a series of disastrous wars to resist foreign invasion, and then by ruthless foreign economic penetration under the aegis of unequal treaties. According to the Chinese historian Liu Ta-Nien, the imperialist spoliation of China by indemnity alone in four postwar settlements in 1842, 1860, 1895, and 1901 totaled 710 million taels of silver, of which the indemnity to Japan in 1895 amounted to 230 million taels, more than three times the whole imperial revenue of China at the time! Such spoliation speeded the development of the invading powers and curtailed China's development.

What was even more far-reaching was that the imperialist powers forced China off her own course of slow but inexorable change by dislocating her autarchic, subsistence rural economy and simultaneously inhibiting the growth of "national" capitalism. China was thus reduced to a debilitated semicolony, neither totally feudal nor totally capitalist. Different regions became virtual appendages of different powers, complicating her economic disintegration. Commercial penetration under foreign customs control was followed by financial domination. Incredibly high interest payments were extracted on foreign loans, secured on China's fiscal revenues and used to service previous external loans, or to finance railways and other enterprises under the aegis of one power or another. The formation of enclaves of political and economic domination by the several imperialist powers in the port cities resulted in the rise of a new agent-entrepreneur or "comprador" class, who served as the Chinese middlemen. It was this class, rather than an indigenous bourgeoisie, who gradually gained manipulative power in the early decades of the twentieth century. The operations, and indeed the survival of this class depended on their links with foreign commercial and financial interests on the one hand, and with the landlords and gentry who controlled the countryside on the other. They evidently had little interest in building an indigenous and self-reliant Chinese economy.

This in part explains why the 1911 revolution led by Sun Yat-sen failed to overcome China's weakness and backwardness. The revolution had overthrown the age-old monarchical system and founded a republic. But in the aftermath, political power and control over economic and cultural development did not go to a new, independent entrepreneurial class strong enough to build an autonomous, self-sustaining capitalism in China. Instead, it fell into the hands of a succession of foreign-backed warlord-bureaucrat-compradors at the regional and national levels, while effective local power in the vast rural areas remained in the hands of rent-collecting landholders and their gentry representatives.

This governing combination of parasitic social classes linked to foreign capital remained unchanged under the two-decade regime of Chiang Kai-shek from 1927–1949. It was characteristic of the regime's traditional approach to development that it laid heavy emphasis on an elitist "tutelage" of the people for constitutional government. Yet such government never came into being despite the 1927 stipulation that the tutelage was to last no longer than six years.

It was also symptomatic that the Kuomintang, like the nineteenth-century Manchu rulers, clearly set its priority on "internal pacification" rather than "external resistance" (*an nei jang wai*) and on civil war rather than social reform, while their rivals, the Chinese Communists, were promoting agrarian reform and an egalitarian society in the areas under their control.

After Pearl Harbor, Chiang Kai-shek issued his blueprint for postwar reconstruction (published in English in 1947 under the title *China's Destiny*). This turned out to be a somewhat wordy homily on five areas of reconstruction: psychological, ethical, social, political, and economic. In it, he mentioned modernization, but based it on the citizen morality prescribed by the Confucian "Four Cardinal Tenets and Eight Virtues" (*ssu wei pa te*). The most fundamental of these, he said, were "loyalty" and "piety" (*chung, hsiao*), which he interpreted as absolute loyalty to the state and absolute piety toward the nation. In both psychological and economic reconstruction, he called for building "independence and self-reliance," but saw industrialization as requiring extensive foreign aid. His program also included a general statement on "equalization of land rights." Along these lines, the National Defense Council in 1944 promulgated its program for economic reconstruction. The basic principles stressed the dualities of planned and free economy, and of state and private enterprise, and the granting of strong inducements to foreign investors, including the abolition (with an eye to inviting maximum U.S. involvement) of all previous controls and restrictions—such as those that prevented foreigners from becoming corporate executives.

It can be seen that the professed goals were "independence and self-reliance" in name, but in practice the strategy was to make possible the shaping of a form of foreign-dominated state capitalism overwhelmingly dependent on external capital and markets—a system roundly condemned by the Chinese Communists as one of direct and indirect exploitation of China's workers and peasants. Kuomintang China's postwar movement in this direction was curtailed, however, by the 1946–49 civil war. Toward the end of Chiang's regime, the economy quickly deteriorated, accelerated by official venality. By July 1948, prices were 2.8 million times those of 1937. No sector of the population, except the top officialdom, was left untouched by the disastrous consequences.

There were many causal factors behind this dismal train of events which wrought such terrible hardship on the Chinese population. But in the final analysis the decisive problem was that power was not in the hands of a social class whose leadership could formulate and put into effect a genuine national program capable of throwing off external domination, and mobilizing China's human and material resources for development.

Current Goals

The empirical lessons of history supported the Chinese Communist Party's strategic concept that development is not possible without social change, and that the road to development is through winning more power for the dispossessed majority. Mao Tse-tung saw the victorious war of liberation as but a preliminary stage, aimed at removing from power those who blocked the creation of democratic forms of development. The power groups who stood in the way were the three "mountains" weighing on the backs of the Chinese people: the feudal landlords, the compradors, and the interests of foreign imperialism.

The 1949 victory, which founded the People's Republic of China, shifted the social locus of *political* power to the worker-peasant alliance (led by the working class). Nationwide land reform in 1951–52 transferred forty-seven million hectares of land to the tillers and led quickly to increases in agricultural production, in peasant consumption and savings, and in the contribution to the national investment fund, though small-scale individual farming limited the scope of such increases and caused a certain amount of polarization in the countryside. In the ensuing four years, a socialist transformation took place. By 1956, 110 million peasant households (96.3 percent of the total) had joined cooperatives, and enterprise ownership in industry had in the main become ownership by the whole people. These changes stimulated qualitative and quantitative advances in production, yet in terms of scale and organization they were not far-reaching enough to meet the needs of rapid, balanced development. Nor was power yet firmly in the hands of the majority of China's producers.

The strategy of promoting further social change as the cutting edge of development, so much emphasized by Mao Tse-tung, did not prevail without an intense struggle within the top levels of Party and government. In retrospect, this formed a consistent pattern of struggle that was bound to culminate in the Cultural Revolution, and must continue beyond into the future. The underlying reality is that the crucial resistance to this strategy now came from those cadres whose commitment to continued revolution had regressed after they had come into positions of privilege and power. In essence, the issue involved differing attitudes on the relationship between *economic growth* and *social justice* as development goals. In 1955, the conservative bureaucrats had raised alarmist calls for deceleration and even reversal in the cooperative movement. In industry, they still adhered to overcentralized planning, and to the Soviet system of a single director in factories, and heavy reliance on engineers and specialists. Their principal argument was that to abandon such tried and tested methods would disastrously affect production and economic growth.

Significantly, Mao Tse-tung responded with the reasoning that his strategy of further, uninterrupted social change was necessary to promote advances in *both* economic and socio-political development which, he said, were dialectically interrelated. He argued that in the conditions of Chinese agriculture, it was mere dogmatic clinging to unreality to insist that the mechanization of agriculture must precede cooperation. He urged that only by instituting cooperation first could the machinery and improved technology needed for large-scale farming be introduced. Equally important were the political implications. He stressed that only by agricultural cooperation could the link between the peasantry and the bourgeoisie be severed, and here his chief concern was to seal off the springs of capitalist restoration in the countryside, and link together the industrial workers and the peasantry on a new, socialist basis.

The "Great Leap Forward" of 1958 was essentially a concentrated attempt to break out of the old conceptual cages concerning development, and pioneer China's own independent path through the activation of the entire people. As such it cast aside the dependency model of "modernization," which stressed imported high technology, professional expertise and centralized management, and irrational, oppressive regulatory codes. Although there has never been any serious proposal that large capital outlays and advanced technology or specialist-manned research and development be dispensed with, the notion that a huge, economically backward country like China had to mark time while waiting for such factors to materialize was a paralyzing fetish that shackled the innovative potential and the working zeal of several hundred million producers eager to change their destiny.

To release this potential and put this zeal to work, the Great Leap Forward shifted the emphasis to principles of self-reliance and mass participation.

In the ensuing euphoria many production records were broken, an enormous amount of what economists call "overhead capital" was created, countless water conservation schemes were implemented, and health, education, and welfare services were extended to remote rural areas. There were also errors due to inexperience, many of which occupied the attention of Western writers. But the principal result of the movement was the discovery of new and faster ways of expanding the capital base and increasing output, making use of the country's vast human and natural resources.

It was at this time that the first major effort was undertaken to implement the dual approaches to development which came to be known as "walking on two legs." This called for equal attention to both industry *and* agriculture, heavy *and* light industry, central *and* local plan-management, large-scale *and* small- and medium-scale enterprises, high *and* intermediate technologies, and central leadership *and* movements of mass participation. These dual concerns reflected a search for the most effective combination of sectoral balance, scale, technology, and managerial democracy in order to bring into play all possible initiatives and resources within a development strategy of self-reliance, independence, and balance.

By 1960, China was able to sum up the experience of testing these dual approaches in a general, long-range policy guideline: "Take agriculture as the base, industry as the leading factor." In terms of national priorities, this came to mean that agriculture held first place, then light industry and heavy industry. Only by giving primary attention to agriculture could the basic problems of food supply, raw materials, and markets be solved on a self-reliant basis, and only by building low-investment light industries could civilian needs be met, and faster capital accumulated for heavy industry. Industry must lead the way to modernization, but it must first serve the needs of agriculture and the peasantry. The terms of trade between city and countryside must be gradually readjusted to help the latter overcome rural backwardness. Health and education must be redirected to reach the peasantry.

Again, it is of great importance to note that the aim of such a framework of national priorities is to provide maximum leeway for achieving both economic growth and social equity. In human terms, what this policy means is that China's industries are not built on the backs of the peasantry, but on a reduced disparity between peasant and urban life. Chinese education contributes to this effort by enhancing the attraction of the less-developed rural areas to young people, conceiving of this as the challenge of the future—the "new frontier." Together with economic and administrative measures, this has halted, and to some extent even reversed, the processes of urbanization. (According to official estimates, some twelve million educated youth from the cities settled in the country following the nationwide movement keynoted by the slogan, "up to the hills, down to the villages.") Such policies also help to instill a national sense of common purpose and mutual concern.

The internal dynamics of industrial enterprises are likewise controlled to reduce problems arising from authoritarian managerial systems. In 1960 Mao endorsed the policies of the Anshan Steel Company—an act which later came to be known as the "Anshan Charter." The policies called for "politics in command," strong party leadership joined with mass movements, and included the famous three-point managerial code: managers are to take part in productive labor, workers are to take part in management, and irrational regulations are to be reformed. These policies were subsequently implemented also at the Taching Oilfield and came to be associated with its name as well.

Other policies, directed along the same lines, include systems of "downward transfer" (hsia fang) in government offices, enterprises, and schools, whereby officials, planning staff, intellectuals, and office workers periodically go down to basic levels of production, in farm or factory, to work with their hands and reestablish contact with the people and with social reality. These are tantamount to refresher courses for acquiring or reacquiring the standpoint and values of the common people. Similarly, the requirement that schools combine productive work with book-learning and operate with doors open to the workers and peasants, is meant to nip elitist tendencies in the bud.

China does not see any intrinsic merit in labor-intensive methods or low-technology applications. Nor is specialization a target of attack in itself. Rather, China perceives the best path to development to involve each person—worker, peasant, student, and soldier—using his or her special competence in one area and acquiring competence in several other areas (in line with Mao's so-called May 7 Road of human development). In this way each individual is to contribute to society and to be self-reliant and not find himself alienated from others in the community. A parallel development is the creation of large numbers of paraprofessionals. The most successful of these have been the "barefoot doctors," recruited from among the peasantry and serving them without abandoning their original roles and work. They supplement but do not replace professional doctors. The same principle has been applied to engineers, scientists, teachers, and so on. The only requirement on professionals is that they make their contribution to the people without concern for their own individual gain.

In this antidisparity policy of development it is not expertise and intellectual pursuits that are combatted, but social status and its tendency to alienate professionals from the people. Under the Confucian tradition such alienation is encouraged—for example, by the saying, "He who works by brain rules, he who works by brawn is ruled." Since this tradition held sway in China for 2,000 years and still acts as a subtle but powerful ideological impediment, it is understandable that the criticism of Confucianism was pressed on such a broad nationwide scale in connection with the repudiation of Lin Piao during the later stages of the Cultural Revolution.

The Cultural Revolution and the Chinese vs. the Soviet Goals of Development

All these people-oriented goals and strategies of development call for stupendous increases in the power of the people. In the struggle for socialist economic growth and modernization, those antidevelopmental factors are combated which (like profits, bonuses, differential wages) provide the incentives for production under the capitalist system. In a China without capitalists, it was the bureaucratic holders of power who resisted the people-oriented developmental strategies. Power had thus to be wrested from their hands.

The goal of the Cultural Revolution was to accomplish this end. Its basic concept, constantly emphasized by Mao, was continuous revolution to retrieve and consolidate proletarian hegemony. This core concept has been applied to the entire system of government, to social production and distribution, to intellectual and artistic endeavors, and to community life. Its philosophy is that in order to emancipate all the people from oppression and privation, the most oppressed and deprived classes must first be able to emancipate themselves and assume the controlling role over modernization. In

China, these classes comprise more than 90 percent of the people and include industrial workers, who form the leading class, and their allies, the peasants who, in turn, are led by the poorest rural strata. Genuine socialist development in the Chinese view requires "democratic dictatorship," that is, power to make decisions based on views from below, and power to compel the compliance of surviving exploitative forces. It requires that this power should be firmly in the hands of the economically least-developed majority. Only such measures will ensure that changes are people-oriented, self-generating, and thoroughgoing. This means "continuing revolution," as the Chinese term it, on a wide front of problems, a struggle over the long term to build up the decisive ascendancy of the goals, strategies, and policies embodying the nonexploitative, egalitarian, and cooperative values and interests of the working people in all spheres of development, whether in economic planning, managerial systems, educational and technological development policies, or the whole, enormously broad category of "culture." A hard and periodically sharp contest is envisaged to displace the control and influence of those classes (landlords, bourgeoisie, and the officials, intellectuals, and professionals oriented toward these classes by political, economic, or ideological ties) which, for historical reasons, still dominate these spheres of work and life and which, by their influence, inhibit the type of development process that can reduce unhealthy disparities while stimulating balanced growth. This, in essence, was the central issue which the Cultural Revolution dealt with, and it explains why this event was of such paramount importance for development. Future cultural revolutions (no doubt on a progressively higher level of sophistication in theory and practice) will very likely be necessary.

The notion that a country on the path of socialist development, after having changed to public forms of ownership of its factories, farms, and utilities, still needs to focus major attention on combating antidevelopmental social forces represents, in the Chinese view, a sharp departure from the road taken by the Soviet Union. Indeed, the Chinese road results in part from the critique of Soviet policies. The present power-holding stratum of Soviet political and economic managers clearly does not admit the existence of any bourgeoisie, new or old, in the Soviet Union. It clings to the deterministic interpretation of the Marxist tenet that the superstructure of ideas and institutions conforms to the economic base, an interpretation that sees conformity emerging at every junction of change automatically, without a long historical process of struggle. Once the socialist economic base has been formed, values and institutions are presumed to adjust accordingly and nothing needs to be done to revolutionize the superstructure. Socialist man having presumably arrived, it remains only to concentrate on speeding up production. This should be done by every economic stimulus possible. Today this includes, and indeed stresses, profit and profitability (as the basic indices for evaluating enterprise performance) and every device for arousing the material interest of the working people. Despite the juridical status of Soviet enterprises as forms of public ownership (which is the principal underpinning for the Soviet claim to be a socialist state), what struck Chinese observers about such a system was its demobilizing effect on socialist human values, its polarizing effect on incomes and human welfare, and its endemic tendency to concentrate actual control over production and distribution in the hands of a small, privileged stratum alienated from the working majority of the population. These tendencies are the dynamics of class re-formation, and distort economic growth in directions which the Chinese regard as antithetical to socialist development.

By contrast, Chinese cadres and the whole population have for some two decades been schooled in Mao Tse-tung's analysis, according to which elements of the exploiting classes continue to exist in socialist society and exert their influence on its development, and their representatives time and again attain office in the top echelons of the Party and the government. They tend to form a new class of bureaucrats in that they act as if they were members of a class owning the means of production.

The Cultural Revolution was to combat such figures of power. In order to clear the path to socialist development, it was and is held to be imperative to fight against such classes, their institutions, and their mentality. To overlook this necessity is to invite regression. Mao issued this warning in the context of a view of socialism as not a static social form, but as a dynamic process of transition that will take "a long historical period" to consummate.

The key goals of the Chinese road of socialist development are: (a) an unswerving adherence to the socialist movement toward ever higher levels of nonexploitative and cooperative society, and (b) on the above basis the creation of a strong and modern production system. These interrelated goals demand that power be wrested from the new "bureaucrat class" and put in the hands of the people and their representatives. There is every indication that the post-Mao leadership adheres to these goals and will continue to pursue them vigorously.

II. Goals in Japan

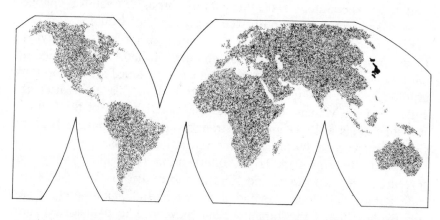

Another Asian giant of history and a major economic power in to-day's world, Japan concentrates almost 110 million people on four relatively small islands off the east coast of Asia with a total land area of about 372,000 square kilometers. Her recovery and growth to major status among the developed countries after defeat in World War II is considered by many almost miraculous. The country is now at a time of decision, weighing the desirability of continuing to pursue goals of economic growth against that of embracing some more social and spiritual values and goals.

Japanese expansionism found strong expression during the period between the Meiji Imperial Restoration (1868) and the Sino-Japa-nese War (1894–95). The slogan "rich country, strong army" key-noted the Meiji Restoration itself. The Restoration took place in a mood of international crisis brought about when, in the latter days of the Tokugawa shogunate, the invasion of Asia by the West became known. It was then that Europe, as well as the United States, became aware of Japan as more than a country of isolated feudal clans.

Thus it was understandable that "rich country, strong army" should characterize the national goal of the Meiji government. Members of the new government were motivated by the belief that in order to avoid colonization, Japan must import Western technology as quickly as possible, and become strong both economically and militarily.

Eastern ethics were to be combined with Western art (*Sakuma Shozan*) and technology was to be added to the mix.

The Sino-Japanese war was generally held to be proof of the correctness of the "rich country, strong army" policy. A "small country by the Eastern sea" won a victory over the "sleeping lion" on the continent. The outcome of this victory brought about a changed consciousness in Japan, and sowed many seeds of trouble.

First of all, although China had earlier been esteemed by the Japanese as a culturally superior country, it had now revealed its military weakness. As a result the Japanese developed a contemptuous attitude toward the Chinese and continued in this even after the collapse of the Manchu dynasty and the establishment of the Chinese Republic. This attitude grew in strength until the Japanese believed their country to be, by far, the superior nation in Asia.

Second, the so-called Triple Intervention—in which Japan was forced by Russia, France, and Germany to return to China the Liaotung Peninsula, which she had acquired in the Shimonoseki peace treaty—humiliated the Japanese, and gave rise to a distorted form of nationalism.

Third, an awareness emerged that since victory had been won at war, there should be a compensation. The Liaotung Peninsula itself had to be returned, but since Taiwan and the Pescadores were in Japanese hands, a large monetary indemnity was obtained. This, and the fact that a foothold for the control of Korea had been established, satisfied most of the Japanese people.

Fourth, the fact that foreign influence was removed from Korea, and that it came under Japanese influence, stirred up Japanese ambitions to advance into the Asian continent.

Finally, the government's "rich country, strong army" policy had been legitimized and all criticism of the government was weakened.

In addition to these developments, the Western powers, which had been regarded as a model of progress by the antigovernment movement toward democratic rights, were now discredited. It was argued that they could no longer be regarded as ideal models because they had attempted to invade Asia. Thus the regime could no longer be criticized through unfavorable comparisons with the West.

The simplistic argument that there was nothing more to be learned from China, and that the Western powers that were looked upon as models were at the same time aggressors, was extremely effective, and the "return to Japan" (*nihon e no kaiki*) theory became well established. The justification for the theory that Japan had come of age in the world was attempted through the Shinto religion. Moreover, a "family-based national outlook" was enlarged to cover all of Asia, with Japan regarded as the older brother to the other Asian countries. This idea grew in strength. The big brother should guide the little brothers and protect them from aggression by European and American powers. Thus the conceit was brought about that Japan was the "Leader of Asia." This idea was blown up until it finally culminated in the extreme notion of "the whole world as one family under Japan's roof." Japan was at the center of the world, with its light shining far and wide to bring peace and prosperity to all.

Current Economic Goals

Japan's extreme nationalism became bankrupt in 1945 with defeat in World War II. The image of "Emperor, State, and People," which the large majority of the Japanese people had come to value, was tarnished, and values disintegrated or became confused. A fixed national goal for this confused period was imparted by one man, Shigeru Yoshida, who was prime minister for seven years after the end of the war. He eliminated the "strong army" part of the policy of "rich country, strong army" and, aiming at economic rebuilding, pursued only the "rich country" part. He looked to the U.S. for defense, and the peacetime constitution, popular sentiment, and economic troubles enabled him forcefully to counter all attempts at rearmament. The theme of "economic rebuilding" was pervasive in postwar politics, and reached its peak with the Ikeda and Sato regimes.

Through almost miraculous economic growth, the gross national product rose rapidly; the government's policy succeeded to a remarkable degree. Unemployment vanished and the material resources of the people became abundant. The high rate of growth, however, was accompanied by environmental pollution and the destruction of nature. One after another, public nuisance (pollution) lawsuits were instituted. The oil crisis at the end of 1973 caused a reexamination of economic strategy and led to recognition of the fact that Japan is a resource-poor country. Consequently a policy of controlling gross demand was hammered out, and the panic caused by the energy crisis was to some extent contained. However, these problems blunted Japan's economic growth, and a low growth rate is now expected to last for some time.

The expansion of Japan's economy was based on large-scale industrialization in a country of relatively small size. Industrial complexes near the Seto Inland Sea, Tokyo Bay, Osaka Bay, Yokkaichi, Minamata, Kashima, Mutsuogaware, and elsewhere produced long-term impacts on air, water, and life forms. A "through-put" economy, of high raw material and energy consumption, and waste from rapidly obsolescent products, contaminated the environment. As capital investment in pollution control increased during the 1960s and 1970s, conflicts between industrial development and environmentalists became a major issue in Japanese society.

Japan depends for most of her natural resources and energy on imports. In 1973, at the time of the oil crisis, Japan imported 99.7 percent of her oil needs, 98.3 percent of iron ore supplies, 85.4 percent of bituminous coal needs, and 100 percent of the required supplies of bauxite, uranium, nickel, and tin. Dependence is also heavy in the area of food and agricultural products. With less than 3 percent of the world population in 1973, Japan imported 10 percent of all agricultural products on the world market. Self-sufficiency in agriculture has decreased as levels of industrialization increased, despite higher yields due to heavy use of chemical fertilizers and pesticides. In 1955 the total agricultural workforce was around sixteen million, whereas by 1963 it had dropped to twelve million and has continued to decrease on the average by 3 percent a year. One reason for the gap between the industrial and agricultural sectors is the income differential which, while now decreasing, is still significant. Other reasons are the expansion of industrial plants over agricultural lands, and the higher profits associated with industrial production.

Although employment rates are relatively satisfactory, the quality of life and the quality of the working environment have not been improved, particularly in small businesses. This is due partly to the emergence of large urban concentrations. People in the Pacific coastal industrial belt are suffering from overcrowding, high prices, and low environmental quality. Urban problems also include lack of adequate housing, public space, and social insurance. The shortage of low-income housing is becoming serious. Plans are being contemplated for decentralizing Japan's economic and political system into more than forty prefectures. Autonomy on this level is expected to be a necessity in the near future.

In 1975, the Council on Economic Affairs, a part of the Economic Planning Agency, published a "Tentative Draft on Japanese Economic Planning in the Latter Part of the 1970s." The list of economic goals in the draft includes:

> Stabilization of commodity prices and full employment;
>
> Security of life and a livable environment by means of social insurance, housing, environmental protection, enrichment of the social stock, education and culture, taxation, public loans, appropriate monetary rates and financing;
>
> Harmonizing with and contributing to world economic development through international trade based on the free market system, cooperation in the area of international balance;
>
> Maintaining economic security and creating the basis for long-term economic development through energy conservation, fostering of agriculture and fisheries, reformation of the industrial structure, reduction of the income gap between urban and rural areas, and the application of science and technology.

The new goals are formulated in the context of Japan's current difficulties with economic recession, environmental pollution, scarcity and high cost of nonrenewable energy and material resources, insufficiency of food supply, and unmanageably large urban concentrations.

Security Goals

Japan conserves a painful memory of World War II. Together with the need to avert international disputes—even in the interest of continued growth and prosperity—Japan has pursued a policy of pacifism in the spirit of Article 9 of its new Constitution. This article states that the Japanese people renounce war as an exercise of sovereign national right. War is renounced as a means of resolving international disputes, as an instrument of national policy, and even as self-defense. Instead, there is to be a system for the peaceful settlement of disputes, sanctions against aggressor nations, limiting or abolishing of arms, and a security treaty organization. As to how, under these provisions, Japan can defend her existence, the Preamble to the Constitution states, "We are determined to maintain our safety and existence by relying on the fairness and faithfulness of peace-loving peoples."

Reliance on the fairness and faithfulness of peace-loving peoples has been subjected to natural erosion since the postwar years. The United Nations could not guarantee an international collective security system, and the superpowers have constantly escalated their military potential. Already in 1950, General MacArthur announced a basic shift in Japan's security arrangements, saying that "we can never interpret this article (Article 9) of the Constitution as completely denying the inalienable right of self-defense against any provocation or attack from the adversary."

Japan regained her independence officially on April 28, 1952, and began to construct a system of democratic self-government. This included creation of a Police Reserve Force and a Naval Defense Force under the unified administration of the Safety Agency. The names were subsequently changed to Safety and Self-Defense Forces.

Japan's Defense Council was established in 1956 and its statement of "Basic Policy of National Defense" was made public a year later. The goals include supporting the activities of the U.N. in promoting world peace; establishing the necessary foundation for ensuring national security by stabilizing people's livelihood and enhancing their patriotism; gradually consolidating the effective defense forces within the limits of the need for self-defense in conformity with national power and conditions; and meeting any aggression from the outside within the framework of the U.S.-Japan security system until the U.N. can effectively perform its functions of stopping such aggression. With respect to nuclear weapons, the government declared the "three nuclear principles": *do not possess, do not produce, do not import.*

Civilian control over the Self-Defense Force is enforced through control by the national assembly, by the cabinet, and by civilians within the Defense Council. However, the Self-Defense Force has been progressively enlarged through four Defense Consolidation Plans, beginning in 1958. The fourth such plan (1972–76) had a budget of approximately 4.63 trillion yens (almost $16,000 million), to maintain and improve a force of some 180,000 men and 39,000 reserves, commanding vessels with 168,000 total tonnage, more than 1,200 aircraft, and up-to-date land, sea, and air weapons capabilities.

Such levels of expenditure and preparedness excite considerable controversy among the Japanese people. It is questioned whether the Self-Defense Force violates Article 9 of the Constitution. According to opinion surveys, an absolute majority of the people regard the Self-Defense Force as a regular military force. Academic circles believe that Article 9, having renounced war even for self-defense, would need to be amended to justify having the force.

Before the creation of the first Police Reserve Force, Prime Minister Yoshida said that the recognition of the right even to self-defense induces wars, and hence he pursued a policy of demilitarization. As the Self-Defense Force came to expand, however, he argued that "a fighting force means a unified capability of effectively waging modern warfare." During the time of the Hatoyama Cabinet, an amendment of the Constitution was advocated and interpretations were made such as "For self-defense, we can even attack the enemy country." Then, as Prime Minister Sato explained, "the Self-Defense Force is needed for self-defense." This statement has been taken as intending the strengthening of a self-defense posture in the 1970s, in the sense of the Nixon Doctrine. A commonly held belief is that even the Constitution is "not denying the self-defense right inherent to a nation" and therefore, being constitutional, the Self-Defense Force should not be regarded as a military force. However, among the opposition parties the Social Party (*Shakai-do*) advocates a demilitarized neutrality policy, the Komei party is for a complete neutrality policy, the Social Democratic Party (*Minsha-do*) is for allowing the stationing of American forces only in an emergency, while the Communist Party is for the policy of armament for self-defense. Except for the Social Democratic Party, all opposition parties claim that the Self-Defense Force is unconstitutional.

This point has been frequently disputed not only in the National Assembly, but also in the judicial courts. In the famous Sunagawa decision (1959), the Supreme Court ruled, "the inherent right of self-defense was not denied in any way and the pacifism of the constitution never prescribed no-defense or no-resistance." It further said, "Taking measures for necessary self-defense is a natural exercise of the right which is inherent to a nation," and ruled that the Self-Defense Force is not equivalent to a fighting force. Nevertheless, a nationwide consensus on Japan's security goals has not been achieved.

The Present Diversity of Japanese Aspirations

In the course of the process of reconstruction and economic development, the Japanese people have consistently demanded improvements in their standard of living. Immediately after World War II the task of the government centered on providing sufficient food to sustain life.

When the basic needs of food, housing, and clothing were assured, the people came to demand further improvements. Whereas the basic demands were widely shared and relatively uniform, these later aspirations took many different forms. They may be summarized under five characteristic types:

the first type focuses on material goods and standards: spacious living quarters, good food, leisure time, and the ownership of the latest cars and appliances;

the second centers on the conservation of nature and the human environment, and the preservation of the cultural heritage. It maintains that a decent life requires clean water and air, natural landscapes, and traditional culture;

the third type seeks the improvement of welfare, arguing that if welfare is extended to the elderly, the infirm, the physically handicapped, widows, and infants, this will bring about a truly fruitful and humane social existence;

the fourth seeks participatory democracy, with a voice in policymaking and in the executive process of national and regional self-governing bodies, as well as in the setting of various national policies connected with industry and labor. It holds that a genuine democracy is established only when such participation is assured;

the fifth type aims at reform in numerous areas of political, economic, and social life. There are those who wish to create new structures through the destruction of present institutions and value systems, and others who seek reform within the existing framework.

However, every political party has advocated policies aimed at a high material standard of living, environmental conservation, removal of public nuisances, economic prosperity, and public participation. Some hold that these have now become the new national goals.

Nevertheless, it must be pointed out that no bounds are known to the first category of demands, namely material demands. At one time it was the dream of every Japanese housewife to have an electric refrigerator, a washing machine, and a vacuum cleaner. This dream has been fulfilled, and now the objects of their cravings are the so-called three C's: car, cooler (air conditioner), and color television.

Even these wants have been practically fulfilled today, and the sights have shifted to traveling abroad, central heating, and more spacious living conditions. Such demands are encouraged by the partially irresponsible campaign promises of the political parties and are manipulated by commercial advertising.

Aspirations in the second category—environmental conservation and removal of public nuisances—respond to national problems. Their fulfillment has led to a lower return on investments on all fronts, beginning with the building of production facilities, as well as to constraints on the use of resources, a rise in wages, and a resulting decline in international competitive strength. Profits are lower and economic growth has become stunted. This has unavoidably caused a worsening of the international balance of payments and a rise in lawsuits. It is a main factor in Japan's present "stagflation."

The third category of aspiration, concerned with welfare, has already given rise to a mentality that has caused the loss of the spirit of self-reliance, and has induced people to take favors from the state. There is a general tendency to expect welfare and shirk responsibilities.

The fourth category, a desire for participation in decision-making, has created confusion concerning where, how, and among whom participation should occur. For example, public opinion research shows that an overwhelming number of people hold that serious issues should be voted upon by citizens and residents. But there is absolutely no debate on how to reflect the voice of individuals in policy formulation before the approval or rejection of policies is requested. There is no dearth of complex issues which require expert knowledge, and there are many open questions associated with each problem. Can a citizen accurately judge the pros and cons? Would his judgment not be irrational or shortsighted? If the results of a vote are considered undesirable, who takes responsibility for that? How would the results of a vote be modified? These and similar questions are posed but not resolved.

After the war the government pursued a policy of rapid economic growth, and after the oil crisis it switched to a policy of stabilized growth. "Social justice" and "improved welfare" are now presented as the new goals. Questions are being raised about both. Can one hope for social justice within the framework of a capitalist economic system? Can it be achieved within a mixed economy, or must one convert to a socialist system? Can social justice take account of individual ability and work ethic, and offer not only equality under the law, but equal opportunity and fair competition?

The expansion of welfare services and guarantees is necessary, but how can one avoid the welfare mentality which seeks to extract all it can from the national and the regional governments? Although the national and regional governments care for the sick and the elderly, many feel that the spirit of sympathy and service of traditional Japan has been lost.

Social justice, increasing levels of wealth, removal of public nuisances, sufficient welfare, citizen participation, and similar issues are not taken lightly. But a lack of sound knowledge of the pertinent facts at present frustrates the clear formulation of Japan's national goals.

Chapter 5

Goals in Latin America

We begin our second, more southerly west-to-east sweep with a review of the goals of Latin American nations and peoples. Most of this vast region is relatively underdeveloped, as indeed are all others we encounter in this part of our world atlas of goals with the exception of Australia and possibly Singapore. The Latin American region was conquered and colonized for the most part by Spanish and Portuguese expeditions in the sixteenth century. Independence was achieved by most of the nations in the nineteenth century. The population is concentrated mainly in the more easily accessible coastal areas and in the cooler highlands. The Latin American population (including Mexico, Central America, the Caribbean, and the countries of South America) is estimated at around 330 million. It is growing at an average rate of 2.8 percent. It is unevenly distributed, with large cities and metropolitan regions, small villages and hamlets, and little in between.

Political life is hectic, colorful, and diversified. During the wars of national independence the descendants of the Spanish conquerors displaced the original Spanish rulers. But the hierarchical structure established by Spain and the Catholic Church was retained. In the

111

absence of a strong central authority regionalism developed, with local political and economic organization. Local leaders (*caudillos*) emerged from the ranks of large landowners and the armed forces, and took over the guidance of political life. Until recently the landed aristocracy dominated most of the rural areas, and is still relatively strong in some countries, such as Argentina, Colombia, and Brazil.

National leaders depended on the support of regional *caudillos,* since the latter commanded the loyalty of the local populations. Functional socio-cultural, economic, and political units tended to be based on extended families with many *compadres*—groups formed by several extended families, and other closely knit groups based on personal ties, family relations, and communal needs. Because of such regionalism, some Latin American nation-states experienced difficulty in integrating their populations and ensuring their allegiance to the nation as a whole.

The constitutions of Latin American states tend to be reappraised after each revolution or major change in regime. Some countries, such as Venezuela, have had as many as twenty-five constitutions. The Dominican Republic has had twenty-three, and five other nations have had ten or more. Discontinuities are frequent in the political life of Latin American nations, but more often than not leave the established hierarchical structure of economic and political life intact. It is mainly the leading persons that are replaced. Revolutions are initiated and carried out in the name of the people, national unity, and the safeguarding of national interests.

Although there are great differences in income levels in the region, the average level of socio-economic development is still low. More than 40 percent of Latin Americans are still engaged in relatively primitive forms of agriculture. Among such rural masses illiteracy rates are high, and marginal existence is not uncommon. Real per capita product has more than doubled since 1957 and is now about $1,000 annually.

Socio-economic rigidity and the inequitable distribution of wealth have produced a pattern of socio-economic stratification in which roughly the upper 1 percent of the people control some 30 percent of the wealth, the next 30 percent control 50 percent, and all the rest share the remaining 20 percent. (See Figure 5-1.)

Urban socio-economic development is normally associated with modernization and industrialization. Brazil, Argentina, Mexico, and

Figure 5.1
Distribution of Wealth in Latin America

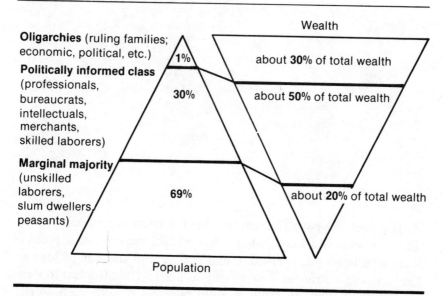

Wealth

Oligarchies (ruling families; economic, political, etc.) 1%
about **30%** of total wealth

Politically informed class (professionals, bureaucrats, intellectuals, merchants, skilled laborers) 30%
about **50%** of total wealth

Marginal majority (unskilled laborers, slum dwellers, peasants) 69%
about **20%** of total wealth

Population

Colombia have succeeded in achieving a rapid rate of industrialization and import-substitution. The smaller nations of Central America, as well as Bolivia, Paraguay, and Ecuador, make but slow progress and continue to rely heavily on imports. Venezuela, as a member of the Organization of Petroleum Exporting Countries (OPEC), is in a privileged position, enjoying considerable oil revenues. All countries aim at integrating the marginal socio-economic classes; developing better use of existing natural and human resources; increasing agricultural productivity; diversifying domestic industry; upgrading the national educational system including skill-training programs; and expanding public and private savings to evolve a self-reliant basis for economic growth. The expressions of these general objectives vary greatly from country to country and are accompanied by more specific goals and expectations, as the following studies indicate.*

* Goals in Latin America are presented under three headings: goals in Mexico; goals in the northwestern countries of South America; and goals in the southeastern countries of South America. These headings reflect regional commonalities and divergences, but are not meant to suggest the presence of three distinct types of nation and culture on the continent.

I. Goals in Mexico

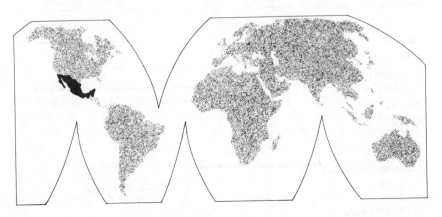

Variety and diversity characterize the Mexican countryside. When Hernán Cortés was asked what it looked like, he crushed a piece of parchment in his fist, released it, and said: This is the map of Mexico. The land surface ranges from swamp to desert, from tropical lowland jungle to high alpine vegetation, from thin arid soils to fields so rich that three crops a year can be grown on them. Barely one-fifth of the land is suitable for cultivation, and of this portion only one-third is irrigated.

Mexico's population is one-fourth pure Indian, over one-half mestizo, about one-tenth pure European, and the rest are of mixed black, European, Indian, and mestizo origins. Indian ancestry is often considered an asset; the pride of Mexicans in the native Indian culture is reflected in the many murals that attract visitors from all over the world.

Despite their proximity to the United States, Mexicans do not suffer from an identity crisis and have not lost a spirit of fierce independence. But there is a deep internal gulf between the rich and the poor. The aspirations of the landless peasants of Oaxaca and the thriving professional middle class in Monterrey, for example, have hardly anything in common. As economic growth further widens the socio-economic gap, the have-nots seek to become integrated into the modern economic system, although they still want to retain their ethnic and regional roots.

The present population of about 63 million contrasts with the 12 million that inhabited the land at the time of the 1911 revolution, and with the 120 million anticipated by the turn of the century. In age level, half the population is under sixteen, half the voters are under twenty-six, and half the technicians and civil servants are under thirty-six. The gulf between the rich and the poor parallels that between the modernized city dwellers and the rural agriculturists; about 14 million people, more than one-fifth of the population, lives in the federal district that includes Mexico City, while three-fourths of the almost 100,000 rural municipalities have fewer than 1,000 people.

Unemployment and underemployment are widespread. Most of the 40 percent of the population who work in the agricultural sector are underemployed. More than three million landless peasants work barely 100 days a year. Many in commerce, government, and domestic or other services are also underemployed, working part-time or occasionally, or engaging in activities which reflect hidden unemployment. About 25 percent are now working in industry and in the energy and construction sectors, but underemployment and the rich-poor and urban-rural gaps remain the major socio-economic problems facing the Mexican leadership.

Political Goals
Mexico's modern era began with the 1911 revolution that ended a quarter century of dictatorship. Some continuity with the previous strong-man–based political system was reflected in the 1917 Constitution, which granted extraordinary powers to the presidency. The president commands an integrated political machinery; the government and the official party—the *Partido Revolucionario Institucional* (PRI)—are essentially one. This party combines in a single bloc the organized peasantry, the labor unions, and the civil servants. It permits, and even encourages, a limited opposition, consisting of three parties, of which one is an offshoot of the PRI, another takes a position to the left of it, and the third to the right. Each is guaranteed a certain number of seats in the Chamber of Deputies, whether the ballot entitles them to that number or not. But the presence of the opposition is of minor significance, since neither the Chamber of Deputies nor the Senate effectively exercises its constitutional powers.

Real power is vested in the president, although his term is limited to six years, and by law he cannot be reelected. He makes all important decisions, usually through consultation with, but not necessarily with the agreement of, the PRI. He also names the seventeen members of his Cabinet, who function as the country's top decision-making body. The outgoing president has a strong say in selecting his successor, since he names the gubernatorial candidates as well as the leaders of the PRI.

The government is aware of the need to renew channels of communication with the broad strata of the Mexican people. Candidates for the presidency visited most parts of Mexico in 1970 and 1976, not only to sound out public opinion, but also to bring the government closer to the people in outlying areas. It had been brought home to the government by student unrest before the 1968 Olympic Games and by independent members of the press that one-man–based, one-party rule will be difficult to sustain unless incomes are more equitably distributed, and the backwardness and poverty of rural and urban shantytowns are relieved. Thus attention has been directed not only to achieving a consensus of the nation's principal interest groups within the Party (and avoiding adversary politics in Parliament) but to the discussion and advocacy of new economic goals.

Economic Goals
Until the drastic devaluation of the peso in the fall of 1976, Mexico's economy had shown remarkable stability, especially in comparison with that of other countries in Latin America. While economic growth solved many problems, it made others worse. Mexico's most formidable economic problem today is the value of the peso, and the highly skewed distribution of income. More than a third of the population lives in abject poverty, often in the midst of rising affluence, burgeoning industries, and within modern cities.

Aware that such stark contrasts endanger political stability, presidents in recent years have sought strategies to assure a more balanced economic growth. There are guaranteed floor prices for key commodities, ceilings on major food prices, and a number of import policies. Despite such measures, the income of the farmers has not kept pace with that of other sections of the population. The government now aims at large-scale modernization of agriculture and the creation of more adequate credit terms.

The government headed by past-president Luis Echeverría clearly stated that it would enter any field of economic activity not sufficiently serviced by private enterprise. The number of government-owned or coowned enterprises has risen from only 100 in the mid-1960s to almost 1,000. The state now accounts for more than half of the total investments. The public and private sectors, however, do not yet see eye to eye on how to run the economy. The private sector takes objection to the state being both an actor and a director in economic processes. While all want to continue the 6 percent rate of economic growth achieved in past years, and all are agreed on the need for a more equitable distribution of income, the immediate interests of the government and the private sectors may come into conflict in a new phase of more selective growth.

Long-range economic prospects are favorable, primarily because of the country's great natural resources. These are being progressively exploited—the image of a beggar sitting on a bag of gold no longer applies to Mexico.

Oil has become a major component in the Mexican economy. Domestic oil fields were nationalized in 1938 and they made Mexico energy self-sufficient in the 1960s. In the early 1970s Mexico became a net oil importer but new finds of oil in the southeastern part of the country have now made it a net oil exporter. With the success of OPEC in mind, the government is seeking to strengthen its international economic position, in order to assure continued economic independence from its wealthy northern neighbor. At the same time the country is developing other energy sources, including coal, uranium, and hydroelectric and geothermal power, the latter facilitated by the availability of hot volcanic subsurfaces.

Foreign Policy Goals
Mexico's foreign policy upholds the principles of the right of peoples to self-determination, noninterference in the internal affairs of other states, and rejection of the use of force to settle disputes, and it seeks economic cooperation wherever possible. The country subscribes to the so-called Estrada Doctrine, which condemns the practice whereby big powers recognize and aid national governments in order to further their own commercial or military interests.

Notwithstanding Mexico's long common border with the United States, and its great dependence on that country for foreign trade and investment, past-president Luis Echeverría remained a major champion of a new international economic order throughout his term of office. He proposed the "Charter of Economic Rights and Duties of States" (see Chapter 9), visited thirty-seven nations in an official capacity, and met with sixty-four heads of state.

Mexico entertains diplomatic relations with almost 100 nations and is constantly engaged in efforts to broaden its international contacts. Major goals are improved economic relations, and the transfer of technology for domestic development. Mexico supports wholeheartedly such proposals as the international regulation of access to sea bed resources, national sovereignty extending 200 miles from national coastlines, and the stabilization of commodity prices in relation to internationally traded manufactured goods. The country is a founder of the Latin American Economic System and is active in the developing nations' Group of 77. It sponsors such institutions as the Open University of the Third World, the Center for the Economic and Social Study of the Third World, and the Latin American Research and Information Office for Transnational Studies.

Cultural Goals

Mexico seeks to strengthen its national cultural identity and to preserve its pre-Columbian roots. The many murals in which the country excels depict national affinities with the revolution as well as with the original Indian culture. The architectural splendors of the past are preserved and made accessible to Mexicans as well as to foreign visitors. Even such modern buildings as those that house the offices of Social Security and the Ministry of Foreign Affairs are decorated with historical relics.

Folk dances and music are being revived, and Indian themes are stressed in the government's efforts to bring traditional Mexican culture to the urban and rural masses. A similar emphasis is placed on literature, but efforts here are hindered by the continuing high rate of illiteracy.

Cultural goals are also espoused to further the cause of tourism, which remains one of the pillars of the economy. Tourism contributes significantly to the accumulation of foreign exchange, and has a sizable ripple effect on all sectors of the economy. But Mexico now tries to attract tourists who can appreciate its culture and identity. It is anxious to guard against the erosion of indigenous ways of life through the incursion of more than 3.5 million tourists a year, mostly from the United States. Hence it organizes and supports thousands of "fiestas" of religious and ethnic origin, and safeguards sites of historical and cultural significance against destruction or misuse.

II. Goals in the Northwestern Countries of South America

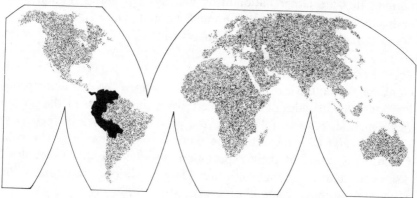

The northwestern areas of the South American continent are shared by Bolivia, Ecuador, Panama, Colombia, Peru, and Venezuela. These countries, known as the "Bolivarian nations," share many of the same socio-economic problems, the same language and religion, similar traditions and cultural organization, and a republican origin born of an independence movement led by Simón Bolívar and generals from these republics at a time when a feeling of unity still persisted. This feeling was subsequently diminished by the difficult topography of this mountainous region, with its slow communications and the emerging nationalism of the peoples and governments. Nationalism has only now begun to yield somewhat in the face of shared economic problems, which have prompted these countries (with the exception of Panama) to form the nucleus of the Andean Pact, which attempts to create a common market for the region and acquire more leverage with respect to the world economy.

Similarities in the social and economic conditions of these countries, notwithstanding variations in levels of income, make for a coincidence of the declared goals of practically all their governments and political parties. These center on economic growth, greater social justice, nutrition and literacy, a higher standard of living, support of the marginal populations, agriculture, land reforms to reduce inequalities in ownership, and peace. Some advances have been made toward realization of these objectives; for example, infant mortality has been decreased and the average GNP has been increased by about 7 percent. These achievements came about despite the diverse political ideologies of the governments and their lack of continuity. At present

only Colombia and Venezuela have democratically elected governments. The other nations of the Bolivarian region are ruled by military
regimes that are either nationalistic and left (in Peru), nationalistic
and center-left (in Panama), nationalistic and center-right (in Ecuador), or nationalistic and right (in Bolivia).

Socio-Economic Goals

Goals in the countries of this region are shaped by dominant problems and the attitudes of the people toward them. Most of the people
feel deprived, both in relation to the privileged classes in their own
countries, and with respect to the more developed nations. The continuing frustration of their expectations produces a sharp feeling of
discontent and impatience with prevailing conditions, particularly the
slow rate of socio-economic progress.

This explains the support given military governments that promise
strong measures to deal with the situation. It also explains their accentuated sense of nationalism. However, extremists are in the minority (no more than 5 to 10 percent of the voters in free elections during
democratic periods show preference for either the extreme right or
left), and most people would agree with a moderately socialist aspiration. In Colombia, for example, only 47 percent of the elite claim
to be opposed to a moderate state control of assets, although 70 percent are opposed among the middle classes. Most people accept the
alternative idea of collective ownership; in one inquiry 84 percent of
those questioned were in favor of it when the question was raised.
They also tend to have a poor opinion of public institutions. Public
education is acceptable to less than half, and public security and
health services to an even smaller proportion.

Religion is no longer generally regarded as a cure for social ills.
In a poll of a representative segment of the population in Colombia,
only 28 percent said that religion was valid and important, while 21
percent thought it was unable to solve current problems. Thirty-three
percent thought it had nothing to do with them. Yet about 40 percent
admitted a need for spiritual values and guidance.

The economies of the region tend to be unstable, and offer a low
level of equity. Half of the population is under sixteen years of age.
The working population consists of three times as many men as
women. The total workforce is usually around 30 percent of the national population. Visible unemployment has oscillated between 6 and
13 percent in Peru, Venezuela, Colombia, and Panama, with higher

rates in Ecuador and Bolivia. But if one takes into account hidden unemployment, and visible and hidden underemployment, some 25 to 32 percent of the labor force turns out to be idle. In rural areas, about 25 percent of the farmers are engaged in no more than subsistence farming. These figures indicate the most marked characteristic of the Bolivarian countries: scarcity of skilled labor, and excess of unskilled unemployed labor.

The distribution of the labor force gives an indication of the importance of the various economic sectors. Nearly 45 percent are engaged in agriculture and fishing, 20 percent in industry and services, and 35 percent in a variety of activities. The industrial and service sectors are more important in Venezuela and Colombia than in the other countries. But the poorest segments of the working class have the least education and the greatest incidence of disease.

Venezuela is the richest country of the region, with reserves estimated in excess of 6,000 million dollars. Her income is from the export of oil which, as an OPEC member, the country has quadrupled in price. Yet Venezuela's economic and social structure is similar to that of the other countries of the region, with high levels of undernourishment, crowding, and illiteracy. The principal problem of the country, according to the president, is that its economy has placed a careless confidence in oil revenues, and neglected to develop its other sectors. There is now a marked effort to promote heavy industry and agriculture, in that order, with the goal of at least supplying domestic needs.

All nations of the region pursue an official policy of traditional-style industrialization, emulating the Western world. For the most part, industry fails to respond to the most immediate needs of health, food, and acceptable standards of life, but follows foreign models that require large amounts of capital and high levels of technology. Examples are the petrochemical, steel, and automobile industries.

More recently, demands have been voiced to develop industries that would absorb more of the available unskilled labor. The governments find themselves in a paradoxical situation. They have to deal with industries created specifically to substitute for imports, but which do not take into account economies of scale, and which also absorb a substantial portion of national savings at the expense of other sectors of greater social benefit.

Consumption patterns have been shaped by United States and European interests and practices. This has had some unanticipated effects.

For example, pressures to increase sales have made for persuasive methods of advertising, and for planned obsolescence, yet the local markets have but a small capacity to absorb the products made and marketed in this manner. As a result, industrial production has been oriented in large measure toward the consumption of luxury goods by the numerically small affluent classes. This has hurt the middle and lower socio-economic classes, who could not afford the goods for which demand has been artificially created. The middle classes tend to overspend, reduce their savings, and incur progressively greater debts.

Governments have tended to protect the industries that cater to demands for unnecessary products by the middle and upper classes, even at the cost of diseconomies. Thus a vicious circle has been created in favor of luxury goods at the expense of essential industries and services. The ill effects are somewhat mitigated by the creation of secondary employment—the use of semiskilled labor to service and repair nonessential consumer goods. The tendency to consume luxury goods beyond the country's economic capacity is a notable characteristic both of the Bolivarian region and of Latin America as a whole.

Such tendencies are reinforced by the traditional values of the culture. Even in poor rural areas, working beyond one's immediate needs is looked upon as avarice and the mark of a hidden desire to dominate. In the mountain regions of Colombia, for example, investigators found that people spend, on the average, 38 percent of their family income on food, 42 percent on the various needs of their social life, and invest only 10 percent in the farming that forms the basis of their subsistence.

Because of widespread poverty, the governments of the region give little thought to long-term strategies of development, attempting rather to quickly achieve at least a minimum level of individual and social well-being. All important economic decisions are in the hands of the governments, four of which are military and two (Venezuela and Colombia) are elected civilian regimes. Even in the latter, the nationalization and control of the principal means of production is advancing. This does not prevent the private sector from exercising influence, but such influence stems from its response to government regulations, rather than from action taken on its own initiative.

State control will probably continue to grow throughout the region and may lead to the creation of a socialist (not necessarily Marxist) economic system, although the currently prevailing mixed economies could continue to exist for a long time.

Population Goals

Indigenous population growth rates in the region are much higher than in the developed world, and may lead to a doubling of the population within twenty to thirty years. Such rates stem from values associated with large families, from *machismo,* which measures a man's worth by, among other things, the number of sons he has, and from the system of extended families. For these reasons it will be difficult, if not impossible, to reduce rates of population increase during the next several decades. Low standards of living, little education, and lack of information contribute to the difficulties, which are further compounded by opposition to birth control stemming from the Catholic Church and the nationalistic and far-left political groups. Bolivia, Peru and, to some extent, Ecuador are formally opposed to population control measures; only Colombia and Venezuela have launched family planning programs, but their effect is yet to be felt.

Major problems arise for the Bolivarian (as for most other Latin American) countries in the area of urban growth. Migration to the cities has been continuous since the beginning of the century. Because of this, together with the high fertility rate, the capital cities are growing at an annual rate of more than 7 percent, and will double in size in ten years. All major cities are ringed by shantytowns built on lands next to construction sites. Shacks in these areas lack even minimal standards of hygiene and security.

The governments are attempting to decentralize the major urban concentrations, but so far have not been successful because of the continuing flow of migrants seeking jobs in the cities. There is a great difference between urban and rural living standards and economic conditions. Improvement in rural conditions is generally frustrated, simply because the economic and political life of each country tends to be concentrated in its capital city.

Food Production Goals

Large areas of the Bolivarian territories are covered by humid, and as yet unexploited, equatorial forests and meadowlands. Their forest reserves are among the largest in the world, but are being wasted or poorly used. Newly cleared lands are colonized for planting traditional crops. Most of the best arable lands are already in use. In mountainous regions there is a danger of soil erosion. When the equatorial forests are cleared, and ecological cycles are interrupted, humid areas become arid zones. Although there are plans for reforestation and conservation, actual practices favor deforestation, and often produce unanticipated adverse results.

Foodstuffs are available within the countries at prices that vary seasonally, in some cases up to 150 percent. Moreover, there are great regional price differences for basic foods owing to the high cost of transportation and the low level of communication between regions. Losses due to deficient storage are high. The difficulties are exacerbated by the needs of the small agriculturalist, who has to sell his crops rapidly after harvest in order to subsist, and thus has little or no bargaining power.

Small-scale farming activities are widely dispersed in mountainous areas. Efforts to improve communication and reduce the cost of transport have not so far yielded significant results. Crops of the modern commercial agricultural sector increase at some 7 percent per annum, while those of the traditional sector increase at an annual rate of about 3 percent. This is barely more than the rate of population increase.

Ecological problems are given low priority because of a lack of clarity concerning what is needed immediately, and what is important in the long term. Renewable and nonrenewable resources have been wasted, and major environmental damage has often been inflicted. Only a few scientists and intellectuals have taken the problems seriously, but they are rarely able to change existing practices.

Foreign Trade Goals

Despite ideological differences among the regimes, major efforts focus on maintaining mutual ties within the Andean Pact. The region has raw materials in large quantity, but their exploitation is often competitive rather than complementary. A similar situation exists with respect to agricultural produce and the attempts of local industry to find substitutes for imports. Monetary policies have rendered commerce among the Bolivarian nations difficult, since some have fluctuating rates of exchange while others over- or undervalue their currencies. Most of the nations depend on one main export item and on a single export market—principally the United States. Venezuela exports mainly oil, Colombia coffee, Ecuador bananas, Peru fish, Bolivia tin, and Panama's earnings come from tolls on the canal. Thus the national economies are extremely vulnerable; their stabilization is one of the goals of joint Andean Pact economic policies.

III. Goals in the Southeastern Countries of South America

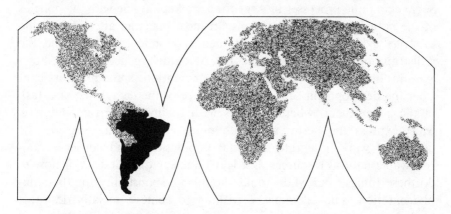

Argentina, Brazil, Chile, Paraguay, and Uruguay constitute the countries of the southeastern half of the continent. These too exhibit some similarities due to their Iberian heritage. They also share borders, and currently all have military governments. The expectations of these countries are akin to those of the developing nations, but their immediate loyalties are primarily confined to the American continent.

The overwhelming concern of the countries of this region is to provide employment, education, adequate housing, and health services for their people, and to integrate their marginal populations into society. Environmental issues do not receive high priority, nor do the wider issues of world security.

Goals in Argentina

Argentina's recent history displays a series of discontinuities in the composition, philosophy, and strategy of government. In the past ten years, there have been eight presidents, and more recently the armed forces unseated the Peronist regime. But the aspirations of the Argentine people remain relatively constant. They range from a home of their own to a piece of land to maintain contact with nature, and they include cultural aspirations and concern for the environment. There is a tendency to look nostalgically to the past, and to assume that the nation's great natural wealth will restore its leadership position on the continent. Despite current problems with violence, excessive inflation, inadequate economic growth, and unemployment, most (if not all) Argentines prefer moderate middle-of-the-road solutions.

Socio-Economic Goals

Socio-economic processes in Argentina are kept in line with the policies of the national development plans. In most plans an attempt is made to strike a balance between continued economic expansion and the redistribution of the national income. Wide divergences remain, however, in the preferred methods of implementation. Some planners consider the development of the infrastructure of the energy sector a task of the government, whereas others wish to involve private industry. Most express the desire to create more employment, upgrade the quality of work, integrate marginal populations, and conserve non-renewable natural resources, but leave unclear the question of how to do these things, and who should shoulder responsibility for their implementation. The dilemma of wishing to achieve socially desirable goals but being reluctant to confront the fiscal responsibilities plagued many Argentine economic projects.

The Argentine political spectrum was, until recently, wide and diversified. It included political parties at the far right (New Force and other conservative groups), right of center (Federal Party and Movement for Integration and Development), broad center (Peronist Movement and Radical Party), left of center (Intransigent Party), and the far left (Authentic Party, Party of Socialist Workers, and Communist Party). Some parties have been proscribed by the military government, and the activities of the others have been suspended. But a new political configuration may emerge eventually, after a return to representative government.

Parties on the left of center attached great importance to labor and social policies. They aimed at providing ample social security through all phases of life. They also wished to have sovereignty over all natural resources, and to legislate foreign investments accordingly.

The parties at right of center favored a liberal economic policy, relying largely upon the free market mechanism. They viewed private industry as the engine of Argentina's development. Accordingly they wished the state to do no more than coordinate and supervise the processes of development.

All parties wove into their programs objectives related to the upgrading of national education, the development of manpower, social mobility, regionalization, and improvement of the quality of life. Agreeing on basic goals, they disagreed on the ways and means of reaching them.

The less partisan national goals now center on reducing emigration, slowing the brain drain, and redirecting internal migration toward selected industrial and agricultural areas. Rural areas, historically the backbone of Argentine economy, are to be revitalized. Goals center on forestation and reforestation, exploration of fisheries, improvements in cattle raising and cereal crops. Agriculture is to be mechanized and its efficiency improved. Agrarian reforms are not contemplated, but ownership patterns are sought that will permit the fullest possible exploitation of fertile lands.

Science and Technology

Establishment of a national research and development capability is high on the list of objectives, especially in regard to food technology, electronics, and low-cost housing. In agriculture hybrid seeds, fertilizers, and harvesters constitute the technological aims, while in the energy sector goals center on the development of nuclear, tidal, wind, solar, and geothermal power. The ambitious technological program also includes goals to evolve research and development capabilities in metallurgy, oceanography, hydrolysis, mining, petrochemicals, transportation, and computer programs. Regional technologies are to be developed to promote the best use of human and natural resources.

The price and supply of energy constitutes a major roadblock in Argentina's drive to modernization. The country has an installed capacity of about 10,000 megawatts, and six new plants will be built over the next five years to add another 5,000. This capacity is based primarily on hydroelectric turbines. The supply lags behind demand by industry, transportation, and consumers. Additional power generation is made difficult by the unclear role of the state versus the private sector. Such uncertainty causes the underexploitation of the country's significant hydroelectric and coal resources. These at present furnish only 10 percent of the nation's energy.

Education

Concern with education is genuine in all segments of Argentina's population. Education is free to all citizens and has been reasonably good. In the past, the drive for quantity eclipsed considerations of quality. During a period when the population increased by 50 percent, the number of registered alumni rose by 125 percent, and university enrollment by 400 percent. Education now accounts for 14 percent of the national budget—the highest percentage in the hemisphere.

A major education goal is to integrate educational programs with societal needs. Education in Argentina is related to child nutrition, hospital service, technical training, and urban development. Illiteracy (now at 8 percent) as well as semiliteracy are to be eradicated, and education is to be begun in the kindergarten. Vocational skill training, however, suffers in most schools from a shortage of physical space and from a lack of qualified teachers.

Foreign Trade Goals

Argentina aspires to solidarity with the other Latin American nations as well as with the industrialized countries of the developed world. According to the present government, the country is basically Christian and Western. This assessment contrasts with the stance of the previous government, which was more nationalistic and more aligned with the developing world.

The neighboring nations of the River Plate basin remain a foremost concern of foreign policy. Good-neighbor policies are prompted by the consideration that this basin is an important source of hydroelectric power as well as a major waterway. Argentine frontiers are well-defined and accepted, with the exception of the Falkland Islands, which Argentina seeks to recover from Great Britain. Disputes may arise in the Antarctic region when the economic potentials of that continent become more exploited.

There is periodic interest in the economic integration of Latin America. The previous government pursued a policy of ideological pluralism which resulted among other things in assigning favorable trade credits to Cuba. The new military government promotes liberal hemispheric relations in a pro-Western context.

Beyond the continent, Argentina's foreign policy focuses on relations with her traditional trading partners, primarily the European Economic Community and North America. Different Argentine governments have disagreed merely in the degree to which the country should be dependent on foreign trade, investment, and technology, not upon the importance of sound international economic relations.

Goals in Brazil

With 8.5 million square kilometers and a population which by the turn of the century may exceed 230 million, Brazil is a large country and confronts all the problems of size combined with diversity. Its population includes black Africans, Japanese, Europeans, and Indians, as well as people from other Latin American nations. The national melting pot creates a unique national spirit. There are, however, great socio-economic disparities.

Brazil is partly a modern technological, partly a primitive artisan society, partly Christian and partly still wedded to magical rituals, such as the *candomble* and *macumba*. Ultramodern medical facilties exist side by side with witch doctors.

The vast marginal populations of Brazil aspire to become part of the monetized economy and eventually of consumer society. Upward mobility often comes suddenly. Thirty percent of the students at the huge São Paulo University come from illiterate families.

Radio and television help bridge the divisions of Brazilian society. Up to forty million people can watch a soccer match simultaneously. Many roofs in the *favelas* (shantytowns) display television antennas even though the basic amenities of urban life are lacking.

Giant urban concentrations and a relatively uninhabited country-side present a further contrast. The disparities are being mitigated by the growth of the middle classes which, according to recent estimates, now comprise about 30 percent of the Brazilian urban labor force. Included in this are the now declining traditional middle class, some formerly rural populations assimilated in the cities, rapidly rising pro-fessional classes, and an intellectual segment aspiring to knowledge, status, and power rather than money.

Members of the armed forces come predominantly from the middle classes. Military schools attract many young people in quest of a good education. The Superior War College is open to civilians coming from the liberal professions, business, and other spheres.

Political Goals
For thirteen years the armed forces have been solidly in power. The military government considers the present type of regime temporary, although no deadline is set for ending it. The ultimate objective is said to be a gradual return to fully representative government.

The present chief of state, whose terms of office expires in 1978, announced his plans to open up the political ambiance by a policy of relaxation of tensions, and a greater degree of civilian political par-ticipation in affairs of the federal, state, and municipal governments. This intention may be thwarted by economic stagnation, caused by severe balance-of-payment constraints, and compounded by the awareness that inflation may be endemic at an annual level of 40 percent and more.

Under such circumstances the armed forces must choose between prolonging Brazil's ephemeral political system, thus strengthening their authoritarian rule, and producing an effective political detente. The credibility of the government, which previously rested upon the economic miracle, may demand a different foundation if rapid growth eludes the nation for a protracted period.

National Integration

Two overriding national goals, development and security, call for bringing together the far-flung parts of the nation. The establishment in Brazil's heartland of the new capital, Brasilia, facilitated vital connections between the northeast, Amazonia, the centerwest, and the economic heartland—the triangle formed by São Paulo, Rio de Janeiro, and Belo Horizonte. Immense highways crisscross the nation, supplemented by railways, waterways, and modern telecommunications networks. There is widespread prospecting for natural resources.

Originally, transamazonic highways and other cross-jungle roads were designed to resettle people in a major effort at colonization. Farming, the raising of animal stock, and forestry were meant to attract new settlers. New crops were planted, such as cocoa, rice, pepper, palm oil, and even fruits and vegetables. Subsequently popular preference for urban clusters induced the government to plan for nine metropolitan regions, to establish many secondary urban nuclei, and to decentralize industry to peripheral regions. The new objective is to prevent the creation of a megalopolis and to aim instead at small cities of some 200,000 people, which can thrive on agro-industry and the processing of natural resources such as copper, nickel, and phosphates.

Socio-Economic Goals

Brazil's government proclaims its basic socio-economic goals in periodic national development plans. The goals concern development, security, and "greatness." These are interrelated. Without rapid economic development, security is threatened. Without security, national integration—the road to greatness—may become impracticable. And without pursuing the goal of greatness, the sacrifices demanded of the nation may be perceived to be in vain.

The plans are mainly economic and technological. They reflect the goals of many population strata but do not mirror any consensus with respect to the timing, priorities, or methods of implementation.

The first plan (1970–74) aimed at rapid and sustained economic growth, whereas the second plan (1975–79) stresses the need for both social and economic achievements. It was almost immediately overtaken by the world oil crisis. This caused a major balance-of-payments problem in Brazil, a country that imports 75 percent of its oil. This made the government put its original quantitative goals on ice, and concentrate on redressing the balance of payments.

The great goals of national planning for the next ten years are: increased supply of energy; a shift away from petroleum-guzzling road transportation; an adequate supply of agricultural products; recuperation of a solid growth rate; and, last but certainly not least, a more equitable income distribution.

While the first national development plan was designed to plug Brazil into the world economy (quadrupling exports in the process), the second plan calls for a greater development of the domestic market. Where the first plan emphasized dynamic industrial capitalism as a means toward modernization, the second plan raises the priority of agriculture. Agro-industry is seen as a bridge between a competitive industrial society and a vigorously expanding agriculture (together with fisheries, forestry, and livestock).

Modernization is seen to depend on the proper use of science and technology. However, while the first development plan relied heavily on importing science and technology, the second plan aims at decreasing Brazil's dependence on imported know-how. It aspires to adapt internationally available technology to local conditions, raw materials, and human skills and needs.

The industrial growth program calls for close collaboration between private and public sectors of the economy. Given the economies of scale and the cost of know-how, it is not surprising that large organizations derive the most benefits from industrial growth. Relatively small Brazilian entrepreneurs are likely to feel that they are being left out. They want to increase their share of the growth at the expense, or with the help, of the state and foreign corporations. This attitude may assume political dimensions if the Brazilian economic miracle wears thin.

Past industrial growth depended largely on cheap imported oil. Since Brazil depends largely on imported oil, continued growth will require a shift from road to rail transportation, the maximum use of

coastal and river transportation, and a greater reliance upon hydro-
electricity and mass transit systems. Brazil's new energy policy is a
victory of pragmatism over nationalism. After twenty years of state
oil monopoly (exercised by Petrobras, whose chief became Brazil's
president), the government invited foreign oil companies to assist
Brazil in exploring new fields. The second development plan calls for
the exploration of shale and offshore oil. In addition the search is on
for new coal mines and for ways to develop solar energy and the
the use of hydrogen as fuel for motor vehicles.

The above goals reflect Brazil's ability to react with flexibility and
pragmatism. Yet Brazil appears to be so fascinated by technology and
industry that she seems to be willing to pay the price in terms of urban
congestion, industrial bottlenecks, and the still widening gap between
the middle classes and industrial elite on the one hand, and the
marginal nonskilled urban and rural workers on the other.

The new priorities are reflected in the transformation of the National Research Council into the National Council for Scientific and
Technological Development. They are also manifest in ambitious
technical-economic agreements with several European countries, including one with the Federal Republic of Germany for the purchase
of equipment amounting to a complete nuclear fuel cycle facility.

Education
The genuine aspirations of the poor segments of Brazilian society are
thwarted by such problems as undernourishment, illiteracy, and
under- and unemployment. The government has launched an ambitious program of adult education (Mobral), which to date has already
taught more than ten million grown-ups to read and write.

It is significant that the second national development plans calls
for annual increases of 5 percent in enrollment for primary education,
8 percent for secondary education, 9 percent for higher education,
12 percent for adult education, and 15 percent for supplementary
technical training. The key to human development is seen to be the
provision of knowledge and training to those who are ready to enter
the labor force. Here the wishes of the people and the policies of
government fully coincide.

Foreign Trade Goals
Brazil's economic "miracle" is temporarily eclipsed by her severe
balance-of-payments deficit. This sudden mutation highlights some

of the country's basic structural flaws. They range from transport problems through endemic inflation, an extreme reliance upon foreign oil, and an equally extreme discrepancy in income distribution, to delays in the institutionalization of government and to urban congestion.

Yet none of these weaknesses in Brazil's structure prevent Itamaraty (Brazil's State Department) from pursuing a long-range policy designed to raise the nation to medium world power status. Foreign policies thus reflect Brazil's foreign trade interests. The European Common Market is acknowledged as the nation's commercial associate. In its relationship with the United States, Brazil seeks a diversification of trade with the focus shifting away from the East Coast. She champions tight economic cooperation with Latin America, on multilateral as well as bilateral bases. Closer ties with the newly liberated African nations, cooperation with Arab countries, and close technical and financial collaboration with Japan are sought. New commercial channels are being created to deal with centrally planned countries, including mainland China.

Brazil financed the huge hydroelectrical complex at Itaipú in Paraguay—a politically sensitive venture, since it is only a few miles from Argentina's border, and may affect the water management of the entire River Plate basin—and is assisting Bolivia in exploiting local oil and natural gas reserves.

Goals in Chile

This country stretches from the hot and arid Atacama desert to islands bordering on the Antarctic, a distance of 4,200 kilometers. It is a relatively narrow band, at one point only 100 kilometers wide, hemmed in by the snow-capped Cordillera mountain range and the blue Pacific Ocean. This physical layout sometimes presents almost insurmountable obstacles to the integration of the national economy.

Chile's ten million people are fairly homogeneous and mostly of European extraction. They share a common system of values even though, politically, they can be sharply divided. Chile is a young, urban, and urbane nation, whose aspirations stem from an ailing economy and intricate politics.

The Christian Democrats won a landslide victory in 1964. They promised to usher in a new era of progress by balancing rapid economic expansion with social justice. Their initial success did not endure. A two-year drought adversely affected agricultural output and curtailed hydroelectrical power, and thereby industrial production. A wavering government failed to bolster the economy. The president all but lost control over his own party as its left wing started leaning toward more radical solutions. Even so, in the 1970 presidential elections, the leftist candidate of the Christian Democrats lost out to his rival of the socialist-Marxist coalition.

In keeping with Chile's democratic tradition, Congress handed the presidential sash to the socialist candidate because, with 36 percent of the nation's vote, he was the first choice of the electorate. The Popular Unity government promised a radical break with the existing economic system through revolutionary change.

The government sought to implement its socialist solutions at a much faster pace than the tottering economy could stand. The mounting imbalances and distortions were compounded by a precipitous fall of the world copper price (Chile's main source of foreign revenue) and by the nation's growing isolation from its leading partners in foreign trade and aid.

The ensuing dislocations prompted ever deeper government interferences. The coalition's originally strong support was eroded as it pushed nationalization far beyond its original plan. In so doing it abandoned sound fiscal management, and caused the cost of living to spiral out of control. In the end economic chaos was widespread. The government, no longer cohesive, reached a degree of political and social polarization which some observers considered to border on illegality.

In the spring of 1973 the armed forces overthrew the government. Chile had not known a military rule since 1925–1931, and had prized constitutional government and a pluralistic society as deeply ingrained traditions.

Political Goals

The military government professes to be nationalistic, democratic, and development oriented. Its democratic thinking is selective and protectionist; its political-institutional foundation is Christian and Western. It seeks a balanced cooperation between the state, diverse groups, and individuals.

The government assumes that the majority of Chileans will go along with restrictions in their personal freedom as the price for law and order and social peace in a world permeated by violence, disorder, and upheavals. It seeks a strong Chile in a strong Latin America, and views strength as the fruit of unity. It is adamant in eliminating all opposition to national unity, and singles out Marxist parties and movements as the number one enemy. This enmity extends to all individual citizens who oppose the government's overriding objectives.

The goal of the government is a moral regeneration of the country, to be achieved by sobriety and a greater emphasis on spiritual needs than on material goods. In this respect the Government does not hesitate to denounce Western-style consumerism when it is "unbridled and soulless." This attitude hardly appeals to Chile's broad, sophisticated middle classes, whose value systems and orientation favor a consumer society.

The government is aware that its image abroad is tarnished, because of its severe infringements on human rights and its lack of credibility. The armed forces justify their rigid stance by attributing many of Chile's social, economic, and political woes to alien Marxist penetration.

However, the government is conscious of the thirst of Chileans for political representation. The president has repeatedly stated that he favors an ultimate return to free popular elections, with mechanisms to ensure that the best elements have access to government—excluding "the enemy." No timetable, however, has been set for a return to representative government.

Foreign Policy Goals

Despite its avowed antagonism to Marxist philosophy, the military government maintains diplomatic relations with Romania, mainland China, and other socialist countries. In general, Chile's international relations are influenced by her foreign trade goals, since the country can no longer be solely dependent on copper, but must vastly increase its foreign revenues.

Chile loosened its ties with the Andean common market, and now favors strong ties with all Latin American countries, especially with neighboring nations and Brazil. It seeks new relations with countries bordering on the Pacific Ocean, as well as with the OPEC nations. Relationships with North America and Europe, her principal trading partners, are to be improved. The country wishes to play an active role in several international organizations and movements, especially at the regional level and the level of the developing world.

Socio-Economic Goals

Upon assuming power, the military government entrusted the making of economic policy to a team of experts steeped in the methodology of the Chicago school of economics. They planned to stimulate investments and economic activity by freeing prices while controlling wages and salaries. Their emphasis was on agriculture, partly in order to feed the urban masses at reasonable prices, and partly to end Chile's classical dependency on imported foodstuffs.

The government expected that a return to the free market mechanism would stimulate production, ease inflation, create employment, attract foreign investments, and diversify the economy. So far, however, the economy has not responded.

Private enterprise has been offered a dominant position in economic matters—a departure from Chile's tradition. Although the private sector has a free rein, the government is ready to step in if its action falls short of promoting economic growth. Yet the Chilean middle and upper classes have long demonstrated a propensity for "imported" consumerism—at the expense of investments in local production.

The national plan aims at reducing the ratio between consumption and investment from a peak of 85–15 to a manageable 67–33 percentage ratio. This is to be achieved by increasing productivity, investing at the expense of redundant consumption, additional fiscal levies, or fiscal deficits. The choice is uncomfortable. If current economic policy misses its target, Chilean aspirations may be thwarted for many years, and national unity may suffer in the end.

The government declares itself anxious to remain in touch with the concerns and aspirations of the people. In order to capitalize on what is constructive in the spirit of the masses, it aims at organizing social groups, such as the Women's Auxiliary Service, and youth clubs, which the *carbineros* plan to set up throughout the national territory. Political groups are to be established eventually through local communities and labor unions, in order to bring local ambitions and concerns to the attention of the authorities.

Goals in Paraguay

Paraguay is a landlocked country. The Paraná-Paraguay river system connects it to the River Plate basin and thence to the Atlantic.

Paraguay's natural seclusion and heterogeneous population have allowed the country to maintain its national identity. This is reflected in the fact that its native language, Guarani, is compulsory, along with Spanish, in all schools including the university. National unity can be traced back to the Triple Alliance War, more than a century ago, in which the country lost 85 percent of its male adults. The Chaco War in the 1930s rekindled the national spirit.

The Paraguay River splits the nation into two highly dissimilar parts. Eastern Paraguay consists of gently rolling country with wooded hills, tropical forests, and fertile grasslands. Western Paraguay, called the Chaco, is a low plain covered with marshes and dense scrub forests. Few people make their home in the Chaco, but because of its good pastures it is used for cattle raising. Most Paraguayans live in the east, in Asunción, the capital, and in fertile rural areas.

Agriculture and animal husbandry employ more than half the population, and cottage industry is still the rule rather than the exception. Emigration to Argentina is considerable; there are more Paraguayans in Argentina than in Asunción.

Paraguay's goals are influenced by a strong executive. The president has been in office since 1954, and his term of office expires in 1978. Concerned over perennial high inflation rates in neighboring countries, the executive maintains stringent controls over monetary expansion. This, together with an outmoded fiscal system, accounts for the slowness of economic progress in the country.

However, the world's largest hydroelectric complex is now being built with the help of Brazilian capital and technology. The generators of the Itaipú dam will generate 10,000 megawatts of electrical power. Another giant generating plant will be erected at Yacyretá through Argentine cooperation. Although the power from these plants will flow in large measure to the sponsoring countries, their operation is likely to change Paraguay's economic outlook. They are the bulwark of the nation's long-range plans, produced by the National Planning Office within the presidency.

Paraguay looks to her neighbors for aid in her development. Exports are promoted, and there is a new emphasis on building the infrastructure, especially in regard to transportation. The hydroelectric complexes are likely to flatten the country's hierarchical socioeconomic system and reduce the domination of economics by politics. The national planning horizons, sketched in the document *Paraguay*

Year 2000, catalyze a longer-term outlook. Awareness is growing of the need for a dynamic population policy, and of the need to diminish the country's dependence on agriculture in general, and on livestock in particular.

Goals in Uruguay

Uruguay, with a territory of 200,000 square kilometers, is South America's smallest nation. About 40 percent of her inhabitants live in metropolitan Montevideo. The country has a good urban living standard, large middle classes, and a high rate of literacy and education.

Notwithstanding a long tradition of democracy, in 1973 Uruguay's armed forces felt compelled to participate in the government to restore law and order. The democratically elected president remained in office, but Parliament was closed down, and the legislative power of the municipalities revoked. The government outlawed the Communist and other Marxist parties and temporarily suspended the others.

The country aspires to economic as well as political normalcy. It recognizes, however, that economic development must precede the restoration of representative democracy. Unfortunately, the economy is slow to respond. It is estimated that more than 10 percent of the population emigrated from Uruguay over the past few years, mainly because of frustrated expectations.

Foreign policy is shaped by a search for balance between the country's two large neighbors, Argentina and Brazil. Because of a common heritage, a common language, a sharing of the River Plate and other factors, Uruguay has traditionally shown more affinity with Argentina. But Brazil's influence is rising. The fact that all these nations have military governments facilitates contacts and understanding, but more specific forms of integration may be called for.

Uruguay's economic future is molded by her trading patterns. The bulk of foreign exchange proceeds from a few commodities, such as wool, meat, and hides, in trade with traditional, mainly European partners.

In its national planning Uruguay seeks to broaden the range of agricultural and industrial output, and to export upgraded natural resources to ensure adequate imports of fuels, lubricants, machinery, transportation equipment, and other industrial necessities. There is an emphasis on reforestation to diminish dependence on imported timber. A similar emphasis is put on prospecting for conventional fuels. Uruguay needs to convince its impatient youth that a more dynamic period of growth lies ahead, in order to stop emigration and exchange apathy for new vigor and interest.

Many segments of Uruguay's society, regardless of their attitude toward the present government, seek modernization as a means of overcoming stagnation in the economy. They are also endeavoring to distribute the economic base more evenly over the national territory, as shown by the Salto Grande hydroelectric complex, offshore oil wells, the iron mines in Zapucay and Valentines, coal mines in various regions and, on the cultural level, by the recent opening of a second university in the north.

Chapter 6

Goals in Africa and in the Middle East

I. Goals in Sub-Sahara Black Africa

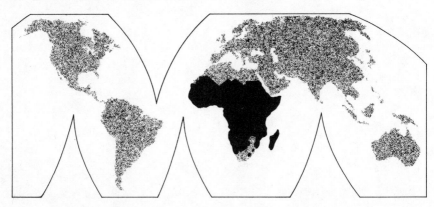

Sub-Sahara black Africa is one of the major areas of the developing world. It experienced colonial domination until recently and still suffers the effects of it. The region contains many states whose cumulative impact on the international scene has become a major force. These states find themselves technologically backward even though they have great human and physical resources, and a rich cultural heritage. They recognize the need for collaboration with the technologically rich regions of the world.

Sub-Sahara African priorities reflect, above all, the basic political-economic conditions of Africans. Many Africans identify themselves with those facing similar struggles elsewhere, and, for some time to come, their priorities and their relations with the developed world may be dominated by the problems they share with other developing countries.

The Basic Problems and Goals of Black Africans

Africans wish to free themselves from all vestiges of colonial, neo-colonial, and racist ties and relationships. Although the political decolonization of Africa is almost completed, the struggle, as Africans see it, is by no means finished. Still to be resolved is the problem of the Republic of South Africa, and that of restoring to the indigenous people their legitimate right to determine for themselves the kind of political environment they will have. Although Africans know that this problem must be solved by themselves, many of them regard the colonial inheritance as a joint responsibility of the international community.

Most African countries face the problem of establishing democratic political systems in their newly independent states. Following the period of decolonization in the late fifties and early sixties, there was considerable internal difficulty harmonizing group interests, both on regional and subnational ethnic levels. Major internal dissensions resulted in civil strife, in movements to recover territory from neighboring states, and in varying degrees of political dissatisfaction. The political institutions needed for genuine democracy, self-determination, and equality did not get time to develop to the level of maturity and complexity the intricate African political environment required. This state of affairs, compounded by various forms of external interference, could cause further delay in creating truly representative governments with a deep sense of accountability and responsibility to the African masses.

The existing political milieu, with one-party or multiparty systems in African political organizations, often could not avoid the alignment of party structures with tribal or regional affiliations. Such alignments had counterproductive results. A number of African countries rejected the idea of the multiparty system, and chose instead a one-party democracy, with mixed results. One of the failures of the African political development process was that it did not find the proper role of ethnic differentiation in constructing wide-based democratic structures. This failure resulted in the release of internal animosities that led to serious conflicts. One of Africa's most widely shared national goals is, therefore, to create political institutions that can establish unity among tribal and religious factions.

A related problem for African countries concerns the role of the political leadership. The decade following the period of large-scale decolonization was dominated by the leaders who spearheaded the struggle against the colonial powers. The task that awaited these leaders after independence was enormous. Most of them achieved concrete goals of political and economic transition within their tenure of office. Others found the tasks too challenging for their meager resources, or overlooked issues that really mattered to their people. In any case, by the time the second and third crop of leaders emerged, in most instances Africans were awakened to the fact that their political institutions were not strong enough to afford smooth transitions of leadership. As a result, African countries succumbed to various degrees of military interventions. Some military-dominated countries are struggling once again to establish political institutions that will assure democratic participation of the masses and genuine self-determination, while in other countries personalized, demagogic, and charisma-based leadership has emerged and holds sway.

Most African countries, regardless of what political system they adopt, contain national elites, middle layers of different kinds, newly emerging working classes, craftsmen, peasants, and farmers and, in coastal regions, fishermen. Their aspirations show certain general patterns, conditioned by their divergent levels of education, dissimilar lifestyles and socio-economic conditions.

The national elites have the most explicit goals and aspirations. On the whole, African elites do not question the values and processes of modernization, but seek to influence its unfolding according to their social and political convictions. An ongoing ideological debate rages among them as the nationalist current interacts with liberal and socialist movements.

The nationalism of the elites exemplifies a profound desire for cultural and political identity to which even the economy is subordinate. But most of them believe that Africa needs a new world economic order. The Western world must review its present ideas of world political and economic matters, and permit Africa to enter into normal relations with other nations under more adequate political and economic conditions.

The middle layers of African countries usually consist of employees, small businessmen, and shopkeepers. Their interest centers on more pragmatic matters. What is important in their eyes is an improved standard of living and freedom of movement in their daily lives. They want the leaders above all to make it possible for them to make good deals. There is a growing middle-class feeling developing among them. The policy makers are attentive to their concern and intend to take account of them in their economic and social policies. In countries such as the Ivory Coast, Togo, and Benin, the middle social layer is particularly dynamic. It is there one finds the women merchants who are so efficient in the markets of large cities.

Workers and craftsmen form a minor social layer whose economic and political weight is still limited. However, the development of class consciousness among workers indicates that in the long run they will have more weight. Governments are taking careful account of their interests, and responding to them in the process of economic development. It is among them that Marxist parties seek and often find their most solid support.

Peasants, farmers, and fishermen constitute the immense majority of the populations—from 80 to 85 percent in most countries. The goals and aspirations of these more or less homogeneous classes are common to all African societies. This group, at the same time, represents the least favored segment of the population, and its demands for improved living standards are a great problem for the countries. The political future of most regimes depends on being able to satisfy these demands.

The countries with the most stable regimes are those where the evolution of these classes is carefully noted by the leaders. It is not by chance that the prosperity of the Ivory Coast is coincident with the success of rural policies. President Houphouët-Boigny himself never misses a chance to declare himself "the first peasant of the Ivory Coast." Nevertheless, the African peasants are profoundly attached to their ancestral traditions, and present demands for the most part are reasonable enough to permit perceptive leaders to satisfy them.

African Regional Goals and Objectives

Goals in French-Speaking West Africa

The languages bequeathed by colonial powers still act as factors dividing groups of nations within the African community. One sector having relatively similar goals and expectations includes the Ivory Coast, Guinea, Mali, Senegal, Mauritania, Niger, Upper Volta, the Popular Republic of Benin, and Togo. Their language is French, and in addition there are several local African languages. The region has a population of about thirty-two million. Independence came to these countries in 1960 (1958 to Guinea) and, although they have since followed their own paths in social and political affairs, persisting similarities permit treating them as a distinct regional grouping.

The mainly agricultural economy of the region has suffered much from the drought of the Sahel. Aside from relatively privileged countries like the Ivory Coast, most countries depend on monoculture. This does not provide an adequate economy for populations bent on progress. In Senegal, for example, despite efforts to diversify agricultural production by planting cotton, tomatoes, rice, and other crops, the peanut crop remains central to the economy. If the commercial harvest reaches 700,000 to 1,000,000 tons, the economy prospers; a drop to 500,000 tons or below causes serious problems for both the government and the urban and rural populations. All these countries are, therefore, concerned to develop forms of industry that will compensate for the natural hazards of agricultural production. Industrialization appears, to the governments as well as to the people, as a necessary step.

The commercial sector is also important for internal as well as foreign markets. West African leaders denounce the manner in which a few rich countries dominate the world economy. They want a serious revision of the unjust economic order which prevails in international relations. They also wish to maximize the value of agricultural products at home. The creation of specialized national industries is a major goal. Industrial development should be based on the processing of local raw materials by small and middle-sized industries, the production of local consumer goods, and the establishment of a profitable industry based on certain favorable factors, such as manpower and energy. The region's governments also wish to promote geological explorations to make possible a rational exploitation of mineral wealth so far unexplored, or insufficiently exploited, by foreign societies during the colonial period.

In the political sphere, the leading parties are trying to overcome three types of internal division. The first is between ethnic groups. There are antagonisms among the groups leading the nation, and there is a desire to unify ethnic groups separated by frontiers established in colonial times.

The second division is between the modern sector of the essentially urbanized population, which is in contact with the Western world, and the traditional sector, which is generally less open to influences of the modern world, and which constitutes the great majority of the population. This second division is particularly serious because so many things separate the two sectors, for example, degree of political evolution and lifestyles (though rural populations now tend to join the urban populations in expressing certain social needs, for example, housing). From this division comes the serious risk of social stratification, full of dangers for the future of the nations.

Finally, there are differences, and even opposition, between interior and coastal regions of the countries. These are due to divergent interests, as well as ethnic and religious differences.

The governments strive to avoid ethnic and regional divisions by generating a network of allegiance and ideological agreement through the single or unified party. In the absence of a national consciousness, the leaders use the political party to express the national idea; supporting the party and affirming its policies are the means of achieving national unity. Thus in Togo, the RPT (Gathering of the Togolese People), mobilizes all the ethnic groups and social classes for the building of national unity centered upon the founder of the party, General Etienne Eyadema. In order to put their political projects to work, the leaders would like to involve all social strata. The most turbulent elements of the population are in a sense restrained by the leaders through the medium of the single or unified party, which tends to mobilize all forces, including the unions. The experiment of "responsible participation" of the CNTS (National Confederation of the Workers of Senegal) is significant. The policy-makers lead the Senegalese unions by integrating their union demands and activities with the economic strategies of the party in power, the socialist UPS (Senegalese Progressive Union). Responsible participation is translated into political posts for union leaders as deputies, ministers, and economic advisers.

In a general way, the governments of these African countries intend to lead their people toward a socialist society. (Only the Ivory Coast is an exception; there the leaders speak of the "happiness of the Ivory Coast" under the aegis of president Houphouët-Boigny.) But African socialism has its own unique goal: It wants to reconcile modern economic theories with the values of black African civilization. Despite variations from country to country, the leaders want to establish socialist parties adapted to black African realities, with a primary emphasis on cultural issues.

Some of the countries have been trying to introduce a form of political democracy similar to the ideals current in Western Europe and North America. The goal is to create a new political experience following a period of domination by the single or unified party. This effort seems to correspond to the desires of the peoples because, as successive coups have shown, they are not content simply to use slogans and follow orders. Where the military have seized power, the previous regimes, which governed through the dictatorship of the single party, have usually failed to meet the deepest wishes of the people; hence they were not supported at the decisive moment. Many leaders now make a point of better aligning their regimes with prevailing currents of political opinion. There is a new movement toward multipartisan regimes, trying to embody the multifold ideals and hopes of the people. French-speaking West Africa is about to take its first steps toward a form of political democracy adapted to its culture and social consciousness.

Preservation of the cultural heritage is a major goal of the region's governments. Concepts such as *negricité* (which can be translated as "negritude" or "black Africanism") and *authenticity* now figure in all the major speeches of the leaders. President Senghor of Senegal is especially bent on making clear to his compatriots the notion of negritude, conceived as the ensemble of the values of black civilization. Negritude is to assure the identity of black Africans within the world community. It is held to be capable of building the civilization of mankind, being both forward looking and constructive.

The achievement of cultural goals hinges on the revision of the existing system. The new system is to express ancestral values, and at the same time to introduce modern notions and skills in order to accelerate economic and social development. The schools are to be made an instrument of development, offering functional literary and technical training. There is new emphasis in school programs on using radio and television, especially in technical fields. The people themselves have a new desire for elementary schooling and practical and technical training. Culture, in its general sense, is as much a concern of West African populations as it is of their leaders.

The desires of the populations for well-being on earth have not replaced a profound feeling of concern for the hereafter. God—or the supernatural in some other form—is always present, both to the city-dweller and the peasant. The religious dimension indisputably gives a particular coloration to the goals and aspirations of the populace. For the middle-class Moslem the greatest hope is to be able to make a pilgrimage to Mecca some day before dying. For the Christian, to go to Rome is the highest dream. As for the animists, they believe it is essential to be constantly in harmony with dead ancestors, as well as with living gods and forces.

Goals in English-Speaking West Africa

This region encompasses Gambia, Ghana, Liberia, Nigeria, and Sierra Leone. These are coastal states having an area of slightly more than 1.3 million square kilometers and a population of about ninety-four million. The population, which is increasing by an annual average of about 2.6 percent, varies considerably in density: There are 13.5 people per square kilometer in Liberia, and 86 in Nigeria.

Ghana, Nigeria, Sierra Leone, and Gambia had common bonds under British colonial rule, and attained independence in the early 1960s. Liberia has been a free state since before the American Civil War, and maintains close links with the United States.

Although all are poor, the economic problems and potentials of each country differ markedly. At one end of the range is Nigeria with a large and diversified agriculture, a growing domestic industry, and new financial resources thanks to the discovery of substantial oil deposits. At the other extreme is Gambia with an economy almost entirely dependent on the production and export of groundnuts. In between are Ghana, with a heavy dependence on the export of cocoa but a great potential for diversified agriculture and more mineral resources, and Sierra Leone as well as Liberia, both exporters of mineral products and having a relatively diversified agriculture. Average per capita incomes range from the equivalent of $300 in Ghana to $75 in Gambia.

The principal problem of these countries is "dependence." They depend first of all on a struggling agricultural sector. Most of the farming is of the subsistence variety, and most of the labor force is engaged in it. Yet considerable food imports are still necessary to sustain their populations. Such imports amounted recently to $300 million for Nigeria alone.

Secondly, the countries are greatly dependent on the international system. Ghana, as already indicated, depends on the sale of cocoa, Gambia of groundnuts, Sierra Leone of diamonds and now also oil. Import and export taxes are the principal sources of state revenue. The basic goal for the region is to break these cycles of dependence and, wherever possible, achieve self-sufficiency.

Goals and aspirations have changed in recent years. During and immediately after the struggle for independence, the main goal was political consolidation and the integration of the various socio-economic classes in the nation. Kwame Nkrumah said, "first seek the political kingdom, and all other things will be added to this." Political instability has marked the evolution of the countries of the region since independence, especially in Nigeria and Ghana. One-party rule and the military still dominate Liberia and Gambia. But, from the mid-1960s to the early 1970s the main goal shifted to promoting economic growth. Ghana's Seven-Year Development Plan (1963–70) projected an annual economic growth rate of 5.5 percent as the basis for the nation's social transformation. A similar note was struck in Nigeria's Second Development Plan.

The goals, however, have changed again: They now focus on the balanced development of the entire social system. Paragraph five of Sierra Leone's current development plan spells out the new goals:

> to preserve political and economic stability as a major prerequisite for uninterrupted and continuous economic and social advancement
>
> to increase the welfare of the broad mass of the population
>
> to achieve a more equitable distribution of wealth and income
>
> to achieve a rapid expansion of the production capacity of the economy
>
> to create the basis for an accelerated pace of economic and social progress
>
> to promote economic and social development through aided self-help methods
>
> to continue and intensify economic cooperation with other West African countries.

The ultimate aim of the development strategy is human progress in terms of better living standards. Hence development is to be brought to the rural masses at the village level and broader popular participation is to be assured in the development process. Economic and social development through "aided self-help" projects is an important feature of the development plan, which also seeks an appropriate balance and cooperation between the private and the public sectors.

Although the goals have shifted to promote social progress, economic growth itself is not disparaged. As a social scientist of the region observed, West Africans need not pass from growth mania to growth phobia. But the region rejects the orthodox tenet that economic development must proceed through emphasis on industry, to the relative neglect of agriculture. Food self-sufficiency is now a prime objective. In 1972 the government of Ghana launched the *Operation Feed Yourself*, and Nigeria initiated the *Operation Feed Your Nation*. Sierra Leone's current development plan likewise accentuates agricultural production.

It is not certain that these countries will continue to concentrate on agriculture in the future. It is clear, however, that they have now adopted a philosophy of development that emphasizes the satisfaction of basic needs of their masses through self-reliant and sustained economic growth. They do not wish to continue measuring economic growth by the classical indicators, but measure it instead by the extent to which the suffering of poverty-stricken masses is alleviated and by the equality with which the fruits of the production process are distributed among their people.

The growth of population is recognized as a hindrance to the developmental process. Liberia, with a population of 1.5 million, noted in its Indicative Manpower Plan,

> Not only will the task of future job creation become more difficult by rapid population growth, but this growth will increase the present dependency burden and the incidence of poverty. Rapid growth also diverts immediate resources from job-creating investment to providing the social services required in trying merely to maintain existing living standards.

With the exception of Gambia, whose population of half a million poses no problems, all governments have educational family planning programs to reduce current fertility rates. These programs are and will continue to be educational and persuasive rather than coercive. The governments believe that rapid socio-economic development is the best way to slow population growth. Nigeria's Third Development

Plan notes that the country has enough national resources for a viable economy and a rising standard of living even for its growing population, and adds:

> Emphasis of policy is therefore being deliberately placed on accelerating the rapid growth of the economy, rather than on direct action to achieve a drastic or immediate reduction in the overall birth rate. It is believed that the high tempo of social and economic development will itself help to accentuate the forces, already at work, which will tend to bring down the birth rate in the long run.

This official view is shared by social scientists even in other countries of the region, where the governments have taken a stronger stance on population control.

Environmental concerns are receiving increasing attention, especially in regard to the conservation of forest, water, and soil resources. The drainage networks of rapidly growing urban slums are to be improved, and it is recognized that atmospheric pollution, as well as the discharge of industrial and human wastes into rivers and lakes, creates pollution problems typical of already industrialized countries. But, because of the low level of industrialization, the threat of industrial pollution is outweighed by demand for industrial goods. Mineral deposits are believed to be far from depleted, and their exploration and exploitation does not cause concern. Aspirations focus instead on providing goods and jobs at the least cost for the rapidly growing populations.

Education is now seen as the key to the desired social transformation. The 1961 Addis Ababa Education Declaration resolved that every African country should aim at universal and free compulsory education by 1980. While this may not prove possible in practice, primary education has become a requirement widely accepted by West African governments. In Ghana, for example, the 1961 Education Act stated,

> Every child who has attained the school-going age determined by the Minister shall attend a course of instruction as laid down by the Minister in a school recognized for that purpose by the Minister. Any parent who fails to comply with the provisions of the preceding subsection commits an offence and shall be liable on summary conviction to a fine not exceeding ten pounds and in the case of a continuing offence to a fine not exceeding two pounds in respect of each and every day during which the offence continues.

Education is not only to become compulsory and free, it is also to become more practically vocation oriented. The present systems serve only the few who remain until graduation, and not the vast majority who drop out. Nigeria announced that it is launching a new plan that includes the development of a parallel system of secondary training schools to retain in the system those who would otherwise leave school, and train them in the needed skills. Ghana will introduce vocational training in 1980, even at the primary level, and permit the student to choose then between further technical training and an academic education. In the latter sphere, the countries are expanding their university systems. Nigeria's three universities are to increase to twelve by 1980, Ghana is planning a fourth institution specializing in agriculture, and Sierra Leone has opened a new university college. Enrollments are modest but increasing. At the three universities of Sierra Leone, for example, enrollment is up from 4,800 in 1970 to 6,000 in 1975.

Traditional culture receives renewed attention. Many feel that years of colonial domination led to an alienation of the elites from the tribal traditions, which are now to be systematically revived. For the present, cultural groups have been formed to entertain visitors to the state with drumming and dancing, replacing more Western-type cabaret entertainments. In Gambia these groups boost an already booming tourist trade.

Cultural renaissance also expresses itself in religious movements. Many African spiritual churches are springing up, and effectively vying with more established Protestant and Catholic churches for membership. African churches aim at delving into the cultural heritage, identifying with it, and avoiding assimilation of Western ideas and habits.

A Sampling of Goals in East and Central Africa

Goals in all parts of Africa focus on the alleviation of poverty, the development of the economy, achievement of food self-sufficiency, and the satisfaction of human needs. These goals are approached in a variety of ways, of which the following sampling, which is illustrative and not exhaustive, gives some indication.

TANZANIAN GOALS

Tanzania, including the mainland Tanganyika and the islands of Zanzibar and Pemba, has a population of fifteen million. Agriculture provides nearly all employment and export earnings. Tanzania's goals are specified by the single political party, TANU. Party and governmental structures fully overlap. Members of TANU are free to participate in all governmental activities whether they are civilians, belong to the military, or are administrators, teachers, or whatever.

The TANU creed holds that all human beings are equal and every individual has the right to receive from society protection for his life and property, and a just return for his labor. But to ensure economic justice, the state must have effective control of the principal means of production, and has the responsibility to intervene actively in the nation's economic life. The state is to ensure public well-being, prevent exploitation by persons and groups, and prevent as well the excessive concentration of wealth. A socialist, classless society is striven for, where all people are workers. Village government (*ujamaa*) is to form the basis of the socialization process, growing from the grass roots to the national level, where the final measures are consolidated.

The TANU creed condemns idleness, drunkenness, and laziness. Everyone must work to achieve a fair distribution of wealth, maintain independence and freedom, and assure self-reliance. The Arusha Declaration of 1967 said, "If every individual is self-reliant the ten-house cell will be self-reliant; if all the cells are self-reliant, the whole ward will be self-reliant, and if the wards are self-reliant the District will be self-reliant; then the region is self-reliant, and if the regions are self-reliant, then the whole Nation is self-reliant—and this is our aim."

KENYAN GOALS

Kenya, a country of 13.6 million inhabitants, also relies on agriculture for the livelihood and employment of over 90 percent of its population. The official goal, pronounced by President Kenyatta in 1965, has been to build democratic African socialism. "We reject," he said, "both Western capitalism and Eastern communism, and choose for ourselves a policy of positive non-alignment." These ideas became the basic philosophy of KANU, the dominant political party. The main features of the desired social model include political democracy, shared social responsibility, various forms of ownership with a wide range of controls to ensure that property is used in the interest of society and its members, diffusion of ownership to avoid concentration of economic power, and progressive taxes to ensure an equitable distribution of wealth and income.

The government is to provide free education in the first four classes of primary school, but the citizens have the responsibility to build schools and encourage their children to attend. The government is to provide the facilities for technical education and prepare plans, but the people must identify the problems of their regions and make specific recommendations through District Development Committees. The government will also extend assistance and credit to industry as well as agriculture, but the citizens must find ways of putting these to beneficial uses and repay the government when required. And the government provides housing sites and services, but the people must build their own dwellings on the assigned locations. The overall policy is to "Kenyatize" the economy. For the people this means sharing responsibilities with the government, but progressively assuming the tasks formerly performed by public officials.

UGANDAN GOALS

Uganda, a country of 9.5 million, has a history of political instability. Each of its several regimes embraced goals of its own. In the post-independence years, government goals favored federation and some degree of monarchic independence. This regime was overthrown by Dr. Obote, who espoused republican goals. He proposed a "common man's charter" with tendencies to African socialism. General Amin overthrew the Obote government in 1971 and installed a military government.

Amin, as Obote before him, has a virtual one-man rule. The defeat of traditional leaders (Kabaka of Buganda) led to a revolutionary government which assigned central authority to the president. The 1967 Constitution provides that the president shall be head of state, head of government, and commander-in-chief of the armed forces. He is to take precedence over all persons, is exempted from direct personal taxation, and is not liable to proceedings in any court.

The 1971 coup brought Ugandan control of all economic operations and nationalization of foreign-owned businesses. The desire to make Ugandan foreign policies independent resulted in the breaking of diplomatic ties with all countries that were thought to interfere in her internal affairs, including Israel, Great Britain, and the United States. Nationals of such countries were expelled. As a result the gov-

ernment has been increasingly isolated both economically and politically.

ZAMBIAN GOALS

Unlike most other African countries, Zambia's economy rests not only
on agriculture but also on mineral extraction and export. Mineral production accounts for two-fifths of the Zambian gross domestic product,
and nine-tenths of foreign exchange earnings. The 1966–71 National
Development Plan was to diversify the economy to reduce dependence
on mining, increase employment opportunities, and raise rural incomes
relative to those in the city; to raise housing and health standards; to
expand social welfare; and to "Zambianize" the economy, i.e., increase
popular participation in economic activities. The focus of development
is "Zambian humanism" as articulated by President Kaunda.

The dominant United National Independence Party attempts to
unify the tribal communities to form a single nation. It wishes to establish a true socialist society based on Zambian humanism, and
eliminate special privileges and inequalities. It also aspires to develop
Zambian arts and crafts, acceptable customs, and the entire national
culture, without entrenching provincialism or tribalism. Only those
who accept these principles of Zambian humanism are accepted into
the Party.

MALAWI GOALS

A small landlocked country with a population of 4.4 million, Malawi
relies almost entirely on agriculture. It has created the Malawi Development Corporation to stabilize prices paid to farmers and provide
them with equipment and materials at or below cost. The Corporation
also aims to improve the quality of crops and implement governmental
policy in regard to food production, processing, and storage, the distribution of seeds, and establishment of experimental farms. It maintains small reserves of foodstuffs, mainly maize, against domestic
shortages.

Systematic aid to farmers is much needed, since only 10 percent of
the active labor force of about 1.5 million are in paid employment.
Aside from those who work in the mining industries of neighboring
countries, the rest—more than a million—engage in simple subsistence
farming. The country has no resources beyond land and people, and
attempts to make these the basis of development.

II. Goals in North Africa and the Middle East

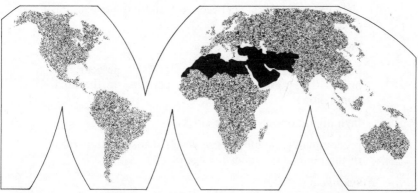

Africa north of the Sahara differs greatly from Sub-Sahara Africa both in cultural heritage and orientation, and current socio-economic conditions. Indeed, North Africa, known also as the Near East, has more affinities with those regions of Asia that are known as the Middle East (although these terms were coined by Europeans for whom the regions were at various distances to the east).

Notwithstanding differences in stages of economic development, social and political sophistication, languages, ethnic origins and climate, and great differences in amounts of natural resources and wealth, the countries of North Africa and the Middle East can be considered a single though differentiated region. It is vast, stretching from Iran, and even Pakistan, to the Atlantic coast of North Africa. Geographically it connects the three continents of Asia, Africa, and Europe. In past centuries, the commodities of the three continents, as well as ideas and inventions, were transmitted across this region, and it was long known as the "crossroads of civilization." The interaction of the Aryan, Sumerian, and other cultures made the region one of the oldest cradles of civilization. A kaleidoscope of cultures, the region is the birthplace of the Judaic, Christian, and Islamic religions.

Some 290 million people now live in the Middle East and North Africa. They belong to more than twenty nations. The following is a summary of their prevailing demographic, economic, religious, social, political, and cultural characteristics.*

---

* The Jews of Israel, most of whom have immigrated from the West, are not included in this summary. Judaism and Zionism are discussed in Chapter 17.

Demographic

high population growth rates (around 3 percent per year, regional average)

high illiteracy rates (between 60 and 80 percent, regional average)

low levels of education

predominantly rural populations (60–80 percent; nomadic tribes are still about 5 percent of the total population)

high migration rates to the cities

predominantly youthful age levels (about 50 percent of the population under the age of 18)

Economic

predominantly agricultural

striving for industrialization

dependent on outside financial or technical assistance

richly endowed with natural resources (not always exploited)

high income in oil-rich nations; low income in others

Religious

dominance of Islam

interpenetration of religious beliefs and rituals with secular values and practices

Cultural

glorious civilization in the beginning; highly integrated and sophisticated civilization during the Middle Ages; decayed and disrupted civilization in the recent past

rich heritage in the humanities (languages, literature, philosophy)

Socio-Political

exposure to direct and indirect forms of colonialism and neocolonialism in the recent past

considerable gaps between social classes

concentration of wealth, capital, and power

autocratic, relatively nondemocratic political systems with centralized planning and decision-making mechanisms

Changing Values and Expectations

All countries of the region are conscious of a need for economic development, which they consider to be inescapable and long overdue. Their sense of urgency stems from an overwhelming fear of falling increasingly behind the growth rate of advanced nations, and from a realization of the abject poverty of the majority of their present populations.

The rapid advance of science and technology in the world, and what is perceived as the compulsive growth-orientation of the West, had a major impact on the region. In its search for new markets, the West has overwhelmed established culture patterns and exploited the mystic values of austerity and frugality handed down through the Sufi tradition. These processes have made the people suspicious of foreign values, and rendered the integration of traditional and modern attitudes especially difficult.

Values considered by Western societies appropriate to the emerging realities of economic, social, and political life gave rise to conflicts in the minds of the people. Brought up on established ethical principles and religious dogmas, they now find their beliefs crumbling. While they search for new frames of reference, they cannot readily identify and accept new forms.

The universal vision and values of traditional Islamic society confront, and often collide with, the self-centered secular vision and values of modern civilization. (See Chapter 17.) In the Islamic vision causality is a combination of the strategic will of God and the tactical freedom of man. The ultimate goal of history is to return to the origins of Holy Justice, not to progress toward some secular utopia. A feeling of predestination is joined in the Moslem mind with a sense of responsibility for the consequences of human action. The present world is seen as a transitory testing ground of character. Real meaning and direction in life must be found in relation to God. The "other world" is, therefore, considered more valuable than this one.

In the fifteenth century, Europeans discovered sea routes to Asia, rounding the Cape of Good Hope. This, and the increased cost of transportation across the Middle East (due in large measure to the insularity of the Ottoman conquerors) led to the increasing isolation of the region. In the nineteenth century Europeans returned in force, following Napoleon's conquest of Egypt. Modern contacts with Europe have left a profound mark on the entire region: It suffered from the

West's technological superiority; it was helpless when confronted with Western military might. The importation of military technology began in the early nineteenth century and has culminated in today's arms imports. Education locally, and in European schools and universities, produced a new elite and diffused European social and economic concepts. The new elite, while influential, is a small minority, consisting of less than .5 percent of the population, and its members are usually replaced in the unheavals that periodically shake these nations.

Today the region is in the throes of a major cultural change. The penetration of European culture has introduced belief in progress and evolution. This has resulted in a negative attitude toward present conditions, and a desire to effect drastic changes.

Notwithstanding the modern orientation toward European culture, there remains an intense commitment to the region's own cultural heritage. As a result of such cultural divisions, and the influence of the Western concept of nation-state, the region is torn both politically and culturally. But gradually a new concept of progress is emerging, which is distinct from the European concepts of colonization, Christianization, and Westernization. A new anticolonial and national orientation upholds the cultural heritage as a valuable element, and interprets past history from a combined nationalistic and cultural perspective.

Most of the national boundaries in the region derive from the political manipulations of the colonial European powers. The people have never before been so separated from one another. Yet the idea that a national culture may be capable of contributing to the integration of nation-states moves national governments to put an emphasis on distinguishing characteristics and on finding their own identities. Nations thus compete with one another for a larger claim on the common cultural heritage. They treat separately with foreign powers and centers of culture. State institutions, which were weak and limited at the end of the colonial period, have not been able to become instruments for collective development and the protection of individual life and dignity.

But the insecurity of the political systems has not slackened state control over the societies nor increased personal freedom. In most states the "permissible" degree of freedom is limited enough to castrate many forms of intellectual activity.

Even the meaning of "revolution" is different in these countries from its meaning elsewhere. The revolutionary attitude in the official philosophy of the governments is mixed with elements of traditionalism deriving from Islam. Governments rely on ethnic and religious feelings, and on the stability of some of the ancient social institutions. In Arab countries, although the influence of socialism is strong, Pan-Arabism and Islam are equally propagated, and in some cases coexist with an orthodox approach. The ideological orientation of the governments profoundly affects the developmental process of their countries, and infuses a mixture of Western or socialist ideas, and traditional or revolutionary concepts.

The "culture of modernism and development" is accepted by the governments of this region. Belief in progress, economic growth, in the goal of improving the standing of living and the rate of consumption is now unquestioned. The discovery of huge reservoirs of oil has transformed this ancient crossroads of civilization into a main artery of the current world energy system. Enormous oil income in some countries but not in others has created a widening gap between them. A handful of the oil-rich countries, with populations totaling about 3 percent of the region, earn about 50 percent of the oil revenue. Larger states, such as Algeria, Iran, and Iraq, which have substantial incomes, also need immense financial resources to sustain their development. While in some desert areas cities resembling those of the affluent West are mushrooming, the main sector of the populations suffers from extreme forms of poverty.

The rise of per capita income among privileged strata has upset the relative equilibrium that marked the poverty of the past. Many individuals among the privileged groups have reached the highest European and American standards of living. Some are living in luxurious self-indulgence. A tendency toward wasteful and conspicuous consumption has developed. Extraordinary political prestige and economic leverage have been attained by the rich. On the other hand, there are entire countries that lack developmental capital and do not possess the resources to attract investment. Hence consumption, indulgence, and waste coexist with destitution and deprivation.

In past centuries the traditional conditions of society and economy produced a frugal population living in harmony with nature, traditional religious prophecies emphasized life after death, and physical hardships were once considered tests of character. But increasing familiarity with conditions in the rich nations now makes for the valuation of wealth and power. Whereas truthfulness, ethical conduct, and humility were traditionally valued, egotism, profiteering, immorality, dishonesty, selfishness, and arrogance are becoming more widespread. Previously a man's value was not measured by the house he lived in; pompous displays of one's worldly goods were not considered virtuous. Today elaborate houses, luxurious vehicles, and indulgent ways of living are beginning to be signs of manly virtue. Where a man's word or a handshake was once a binding contract, now contracts may not compel acceptance even when legally drawn up.

Among the broad strata of the population, the belief that catastrophes, wars, epidemics, and social status are unavoidably the will of God is not totally dead. A significant, though decreasing segment of the population still considers historical events the result of metaphysical causes. Those who view the world in this way have a sense of helplessness, wonder, and drama, rather than the ability to predict and control. But an awareness is also emerging of the possibility of influencing the course of things through self-reliance, perseverance, and hard work. The new economic realities in the resource-rich countries have demonstrated the importance of planning, forecasting, and influencing the future. Analysis of events and conditions, and the search for alternative policies are gradually replacing the conjectural, intuitive, and fatalistic attitudes of the past.

Analogous changes are occurring on the level of family life. The patriarchal family has traditionally been the elemental unit of tribal, rural, and even urban societies in the region. Today respect for women and children is increasing, but the father continues to be the source of rational guidance, the mother being seen as the source of love and emotion.

The scars of colonial and neocolonial times are shown in a distrust of authority and a suspicion of powerful people and organizations. In the same vein, there are persistent misgivings in regard to Western political systems, and sympathy for all deprived nations. There is also a fear that manipulations by state bureaucracies and international business will result in cultural homogenization and the loss of distinct identities.

Current Goals
Since poverty is still widespread, the main goals concern the allocation of wealth and the distribution of power. Because income from oil in the resource-rich countries flows to the governments, the latter do not rely on the affluent classes for survival but can afford to seek the support of a broader segment of the population. Thus human needs

are given more attention, as aspirations expand from the goal of sheer physical survival to the broader objectives of social, economic, and cultural well-being and achievement.

GOALS OF THE GOVERNMENTS

Political

maximization of internal as well as regional political power

maintenance of political stability

promotion of integrated nationalistic feelings

centralization of internal control over political activities

increasing diplomatic alignment with the region and extensive political relations with outside powers

nonalignment with major power blocs but leaning toward the one or the other

modernization of the armed forces for domestic as well as regional employment

authorization of controlled political participation

expansion of power base among the rural and urban masses

rapid interpenetration with developed world economies

creation of a broader middle class

Economic

maximization of short-term economic growth

rapid industrialization

relative self-reliance in food and agricultural production

improved international balance of payments

creation of more jobs (in some countries through expansion of labor-intensive industries)

land reform

partial employee and public ownership of economic institutions

investment of excess capital (in oil-rich countries) in foreign economies more equitable distribution of income (All states claim to strive toward a guaranteed minimum standard of living but most give first priority to military strength. Some assign a bigger share of the state budget to programs that serve the "average" citizen than the urban middle classes, but bank loans, hospitals, schools, and public services serve primarily the latter.)

Socio-Cultural

eradication or reduction of illiteracy through mass campaigns of alphabetization

expansion of higher education

creation of a modern national welfare system (within the constraints of the above-noted economic goals)

urbanization, and the creation of larger and more centralized rural communities

integration of the various subcultures, and ethnic and religious minorities, in the national culture

revitalization of traditional arts and crafts

limited control of population growth (some governments, and even elites and intellectuals, believe that there is a direct correlation between population size and national economic, political, and military power)

settlement of the remaining nomadic tribes

Environmental

preservation of forests and pastures

pollution-prevention planning

exploration and exploitation of natural resources (oil, copper, iron, etc.)

GOALS OF INDUSTRIALISTS, BUSINESSMEN, ENTREPRENEURS *

Political

support and appeasement of the regimes

---

* Private business corporations and elites are relatively influential in both the modern and the traditional states. Some local interests reflect those of international business; the region has long been dominated by powerful oil companies and international banks. The superaffluent business elites have little interest in the long-term prospects of the region, being concerned primarily with their own wealth and power.

encouragement of political stability (except where regimes are unfavorable to business interests)

creation of pressure groups in support of their own interests

if necessary, buying and corrupting public officials

Economic

absorption of rapid economic growth

penetration of internal and external markets

encouragement of joint ventures with foreign firms and business interests

decrease in the dependence on local labor by creating capital-intensive industries

maximization of short-term financial gains

accumulation of wealth as a safeguard against an unpredictable future

Socio-Cultural

encouragement of development of indigenous markets by increasing consumption needs and demands

exploitation of the present values of the people for purposes of marketing

Environmental

rapid exploitation of natural resources (with apathy toward problems of pollution)

GOALS OF THE INTELLECTUALS

more tolerance for the beliefs, values, arts, institutions, and rituals of the people

greater influence on the regimes through opportunities for political participation and the voicing of criticism

more respect for civil rights, social justice, and equality of opportunity and treatment

resistance to political, economic, and cultural influences of the developed world full employment, and incomes commensurate with the changing costs of living; improvement in general quality of life

cultivation and achievement of popular support

GOALS OF THE PEOPLE *

improvement of their own socio-economic conditions, including more food, better housing, more and better services in the areas of health, welfare, and education, and more credit and job opportunities

The Middle East and North African region is currently experiencing an explosion of expectations. People who in the past were accustomed to poverty and underdevelopment, and considered this an act of God, are now awakened and believe that their condition is not the result of God's will, but of the exploitation of their national wealth by the "great powers" and the "developed world." This rise in expectations creates immense pressures on the governments for rapid reforms and an accelerated pace of development.

There are traces of overcompensation in the current expectations. Many wish to gain, in a short time, what they have done without for long. Power and wealth are sought by many through access to higher education, and the institutes of higher learning are faced with immense demands. Poor families attempt to provide opportunities for higher education for their children, sometimes even at the expense of selling their belongings. Unfortunately, this potentially positive development often turns into a drive to win certificates and diplomas by young people who assume that these will entitle them to greater material rewards as their undeniable right. People look for the causes of their deprivation and frustration outside themselves and have little patience for learning the ways and means of achieving power and wealth. They admire the performance of some groups and individuals who, taking advantage of the system's loopholes, its bureaucratization and corruption, have become conspicuously successful. These tendencies reinforce corruption in the bureaucracy, which remains, together with the influence of the developed world, the main obstacle to development.

---

* Since in most countries of the region the masses of the people still live at or near subsistence level, their goals focus on the satisfaction of their most pressing and basic needs with little attention to social, political, economic and cultural goals and objectives not directly related to matters of survival.

Chapter 7

Goals in India and in Southeast Asia

I. Goals in India

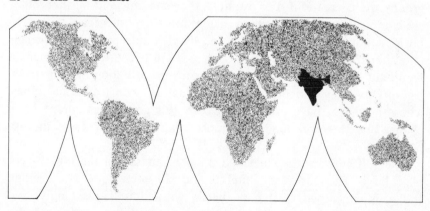

The Union of India extends over three million square kilometers and consists of twenty-two states and nine union territories. It has a population of almost 600 million people who speak as many as 14 officially recognized languages and some 831 dialects, of which 706 are spoken by groups of more than 100,000 people.

India is a multiracial, multireligious society with many caste and class divisions. Indian independence from British rule was achieved in 1947, and India's present political system has been in existence a mere twenty-five years.

Goals and Aspirations of the Indian People

In spite of great poverty and widespread illiteracy, the 600 million Indian people are slowly becoming socially and politically conscious. Through political electioneering and the village self-government system, they are becoming aware of the possibilities and consequences of their participation in decision-making at local, state, and national levels.

Different social groups entertain different goals and aspirations, however. We examine four major strata of Indian society—the elites, the typical masses, the traditional tribes and castes, and the religious groups.

Indian elite groups fall into several categories: the power elite, including members of legislative and other elected bodies, the economic and business elite, the professional elite, the administrative elite, and the socio-cultural elite. Each of these groups is composed of two segments, the traditional and the modern. The traditional elites have been considerably weakened by the present system; the new elite groups are its creations. For example, the economic and business elites are composed of former princes, feudal lords, and members of the old business houses, as well as of the newly rich entrepreneurs. The new elites hope for the maintenance of the system because it has benefited them, and because its continuation means perpetuation of their privileges. Thus they support the present regime. The traditional elites, whose privileges have been curtailed by this government, hope for a change and therefore tend to support some of the parties of the opposition.

The gulf between the elites and the great masses of the Indian people is large. The masses are illiterate and extremely poor. The average Indian is concerned most immediately with himself, his family, and his livelihood. He leads a hand-to-mouth existence, and his long-term concerns are tied up with his own old age. When he is old and ill, he can look for sustenance only to his family, relatives, and friends. The majority of the people, preoccupied with such problems, are not much concerned with wider social or political issues. Moreover, their religious beliefs have tended to reinforce the traditional attitude of resignation to the existing state of affairs. The average Hindu believes in the doctrine of karma and rebirth, and accepts his present condition as preordained and just.

These attitudes are undergoing change. Through political campaigning and electioneering the masses have been educated about the constitutional provisions and now have hopes and expectations that were previously unthinkable. They have begun to demand a social position on the basis of their own achievement. Poverty and discrimination based on birth are no longer considered preordained by fate. People have begun to realize that their condition can be altered only by their own efforts and achievements. Accordingly, the goals and aspirations of the masses are rising. Most of them agree on the necessity of eradicating poverty and establishing an egalitarian socialist society.

The tribal segment of the Indian population has a separate identity within the social system, and is far removed from the mainstream. In this sector there are not only the 302 scheduled tribes totaling some thirty-eight million people, but also the 805 scheduled castes with eighty million. Together they account for more than 20 percent of the population. This segment has been the most neglected, discriminated against, and suppressed.

The tribal segment is the least aware of the changes taking place in India. The tribes are also the least concerned about such matters—they live in a world of their own. The government has a twofold responsibility with respect to them: to motivate them to desire better ways of living, and to provide opportunities to achieve them.

The major religious groups in India are Hindus, Moslems, Christians, Sikhs, Buddhists, and Jains. The Hindus constitute 82.72 percent of the total population. The Moslems constitute 11.21 percent, the Christians, the Sikhs, the Buddhists, and the Jains are only 2.6, 1.89, .47 and .41 percent respectively. (Not all the people who belong to the various religious denominations are active practitioners of their religion, of course, or actively engaged in promoting its cause.)

The active religious groups have three major goals: to contribute to the continuation and perpetuation of their religious system; to promote the inner satisfaction of the individual adherents by catering to their spiritual and "otherworldly needs"; and to assure group solidarity and the satisfaction of the basic needs of their members.

Indian history is replete with cases of conflict and suffering inflicted upon millions of people in the name of religion. Therefore one of the current ideals of the religious groups is to live in harmony and peace with one another. Under the national policy of secularism, all religious groups are accorded freedom to pursue their religious and spiritual objectives. Small religious groups are given special privileges to safeguard their interests.

Continuity in a particular religion as an institution is based on strict conformity to its values and norms. However, because of industrialization, urbanization, increasing contacts with the rest of the world, and divergent political ideologies, religious beliefs and practices are on the decline in India. This is viewed as a challenge by leaders of the religions, who are deeply engaged in efforts to promote their values and beliefs. Temples, mosques, churches, and gurudwaras are being modernized, and many adjustments made to suit present conditions.

Goals of the Indian Government

The goals of the government are rooted in the ideas of Mahatma Gandhi and Jawaharlal Nehru, as is the Constitution itself. The latter, proclaimed on January 26, 1950, is designed to establish a democratic and secular state in which sovereignty is vested in the people, equality of status and opportunity are assured, women are given equal rights, untouchability is abolished, and the poorer and less influential segments of the population are offered extra protection.

The first general election was held in 1951–52, based on universal adult franchise. Since then four general elections have been held in which millions of people participated. These processes helped in the political socialization and education of the masses, and imparted a sense of democratic values. Programs of community development, the system of *panchayati raj* (village self-government), and elected municipal governments decentralized power and raised the autonomy of villages and cities. Although India is still far from achieving the ideals of freedom and democracy as set forth in the Constitution, the country is making progress in that direction.

Current goals focus on the attainment of a basically socialist order. Socialism in the Indian context is not the same as socialism anywhere else; it means, first and foremost, the abolition of poverty and discrimination, and the reconstruction of Indian society on the basis of egalitarian values and the Gandhian principle of general welfare (*sarvodaya*).

There are major inequalities today in India. There is a considerable amount of hidden wealth and many pockets of affluence. People still indulge in luxurious living in the midst of great poverty. The government is keenly aware of the problem, and is attempting to redistribute incomes and resources through such measures as the nationalization of banks, liquidation of traditional privileges, and land reform.

Because of glaring inequalities—including the curse of untouchability which still affects about 125 million people—India perceives socialism as the basic long-term goal. Already in 1954, under Nehru, the Indian Parliament accepted a "socialist pattern of society" as the national objective. It was decided that the criteria for determining the lines of advance would be social gain and greater equality in income and wealth, not private profit. The country would strive to achieve a socialist economy, efficient and progressive in its approach to science and technology, and capable of growing steadily to a level at which the well-being of the masses could be assured.

The benefits of economic development were to accrue more to the less privileged sections of society, and a progressive reduction in the concentration of income, wealth, and economic power was to be achieved.

Pandit Nehru and Mahatma Gandhi had different ideas on socialism. Nehru was captivated by the efficacy of the Soviet and other socialist countries in overcoming poverty. As a humanitarian, Nehru wanted to eradicate poverty and social discrimination as early as possible. He thus advocated socialism of the Soviet type. Yet he did not wish to sacrifice the values of democracy. So he appealed to the people for their cooperation to bring about a grass-roots-motivated socialist society.

Mahatma Gandhi's concept of socialism was based on the principles of *sarvodaya*. The goal of *sarvodaya* is to bring about a nonviolent transformation of the social system to ensure the greatest good of all.

Thus, whereas Nehru and Gandhi, great humanitarians and makers of modern India, both wanted to achieve socialism, they differed in their choice of the means. Current governmental policies, proclamations, and practical measures by and large reflect Nehru's socialist ideas, while the Gandhian ideas have been kept alive by the *sarvodaya* movement.

In matters of foreign policy, nonaligment as well as peace, friendship with all countries, and the welfare of humankind are the government's stated goals. There are understandable reasons for India's policy of nonalignment. The country attained freedom after a struggle for independence that lasted over half a century, and has remained concerned over the intentions of former colonial powers. Today India is unwilling to compromise its hard-won independence, even in exchange for much-needed assistance.

Being one of the poorest countries in the world, India needs help from other countries to sustain and promote her plans for social and economic reconstruction. But the government objects to aid given with the ulterior motive of controlling or influencing national policies. It also realizes that India's problems cannot ultimately be solved by international charity. Thus the concepts of *swadeshi* (home-made goods) and "self-sufficiency," so much emphasized during the freedom struggle, continue to have great significance. The present planning and economic policies of the government are based on the principle of minimum dependence on foreign resources, maximum use of indigenous resources, and promotion of self-sufficiency in all spheres of production. Therefore, in international affairs, India follows a policy of nonalignment with any superpower or power bloc, and nondependence on any foreign country.

Plans and Goals of Economic Development

Planning for the social and economic development of India began in 1950 when the Central Planning Commission was set up and the first five-year plan inaugurated. The country is now engaged in the fifth such plan (1975–79).

Removal of poverty and attainment of self-reliance are the two major objectives of the present five-year plan. A major thrust of its policy is to provide vastly expanded opportunities of employment to the poor sections in general, and to the agricultural laborers and small and marginal farmers in particular. A national program to meet the minimum needs of the poorest and weakest sections of society has been formulated. The plan aims at accelerating the growth of agricultural and industrial productivity and provides for a noninflationary financing of development. It also aims at raising the consumption standard of the lowest 30 percent of the population, and achieving a 5.5 percent annual growth in the national product.

Per capita monthly income in India is about Rs 700 which, at 1976 rates of exchange, is equivalent to approximately eighty U.S. dollars. Total unemployment is in the area of 50–60 million people, or about 10 percent of the population. This figure does not include many millions who are underemployed or seasonally unemployed. In view of these conditions, current economic policy aims at increasing the national income and reducing the level of unemployment. Progressive taxation schemes—such as income, wealth, gift, urban property, and company profits taxes—are imposed to create a more equitable distribution of income. Banking, credit, and investment policies are aligned with these goals.

Population Goals
The latest census, taken in 1971, reported an Indian population of 548 million people. Compared with 1961, when the population was 439 million, this represented an increase of almost 25 percent. The current population is thought to be between 610 and 625 million and is increasing by about 14 million people a year. The increases are attributed to better health conditions, control of epidemics, efficient handling of famines, the slow impact of family planning measures, a low death rate, and a lack of decline in birth rates. In 1961 births were occurring at an average rate of 23 per thousand per year, producing an annual population increase of 19 per thousand. Infant mortality was reduced from 250 per thousand births in the early part of this century to 146 per thousand live births in 1976. While there is little change in the birth rate, the death rate declined sharply during 1951–60. In 1961 the life expectancy at birth was 41.9 years for men and 40.6 for women; now it is 47.1 for men and 45.6 for women. Population density per square kilometer rose from 142 in 1961 to 178 in 1971.

The government is aware of the dangers of the population explosion. Since independence, agricultural production has doubled, but this gain has been wiped out by the 250 million increase in population. Given current levels of technology and availability of resources, India cannot increase food production beyond narrow limits. It is now recognized that the solution to the problems of poverty, unemployment, and economic underdevelopment must include effective measures of population control.

The government gives top priority to such measures. In the five-year plans, family planning has been given increasing emphasis and importance. The fifth plan provides 5,160 million rupees for family planning programs, compared with 2,800 million rupees in the fourth plan.

The goal of the family planning program is to reduce the annual birth rate from about 39 per thousand in 1969, to 30 per thousand by 1979 and 25 by 1983–84. The target of the program is to protect about forty million couples in the reproductive age group from unwanted fertility. (So far sixteen million such couples have been protected.)

The family planning program is implemented through the state governments, but fully financed by the central government, and assisted by the Central Family Planning Council, the Research Coordination Committee, and several voluntary organizations. The program consists of I.U.D. and sterilization services, free distribution of condoms and pills, abortion, a postpartum program, and training in family planning. Universities, several research institutions, and individual scholars are actively engaged in evaluating the programs, and looking for effective methods of population control.

In April 1976 the government announced the National Population Policy, which puts into effect more stringent measures for the strict implementation of the family planning program. The age of marriage has been raised and compulsory sterilization measures by state governments are permitted.

In the first few months after the new measures were implemented the international press reported some highly coercive practices. Two million Indians had been sterilized by September 1976, including 80,000 in the capital, New Delhi. Heads of government departments were required to show that their staffs included a certain quota of "sterilized people." Civil servants were required to be sterilized if they already had two or more children, but zealous officials were also reported to be threatening underlings with loss of jobs or promotions if they did not become sterilized, though they did not yet have two children. Children were said to be barred from enrolling in public schools if they could not show a certificate that their parents had been sterilized. In New Delhi 18,000 school teachers were reported sterilized in the first four months of the program's existence. Some intellectuals charged that officials in rural areas threatened to cut off water or electricity if a village or district failed to meet its quota of vasectomies. Poor people were, it was reported, enticed to sterilization camps by a bonus of 10 rupees (a little more than one dollar) and were given a certificate of sterilization which also assured them that the vasectomies, "performed by first-class surgeons," did not affect their sexual potency. The goal was to perform some six to ten million vasectomies within the first year of the program.

Agricultural Goals

India is a predominantly agricultural country. About 75 percent of the people depend on agriculture and allied sectors for their livelihood; agriculture accounts for 50 percent of the national income, and there are about 78 million cultivators and 47.4 million agricultural laborers.

Though food self-sufficiency is the goal, it is yet to be achieved for a variety of reasons. For one thing, the vagaries of weather affect grain production. Secondly, increase in population causes serious difficulties, along with problems of food waste through socio-cultural practices and food habits, and destruction of grain by mice, rats, birds, and pests. India imports grain, but even so, nutritional levels are both qualitatively and quantitatively low.

Indian agriculture was semifeudal at the time of independence, with intermediary tenancy, middlemen, and a heavy concentration of lands and equipment in a few private hands. The five-year plan accorded priority to progressive reforms. The present plan has the twin objective of increased agricultural output and social justice for the farmer. These objectives are pursued through such measures as abolition of intermediaries, tenancy reforms, a ceiling on and consolidation of holdings, distribution of land to the landless, agricultural credit supply, fertilizer supply, multiple cropping, supply of high quality seeds, storing and marketing facilities, introduction of minimum wages in the agricultural sector, improvement of animal husbandry, and agricultural education.

Health Goals

Poverty is usually accompanied by low levels of health in the population. The poor health of the people of India is attributed to unhygienic environments, inadequate and nonnutritious diets, improper housing, unsafe water supply, improper disposal of human waste, lack of medical care, and absence of health education.

The government's health program includes the control and eradication of communicable diseases, curative and preventive health services in rural areas through the establishment of primary health centers in each community development block, and augmented programs for the training of medical and paramedical personnel. In the fourth plan, subdivisional and district hospitals were strengthened to serve as referral centers for the primary health centers.

In the current fifth plan the aim is to provide at least minimum public health facilities, integrated with family planning services and nutrition for especially vulnerable groups—children, pregnant women, and nursing mothers. The accent is on increasing the accessibility of health services in rural areas; correcting regional imbalances; intensifying the control and eradication of communicable diseases, especially malaria and smallpox; qualitatively improving the education and training of health personnel; developing referral services by providing specialists in upgraded primary health centers in rural areas; and removing deficiencies in district and subdivisional hospitals.

These programs are backed by a budget of Rs 7,960 million during the current plan.

Housing Goals
In most countries of the world, housing is essentially an urban problem, but in India it is a problem also in rural areas. Not only is there an acute shortage of housing but what housing is available is substandard. In cities the housing shortage is primarily due to population increase and haphazard patterns of growth. In the country it is due to poverty and ignorance. A study by the National Building Organization indicated a pressing shortage of 15 million units—3.8 million in cities and 11.2 million in the country. This is a conservative estimate. According to unofficial sources, the housing shortage is of the order not of 15, but of 50 million units.

The government is aware of this problem and has undertaken a series of measures for its solution. These include urban development and town planning, slum clearance and environmental improvement, various social housing schemes, schemes for financing by the central and state governments, and assistance through the National Building Organization and the National Building Construction Corporation. In 1976, the government was considering setting up a separate Rural Housing Corporation.

The overall goal of the housing policy is to remove the current shortage by providing dwellings with standard facilities in congenial environments. Because of the magnitude of the problem and lack of funds, this cannot be achieved in the near future.

Educational Goals

Educational policies aim at bettering a disastrous situation. Up to 70 percent of the population is illiterate and, except for certain urban areas, educational services are poor. The people often keep their children away from school, since they are needed around the house and on the farm, and teachers, being poor themselves, do not have high social status as Indian teachers had in the past. Language problems create further difficulties. When Hindi replaced English as the national language, non-Hindi-speaking people protested. The controversy became acute enough to threaten the unity of the nation. The government resolved it by adopting the three-language formula. Accordingly, people in each region are to study three languages: Hindi, English, and their regional language. Where Hindi is the regional language, they study one of the South Indian languages.

The current goals of the National Educational Policy include free compulsory education up to the age of fourteen; improved socio-economic status and training for teachers; implementation of the three-language formula in all schools; improved science education; better training and education for agriculture and industry; and better quality and quantity of inexpensive textbooks.

About 6 percent of the national income is now earmarked for education. The aim is to educate 97.1 percent of the children in the 6–11 age group; 47.1 percent in the 11–14 group; 26.1 percent in the 14–17 group; and 6 percent in the 17–23 group.

Goals of the Twenty-Point Program of the Prime Minister

Since the country was not making adequate progress with respect to the goals of the five-year plans, and inflation, unemployment, and various economic problems began to mushroom, the prime minister announced a decisive twenty-point economic program for India in July 1975, shortly after she declared the national emergency. The program spells out the objectives which the government holds essential for stability and progress in India:

reduction of prices, display of stock position, procurement and distribution of essential commodities and enforcement of strict economy in government expenditure

implementation of agricultural land ceilings and redistribution of land provision of house sites for landless and weaker sections

aboltion of bonded labor

liquidation of rural indebtedness

implementation of laws of minimum wages for agricultural labor

better irrigation systems for greater productivity

more power generation for greater productivity

new development plan for the handloom sector

improvement in the quality and supply of clothing

socialization of urban and urbanizable land

property valuation and punishment of economic offenders

confiscation of smugglers' properties

liberalization of investment procedures and action against misuse of import licenses

worker participation schemes in industry

national permit scheme for road transport

income tax relief for the middle class

provision of essential commodities at controlled prices to students

provision of textbooks and stationery to students in hostels

new apprenticeship schemes to enlarge employment and training opportunities, especially for the weaker sectors.

This program is enforced by the central and state governments, and by governmental and voluntary agencies with all the power at their command.

Goals of the Opposition

A number of opposition parties exist in India, several of which arose from splits within older parties. Their ideologies range from the extreme right to the extreme left. No party has yet become a serious rival to the ruling Congress Party on the national level, although a few succeeded in forming local governments in some of the states. The Congress Party is in power at the national level and in all regions except Kerala (where it is in coalition with the Communist Party of India).

The basic goal of most, but not all, of the opposition parties coincides with the ruling Congress Party's desire to build a form of socialism in India.* The opposition parties perceive this as a necessity to overcome the oppression of extreme poverty, coupled with

---

* The major opposition parties and their philosophies are the following:

Congress (old) which came into being in 1969 as a result of a split in the Indian National Congress. It functions as an opposition party more on account of a conflict of personalities than of ideologies—its basic philosophy is similar to that of the ruling Congress Party;

the Bhartiya Jana Sangh, popularly known as the Jana Sangh, with a strong nationalistic, Hindu, and anticommunist orientation;

the Bhartiya Lok Dal (B.L.D.), formed in 1974 through a merger of seven parties of shared ideologies. This party champions the creation of a welfare state based on a free enterprise system and opposes communism and centralized planning;

the various Communist Parties of India: the original CPI, the CPI (M) (Marxist), and the CPI (ML) (Marxist-Leninist). The latter was formed by extremists in the CPI (M) and is led by activists from Naxalbari in West Bengal. The CPI itself is aligned with the Soviet Communist Party, supports the ruling Congress, and is in coalition with it in the state of Kerala; the Marxist faction is in opposition and professes to follow a policy independent of both the Soviet Union and China, while the Marxist-Leninist faction stands for immediate, violent class war and the founding of a communist society in India based on the Chinese model;

the Socialist Party of India (S.P.I.), which aims at establishing a democratic socialism similar in nature to that envisaged by the ruling Congress but divergent in its strategies of implementation;

the Dravida Munnetra Kazhakam (DMK), a strong regional party in the state of Tamil Nadu (formerly Madras) with influential representation in the national Parliament. It is against orthodox Hinduism and domination by the Brahmins, promotes the cause of the rest of the Hindu population, and strives for greater autonomy for the different states of the Indian Union;

the Rashtriya Swayam Sevak Sangh (known as R.S.S.), an orthodox militant Hindu organization with the avowed objectives of protecting Hinduism and creating a glorious Hindu nation. Although it professes to be a purely cultural institution, it has a political orientation and supports the Jana Sangh;

the Moslem League, whose objective is to safeguard the interests of India's Moslem population;

the Anand Marg and the Jamaat-e-Islami-e-Hind. These are religious organizations as well, with political aspirations and tactics considered extremist by the government.

social injustice. However, their short-term objectives show major differences. The range of the opposition parties in India falls into two categories. In one we find those who do not subscribe to the basic goals and objectives of the ruling Congress Party, and strive to seize power in order to create a different social order. In the other category are those parties that subscribe to the goals and objectives of the ruling party, but favor partly or entirely different means of achieving them.

Notwithstanding ideological differences, several opposition parties joined together in 1975 to form a united opposition, thereby hoping to wrest power from the Congress Party. They accused it of corruption, betrayal of the public trust in reneging on election promises, and failing to remove massive poverty. Agitation was first launched in the states of Bihar and Gujarat and soon spread to the entire country. In response, the government declared a national emergency. Most of the opposition leaders were imprisoned, censorship was introduced, and fundamental rights guaranteed by the Constitution suspended.

II. Goals in Southeast Asia

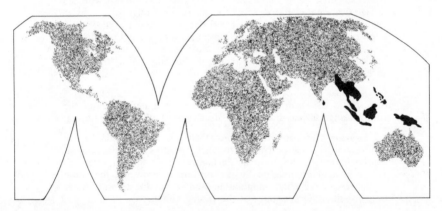

The next, and in our survey the last, great developing area of the world to be considered is Southeast Asia. This vast region encompasses nine countries on the rim of the Asian continent, from Burma in the west to the Philippines in the east. Some 300 million people live in this region, which has 4.6 million square kilometers of land. While the average density of the population is only about 68 persons per square kilometer, in reality population density varies widely and ranges from the densely populated island of Java in Indonesia, and

Table 7-1
Sub-Regions of Southeast Asia

Primordial Ties

Race	Religion	Language
MALAY	ISLAM	MALAY
Malaysia	Malaysia	Malaysia
Indonesia	Indonesia	Indonesia
Philippines		
	BUDDHISM	
	Laos (Theravada)	
	Khmer Republic	
	(Theravada)	
	Burma (Theravada)	
	Thailand (Theravada)	
	Viet Nam (Mahayana)	

Colonial Ties

Colonial Regime	Colonial Language and Education
FRENCH	FRENCH
Laos	Laos
Khmer Republic	Khmer Republic
Viet Nam	Viet Nam
BRITISH	ENGLISH
Burma	Burma
Malaysia	Malaysia
Singapore	Singapore
	Philippines

Modern Ties

ASEAN	Communist Ideology
Thailand	Laos
Malaysia	Khmer Republic
Singapore	Viet Nam
Indonesia	
Philippines	

the Red River Delta in Viet Nam, to the sparsely inhabited hills and rain forests of Borneo.

Southeast Asia, a conventional designation adopted only in the last quarter-century, includes groups of countries which have diverse cultural characteristics, most of which were handed down from history. Theravada Buddhism is the major religion in Burma, Laos, Cambodia, and Thailand, while Mahayana Buddhism (the Chinese variant) dominates Viet Nam. The Malays of southern Thailand, the Malays and many of the indigenous peoples of Malaysia, most Indonesians, and many of the inhabitants of the southern Philippines are Moslem. Three countries of the area were subjected to British colonialism (Burma, Malaysia, and Singapore) and three to French (Laos, Cambodia, and Viet Nam). Of the remaining three, one was dominated by the Dutch (Indonesia); one by both the Spanish and Americans (the Philippines); and one succeeded in avoiding colonial domination largely because it served as a buffer between British and French colonial interests (Thailand).

The languages of Laos and Thailand are related and similar; Malaysia and Indonesia share mutually intelligible national languages; most of the dialects of the Philippines are related to the Indonesian and Malaysian languages as members of the Malayo-Polynesian family (though the elites speak English, and occasionally Spanish). Vietnamese borrows heavily from Chinese; and Singapore is rapidly becoming English-speaking even at the street level. In anthropological terms, the great Malay arc extends from southern Thailand through Malaysia, Indonesia, and the Philippines, though the accretions of more recent history (through colonialism and religious conversion) have tended to obscure these similarities.

Finally, in more recent years, Laos, Cambodia, and Viet Nam have shared political ideologies with some common basic premises; Thailand and the Philippines were members of the Southeast Asia Treaty Organization; Thailand, Malaysia, and the Philippines were part of the now superseded Association of Southeast Asia; and today Thailand, Malaysia, Singapore, Indonesia, and the Philippines are all actively involved in ASEAN, the Association of Southeast Asian Nations. Thus, many mutually reinforcing and some crosscutting subgroupings may be identified. For this reason the objectives of these subgroupings and the countries comprising them will be discussed more frequently than the objectives of the region as a whole.

Goals of the National Elites

National Survival Goals

Except for Indonesia (two million square kilometers) all Southeast Asian states are small, ranging in size from Burma (678,000 square kilometers) to the diminutive island republic of Singapore (581 square kilometers). While most have the potential for significant development, thus far most performances have fallen disappointingly short of expectations. By comparison with Africa and India, few Southeast Asian states are truly poor, but today only Singapore can be described as a member of the family of developed nations, and even here some reservations still must be voiced.

As small and still underdeveloped nations, the countries of Southeast Asia are vulnerable to forces frequently beyond their control. Because of their sense of vulnerability they regard continuity, security, and predictability as ends in themselves, rather than as means for attaining some loftier goals. The communist states of the region seek security by becoming part of a larger worldwide fraternity; the ASEAN group seeks security by unity of purpose despite diversity of means and styles; and Burma withdraws into itself in the hope that it can escape being swallowed up by greater powers.

The fragility of the states of Southeast Asia owes at least as much to internal factors as to the external forces that seem so threatening. This is not well recognized by the elites within these states, though in almost every country of Southeast Asia it is possible to identify at least one basic, internal dynamic characteristic that seems destined to lead eventually to some fundamental, and probably revolutionary, changes. Family-based social organization among the Filipinos, for example, while contributing to continuity in the Philippines, is also a source of corruption and inefficiency, and widens the gap between the haves and the have-nots. Malaysian economic progress owes much to the presence of the Chinese, but Malays and Chinese have difficulty living together in harmony, either in conditions of poverty or prosperity. The Thai genius for compromise and accommodation kept their land free from foreign domination for centuries, but domestically it has done little to help the country realize the potential it seems to have. U Nu's admirable and lofty ideals were translated into a debilitating mysticism that led Burma into an economic disaster, from which the present leadership seems reluctant or unable to extract

the country. The Lao elite, each segment of which has strong traditional ties to identifiable groups in the countryside and in urban
society, are still in disagreement over the dimensions of the Lao nation. The great Khmer tradition provided Cambodia with a cohesion
almost unique in Southeast Asia, but even this has recently proved
fragile in the face of the stresses of war and politics. The dynamism
and vitality of Vietnamese nationalism is now well proven; that it
can overcome its geographic divisions and its legacy of north-south
rivalries is less certain. The people of Singapore have demonstrated
their energies and abilities, and the genius of the leadership lies in its
skill in harnessing these attributes to achieve identified and carefully
conceived objectives. The rapidly changing face of the island and
its prestige abroad are vivid testimonies of the success of both the
people and their leaders. In the future, however, the country may
have to pay a high price for its tight organization, discipline, and
management. Indonesia's "potential" is well recognized, but in Southeast Asia its ability to lead is questioned and, internally, continuing
tribal ties have contributed to corruption and thus far have made it
impossible for Indonesia to put its own house in order.

The territorial survival of the countries that comprise Southeast
Asia is not seriously questioned, for there have been few threats to
the geographic integrity of the individual countries. The survival of
the ideas, institutions, social classes, and leadership that today are
identified with each of these countries is a different matter. The elite
of each country feel threatened, and while many seem to have wrongly
identified the major threat, it is nevertheless true that their vulnerability is an objective fact. In such a setting the primary objectives of
the countries of the region are understandably related to their own
desire to survive.

Goals of National Integration

Most of the states of Southeast Asia emerged on the international
scene as individual political entities, marked by considerable internal
fragmentation. In each state there was a great gap that separated the
wealthy few from the many poor. With few exceptions linguistic differences presented major obstacles to effective communication between
the government and the governed, and even among people of the
same class living in different parts of the country. In many countries,
particularly the states of mainland Southeast Asia, highland minorities

had traditionally been exploited by colonial governments administered almost exclusively by lowlanders and foreigners. Every country also had its ethnic and religious minorities, some of which dominated for a time (like the Catholics in South Viet Nam), and some of which threatened to become the majority (like the Chinese in the old Federation of Malaya).

Most educational systems taught the elite to speak the colonial language while the masses were permitted (or required) to function in their native tongues. Only in the Philippines after 1898 did the colonial language serve as the medium of instruction at all levels and for all people, and even here many Filipinos outside Manila did not gain functional literacy in English even after secondary school graduation.

Every country in Southeast Asia inherited one capital city which served as the center of colonial commerce and administration, and was usually the point of entry for Western ideas, fads, and technologies. The gap between the city and the countryside, particularly the capital city and the countryside, was so great that it defied quantitative comparison. The colonial governments in Southeast Asia only occasionally penetrated significantly into the rural areas of each country. Rarely did national elites have either the need or the desire to go into the countryside and when they did, they went as ruling authorities, not as public servants. Rural leaders, on the other hand, were viewed by their followers more as buffers against the threatened encroachment of national administration than as a link between the government at the top and the governed at the bottom. A village headman was supposed to impede integration, not to facilitate it.

In settings of such diversity, integration naturally assumes a high priority. Supporters of integration must be mobilized, and minorities and majorities outside the circles of the elite must be incorporated into the nation. Most states of Southeast Asia have experimented at one time or another with the institutions of Western-style democracy, including political parties and elections, but most have become disillusioned by the inefficiency and uncertainty of the process, and have abandoned it in favor of other approaches which, it was hoped, would be more effective. Today almost every state in Southeast Asia has significantly improved its capability for penetrating into the countryside through rural development programs, the military and police, the media, patronage politics, or other more traditional means. Such tactics of penetration have mobilized people as much against the regime as in support of it.

Breaking down social and class barriers has proven more difficult, and if it does not succeed, further internal disruption could result. Shans and Karens are proud that they are not Burmans, and they resist pressures to change their identities. Malays in the Moslem provinces of southern Thailand look longingly at the Malay-dominated government of Kuala Lumpur, and with resentment at the Thai-dominated government of Bangkok. The Chinese of Malaysia have little interest in converting to Islam, and the indigenous peoples of eastern Malaysia (Borneo) often resent the heavy hand of Kuala Lumpur politicians who try to force them to "rediscover" their nonexistent Malayness.

Integration within nation-states is a major goal throughout Southeast Asia. It has not been attained as yet more than partially in any country. While it is virtually impossible without politically mobilizing the people, such mobilization can also lead to an opposition that resists attempts at integration.

Goals of Economic Development

Some Southeast Asian countries have recognized the deficiencies of Western development models but most of the noncommunist countries of the region have nevertheless chosen to try to emulate them even where the risks involved are recognized. In the eyes of many leaders, facing up to problems of pollution, alienation, urban violence, and other appurtenances of the Western development process can be deferred until the benefits of development are closer to realization. In recent history colonial powers have razed forests, defaced the earth, built sometimes ugly and frequently unhealthy cities, and contributed in many other ways to economic development allied with environmental decline. Today, the process may continue in many countries, but now such exploitation is at least done in the name of the sovereign people of the countries, if not always for their benefit. The objective, enunciated with varying degrees of certainty and clarity, is economic development to the point of self-sufficiency (or symbiotic interdependence, depending upon the strategy), leading eventually, it is hoped, to genuine national prosperity.

In adopting Western development models, the noncommunist countries of Southeast Asia have nevertheless maintained something of their unique character, although few of the elites consciously advocate more culturally continuous strategies.

Goals of National Identity

Of less pressing importance than integration, but connected with it, is the quest for identity and stature. Southeast Asian leaders are struggling to prove that their delineated borders are meaningful in other ways than as conventional demarcations of European power plays. The "we-they" dichotomy, which lies at the heart of the quest for nationhood, is still variously defined within the countries of Southeast Asia. For the elite, "we" ideally would include all fellow countrymen, but for many of these fellow countrymen there are large groups of persons residing within the territorial borders (perhaps even the elite themselves), who are among those identified as "they," rather than "we."

Not only must the leaders of Southeast Asian countries convince their followers that they belong to a larger national family, they must also convince others that their country has a place in the regional and supraregional international orders. Each state of Southeast Asia, largely in its own idiom, has been struggling to prove its *raison d'être* to the powers beyond its borders. Manifestations of this quest are to be seen throughout modern Southeast Asia beginning with the independence movements of Indonesia and Viet Nam, and extending to such recent events as the Thai-American confrontations (provoked by an historically powerful Thai military establishment highly sympathetic to Pentagon requests), Vietnamese fears of Chinese interference (fears that have been translated into rediscovered friendships with the USSR), Filipino outbursts against American bases (immediately following the demise of the pro-American Saigon regime), and ASEAN bickering over the creation of a common market (which appears to some to threaten the warrant for the separate identity of member states).

Extraterritorial Aspirations

Several states in Southeast Asia pursue territorial objectives beyond their own borders. Although most states harbor such extranational ambitions to some extent, several countries have formulated and pursued foreign policies that have had considerable impact on some of their neighbors. Indonesia's dreams of an Indonesia *Raja,* comprising all of the Malay-populated countries of Southeast Asia, were confined to the heady days of the Sukarno era that spanned the two decades between the mid-forties and mid-sixties. Yet Sukarno was probably more a voice, articulating the details of such a future, than the architect of the vision itself. Many Indonesian and some Malaysian leaders have shared this dream for the future. The quest for sovereignty over West Irian, the "confrontation" of the newly created Malaysia, and the philosophical underpinning of the Maphilindo Agreement were authored by Sukarno, but the march into Portuguese Timor, and the recent reluctance to accept any non-Indonesian initiatives in ASEAN were events in the same tradition that occurred long after Sukarno was dead and his regime discredited.

Malaysia too, has had extranational ambitions. The very creation of Malaysia from the underdeveloped territories of Borneo and the relatively well-developed states of Malaya and Singapore was couched in language reminiscent of the rhetoric of American "manifest destiny." Although many Malaysians have since had second thoughts, in 1961–63 it was not easy to find leaders in Malaya who did not agree with Tunku Abdul Rahman that the union of the Malay peoples of the region was desirable because it was natural, and indeed because it was inevitable. Of course, when Malaysia's "manifest destiny" came into conflict with Sukarno's vision of the Indonesian *Raja* the result was confrontation and Sukarno's militant "crush Malaysia" policy.

Today, Viet Nam's extranational ambitions are feared in many parts of Southeast Asia. It is ironical, but instructive, that while Viet Nam fears the "Chineseness" of China, many of the Southeast Asian leaders fear the "Vietnamness" of a unified Viet Nam. For the Vietnamese, "Chineseness" implies a view of the world that places the middle kingdom at the hub of the international order, and displays an arrogance about the foreordained superiority of all things claimed by the Chinese as part of their own national past, present, and future. Thus, as the Vietnamese view the situation, China is a threat because Chinese objectives cannot (and, according to the Chinese, even need not) be compromised, but only postponed when necessary. The Chinese regard these objectives (again, according to the Vietnamese view) as right and appropriate, if for no other reason than that they are Chinese. Yet, for many Southeast Asians, Viet Nam poses similar policy problems. Although it is not frequently discussed, most leaders seem to feel that the "Vietnamness" of Viet Nam constitutes a threat. It is one that is not as likely to manifest itself in the form of physical assaults by the military, as it is to manifest itself more subtly, in the form of the supposed infallibility and even historical inevitability of Viet Nam's deep-seated social and political objectives.

Goals of Subnational Groups

Racial, Tribal, and Linguistic Divergences

Many of the national goals of Southeast Asian countries outlined here are less important, meaningful, and relevant to their diverse subnational strata, and some may even conflict with local and regional aspirations. Highlanders, for example, are still more concerned with their survival throughout the region than with the goals of the national elites, and resist influences from the lowlands. Because of linguistic and cultural affinities, many feel closer to their neighboring highland cousins (even when fighting with them) than to their lowland governors. Even among those who have ventured from their homes and migrated to the cities (particularly in Thailand), much of the tribalism that characterized their lives in the mountains continues. The world in which the highland tribes live may have expanded in recent years, but rarely, if ever, does their outlook approach the breadth of the view common to the leadership in the capital cities. Even in the developed world it is not uncommon for the provinces to be more "provincial" than the capital city, but in Southeast Asia the gap has become qualitative—it permeates all aspects of living, and is not measurable by economic indicators alone.

The fourteen to sixteen million Chinese of Southeast Asia constitute a small but important minority. Most are recent immigrants (coming in the late nineteenth and early twentieth centuries), and have resisted alienation from Chinese culture. Despite their determined resistance, the loss of their cultural heritage has proceeded with varying degrees of speed and thoroughness in the various countries of Southeast Asia. However, this process has not always meant the loss of a Chinese identity, which seems far more resilient than the culture it originally symbolized.

The communities formed by Southeast Asia's many Chinese minorities are highly diverse, even internally. Most of their members have experienced both oppression and discrimination in the past and the threat of such treatment still exists. There is historical evidence that their fears are not groundless. In such a setting, survival was always a primary objective, but success in the face of great odds often became a secondary objective in itself. Coming, as most immigrants did, from a world of a different tradition, there was little they could learn or assimilate from the local culture that could display their degree of success in their new surroundings. Because of the hostility that met

them, it was impossible for them to climb the political and social lad-
ders. Thus, success came to be measured on a purely materialistic
scale, and the acquisition of wealth came to be viewed by many Chinese
as an end in itself. Among today's youth, changed political and social
conditions have altered their outlook (often to the sorrow of their
parents), but much of the old motivation toward highly materialistic
objectives remains intact.

Language is usually related intimately to culture and identity. Almost every state of Southeast Asia has been forced to select a national language, and the choice has often been determined by the elite
on the basis of the language in which they themselves are most comfortable. This places those who function less well in the national
language at a distinct disadvantage, and those who cannot use it at
all may feel completely outside the system. It has been fairly common,
particularly during the period preceding and immediately following
independence, to find that subnational communities have demanded
recognition of their own tongue, along with the chosen national
language.

Religious Aspirations

Religion is another factor that significantly affects the objectives
chosen by many Southeast Asians. No religion in Southeast Asia is
confined to any one country, and no country is without its significant
(and sometimes troublesome) religious minorities. Many examples
could be cited, but two cases involving the predominant religion,
Islam, stand out in recent history.

The "great Malay arc" extends from southern Thailand, through
peninsular Malaysia, along the coastlines of Indonesia and eastern
Malaysia into the Philippines. For the most part, the Malay people
of the arc are also Moslem, but at neither end of the arc do religion,
race, and political boundaries neatly coincide. The three southernmost
provinces of Thailand are predominantly Malay, and at various times
in history (most recently during the Japanese occupation of Southeast
Asia) they have been treated as part of the Malay states on their
southern border. Although the Thai language is spoken by most people in southern Thailand, Malay is also common and is the language
many Thai Moslems use at home. The south has traditionally been
given low priority in almost all Thai development projects, and even
today many residents feel that the Bangkok government cares little
about the underdeveloped condition of the Malay provinces. On the

other hand, the Thai Moslems can see the benefits flowing to Malays just to the south through the Malay-dominated government in Kuala Lumpur. Some have traveled across the border and have seen the Malay gains firsthand; others observe Malay progress on television received clearly from TV Malaysia's northernmost relay station; still others hear stories, probably embellished somewhat, from family and friends. The end result is that a traditional suspicion of the Bangkok government on the part of the Thai Moslems is reinforced by their envy of the happier conditions of their cousins a short distance to the south. The desire for separation in southern Thailand is an issue that is always present, and it becomes important from time to time when conditions at home are unfavorably compared to those in Malaysia.

At the other extreme of the Malay arc the situation is even more difficult. The Philippine armed forces have been fighting against a full-scale revolt in the south, and while religion is only one piece in a complex mosaic of difficult issues, the Moslem-Christian dichotomy is the main way insurrectionists are distinguished from the government. The situation has been complicated by the great sympathy shown toward the Moslem rebels by the state government in Sabah (led until recently by a militantly supportive Moslem, Tun Mustapha bin Dato Harun). In fact, it has frequently been alleged that Sabah under Mustapha was a major trans-shipping point for arms supplied by Libya, and Mustapha showed no hesitation in stating his personal views on the correctness of the Moslem insurrection.

The objectives of the Thai Moslem minority at the western end of the Malay arc are difficult to assess with certainty. It is apparent that discontent with the status quo is fairly widespread and that there is considerable support for secession from Thailand and association with Malaysia. However, Malaysia has been careful not to signify any support for such a movement, and without Malaysian approval little can be accomplished.

The objectives of the Philippine Moslems have been much more clearly stated. The Moro National Liberation Front wants independence from the Manila government, though it might settle for almost total autonomy within a federal system. Because of the size of the Moro minority and the large area encompassed, political support from Malaysia's Moslems is seen by the Moros as less important than in the case of the Thai Moslems, but in fact their Sabah neighbors have provided such support in the past, probably against the wishes of the federal government in Kuala Lumpur.

Business Objectives

Historically most of the entrepreneurs found in Southeast Asia during the colonial period were alien to the indigenous societies, and the lingering effects of this are readily apparent today. The top entrepreneurs were usually colonial businessmen, but just under this stratum, and occasionally almost on a par with it, were to be found migrant Chinese (throughout Southeast Asia) and Indians (in Burma and Malaysia). Today many colonial businessmen have been replaced by native entrepreneurs and bureaucrats, but there are many private European and American investors now in noncommunist Southeast Asia. The growth of multinational corporations has also introduced a new element of alien entrepreneurship into most Southeast Asian economies. In Burma most of the Indians have been expelled and the Chinese influence considerably reduced. Elsewhere attempts have been made to reduce the Chinese-controlled segment of the national economies, but these attempts have met with only limited success.

Today the "alien" entrepreneur (who may be regarded as such even though he is a citizen) is still much in evidence throughout Southeast Asia, particularly in the Philippines, Indonesia, Malaysia, and to a less extent in Thailand. Many of these entrepreneurs retain transnational ties, chiefly through relatives living in other countries, and capital is often transferred quickly, efficiently, though sometimes illegally, through these informal channels. For many of these alien entrepreneurs the accumulation of wealth continues to be a goal in itself, and to accomplish this end they need a fair degree of political stability and predictability, a minimum of official harassment, and loosely structured national governments that will not be too efficient in enforcing all the antialien or pronative economic legislation that exists in the statute books.

Only Thailand in Southeast Asia has a long history of significant native entrepreneurship, and this may be attributed to the absence of a colonial experience. The Chinese migrated to Thailand, just as they did to other parts of Southeast Asia, and once there they tended to work through and identify with the ruling class, as they did elsewhere in the region. However, the ruling classes in Thailand, in contrast to those in other countries in Southeast Asia, were indigenous, not foreign, and thus it was in the best interest of the Chinese entrepreneurs to emphasize their local ties rather than their alien connections. While Chinese entrepreneurs may be readily identified in Thailand today, they carry less weight than the native Thai and the Thai-Chinese, many of whom no longer recognize their Chinese ancestry.

The Philippines witnessed the growth of a largely Spanish-Filipino mestizo entrepreneurial class, stemming from the landed aristocracy of the Spanish colonial period. Today most of these are regarded as indigenous (though in fact their roots are often as alien as are those of the Chinese), and most have become part of the ruling national elite.

Throughout Southeast Asia the indigenous entrepreneur is often a recent product of economic and social policies designed to divert some of the national wealth from aliens to natives. Every country, including pre-1975 South Viet Nam, Cambodia, and Laos, has adopted policies limiting the activities of the alien entrepreneurs (Europeans and Chinese alike, in some cases) for the benefit of the indigenous economic elite. Such policies have been implemented with widely varying degrees of effectiveness, but the end result has been a dramatic increase in the number of indigenous people now actively involved in the modern economy. In some cases efficiency and effectiveness may have suffered, and the opportunities for corruption may have increased, but new entrepreneurial classes have nevertheless emerged. These new classes are usually greatly indebted to the existing regimes, and most have a vested interest in their continuation. Thus, their objectives are likely to be couched in conservative terms, mostly favoring the political status quo and an improving business climate.

Aspirations of the People

The rural masses of Southeast Asia, as elsewhere in the developing world, have little opportunity to articulate general objectives. One can only surmise that their overall goals are in fact a collectivity of individual aspirations—each highly personal, specific to the family involved, and limited by the constraints of the environments in which they must live. Problems of birth, death, sickness, marriage, food, housing—and finding peace of mind when these do not measure up to hopes and visions—these things probably dominate the lives of the common people of rural Southeast Asia and afford little time or stimulus for contemplating loftier and longer-range objectives. Occasionally a Sukarno, Ho Chi Minh, Sihanouk, or Magsaysay may come along and incite the rural people to expand their horizons beyond the immediate world in which they live but, for most, life goes on with the setting and seeking of attainable goals and objectives, which can rarely escape the limits of the highly personal world in which they live.

City dwellers live under more diverse conditions and their goals and aspirations are correspondingly diversified. Life in present-day Hanoi and Phnom Penh is entirely different from life in Singapore and Manila. The rapidly growing middle class of Singapore shows many of the signs of affluence familiar to the West: better health and problems of obesity, much leisure time but difficulty in filling it meaningfully, a love for cars, and a tendency to be complacent about the future. By contrast, the people of Phnom Penh are not complacent about their future because the past decade has forcefully demonstrated how uncertain life actually is, and how fragile are one's familiar institutions. For the urban masses of Hanoi life may have returned to near normal after the dangerous days of the late sixties, but Viet Nam is still a country psychologically prepared for a protracted struggle against overwhelming odds. Hanoi relaxed only slightly following the collapse of the Saigon regime and austerity is still much in vogue. But it would be impossible to describe the mood in Manila, even in the early days of martial law, as one of austerity, and today life is very much back to normal. Night clubs are busy, traffic is snarled, pollution at peak hours makes the air almost unbreathable, and shops are stocked with luxury imports and a growing inventory of locally produced goods. Most of the wealthy have maintained their positions despite martial law and recession, Roman Catholic masses are well attended, and the squatter area seems neither to have grown nor shrunk despite a distressingly high population growth rate.

Chapter 8

Goals in Australia

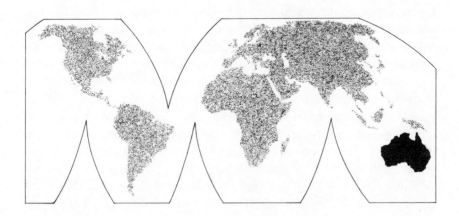

Distance is as characteristic of Australia as mountains are
of Switzerland. By sealanes or airlanes most parts of Australia are at least 12,000 miles from western Europe, the
source of most of Australia's people, equipment, institutions and ideas. The coastline of Australia also stretches
for 12,000 miles and the coast encloses as much land as the
U.S.A., excluding Alaska. The distance of one part of the
Australian coast from another, or the distance of the dry
interior from the coast, was and is a problem as obstinate
as Australia's isolation from Europe.

This opening paragraph of Geoffrey Blainey's 1966 economic history of Australia, *The Tyranny of Distance,* gives some insight into
one of the most important influences on Australia's past, present, and
future development, and not just in economic terms. The sheer isolation of a population of only thirteen million on this huge island continent, so far removed from their European origins, has fashioned a
society with an almost fierce desire for economic and cultural independence. Yet the very smallness of its population, and the proximity
of relatively giant countries of totally different racial and cultural
backgrounds and markedly different economic status, is a major

moderating factor in determining Australia's view of its role in the world economic and social system.

The Lucky Country

To most Australians, it is an understatement to say that they are indeed inhabitants of the "Lucky Country." In less than 200 years, a continent sparsely populated by nomadic aboriginals has become the home of one of the world's most highly urbanized societies. In anyone's terms, much has been achieved by the descendants of the handful of convicts and settlers from England that gave the Australian continent its first permanent European residents.

Australia's natural resource wealth is substantial. Vast deposits of bauxite, iron ore, coal, and uranium have been discovered, and despite a recent slowdown in the rate of discovery and development, it seems that much of the continent's potential in minerals has yet to be found or developed. A relatively modest exploration program has given Australia the promise of becoming self-sufficient in energy products, and has identified major natural gas resources. The country is already the world's largest supplier of bauxite, the third largest of iron ore and zinc, and fifth largest of nickel. It also has significant copper and coal production.

Australia is also a major producer of rural products. The total rural output is about $6,500 million annually. Australia accounts for 60 percent of the world's merino wool output, 30 percent of the greasy wool output, and a significant part of world export trade in meat, wheat, and sugar. In total, about two-thirds of Australia's rural output is sold on world markets.

Industrially, Australia also has all the features of a self-sufficient economy, and manufacturing employs about one-quarter of the total workforce. It has its own steel and nonferrous metal industries, produces most of its consumer durables and manufactures a wide range of chemical and petrochemical products.

The industrialization of the Australian economy started in earnest around the turn of this century, but up to the 1930s manufacturing accounted for only about one-eighth of the gross domestic product. Following the Great Depression, manufacturing growth was rapid and generally uninterrupted, largely because of the effective use of tariffs, and the participation of the government in joint ventures in strategically important sectors. The major thrust toward today's integrated and essentially self-sufficient industrial sector came as the result of World War II, during which both production and imports were subject to direct controls. A close collaboration evolved between government and private enterprise, and continued into the postwar years.

Australia's population, after a quarter-century of large-scale migration from Europe to support economic development, is now thirteen million. Today Australians generally accept the objective of zero population growth (ZPG). They were among the early users of the pill, and essentially materialistic values have resulted in a major shift in birth rates. Thus Australia is in the fortunate position of being able to regulate its own population size very closely, by turning on or off the migration "tap." ZPG appears to be very much within reach.

Few Australians lack effective access to free basic education, and although poverty still exists (largely owing to the high degree of urbanization), a major part of the population enjoys the "Australian dream": each family in a single, relatively comfortable dwelling, a steady job, many opportunities for outdoor leisure, and a large degree of individual freedom. In the world context, Australia is indeed a "Lucky Country."

Goals in the Recent Past
Australians set about the task of achieving economic prosperity in a determined way. The basic economic objectives, set in a government white paper at the end of World War II, gave a fairly clear picture of what Australians wanted to achieve in the following quarter of a century.

The 1945 white paper set out one central objective of national policy—full employment. Other key objectives were rising living standards, a high rate of economic and population growth, stability in costs and prices, external viability, and a more stable, predictable economic environment. It captured remarkably well the aspirations of the contemporary community. Its focus was largely—in fact, essentially—on material values, and it gained widespread support. It provided a fresh vision for a country that was underdeveloped, and that had faced the prospect of world conflict reaching its shores not long after it had suffered a depression. It thus expressed the fundamental values shared by all at that time.

The white paper provided a framework for policy making that lasted for twenty-five years. It placed particular importance on the dignity of the individual, basic equality, a free society, improved material well-being, and the opportunity, in fact the basic right, to work.

Such was the background to the growth and development of Australian society in the twenty-five years after the war. The young and vigorous nation prospered. Its efforts were focused successfully on material values, it was inward looking, and it was determined to achieve and sustain economic self-sufficiency.

The Search for New Goals

The 1950s and 1960s also gave Australians a sustained period of political stability. A conservative government held power for a record twenty-three years, but Australians then started to question some of the ingredients that had brought success. National sovereignty became a major issue again, as more people became aware of the extent to which foreign investment had featured in Australia's development, and as conventional strategic alliances brought the frustration of participation in unconventional and unsuccessful wars. The longstanding domination of conservative politics began to be questioned, largely on the grounds that government was no longer reflecting the Australians' basic desire for openness in policy making and their concern for minorities. Part of this process of reexamination led to the election of a trade union–backed Labor government in 1972. Then followed a period characterized by an almost frantic search for new goals aimed at the achievement of a truly egalitarian society, greater expression by the community of concern for all its individual members, and the establishment of closer economic and strategic ties with the established and emerging nations of Southeast Asia.

These emerging goals were communicated by the Labor government to a Green Paper Committee in 1974. From a large collection of official documents, the committee distilled the following general statements:

> The purposes and basic goals of the Australian Government are to provide for and improve the well-being of the people of Australia through:
>
> > equality of opportunity so that all persons, without discrimination, may live a full and satisfying life
> >
> > full employment

rising and generally enjoyed standards of living, with
stability in costs and prices

freedom of choice and personal independence for individuals, consistent with the rights of others

national sovereignty

responsive, helpful, mature relations with other nations

viability in external economic relations

conservation of the environment so that Australia's natural and historical heritage is protected and enhanced.

In the opinion of the Governmental Industrial Green Paper Committee, Australian industry should aim at:

improving the working of the economy so that an increased
GNP per capita is available to support rising community
aspirations, using resources in the most efficient way compatible with enhancing the community's well-being

improving the quality of worklife to match the expectations of Australians for dignity and fulfillment in their
work, including of course the right to work

encouraging social cohesion by helping adjust expectations
to reality and developing shared aims and ideals

increasing the involvement of Australians in systems of
decision-making so that all can be confident that the system
is working fairly, by further decentralization of decision-
making in government, firms and unions

building a capability to adapt to any further change into
institutions and processes of policy formulation.

Although these goals had much in common with those expressed
in the 1945 white paper, they reflected the growing concern of Australians for recognizing a "wider world"—not just in terms of more
interest in other nations, but more concern for nonmaterial values.
However, as the newly elected Labor government was to discover less
than three years after taking office, its concern with this "wider world"
in a seriously worsening economic situation produced a massive reversal of its electoral support. The Labor government was defeated by
a record margin by an opposition whose platform was largely focused
on achieving a rapid return to the economic prosperity of the 1960s
and on reducing the involvement of government in community deci-

sion-making. This latter policy direction was made clear by Malcolm Frazer (then opposition leader) in a speech in Perth, in September 1975:

> The goals of Australians should be set by Australians in the course of their own lives. Government is the focus of common but limited goals. It does not, and should not, set detailed goals for individuals. Government has the job of aiding people in pursuit of their diverse objectives and minimizing the imposition of uniformity and conformity. . . . Government is not the embodiment of the community. It is a set of institutions within a wider society.

Australian Goals Today

Australians have not progressed much, in recent years, toward achieving a national consensus on goals and objectives. In some ways, the goals of Australians in 1977 are not much changed from those of ten or twenty years ago. Yet in other ways, a change in goals has taken place, a change toward much deeper concern with contemporary regional issues. Australians now seem more willing and able to debate deep social issues—the conservation of resources and the environment, the control of the uses to which uranium exports are put, the role of trade unions, the quality of working environments, to name only a few. It also seems to have become more important to discuss growth, immigration and Southeast Asian security, less in polarized political terms however, and more in terms of where Australia fits into a changing region. It may even be said that Australians have now become more concerned with change itself, and the need to adapt to change within both the Australian and world societies, with an emphasis on the quality of the path chosen and its future sustainability.

The 1974 green paper may have represented a watershed in the development of Australian goal setting. A group of men with diverse political, social, and economic beliefs found after nearly a year of research, investigation, discussion, and deliberation that most of their individual aims were held in common. It may be that Australians are developing a capacity for goal setting that can bring about a community of effort, and a social cohesion capable of addressing important domestic issues.

However, Australians still devote relatively little effort to crystallizing their aims in the global context. Regional strategic security issues are becoming more important politically, but most individual

Australians still find it difficult to become deeply concerned about such matters. The arguments for and against various mineral resource management policies are of concern to most Australians, but mostly in the context of preserving Australia's economic and resource options, rather than in terms of the role these resources might play in serving mankind's developing needs. The debate on future immigration policy is focused largely on its domestic impact, because most Australians regard as somewhat unreal the possibility of the Australian continent providing a home for countless millions from the nearby overpopulated Asian countries. This attitude is based not only on the question of sheer numbers, but also on the racial differences in a society that has always valued homogeneity in its racial and economic composition. On the other hand, Australian adaptability is reflected in the signing of the Treaty of Friendship and Cooperation with Japan. Just over thirty years ago, it seemed totally inconceivable that these two nations could go beyond trade ties and sign a treaty which formally recognizes that each has a deep interest in the continued stability of the other, both as a supplier and as a market. As recently as the early 1960s, successful Australian election campaigns featured a heavy emphasis on the "Red Menace" to the nation's north, yet in the mid-1970s Australia is actively cultivating its mutuality of interests with the People's Republic of China.

These changes, which are reflected in the policies of both major Australian political parties, have taken some time to come about, but the effects will be durable and far-reaching in terms of Australia's regional goals and aims. They are also embodied in the prime minister's foreign policy speech on June 1, 1976:

> In our relations with other countries, the ideology of regions is not irrelevant but it cannot be the guiding principle of our policy. While common values and attitudes may serve to make cooperation easier, their absence need not preclude such cooperation if there are parallel interests. Whatever the basis of a regime, whatever the organization of its domestic government, the chief determinant of our relations will be that country's approach to foreign relations, how it meshes with ours, and of necessity the extent of the interests we share.

It is difficult to predict how deeply and quickly Australians as individuals will become concerned about outward-looking goals and aims which address the global, or even regional, issues facing man-

Section 2:
An Atlas of
International and
Transnational Goals

The circle of major actors on the contemporary scene is no longer confined to nation-states, their governments, and populations. A growing number of increasingly important international organizations, multiregional religious groupings, and multinational business corporations have emerged and taken their place among the important decision-makers. Following our overview and summary of national and regional goals, we now turn to a consideration of the goals pursued by such international and transnational bodies.

Their great number and diversity make it impossible to comment on them all, or give a full account of their goals in the modest space at our disposal. We do offer, however, a representative sampling, beginning with the United Nations and the International Labour Organisation, and taking in turn the World Council of Churches, representing some 285 Church bodies, and the single most influential

Church, the Roman Catholic, and ending with the goals and objectives of today's giant multinational corporations.

The goals of such international and transnational bodies are not
those of nation-states any more than the goals of nation-states are
those of individual persons. At each level of organization we find the
range of human goals represented in different forms. In an international or transnational setting, local and national goals become elements in the calculation of objectives that are wider-ranging in a
geographic, and sometimes also cultural, sense. These often influence
the definition and implementation of national and regional goals, and
play an important part in the determination of mankind's future.

Chapter 9

Goals of the United Nations and of the International Labour Organisation

I. Goals of the United Nations

Founded in 1945, the United Nations is today in a transitional stage: It is neither merely a league of purely sovereign nation-states, nor a supragovernmental organization exercising authority over the world's nations. Member states themselves are ambivalent toward the U.N. On the one hand, they would like to see world problems and difficulties resolved. On the other hand, they are unwilling to grant the U.N. the means to implement solutions they themselves agree upon. Hence, at the present time, the United Nations is something between a forum for the joint discussion of mankind's goals and a functional coordinator and implementor of the goals.

The goals discussed at the United Nations are not simply the national or popular goals of the member states "writ large." The U.N.'s transnational goals concern first and foremost (though not exclusively) world security, human rights, the world economy, development, world food, health, and population, the environment, and international law.

World Security Goals

Founded in the immediate aftermath of World War II, the United Nations was seen, at least by most of its founders, as primarily a peacekeeping machine. The particular format then decided upon—a concert of great powers acting *unanimously* to stifle aggression—broke down almost immediately with the falling out of the wartime allies. No new format has since been seriously suggested to take its place. The general failure of the most powerful members of the community to agree on how to police the international neighborhood has left it open to disorder and calamity, yet no one feels the time has come to elect a U.N. lawkeeper.

Although "collective measures" as delineated in the United Nations Charter have not worked, members have remained committed to the basic goal of maintaining peace and security through the United Nations. At its twenty-fifth anniversary session the U.N. adopted, for instance, a "Declaration of Principles of International Law concerning Friendly Relations and Cooperation among States in accordance with the Charter of the U.N." This document was regarded by some as an historic elaboration of the Charter principles, in particular those concerning use of force, international disputes, and intervention. Thus the members from time to time try setting forth, in more detail, codes of conduct and behavior designed to translate existing *intra*national norms to the *inter*national arena.

Disarmament
Although disarmament and the regulation of armaments are not given much space in the Charter, no goals have been pursued more ardently in the United Nations, nor has any goal proved so elusive, despite the danger of worldwide holocaust, and the world economic drain caused by armaments spending. The primary statement of goals and principles related to disarmament was produced in private talks between the United States and the Soviet Union, and adopted by the General Assembly in 1961. General and complete disarmament was the aim, in stages, under "strict international control." An International Disarmament Organization, not subject to veto, was to have unrestricted powers of verification. The principles include at least passing recognition of the need for progress in strengthening the institutions of peacekeeping and the peaceful settlement of disputes. The same requirement is spelled out in a "Comprehensive Program of Disarmament," recommended by the Assembly to the Conference of the Committee of Disarmament in 1970, which called for parallel negotiations on both disarmament and on peacemaking machinery.

Although a number of disarmament-related treaties have been adopted in the United Nations, only one—that dealing with biological warfare—has actually succeeded in abolishing a weapon. Other measures have been, in essence, *nonarmament* measures, which attempted to exclude either territories or weapons from future arms races.

One example of the latter was the establishment of nuclear-free zones, such as that covering Latin America, although the primary candidate for nuclear weaponry (Argentina) is not a party to the agreement. Nuclear-free zones are enjoying a high degree of interest at present, with more or less serious proposals being made for the South Pacific, Africa, South Asia, and the Middle East.

Included also in the nonarmament category are the "no bombs in orbit" treaty, the treaty which prohibits permanent nuclear weapon installations on the sea floor, and the nuclear nonproliferation treaty. Such measures are of relatively small significance in themselves, and for the most part have serious weaknesses, yet they are potentially valuable because they can contribute psychological momentum toward further agreements. If the psychological context changes, or the momentum is lost, such measures alone are a frail barrier against a resurgent arms race.

Control of conventional arms is an even more vexing problem. Major industrialized countries are enjoying the financial benefits of massive arms sales. Recipients want arms for purposes they consider legitimate, such as ending colonialism, promoting national liberation, and defending newly won independence. Why, they ask, should they accept any self-denying ordinance, when the two major contenders in the arms race have taken no steps at all to reduce arms? The major powers have reacted with distaste to the annual appeals of the General Assembly for arms-cut arrangements, and for steps toward disarmament. They have considered such appeals to be out of order, and have characteristically kept their more serious discussions on such matters outside the U.N. framework.

Although the guidelines for a general disarmament scheme are fairly well understood by member states, the requirements of an alternative security system are not so well understood or accepted. Yet only an alternative security system, instrumented through the world organization, could make disarmament feasible. Neither a world security system nor disarmament can be envisaged apart from a sharply increased commitment to build a world society based on a growing sense of solidarity among nations—a goal which will be discussed in Part III but is beyond the scope of current U.N. consideration.

Peacekeeping and Settlement of Disputes
Within the framework of peacekeeping by the United Nations forces, a vitally important new principle has emerged. It is the principle of *interposition*, in which U.N. forces are charged with the responsibility for separating warring parties, and preventing or halting conflict while the dispute goes to the conference table. While now taken for granted, the interposition principle is in no way alluded to in the Charter, and represents a major advance beyond the notion of the United Nations as a mere instrument for organizing successful punitive war against countries identified as "aggressors." It represents the advance of law enforcement over committee agreement, and a successful translation to the world level of a recognized norm within nation-states.

On the other hand, while the U.N. Charter nominally requires that disputes be settled peacefully, and suggests some approaches to disputing parties (negotiation, conciliation, mediation, and so on), no permanent mechanisms are provided other than the possible convening of the Security Council, or of ad hoc bodies of the Council. Although the goal is stated, it is not implemented. The brightest spot in dispute settlement is the evolving use of the "good offices" of the Secretary-General, functioning confidentially and effectively behind the scenes.

In summary, the requirements of a world security system are given weak acknowledgment as goals of the world community at the United Nations, but are not treated like the recognized security requirements of nation-states and regional organizations.

Human Rights Goals

The United Nations has in most respects successfully translated nationally held norms on treatment of human beings to the world level. Since its founding the U.N. has been active in codifying norms based on acceptance of the worth of the individual human being and his right to those conditions which improve his chances to realize his potentials. More recently, a new emphasis on collective human rights, and particularly on economic rights, has emerged.

The two major U.N.-inspired human rights instruments—the International Covenant on Civil and Political Rights, and the International Covenant on Economic, Social, and Cultural Rights—were completed in 1966 and became effective in 1976. They are not as liberal as the first great United Nations accomplishment, the Universal Declaration of Human Rights, but that is to be expected because, unlike the Declaration, they are regarded as legally binding obligations. Other U.N. instruments include conventions on genocide, racial discrimination, refugees, stateless persons, political rights of women, nationality of married women, consent to marriage, slavery, forced labor, discrimination in employment, equal pay for men and women, discrimination in education, and others.

Two United Nations documents, the Covenant on Civil and Political Rights, and the Convention on Racial Discrimination, contain the possibility of individual petitions over the heads of governments to an international body, in effect, a supranational appeal.

Thus the United Nations has gone far beyond the mere mention of human rights in the Charter, by successfully establishing planetary codes for the treatment of human beings. On the implementation side, the picture is not so encouraging. Here, national sovereignty interferes with success. Nonperformance has given rise to frustration and the proliferation of violations. The U.N. machinery for the implementation of human rights is weak, overlapping, and redundant. The accused nations can successfully raise the charge of "internal interference," unless the targets, such as colonial powers, are politically acceptable to a majority.

One of the great successes of the United Nations has been in guiding peoples out of colonialism into independence—thus implementing its Charter references to the "self-determination of peoples." It is essentially this success which has led to the achievement of near-universal membership in the U.N.—from 51 states in 1945 to 144 in 1976. The principle of self-determination may not always be honored, but it is among the most deeply established planetary norms.

World Economic Goals

While the United Nations has been engaged in various kinds of economic assistance almost since its inception, it is only recently that an effort has been made to establish global norms. The basic element is a plea for equity in access to resources, trade, and technology. Just as bills of rights and responsibilities have already been delineated for nations in other fields, the U.N. is now attempting to spell out a basis for cooperative, friendly, and just economic relations among states.

Two major instruments were adopted by the General Assembly in

1974, though they were not universally hailed. The first was the Declaration and the Programme of Action on the Establishment of a New International Economic Order, adopted by the sixth special session of the General Assembly, and the second, the Charter of Economic Rights and Duties of States, adopted by the twenty-ninth regular General Assembly. Most industrialized states feel that, in the attempt to redress present injustices, the developing countries have gone too far—particularly regarding "sovereignty over natural resources" and terms for nationalization. Even so, there is no doubt that these were landmark statements of principle. Although not formally agreed to by all states, these principles have already become a tacit part of their thought and strategy. This was evidenced, for instance, in the radical shift in the U.S. posture between the sixth and seventh special sessions of the Assembly, from a stance of total confrontation to one of offering constructive proposals.

Among the major principles contained in the two documents are these, stated in the Declaration:

> We . . . proclaim our united determination to work urgently for the establishment of a new international economic order based on equity, sovereign equality, interdependence, common interest and cooperation among all States, irrespective of their economic and social systems, which shall correct inequalities and redress existing injustices, make it possible to eliminate the widening gap between the developed and developing countries and ensure steadily accelerating economic and social development and peace and justice. . . . The prosperity of the international community as a whole depends upon the prosperity of its constituent parts.

Development Assistance

Development assistance is highly institutionalized in the United Nations. There is a well-established commitment to raise the level of well-being of less fortunate peoples and nations. The underlying assumption clearly is that humanity is not divisible into superior and inferior peoples, whom it is appropriate to treat in different and inequitable ways. Through a combination of assistance and self-help, people everywhere should have access to economic well-being and dignity.

Development assistance programs are now placed under an umbrella agency—the United Nations Development Programme (UNDP).

The programs have been through several "agonizing reappraisals," and there was a recent undertaking to double their capacity for handling assistance. They are also increasingly taking into account local needs and wishes, and allowing for the participation of recipients. In approving, in principle, $2,065.7 million as an "indicative planning figure" for UNDP aid in 1977–81, the program has focused "as never before" on the poorer countries.

As is the case with so many U.N. agencies, the existence of UNDP expresses international intent and registers a value commitment, but development assistance funneled through United Nations programs is still but a small percentage of that channeled bilaterally from rich to poor countries—the former seeking political returns on their help.

Other related bodies include the United Nations Conference on Trade and Development (UNCTAD), and the Industrial Development Organization (UNIDO). UNCTAD's work has helped establish the fact that *terms of trade* are at least as significant as grants and loans for development aid. Especially for undiversified, single-product countries, terms of trade can make or break the local economy in a season (and, incidentally, render recipient countries incapable of making repayments on development loans). UNCTAD also tries to provide participation by Third World countries in the redesign and regulation of the *world monetary system,* which up to now has been established and run by the financially most powerful states, with their own interests strongly in mind. Here again, as throughout the world economic field, equity and participation are the watchwords under which efforts are mobilized toward a new world economic order.

UNIDO has the task of catalyzing industrial development in the developing world. The agency's existence is undoubtedly a reflection of the belief held by many countries that the quick way to economic well-being and a high standard of living is to industrialize, and achieve locally the production of goods now found in industrialized societies. There may be some important fallacies in this assumption, just as there have been in traditional approaches to development aid. Nonetheless, the attempt by the international community to respond to this assumption has involved an underlying value decision about the responsibility to assist the underdeveloped countries toward economic self-sufficiency.

The U.N. has frequently used (and is in danger of overusing) the technique of naming days, years, and decades as times of emphasis on a particular subject or problem. The first Development Decade ran from 1960 to 1970, and was more important for what it revealed than for what it achieved. The second Development Decade, 1970 to 1980, has also provided a valuable means of studying and focusing world attention on the prevailing trends of economic growth, trade, and aid for Third World countries. Targets were set for both decades. The midterm review shows that only one country, Sweden, has thus far reached—and even surpassed—the target of aid commitment on schedule: .7 percent of GNP. Some countries, such as the U.S.A., are sliding further away from it—the U.S. is now at about .4 percent of GNP. Here again, as so frequently, endorsement of a goal is coupled with inadequate implementation. The schedule of commitments by donor nations toward development aid, their performances in frequent pledging conferences for various purposes, their attitudes toward the miniscule U.N. budget and toward payments for past and present peacekeeping arrangements, provide an all too accurate index of their real adherence to the world community values they profess.

A significant role is played in development by the World Bank group. The World Bank acts as a conventional lender of funds, principally for projects essential to the economic development of member countries. Loans on favorable terms below commercial rates are granted to governments and (with government guarantees) to private enterprises and public agencies.

The International Development Association (IDA) lends on minimum terms. It provides finance on terms which are more flexible and bear less heavily on the balance of payments of recipient countries than do conventional loans.

The International Finance Corporation (IFC) assists private enterprise. Its operations include loans, equity investments, and underwriting and standby commitments covering the sale of securities issued. The IFC does not require or accept government guarantees on its investments.

Because the funds involved are substantial, the World Bank group, unlike some of the underfinanced U.N. agencies, is a major element in international affairs. Funds lent by the Bank and IDA in 1973 totaled $3,408 million. The activities of this group of agencies corresponds quite accurately with the same kind of help provided to depressed cities and areas within member states by their central governments. This type of assistance, and the implied value of providing aid and assistance on a self-help basis, has been successfully translated to the level of the world community.

Energy Development and Regulation

While the United Nations has yet to play a very significant role in the development or regulation of energy, there are two areas in which its development has been important. One concerns nuclear, and the other geothermal, energy. The U.N. has provided leadership both in exploration and in exchange of information about geothermal energy through conferences and occasionally through *in loco* meetings.

The International Atomic Energy Agency (IAEA) is rapidly gaining in significance as the spread of nuclear materials and capabilities accelerates. The agency provides training in nuclear technology. It also operates a safeguard system against diversion of nuclear materials from power reactors to weapons uses. More recently, it has been approaching the question of "peaceful uses" of nuclear explosives. The spread of the safeguard system, and its strengthening and acceptance by additional countries, are absolutely decisive in the halt of the spread of nuclear weapons and, ultimately, in the denial to terrorist groups of access to nuclear materials. In the nuclear power field, the agency is not exactly a disinterested party. It tends to advocate nuclear power fission reactors as the short-term solution to energy shortages. In relation to the question of assisting nonnuclear countries with peaceful nuclear explosions, the agency has been handed a thankless task and it is to be hoped governments will not demand that the matter be seriously pursued.

Plans for direct ownership and control of nuclear energy by the organization foundered at the start, but the IAEA is in fact picking up, little by little, some of the safeguarding and monitoring (if not regulatory) responsibilities. A process of evolution here may have to continue, since regulation of nuclear traffic is yet another vital function quite beyond the capability of member states.

World Food Goals

The concept of "triage"—of aiding only those groups or persons who can clearly respond to help—has not guided the United Nations responses to world food shortages. The U.N. has been committed for many years to stimulating food production, directing contributions of food to areas of shortage, and itself distributing food when other donors were suspect. The principle is clear—that persons in need shall not be denied food if it is available. The elevation of this principle to the world level is now well-established.

The main organ of United Nations involvement with food problems is the Food and Agriculture Organization (FAO), which came into being in 1945. It is charged with raising levels of nutrition, improving production and distribution of agricultural products, and bettering the condition of rural populations. With the disappearance of world food surpluses, and with the impact of energy price increases on the "green revolution" and its intensive and expensive modes of cultivation, the FAO's activities have been supplemented by new functional units. Several are related to the major World Food Conference held in Rome in 1974. One is a World Food Council to monitor and stimulate food deliveries, among other things. A second is an Agricultural Development Fund to assist in expanding agricultural output in developing countries. The international community has not yet accepted the notion of a centrally managed world food bank, but individual nations are asked to hold reserves against a world food shortage. Contributions totaling $523 million have been promised by forty-three countries for the 1977 to 1978 World Food Programme, with further contributions from the European Economic Community and other major contributors expected. The target for the period is $750 million.

The response of member states to food shortages has generally been more immediate and generous than their response to many other global human problems. There is, it must be supposed, a basic identification with the hunger of fellow human beings; the international community shows signs of developing a conscience with regard to world food supplies.

Goals of Health and Basic Well-Being

Another fairly noncontroversial area of U.N. involvement has been that of worldwide health and disease. The principal agency within the United Nations system for these issues is the World Health Organization (WHO), established in 1948. Its most widely-known successes have been control of communicable diseases, including malaria, smallpox, and trachoma. (Some demographers now feel that family planning should have preceded worldwide efforts on food and health, the very success of which has contributed to soaring population rates.) WHO is also active in fields of environmental health, public health service advice and planning, education and training, and research on animal diseases and the standardization of biological substances. One problem of present concern to the agency is the high rate of "brain drain" among doctors, and efforts are being made to control what the agency calls the "undesirable migration of health manpower." The commitment of the community of nations to the achieving of global health is well established and has shown remarkable results. The working budget of WHO for 1977 is $146.9 million.

Allied to problems of health and disease is the task of disaster relief. U.N. involvement on an ongoing basis is relatively new. UNDRO, the United Nations Disaster Relief Office, was established only in 1971, on a minimal basis. Its primary tasks were seen as the coordination of the efforts of other agencies and groups, the promotion of stockpiling, and the provision of technical assistance in advance planning for disaster-prone areas. The office has quickly captured the imagination and respect of members, and is expanding its budget and activities. The U.N. system has provided a global focus which has greatly facilitated the work of this agency. Recently it secured a portable satellite ground station which can be flown into disaster areas and directly coordinate relief efforts.

The many activities of the United Nations in relation to dangerous drugs are not widely known. Here again, the international focus has proved extremely useful. The major organ at present is the Commission on Narcotic Drugs, which supervises agreements, suggests new machinery, and prepares needed conventions. Two technical organs are the Permanent Central Narcotics Board and the Drug Supervisory Body, which exercise controls over the production and requirements of narcotic drugs.

The U.N. agencies have a close working relationship with the International Criminal Police Organization (INTERPOL). The problems of the United States with opium derivatives, marijuana, and psychedelics have led to new conventions, and to a sudden spate of activity in the General Assembly concerning drugs.

The United Nations has a highly respected record in the protection and resettlement of refugees. U.N. aid for Palestine refugees began in 1948, and is now focused in the United Nations Relief and Works Agency for Palestine Refugees in the Near East. This body provides food, shelter, and education for around two million persons. Financially it is poorly supported by members. Many hundred of thousands of other persons have been cared for by the present major U.N. office concerned, the High Commissioner for Refugees.

Here again, the mobilization of international concern, beginning with refugees from World War II, and continuing with refugees throughout the world (whether Bangladesh, Sudan, or Middle East) has been notably successful.

Another area where significant success has been attained is care for the least privileged of the world's children. The United Nations Childrens' Emergency Fund (UNICEF) has become one of the permanent and most respected U.N. agencies. Originally created to provide emergency relief for children victimized by World War II, it has gone beyond health and disease control for underprivileged children in many parts of the world, to the provision of nutrition, social services, and education. The international community appears to have recognized the importance of a commitment to the well-being of its children as heirs and purveyors of human destiny.

World Population Goals

The United Nations has only lately taken up the question of population control. Constraints of custom, attitude, and religion played a part in delaying a U.N. role in this question. The Fund for Population Activities was not adopted by the General Assembly until 1972. The twenty-fifth General Assembly declared 1974 to be World Population Year, and an important World Population Conference took place that year in Bucharest. As with the Stockholm Environment Conference, the meeting served well as a sensitizing mechanism to a globe surfeited with uncared-for people. Earlier conferences on population convened by the U.N. had been essentially meetings of experts, primarily in the field of demography.

In Bucharest, the industrialized nations emphasized the fact that developing countries' gains in agriculture and industrial production were being wiped out by their increasing populations. The developing nations maintained that economic and social development were integral to any successful modification of population practices, and that population could not be treated as an isolated phenomenon. Nonetheless, there is no doubt that awareness of population pressure as a global problem of great immediacy was greatly heightened. The Fund for Population Activities' program is steadily growing, and it is providing technical assistance and advisory services to many governments.

Modification of population trends remains a touchy subject. The steady, noncontroversial approach of the FPA is bypassing many heated and partisan discussions, and could become a major tool in training human beings to face up to the facts of their own productivity on a spaceship of finite dimensions.

World Environmental Goals

In the case of environment and pollution, as in the case of several other major world problems, substantial U.N. involvement was inaugurated with a general world conference, and is of quite recent date (1972). No aspect of this and subsequent conferences has been more vital than the degree to which they have served as global sensitization mechanisms. Until the Stockholm Environment Conference, environment, ecology, and pollution were regarded by most of the world as a Western industrial curiosity. The interest of developing nations was captured when the new agency, the United Nations Environment Programme (UNEP), was located in Nairobi, Kenya—the first U.N. agency to operate in the developing world. Its programs are helping to instill notions of world community and shared responsibility, not through exhortation, but by simple presentation of evidence of the organic interrelatedness of all the elements of the global ecosystem.

UNEP efforts are thus far germinal. A Global Environment Monitoring System (GEMS) is being established, and certain initial target problems are being identified. Dimly on the horizon is the more problematic, but essential, task of setting guidelines for national behavior and international standards. Once proposed, they will undoubtedly remain as recommendations for a considerable time before being written into binding treaties.

World Law Goals

Despite the hedging of member states, the United Nations has become a force in its own right in the development of international law. The U.N. is regarded by many authorities as laying down the rudiments of international common law. In effect, this means establishing planetary norms of behavior. These norms, as in any developing system of law, only gradually become accepted in practice, and only by later community agreement finally become enforceable law. This process is operative in the codification of planetary norms of human rights discussed above, and is beginning to be visible in the development of global economic norms. In 1974, after nearly fifty years of international effort, a definition of "aggression" was completed at the U.N.

Aggression is a key word in the Charter, for upon it depends Security Council action against wrong-doers. The definition critically assists Council decisions about when to activate its "enforcement" prerogatives.

Some lesser contributions to world law are also being made in other areas. In 1971 the General Assembly accepted a Convention on International Liability for Damage caused by Space Objects. The convention fixes responsibility for compensation upon the state from which the space object originated and establishes a Claims Commission to deal with disputes. Perhaps more important than the convention itself is the acceptance of the principle that laws agreed to by the international community are applicable to member states.

One of the most heartening among recent developments was the adoption by the General Assembly in 1970 of the principle that the resources "of the seabed and subsoil thereof"—beyond national jurisdiction—are the "common heritage of mankind," not the property of any state or group of states. Some members have hailed this step as the establishment of a new legal principle of great importance. Its impact is being diminished by the rapidly increasing claims of states to wider jurisdiction over the waters, soil, and resources off their coasts. This discussion, taking place during the sessions of the Law of the Sea Conference, provided a detailed (and not a very encouraging) commentary on the attitudes of states towards principles of community, as against principles of individual exploitation.

The "common heritage" principle, however, will live on. Indeed, it is even being considered for a draft treaty on the resources of the moon.

The attitudes of states toward the International Court of Justice and its statutes likewise provide an index of their commitment, or lack of it, to international legal procedures—in particular, their acceptance, and the conditions of their acceptance, of the so-called compulsory jurisdiction clause. Under the terms of this clause, any state may at any time declare that it accepts as compulsory the jurisdiction of the Court in all legal disputes. Far too few states have made such a declaration, and most of those which have, have hedged them with reservations largely nullifying the undertaking. The norm is set up; it stands there in the statute. What is being registered is the current ambivalence of states toward binding international legal processes, and toward third-party involvement. The court itself is enjoying a mild renaissance since its ruling on South Africa and Namibia, and has had before it such cases as the United Kingdom-Iceland "cod war," French South Pacific nuclear tests, and the Spanish Sahara.

The United Nations system has achieved the beginnings of an international legal order. While many of the enunciated principles are partly compromised from the outset, and the codifications are far from perfect, a structure has been slowly built up, and a willing membership could certainly activate and gradually perfect it, should it wish to do so.

II. Goals of the International Labor Organisation

Created in 1919 with a mandate for the promotion of "peace through social justice," the International Labour Organisation (ILO) has actively striven to achieve this goal throughout its existence. On its fiftieth anniversary, its efforts were acknowledged by the award of the Nobel Peace Prize.

Recognizing that lasting peace depends largely on the social and economic well-being of the world's peoples, the ILO's educational and operational activities have been directed to promoting social justice through the amelioration of the conditions of life and work for the working men and women of the world.

The ILO seeks to promote peace through the eradication of poverty and inequality. This primary goal entails several subsidiary operational goals, including the advancement of human rights, the improvement of working conditions, tripartism (cooperation between employers, workers, and governments), and the promotion of world employment opportunities and solidarity.

The Advancement of Human Rights

In recognizing that the achievement of material well-being is meaningless without the simultaneous free spiritual development of the individual, the ILO anticipated by several decades the U.N. Declaration of Human Rights, and its International Covenant on Economic, Social, and Cultural Rights. The Constitution of the ILO, signed in 1919 and reaffirmed in 1944, declares,

> All human beings, irrespective of race, creed or sex, have the right to pursue both their material well-being and their spiritual development in conditions of freedom and dignity, of economic security and equal opportunity.

The ILO was thus mandated to bring together governments, employers, and workers for united action in the cause of social justice, to protect the rights and dignity of the individual worker and his or her family.

Four major groups of conventions have been achieved through ILO activities: the Convention on Forced Labour (1930) and Abolition of Forced Labour (1947), which guarantee freedom from forced labor; the Equal Remuneration Convention (1951) and that on Discrimination in Respect of Employment and Occupation (1958), which provide for freedom from discrimination; the Right of Association of Agricultural Workers Convention (1921), and the Conventions on Freedom of Association and Right to Organise (1948) and on the Right to Organise and Collective Bargaining (1948), which assure freedom of association for workers; and finally the Employment Policy Convention (1964), offering protection against unemployment. The entire body of ILO Standards is dedicated to the promotion of human rights. The organization's operational activities facilitate the implementation of the principles at the national level through technical cooperation programs. These include assistance in the formulation of labor legislation, the creation of fair and safe working conditions, the organization of social security schemes, the development of labor administration and labor manpower relations, and the promotion of worker education.

The Improvement of Working Conditions

A vast body of conventions and recommendations spanning all the decades of the ILO's history justifies and endorses its educational and operational activities aimed at improving conditions of work. The standards attempt to regulate various aspects of working conditions, such as hours of work, health and safety, paid vacation, and to provide for the workers a maximum of economic protection in any given socio-economic context by guaranteeing minimum wages and establishing various schemes of social security and insurance. Instruments for achieving these aims are various national institutions, such as trade unions, labor departments, employers' organizations, and rural cooperatives, as well as the ongoing World Employment Programme (WEP). The organization assists developing countries to devise and apply social policies, for example in the setting up of pension funds and social security and insurance schemes, and in establishing regulations for the improvement of working conditions.

The organization has been criticized for treating the concept of "working conditions" in the abstract, and thereby overlooking the fact that such conditions are relative to the socio-economic and political conditions of individual countries. There do not seem to be any "standard packages" which could be offered to and implemented by all nations. In some cases the standard-setting activities of the ILO have actually hampered development, as standards adopted enthusiastically at its Geneva headquarters turned out to be unsuited to the socio-economic development of given countries. An example of this was observed in Colombia in 1969. An ILO mission was obliged to conclude,

> the total effect of labor laws in Colombia (and this applies throughout Latin America) is to give great security to a small minority of the working class at the cost of great insecurity for the remainder.

The ILO now attempts to rethink the direction and scope of its activities related to world working conditions. The recently launched International Programme for the Improvement of Working Conditions and Environment (PIACT) seeks to refocus the interest of countries concerning the already long-standing problems of the work environment.

Cooperation through Tripartism

ILO's tripartite structure is unique among international organizations. The organization grants employers, workers, and governments equal shares of responsibility, and upholds the principle that divergent interests in labor relations should be reconciled through discussion and consultation. The representatives of employers and workers have kept the ILO in touch with the realities of the workplace, as well as with the concerns of the major economic and social groups affecting labor conditions in nations. Albert Thomas, the first Director-General, likened the organization to a machine in which employers, workers, and governments are respectively the brake, the accelerator, and the engine. The workers give the ILO its humanistic bent, the employers force it to consider the practical implications of actions, and the governments call attention to the problems and opportunities of implementation.

However, the real decision makers of nation-states are not always present or influenced by the workings of such ILO groups as the International Labour Conference. Thus some of the impact of international decisions is lost in the transmission to national forums. Moreover many strata of the working populations—especially the rural agricultural strata of developing countries—are not properly represented, and there is some question whether the ILO can cater to their needs. While the concept of tripartism is excellent, it is not fully representative and its implementation leaves much to be desired.

Through its expanding technical cooperation programs, the organization seeks to increase the scope of national participation. It offers training for trade union leaders, government officials, and employers, it assists in the development of trade unions, labor ministries, and employers' organizations, it is helping to draft labor legislation and to set up industrial and labor relations systems, and it is aiding in the creation of cooperatives and other institutions to permit the fullest possible involvement of rural populations in the social and economic life of nations.

Employment Promotion

The ILO has established the promotion of employment as a priority goal of workers, employers, and governments of most of the member countries. The organization's contribution toward this goal is twofold. In the first place, most of the expanding technical cooperation programs are devoted to the development and fullest possible utilization of the human resources of member states. Industrial and rural vocational-training programs, management-training projects, and assistance with rural and urban development schemes illustrate the scope of ILO activities.

Secondly, the ILO helps world employment through its own World Employment Programme. This notes that hundreds of millions in the developing countries are left behind in the drive to build modern economies, and it insists that employment must be at the heart of all projects of economic and social advancement. It seeks to ensure that all people participate in the tasks of nation-building, and thus receive a fair share of the fruits of economic and social progress.

The ILO's Employment Policy Convention (1964) declared:

> With a view to stimulating economic growth and development, raising levels of living, meeting manpower regulations and overcoming unemployment and underemployment, each member shall declare and pursue, as a major goal, an active policy designed to promote full, productive and freely chosen employment.

The World Employment Conference of June 1976 reviewed the work so far done under the World Employment Programme and underlined the necessity of making the satisfaction of basic needs a priority goal of the world community during the next twenty-five years. The conference called on individual countries and the community of nations to strive to satisfy the minimum requirements of the poorest segments of the population.

Promoting World Solidarity

The precept guiding ILO activities is that "poverty anywhere constitutes a danger to prosperity everywhere." Thus the socio-economic interdependence of the nations of the world today is well recognized, and concerted action is demanded in the interest of peace and social justice.

Through its tripartite structure, its universality, and its wide range of normative and operational activities, the ILO seeks to demonstrate in practice that collective action is more effective than the sum of the efforts of individual countries acting on their own. As its Director-General David Morse wrote,

> The ILO, acting in concert with the other organizations
> of the U.N. system is, therefore, above all a living testi-
> mony to the ideal of the solidarity of mankind.

Research on various aspects of the problems and opportunities of world solidarity is now promoted by the affiliated International Institute for Labour Studies, which organizes conferences and offers stipends for work on relevant topics.

Chapter 10

Goals of Multinational Corporations

Multinational corporations (MNCs) represent a key force in the international business world, and a major influence in the conduct of world affairs. Of the 100 wealthiest entities on the international scene, well over half are corporations.

MNCs vary widely in structure, style, and operation; they differ in the scope of their business (mining, agriculture, manufacturing, services, banking, etc.); and while they are known as multi- or transnational enterprises, each still calls one country its "home." It is chartered by a government in its home country and it reflects that country's particular culture and values.

The avowed goals of such corporations are usually too broadly stated to be useful in understanding their real operative purposes. For U.S.-based multinationals, for example, the published goals tend to be something like the following:

The basic objective of XYZ Company is to operate a vigorous, growing, diversified, and profitable business in the balanced best interest of its customers, shareholders, employees, suppliers, and the economy at large by generating earnings and profits at levels which will assure payment to shareholders of dividends sufficient to warrant their continued investment in the Company and at the same time sufficient for retention of funds in the business to assure growth and improvement.

Such general statements are often supported by a list of more specific objectives which derive from, and are intended to support and amplify, the basic goal. Typically, these more detailed statements aim at specifying the nature of corporate responsibilities to the various constituencies of that company, for example,

customers: ". . . to design, make, and market all company products and services with good quality and with inherent customer value, at fair prices . . ."

employees: ". . . to provide good jobs, wages, working conditions, work satisfactions, and opportunities for advancement . . ."

the public: ". . . to adapt company policies to meet continuously, progressively, foresightedly, and voluntarily the social, civic, and economic responsibilities commensurate with the opportunities offered by the size, success, and nature of the business and of the public confidence in it as a corporate enterprise."

Such statements, however, are more indicative of good intentions than of operational goals. Occasionally we come across a more descriptive and helpful statement, such as the following:

energetically to seek and develop opportunities for accelerating profitable growth both at home and abroad, with particular emphasis in fields where the company may occupy an advantageous position because of raw materials, facilities, or management skills

the importance of change is recognized, and constant attention shall be given to expansion in areas with long-range growth and profit potential, and to the identification and elimination of declining and less profitable products and activities.

Clearly, these examples are only illustrative of the range of possibilities, rather than exhaustive. Yet, by analyzing such statements and the speeches of executives, and comparing them with the inferences drawn from the performance of the corporations, we can list a number of general conclusions about corporate goals and managerial behavior.

Growth and Profitability

These are the prime objectives and motivational forces of MNCs. As dynamic institutions and creatures of an industrial culture (whether

Western or Japanese), they are deeply imbued with a growth ethic. "To be is to grow," is a cardinal belief that pervades their policies and actions. Not to grow is equated with stagnation and decay. In this belief they take their cue from the societal values of the industrial culture, and from adherence to the philosophy of a market economy. Growth is seen both as a route to, and in need of discipline by, profit (since "profitless growth" cannot be sustained for long).

Tension between Short-Term and Long-Term Goals

On the one hand the MNC—any corporation, for that matter—is in business for the long term. It has a steady, declared interest in its own continuity, and no management willingly elects to preside over the demise of a business. On the other hand, the managerial calculus is excessively weighted in favor of short-term measurements; and the corporate annual report is something of an anachronism, being a continuation of an annual accounting of the crop cycle of an agricultural society. Quarter-by-quarter profitability is seen as a prerequisite for maintaining the vitality of an organization in order that it may have a long-term future. The tension is acute, and made more so by the fact that, in the inflationary environment of modern industrial societies, a heavily discounted *future* benefit provides only a weak motivation for *present* actions.

The Interests of Multiple Constituencies

Corporations have to serve customers, employees, owners, suppliers, and other groups and interests. A major challenge to managerial decision making is to balance the interests of the various claimants on a company's output. For an MNC, the balancing act is made more complex by the diversity of national interests that it has to factor into its calculations. Increasingly, too, these constituency interests are being "institutionalized" in a wide variety of unions, employee associations, consumer organizations, and environmental and public interest groups (not to mention governments) so that their influence is no longer left entirely to the discretionary recognition of their claims by corporate managers.

Responsibility to the Owners of the Business

This means, predominantly, owners in a single country. In the final analysis responsibility to the owners is viewed by managers as their *prime* responsibility. It is not merely a matter of legal responsibility (the corporate charter expressly delineates a line of responsibility from managers through directors to stockholders); it is also a philosophical preference, rooted in the notion of capital property rights. This holds good even where it is the government or the employees that are the owners. In each case ownership rights are linked with investment in the business. An exception is to be found in cases such as German codetermination, where employee representation on the board of directors is divorced from ownership. The very term "owners" (though in most cases "investors" is a more appropriate description) reinforces the idea of a predominant claim, to be matched by a correspondingly major responsibility on the part of managers.

The Primary Goals of Growth, Profitability, and Efficiency

Growth and profitability are the primary objectives of MNCs. The pairing of these two goals is not fortuitous. Contrary to the assertion that profit maximization is their *sole* objective, MNCs frequently balance growth and profitability as relatively equal corporate goals, or even place the prime emphasis on growth, in terms of expanded output, new products or services, increased market share, or entry into additional markets. The search for growth is continuous. The aim is to match the particular strengths of a corporation in technology, marketing, or manufacturing, with new or expanding markets created by consumer needs of growing populations, or by governmental development projects (in energy, materials, or infrastructure).

The corporate search for growth is both selective and conditional. While, in *aggregate*, the MNCs' growth may seem undifferentiated (simply because their aggregate range of activities is so comprehensive), the process for any one company is, in fact, highly selective. The selection process is conditioned by assessment of such factors as corporate and competitive strengths and weaknesses, relative market growth rates, availability and cost of resources, including capital, and profit expectations. At any given time most MNCs find themselves with more options than resources. They have, therefore, to establish their own systems of selection criteria and priorities for allocating these resources.

A major debate, and a potential source of friction, revolves around the question whether, and to what extent, these internal criteria and priorities coincide with those set by nations via the political process. It is, of course, entirely possible for MNC and national goals to be in harmony (or at least reconcilable) but, as Kurt Waldheim, U.N.

Secretary-General, has noted, "it is necessary to *search for* the coincidence of national and corporate interests rather than to *assume* it"
(emphasis added). While in general terms one might reasonably
assume a broad approximation of corporate goals to national goals
(at least those of the "home country"), in any specific instance there
can be sharp divergences; and very few would subscribe to the half
of Charles Wilson's statement that goes, "What's good for General
Motors is good for the country." (The first part of that statement was,
"What's good for the country is good for General Motors.")

In selecting and in implementing corporate strategies for growth
and profitability, the related goal of efficiency (or productivity) comes
into play. To achieve profitable growth, the MNCs stress the efficient
use of resources—human, material, energy, land, and capital. There
are, of course, other strategies for achieving growth and profitability
(e.g., product innovation, market segmentation, improved service),
but once the strategy has been decided, efficiency becomes the desired, and often the decisive, factor. In this context productivity can
be colloquially defined, from a corporate point of view, as "securing
maximum output from a given input." Profitability is based on the
principle of efficiently conserving scarce or expensive resources—
again, essentially from a corporate viewpoint.

A number of important, even though obvious, points should be
made about this economizing (or conserving) process:

Historically, the costs of most resources have been set by the inter-
play of market forces of supply and demand. Price, in other words,
has effectively been the measure of scarcity.

The price of a given resource has tended to vary considerably, not
merely over time, but also among countries and regimes within
them.

As a result there can be strong competition at any given time among
providers of a resource (especially of labor, energy, and materials),
and there can thus be a corresponding range of alternative choices
for the users of these resources.

Over time the relative costs of the various resources have tended
to shift, sometimes dramatically. Thus, substituting cheap energy
for expensive labor may cease to be an economizing strategy when
the relative costs of these two resources undergo a major change.

Until fairly recently, some resources—mainly air and water—have been considered "free goods." The use of these resources has not been factored as a cost in the production equation.

These facts have had an important bearing on the choice of corporate goals and strategies. In the first place, MNCs have had, and have striven hard to maintain, considerable flexibility in optimizing the mix and cost of resource usage. To improve productivity, they have not only shifted the relative weightings within the resource mix, but also changed their sources. They sought to identify the "national comparative advantage" of various countries, and so tended to reinforce the adoption of specific resource strategies in given nations (for example, the tendency to specialize in producing raw materials, or developing labor-intensive manufacturing operations). This has been both a response and a contribution to the emergence of an increasingly complex and interdependent global economy.

Second, because the real costs of supposedly "free goods" and "negative externalities" have not been accounted for, many manufactured goods have enjoyed an unwarranted cost advantage in their competition with services (which tend to be more labor intensive, yet less polluting and resource consuming). This fact has obviously influenced the selection of corporate priorities and growth targets.

Third, the production and distribution system has developed in a linear mode (straight throughput) rather than in a circular one (recycling).* This has been an "economically logical" response, by both corporations and nations, to the desired goal of raising the material standard of living, in the light of the existing system of resource use accounting.

Recently, however, major changes have occurred both in "internalizing" the costs of pollution and waste disposal, and in the relative costs of various inputs (energy, labor, capital, materials). These changes have delivered major shocks to the economic system, upsetting many corporate strategies and objectives. Thus, while the basic goal of efficiency and productivity remains essentially unchanged, a major reoptimization process is under way to achieve it under circumstances changed, in part by market action, and in part by the political process.

Corporate resistance to this legislated "internalizing" of external costs has been directed not so much against the legislated goals of

---

* See Chapter 14 for details.

environmental protection, as against what companies see as the excessive pace and inconsistencies in implementation, together with a neglect or blurring of certain key "trade-off" decisions. Despite an innate opposition to further government regulation, most companies recognize that, if society opts for a pollution-free environment, there is merit in having legislation which establishes uniform standards, penalties, and incentives, thus equalizing conditions for all competitors within a given country. (There has, however, been opposition, and not only from corporations, to establishing goals of "absolute purity," or zero discharge of pollutants in some cases, on the grounds that the exponential increase in costs to eliminate the final elements of pollution is out of all proportion to the societal benefits, and the environment can cleanse itself of small amounts of pollution.)

Problems arise, however, when some countries establish lower standards than others, and some require no standards. These countries thus achieve competitive advantages for companies within their jurisdiction. Following the economizing process to its logical conclusion, MNCs that might be put at a disadvantage by higher standards can be expected to weigh this factor, along with many others, in decisions about plant location. In an increasing number of instances the balance may be tipped in favor of the site with the lower standards. To the extent that this "competitive advantage" accrues mostly to developing countries, it may work in support of their goal of industrialization. It is questionable, however, whether this would provide the optimum mix and scale of industries for their purposes.

It is worth noting, finally, that many companies have made a "virtue out of necessity" from this new concern with environmental protection. Some, responding in the traditional way to new markets, have seized the opportunities created by legislation to become suppliers of pollution control equipment. Others, acting on the equally traditional incentive to economize, have been forced to reexamine their production processes and in so doing have discovered (as Dow Chemical did) that pollution is, in effect, a wasted resource that can be captured to produce valuable by-products.

The Secondary Goals of Global Rationalization
The primary goals of MNCs entail the secondary goal of "global rationalization" with respect to their research, engineering, manufacturing, marketing, and service systems. This carries economic rationality to its logical conclusion, building on global interdependence and na-

tional comparative advantage. Fundamentally, pursuing this goal reflects the twin instincts of MNCs—to search out lowest-cost inputs
consistent with their desired standards of quality and efficiency; and
to find or create new markets. In the process, the companies learn to
operate on a global basis, crossing national boundaries in the search
for these inputs and markets.

A complex system of interrelated operations exists already in the
developed world, so the impact of future global rationalization may be
felt more in the developing countries. The magnitude of the change
in its wake will be incomparably greater for the developing countries
than for industrialized nations.

There appear to have been at least three stages in the evolution of
the goals of MNCs with respect to developing countries over the past
two or three decades:

STAGE 1

Developing countries as sources of raw materials. This stage might
be said to represent the "age of the extractive MNCs." Companies
went where the materials were, extracted them from the earth, in
some cases did some refining in these countries, but exported the
output, mainly to the developed world.

STAGE 2

Developing countries as bases for manufacturing. This is a strategy
employed mainly, but not exclusively, by U.S.-based MNCs faced
with competition from other corporations with lower unit labor
costs. Lower wage rates in developing countries attracted the establishment of manufacturing and assembly plants requiring relatively
low technologies, with exports aimed at the U.S. or other developed
countries.

STAGE 3

Developing countries as growing internal markets. The expected
slowing of economic rates of growth in developed countries now
serves to focus the attention of MNCs on the faster growth potential
for consumer and industrial products in a number of Third World
countries.

The description of these three stages is oversimplified, and in reality
they are to some extent overlapping. But there has been a significant
shift in the thinking and goal-setting process of many multinationals.

There is an essential difference between stage 1 and stage 3 in terms of the impact of corporate goals on developing nations. It is one that accords with a distinction between extractive and manufacturing (and financial and service) MNCs.

Manufacturing companies are far more likely than extractive industries to have a compelling interest in raising the purchasing power of the masses in the countries where they operate. Whereas extractive companies are predominantly oriented toward *exports,* manufacturers are more likely to set as one of their goals the development of *internal* consumer and industrial markets which they can then serve.

The distinction between extractive and manufacturing corporations also relates to the problems of population control and distribution. Historically, rising living standards and increasing industrialization have been associated with slower population growth. While expanding population would seem to be in harmony with corporate growth objectives, these objectives are, in fact, best furthered by increases in per capita income. Thus, growth in income rather than growth in overall population size is the national goal that most MNCs would seek to promote.

On the population issue, a second distinction between extractive and other corporations relates to the question of population *distribution.* Simply stated, extractive industries locate where the materials are (generally, in remote nonurban areas); while manufacturing and services industries locate where the markets, i.e. the people, are. Therefore the operations of extractive industries and of "agribusiness" NMCs, whose products and services promote greater agricultural productivity, tend to support "deurbanization;" while manufacturing and service operations tend to promote the migration of people to the cities. These effects, however, are not part of MNC goals and planning since corporations do not normally base their siting decisions on considerations of national and demographic patterns.

Recent Changes in Corporate Planning and Goal Setting

Until fairly recently much of the expansion, and many of the activities, of MNCs resulted from a piecemeal approach to planning, in which immediate opportunities were seized and crises avoided, or at least mitigated. Corporate goals tended to be incremental and short-term responses to a series of external stimuli. Thus, an almost overnight awareness of the consumer market potential in Western Europe caused a lemminglike drive on the part of U.S.-based MNCs to "go

European" in search of growth opportunities. A sudden surge in raw material prices, or an interruption of supply, gives rise to a proliferation of "backward integration" moves, in an effort to ensure continuity of supplies. New environmental or antidiscrimination legislation leads to a hasty building-in of new goals for plant or product design, manufacturing processes, or personnel administration, to avert the penalties of noncompliance or the onset of class-action suits.

No doubt, much of this incrementalism represents a desirable flexibility and adaptability to unforeseen events. Also, as we shall see, there are exceptions to this generally short-term approach, in the form of commitments to computers, nuclear power, resource development, and the like. But too many goals are set without a full consideration of their resource requirements, their true costs (financial and otherwise), or even their impact on the company. In the 1960s too much reliance was placed on a euphoric belief in growth and the expectation that, in the words of John F. Kennedy, "a rising tide lifts all boats."

In the sober environment of the 1970s a new and more cautious approach to goal setting and resource allocation is emerging in the form of corporate commitments to strategic planning. More and more of the larger MNCs are adopting a form of planning that enables them to take a longer-term, more holistic view of their business and its environment. Their aim is to force serious consideration of corporate goals in relation to a specified mission, and to allocate resources in a more rational and disciplined manner, in accordance with a set of established priorities and criteria.

The longer-term, holistic approach to business and its environment encourages a recognition of the social and political, as well as the economic and technological, aspects of the global environment relevant to business; of the corporation as a subsystem of this *total* environment; and of the need for a better balance between short- and long-term goals.

The emphasis on defining the "mission" of the corporation, as the first step in planning, motivates an explicit consideration of its basic *purpose,* and stresses the need to relate specific goals and objectives back to it. In such an exercise it becomes apparent that "profit maximization" is wholly inadequate, not merely as a public relations motif, but also as an operational statement of the basic purpose. Once corporate goals are examined in this manner, the need to identify national and even global goals—so that the harmonizing of system and sub-system goals can be improved to the benefit of both—becomes more obviously a matter of corporate self-interest.

The disciplined approach to all resource allocation, not just capital, makes more likely a differentiated and highly selective approach to growth. It also creates a better awareness of the true cost of resources, and offers some clues as to the "reoptimization" that is now being sought.

Much more is now being internalized in the multinational corporation than just the cost of "negative externalities." Public policy considerations, societal expectations, and national goals are coming to be as routinely factored into corporate decision making as are return on investment and market share, precisely because the former are becoming the prime determinants of the latter.

Without being overoptimistic about the new trend toward strategic planning, it is reasonable to hope that it may contribute in a major way to developing a fuller sense of "global systems thinking" in today's major multinational corporations.

Examples of New MNC Orientations

There is evidence that, although a full turnabout from previous short-range, profit- and growth-oriented practices has not yet occurred, many MNCs are actually opting for longer-term and more globally conscious strategies. These center around the following: the decision to invest; the utilization of appropriate technologies and production methods; environmental acceptability; plant location; and control of the financial, business, and technology practices and personnel policies of subsidiaries.

Traditionally, MNCs have invested wherever the rate of return on investment was the highest. As a result, the more dynamic and faster-growing regions of the world received most of the investment during the era following World War II. Canada and Western Europe received the lion's share of direct foreign investment, originating primarily in the U.S.A. The Third World received less than one-third of total investment, mostly in raw material extraction, an industry usually providing a very high rate of return on investment.

The slowdown of economic activity in the West, together with increased political stability and an accelerating market size in the developing world, caused a surge of direct foreign investment in manufacturing at rates of return on investment comparable to, or occasionally less than, that obtained in the developed countries.

European and Japanese MNCs have a slight edge over their U.S. counterparts in this regard. In 1971, U.S. MNCs had only 46 percent of their subsidiaries in the Third World while Japan had over 90 percent, and France and Italy had 66 percent and 74 percent respectively. Nestlé states that "the growth in absolute value terms of the activities of the Nestlé companies in the developing countries is considerable and continuous; their combined turnover increased from 428 million Swiss francs in 1950 to 3,568 million in 1974." Philips, Unilever, and Shell are all stepping up their penetration into Third World markets as well.

Regarding the rate of return on investment it seems that the "Age of the Quick Payback Period" is over. Unilever, for example, reported that in 1975 the rate of return of its subsidiaries operating in the developing world was the same as that of the rest of the company. IBM told the group of Eminent Persons two years ago: "We go into a developing country and operate at a loss. . . . In the country of one of the members of this panel, for example, we went for eleven years without profit."

A comparable shift is occurring with regard to the utilization of technologies and production methods. In the past, managers operating under the unique conditions of rapid economic growth (large and affluent market, tight labor supply, cheap raw materials and energy, etc.) devised production technologies to produce large quantities of products via an increasing substitution of machine power for human muscle power. Successful substitutions at home were then "exported" or "diffused" into regions of the world characterized by small markets and abundant labor supply.

There is now considerable evidence that some MNCs are reversing this trend. One of the most noteworthy examples is Philips Company, the Dutch multinational which has facilities in forty-two developing countries. Philips' philosophy is summarized below:

> In several countries, now referred to as developing countries, Philips enterprises were already established before the Second World War. In most of those countries the home market was too small to make large-scale production an economic proposition. Where the closed economies nevertheless made it desirable to establish production plants, different techniques more suitable for smaller production runs

were needed. For this reason a pilot plant was set up over twelve years ago at Utrecht (Netherlands) for the special purpose of converting manufacturing processes to simple techniques better adapted to the production of smaller series. In this pilot plant, where employees from developing countries are trained to become plant managers, it is not only machines and tools that are adapted but also, for example, administrative procedures and methods of inventory control. This is done in a situation colsely resembling that encountered in developing countries. In many cases this has accelerated the start of production in developing countries without causing the national Philips organizations to run into serious problems of adaptations on the spot.

General Motors Corporation has concentrated recently on providing more appropriate products for developing countries. An example of this effort is the Basic Transportation Vehicle (BTV) described below, which is designed for economies with less than $400 per capita:

General Motors has developed what we call a Basic Transportation Vehicle. It is a low-cost product requiring a minimum of sheet-metal fabrication and designed with emphasis on the ease of its assembly, repair, and operating cost. All components except the major highly engineered components such as the engine and transmission, are being produced locally. We are drawing on the high-volume production of our subsidiary in Great Britain to provide these components for this new vehicle at low cost. The Basic Transportation Vehicle is currently being produced in Malaysia, Portugal, and the Philippines, and we have plans to make this vehicle available in other countries in the future. The BTV in Malaysia is selling at a price over 30 percent lower than that of an imported small pick-up truck, our closest competition, pricewise, in that country.

Ford Motor Company has launched one of the most innovative and most promising production strategies, known as "complementation":

Ford's ability to source internationally, and particularly between its own affiliates, creates new possibilities for smaller countries to participate in the benefits of industrialization. One difficult but potentially very beneficial method is product complementation between Ford companies in different countries, with each contributing complementary parts and components and performing assembly operations. Through such complementation programs countries whose domestic markets are too small to justify the investment required to achieve mass production efficiencies can nevertheless begin to industrialize by manufacturing and exporting one or more components in high volume. The net result of such programs is additional employment, a manageable level of local investment and a locally assembled vehicle in each of the participating countries at a reasonable cost.

Recently Ford embarked on a modest complementation program which presently involves Australia, Thailand, Taiwan, the Philippines, and Argentina, to build the Fiera, an all-purpose, low-cost vehicle for nations reaching for growth. With the help of teams of Ford manufacturing, management, and purchasing specialists, Fiera components now are being produced by more than 150 suppliers in the Asia-Pacific area. The Fiera was first introduced in the Philippines in late 1972 and is now being marketed in the Philippines, Thailand and Taiwan. In its first year on the market about one-fourth of all Fiera sales were to customers purchasing their first motor vehicle.

There have been numerous other examples of MNC attempts to tailor product and/or production technology which would prove to be more appropriate for small and less developed countries. Apparently moved by E. F. Schumacher's Intermediate Technology Group, John Deere, the large agricultural implement producer, has examined the technical and economic feasibility of building a unique tractor for small farmers in developing countries on several occasions. In 1967, a senior Deere engineer studied the possibility of retooling the 1937 Model H tractor for the developing nations. The estimated list price of this tractor would have been only 55 percent of that of the 1020 tractor introduced in 1965. In 1971 Deere's Waterloo unit made a feasibility study to design a two-wheel walking tractor for developing nations. Included in the design goals for the tractor were the use of some highly tooled components from Deere along with many components to be made by local manufacturers in developing nations. Although functional performance was developed for all of these projects none was economically feasible and therefore whatever production and marketing took place had to be discontinued. Ironically, most of the small walking tractors are presently used in Japan and Western Europe.

Environmental acceptability has been added as a third dimension to managerial decision-making along with technological and economic feasibility. Most MNCs, anticipating the worldwide dissemination of environmental awareness and legislation, have incorporated environmental considerations into their objectives. Shell, for example, lists as one of the three objectives of refining ". . . to reduce the emission of pollutants and so avoid affecting the environment." U.S. multinationals such as Dow Chemical, Du Pont, Union Carbide, and others began their own pollution control programs before the Mexican environmental law took effect in 1971. General Electric recently agreed to an innovative settlement regarding its pollution of the Hudson River. The company agreed not only to reduce its discharges into the river but also offered to pay $3 million toward restoring the river's purity.

The decision concerning plant location has also undergone considerable transformation. The conventional philosophy of locating a plant in or near a big city where adequate communications and labor supply are located (which, in turn, has contributed to the immense problems of urbanization) is giving way to more interest in rural development. While there exists considerable reluctance to locate a plant outside the big metropolitan area when economic factors do not dictate such moves, numerous MNCs have either initiated or supported governmental plans to develop rural areas.

Since the mid-1950s, the Shell Oil Company has been engaged in a specialized form of rural technical assistance which began in Italy at Borgo a Mozzano in Tuscany, and has subsequently been followed in other countries such as Venezuela, Portugal, Trinidad, Nigeria, Thailand, and Ethiopia. Nestlé, as well, takes considerable pride in explaining its activities in the developing countries: "There have, of course, been benefits for the company, yet by creating a source of permanent wealth for milk producers in regions far from industrial centers Nestlé has furthered industrialization with effects on the regional economy which are now established facts."

On the governmental side, most governments either delay or deny permits to start a new facility or to expand an existing one in heavily industrialized areas. Brazil and Venezuela are the most notable examples of governmental efforts to move industry out of the big city and into the interior.

Last but not least, changes are also taking place in regard to the control of subsidiaries. Control over a subsidiary's activities can be exercised either through financial ownership, restrictive business and technology transfer practices, or assignment of parent nationals to key managerial positions. It was a common practice for most U.S. and a few European MNCs to insist on absolute control over a subsidiary's activities through 100 percent ownership, restrictive technology transfer and business practices, and placement of parent company expatriates in key managerial positions.

Recently, because of pressures by host governments and most importantly, because of the considerable successes of Japanese and European MNCs in joint ventures, most MNC's are adopting a policy of granting more freedom to their affiliates outside their national borders. Nestlé, for example, has a formal policy not to own plantations, agricultural land, farms, or livestock—a practice commonly followed by most U.S. MNCs who believe in vertical integration. John Deere Company's Argentinian subsidiary is headed by a native Argentinian. Nestlé, Caterpillar, Union Carbide, IBM, Philips, Ford, General Motors, and other large multinationals now employ expatriates as less than 1 percent of their total overseas manpower.

These examples of more forward-looking strategies by some large multinationals should not be taken as a general assertion that the various national and international business interests have exchanged their traditional profit, growth, and efficiency orientations for broad-based humanistic concerns, but only to illustrate the interdependence of changes in society's values and goals and those of its business groups and interests. In many cases, large businesses continue to be concerned with traditional profit and growth motives, and practice year-to-year assessments of progress with respect to them. They do, however, show flexibility and adaptability in strategies when faced with changing conditions, and these qualities could be harnessed to create more long-term benefits for the international community.

Chapter 11

Goals of the
World Council of Churches
and of the
Roman Catholic Church

I. Goals of the World Council of Churches

The World Council of Churches is an organization of some 285 Churches in all parts of the world. Any Church is eligible for membership if it accepts the Council Basis: "[We] confess the Lord Jesus Christ as God and Saviour and therefore seek to fulfill together the common calling to the glory of the one God, Father, Son, and Holy Spirit."

Cooperation among various Christian Churches in promoting peace and justice began with a 1925 meeting in Stockholm. The World Council became associated with the International Missionary Council in 1948, and the original concept of an "association" was replaced with the more powerful notion of "integration" in 1961. The purpose of integration was seen as the need to manifest the unity of all Christians everywhere. In 1968 the ecumenical movement expanded from a mainly pan-Christian movement and began increasingly to embrace the non-Christian communities as well.

The World Council's goals today center on promoting all social, political, and economic factors which could help bring about social and spiritual renewal. In the Fifth General Assembly, held in Nairobi in 1975, the Council identified the following major world concerns:

the liberation of women, the dissatisfaction of peoples seeking more political and racial freedom, the use of increases in GNP by strong national governments to develop technological and military complexes, the instability of the 200-year-old world monetary system, the population explosion, the ecological problem, and the increasing gap between rich and poor countries.

The World Council of Churches responds to these problems by setting up "units" to study the issues. The currently operating units are concerned with Faith and Witness, Justice and Service, Education and Renewal, and Communication. Some have several commissions or subsections, and within them are a number of working groups concerned with specific tasks. They are complemented by a general Humanism Studies Programme.

Ideas and recommendations flowing out of the work of these task-forces deal with a wide variety of topics, ranging from the meaning of unity in the contemporary world and problems of communication between different faiths, to concrete issues concerned with science and technology. Some of the Council's major goals and suggestions are reviewed below.

Goals for Assisting Development

The Council devotes special attention to the problem of development, and its desirable and undesirable consequences. It stresses that man is the focus of development and people must not be treated as objects to be manipulated. Development itself must become a process of increasing economic and social justice in the world community.

Development must not connote acquiring limitless resources but the sharing of those that are available. A 1974 conference in Bucharest suggested that Christians are rediscovering that justice means sharing. They can and should find fulfillment by applying their ascetic tradition to political programs dedicated to redistributing the world's resources for the common good.

Justice, it was pointed out, is a universal concept that includes nature as well as human society. It calls for an awareness of the interdependence of people among themselves and with their natural environment. "We—human persons—need each one of us in the community of mankind. We—mankind—need nature as part of the community of creation. We—creation—need God, our creator and re-creator."

In a world of interdependence, where great economic, social, and political power is amassed and is supported by sophisticated technologies and organizations, it is important (the Council feels) to emphasize that some "traditional" freedoms—of individuals as well as of social classes and nations—have to be subordinated to the common good. It notes that freedom of conscience and of creativity become extremely precious for those who feel themselves reduced to insignificant fragments by powerful states and labor organizations.

According to the conference reports a necessity in all societies is the safeguarding of a certain harmony between personal freedom and social responsibility. It is also necessary to recognize that economic growth is a means, not an end in itself. One should distinguish between political choices that call for centralized decisions, and others which can be made by local communities. It was thought to be equally important to distinguish between areas in which individual profit should yield before social need, and areas where a person's conscience must be held inviolable. The World Council called for participatory decision making through more appropriate institutional structures, and for changing the aims of developed countries, especially with regard to consumption. Minimum human needs must be specified, and development must be assessed not in terms of rising GNP but in terms of quality of life and social justice.

The Faith and Witness Unit's section concerned with "Studies on Church and Society" is particularly interested in the role of science and technology. This stems from the recognition that science and technology "place in man's hands the power to control and change his natural and cultural environments and even to alter his own biological nature. . . . The revolutionary element in our situation is that man not only has the power to do these things, but has begun to do them and must live in constant awareness of his new power." Technology, it is said, is neither neutral, nor can it solve all problems. Its just and humane application requires that every individual participate to the extent of his abilities in deciding its uses.

The 1975 report on "Social Responsibility in the Technological Age" stated,

> The responsibility that now confronts humanity is to make a deliberate transition to a sustainable global society in which science and technology will be mobilized to meet the basic physical and spiritual needs of people to minimize human suffering and to create an environment which can

sustain a decent quality of life for all people. This will involve a radical transformation of civilization, new technologies, new uses for technology, and new global economic and political systems.

As a result of its deliberations, the Council body recommends the following goals for member Churches.

Energy Conservation

The churches in the industrialized countries should challenge present patterns of energy consumption in order to extend the useful life of nonrenewable energy resources and to assist the movement toward a low growth energy economy in those countries.

Nuclear Energy

The churches at the national level should lobby for more effective safeguards in the control and operation of the nuclear fuel cycle to ensure that there is a reduced risk of diversion of strategic weapon materials; in addition there is a need to press for more serious investigation of the long-term disposal of radioactive wastes by those responsible for the management of nuclear power programmes.

Alternative Energy Technologies

Since there are inevitable grave ethical problems involved in the application of nuclear energy, the churches and individual Christians should promote sufficient funding and moral support for research and development of renewable sources of energy, e.g., solar, wind, and wave.

Ethical Obligations in the Sustainable and Just Society

The Churches should examine very carefully the implications of a movement toward a sustainable and just society as this embodies many significant structural changes in the patterns of food production, energy consumption, employment, population, housing, and transport in both developed and developing countries.

Science and Faith

It is important that the Churches encourage scientists and technologists to develop socially responsible new directions for modern societies. This encounter should focus on issues of science and faith and on the ethical implications of specific scientific and technical activities.

Ethical Dilemmas in Biology

The Churches and the Christian Medical Commission of

the World Council of Churches should further study the
ethical dilemmas and theological perspectives relating to
recent discoveries in the biological and medical sciences.
This study should include a fresh consideration of the
meaning of the concept of the sanctity of human life.

A 1976 report by a working group concerned with the uses of
energy suggests that a 100-year time horizon must be adopted to deal
with the energy problems facing mankind. The group has not decided
on what energy option to advocate but calls for the thorough study
of available options in the areas of renewable energy sources.

In assessing the long-term problems of development, the Nairobi
conference recognized the importance of the following "struggles" of
contemporary peoples: the struggle for social justice through new
socio-economic and political structures; for a society in harmony with
nature; for a more human mode of life in a world increasingly dominated by science and technology; and for self-reliance. The task forces
raise this problem: Can development, as a process in which economic
growth, social justice, and self-fulfillment are interrelated, be initiated
by peaceful means, or does it require an abrupt break with the present
system of international relations? Present disparities between rich and
poor nations help to perpetuate patterns of exploitation as well as
poverty, and the abuse of the environment. Hence it is felt that

Development of a new type cannot, in short, be considered
apart from movements for liberation and social justice.
These movements should receive the support of the
Churches at all levels. . . . It has become evident that the
improvement of the development process requires more
than a transfer of resources. It requires a deeper commitment with the poor and a realignment with the oppressed,
expressed in attitudes, beliefs and action in solidarity. . . .
The Churches should recognize the real capacity of the
masses to achieve their own development when they are
enabled to express and act with their own power.

The Council suggests that answers must be found to these questions:

How can the overuse of the world's common natural resources by
the industrial nations be critically appraised and corrected by representatives of the world's poor?

What is the sustainable minimum living standard for all people on
earth (food, clothing, housing, education, etc.)?

What rate of use of the earth's natural resources (renewable or nonrenewable) would this minimum living standard permit?

What use of these resources can the earth's ecological system sustain without further damage?

How can a common search for alternative raw materials and technologies be carried out with the effective participation of representatives of all inhabitants of this earth?

The World Council of Churches advocates the creation of a just and sustainable world society, in which the inequalities between rich and poor are eliminated through more awareness and greater power of decision by the majority of the human community. Thus the Council argues for the decentralization of power, a positive change in world balances, and the use of humanly appropriate technologies.

Goals for World Peace and Human Rights

The Council appointed a Commission on International Affairs to promote the following ideals and processes concerned with peace and security: peace with justice and freedom; the development of international law and institutions; respect for human rights and fundamental freedoms (with special attention to religious freedom); international control and reduction of armaments; the furthering of economic justice through international economic cooperation; the acceptance by all nations of the obligation to promote the welfare of all peoples and the development of free institutions; progress toward self-government in still-dependent territories; and the international furthering of social, cultural, educational, and humanitarian enterprises.

The Council urges that the danger posed by the arms build-up necessitates a broad change in social values. In particular, it urges the reallocation of resources now committed to arms, in order to further the development of poor and disadvantaged nations, and to increase their self-reliance. It appeals to international organizations to enforce arms-control and -limitation agreements, and to reach new agreements on the banning of chemical weapons and the control of arms production and trade. The Commission's document on disarmament states: "One contribution Christians have to make is to help combat the apathy and hopelessness which tend to undermine the struggle for genuine world disarmament."

World peace hinges also on respect for human rights. Respect for human rights is, in fact, a precondition of human survival, according to a 1974 Basic Programme Paper of the Commission on International Affairs. The Council takes an "integral" approach to the question of human rights, concering itself with such matters as the struggle against white racism and *apartheid*; Church participation in economic and social self-development; and recommending changes in the international structures which oppress underdeveloped nations and nonwhite majorities or minorities in both developing and developed countries.

The Churches must insist that *all* human rights be respected, as viewed from every cultural perspective. The ecumenical movement must see human rights not only from the perspective adopted in the United Nations Declaration on Universal Human Rights, but also from the viewpoints of peoples whose cultures, socio-economic traditions, and political structures are different from those of the developed nations. The Council wishes to correct three mistaken ideas about human rights. The first is that human rights concern only individual freedoms—i.e., that they are not applicable to groups and communities. This idea has its roots in nineteenth-century liberalism and has been promoted by Churches that emphasize "individual salvation." In reality, however, violations of human rights occur in entire sectors of society, and must be eliminated in the social context. The second mistaken idea is that the human rights question is "nonpolitical." The Council believes that human rights are a political matter, "like every attempt of man to realize the human potential with which the Creator endowed him." The third idea to be corrected is that standards of human rights apply only to "others" while "our" situation is different. International cooperation is required to ensure the truly universal application of human rights standards.

Relations Between the World Council of Churches and the Roman Catholic Church

Before the pontificate of John XXIII the attitude of the Roman Catholic Church toward the World Council was reserved, but in recent years a limited cooperation has evolved.

The Pontifical Commission *Justitia et Pax* has set up a Committee for Society, Development, and Peace (SODEPAX) jointly with the World Council. Catholic theologians have participated in the Council's Faith and Constitution Commission, and a Joint Working Group has been created. Observers from each attend the meetings of the other. Yet, despite declarations that the moment of encounter has been replaced by one of dialogue and ecumenical fellowship, there are difficulties in "witnessing together"—i.e., in reconciling the Roman Catholic Church's emphasis on its own identity, and on its considerable international hierarchical authority, with the status of a Council which receives its authority only from its members. International legal recognition accorded to the Holy See also makes international cooperation with other Churches more difficult, especially in relation to the United Nations.

The Roman Catholic Church decided not to request membership in the World Council in Nairobi in 1975. It opted, however, to continue joint activities through SODEPAX and the Joint Working Group.—In view of the fact that the Roman Catholic Church and the Holy See command considerable spiritual authority in the world, and define and pursue their own goals, we devote a separate section to describing and analyzing them.

II. Goals of the Roman Catholic Church and the Holy See

The world community pays renewed attention today to the ideas and policies of the Catholic * Church, especially in relation to issues involving the entire human community. The Catholic Church, and its historical embodiment in the Holy See, have an influence not only on Catholics but also on the faithful of other religions, and on the governments of a majority of nation-states. The will and word of the Catholic Church and the Holy See reaches millions. Despite their lack of economic and military power, they constitute distinct forces in today's world which merit special attention and analysis.

Official Catholic goals are discussed here in relation to issues of broad human concern rather than those of more limited theological interest. They include several of the issues raised by the international community at the United Nations: human rights, the economy, population, and peace and, in addition, such issues as personal conduct, and relations with members of other faiths and with atheists.

---

* In this report the word "Catholic" refers specifically to those Churches and individuals who acknowledge allegiance to the See of Rome. There are other ecclesiastical entities which regard themselves as holding the historic Catholic faith, but do not acknowledge allegiance to Rome, notably the worldwide Anglican Communion, and the Eastern Orthodox Churches, among others.

Goals Concerning Human Rights

Human rights emerged as a world issue during the pontificate of John XXIII. During this time the Catholic Church emphasized that every human being is a "person"—by nature endowed with intelligence and free will. This human person is subject to rights and duties that emerge "immediately and simultaneously" from his nature, and are therefore "universal, inviolable and inalienable."

The goals of the Catholic Church thus relate to the inalienable rights and duties of every individual, since "by his innermost nature man is a social being, and unless he relates himself to others he can neither live nor develop his potential." As interrelationships among men increase, and since they will increase still more in the future, the Holy See exhorts all nations and races to set aside their differences in an endeavor to achieve the shared development of every human being. The human person is indeed the beginning, the subject, and the end of all social institutions regardless of race, sex, or religion. All men are fundamentally equal. All have the right to existence, to physical inviolability, and to a sufficient quantity of those things that are indispensable to the satisfaction of their needs.

Goals Concerning Personal and Family Life

Love is the supreme end of all human experience. This is the concept that underlies the Catholic Church's view of matrimony. This concept includes love of God (the highest object of love) and, at the same time, love of one's neighbor.

Conjugal love within the family is for purposes of procreation. Sexuality, the Church points out, is by its very nature oriented toward an end that transcends the individual, namely the survival of the human race. Procreation is a moment of giving. "Children are the most precious gift of matrimony and contribute to the greatest extent to the good of the parents." Thus "the Church holds that every matrimonial act must remain open to the transmission of life," in responsible parenthood.

The Church draws a sharp distinction between legitimate and illegitimate forms of family planning. The following are legitimate:

therapeutic means, necessary to treat diseases of the organism "provided that said impediment is not directly willed, for any reason" recourse to infertile periods—"it is right to take account of the natural limits immanent in generative functions . . . in order to regulate births without in the slightest offending moral principles"

The following are considered illegitimate:

direct sterilization, whether permanent or temporary, of either the man or the woman

any action which, in advance of the conjugal act, or in accomplishing it, or in the development of its natural consequences, proposes as its aim the prevention of procreation

the direct interruption of the generative process once it has started, and above all direct abortion, even if procured for therapeutic reasons.

In the Church's view the possible consequences of illegitimate means of family planning are extremely grave. There could be an increase in conjugal infidelity, with the resultant lowering of moral standards, and above all there could be harm to the younger generations. There could be loss of respect for women through considering them "as mere instruments of egoistic enjoyment." The Church warns that the sanctioning of illegitimate means of family planning could put a weapon in the hands of public authorities who could "impose on their peoples . . . the method of contraception considered by them as the most effective."

The Catholic Church is not unaware of the gravity which the problem of population growth presents today. "The problem is extremely complex and delicate. The Church recognizes its manifold aspects. But it has to uphold God's law, and it must proclaim this law in the light of scientific truths." The new document of CEI (Italian Episcopal Conference) on sexual matters takes an even harder line. It condemns every sexual activity which does not take place within the bonds of marriage, including premarital and extramarital relations, homosexuality, and masturbation.

The Catholic Church proposes to:

make immediate provision for a timely sexual education in line with Christian morality

provide clear indication as to conjugal morality

set up on a wide scale premarriage and marriage counseling bureaus of proven Catholic faith provide adequate assistance in cases of illegitimate or dangerous maternity.

Socio-Economic Goals

According to Catholic ethics, profit should be shared by the two co-producers, capital and labor. The worker's wage should enable him not only to survive, but to lead a dignified life.

Profit is not to be taken as the driving force of economic progress. The concept of competition as the supreme law of economics is to be rejected, along with private ownership as an absolute. Capitalism is not condemned *in toto* as long as it safeguards the common good, which is the yardstick and the aim of economic freedom. Therefore capitalism (though not laissez-faire capitalism) can be a valid approach to economic problems.

It is society's duty to ensure that every individual can find work. The right to work is treated as a moral necessity. Paul VI stressed the need to create "an authentic international labor law, applying to all peoples." To this must be added the duty of humanizing work to develop the person, the focal point of Christian social ethics. Indeed, work "must be assessed and treated not as though it were an item of merchandise, but as an expression of the human person." Work is both a privileged aspect of the union among men, and a promoter of fraternity. Wages should neither be left to the laws of the market, nor decided arbitrarily, but "fixed according to justice and equity," i.e., according to need and effective service to the community. These vary from country to country.

The Catholic Church's position on economic issues differs markedly from both the capitalist view, where the basic concept is profit, and the Marxist theory, which regards labor as the sole source of production. The Church interprets the class struggle differently—it claims that the struggle is not so much the conflict between the classes as the matter of the quality of their relations. Every effort should be made to change these relations, in order to build a human community, rather than to aim at artificially achieving a single class level.

The Church affirms the legitimacy of private property, which stems from man's right to use the assets of the land. Private ownership is the natural means for man to exercise his sovereignty over these assets. Property is an extension of the person. Private ownership also fulfills a social function, which stems from the right to property. The problem is to reconcile this right with the higher exigencies of the universal allocation of benefits to increase the common good. Thus the state and other public agencies may acquire property, when necessary for the common good, but may not do so with the intention of reducing or eliminating the property of private individuals.

Nationalization or appropriation by the state of an economic resource cannot be a final and universal solution. The common good must be made available to all members of the community in varying degrees according to their tasks, merits, and conditions. Promotion of the common good is the link between individual and society. The principles of the common good are rooted in justice on the natural level and charity on the supernatural level. Public powers are to give special heed to the poorest segments of the population, applying the principle of solidarity as the moral responsibility of the privileged.

The whole field of economic activity is now regarded by the Church as a search for worldly well-being, since it forms part of man's complete development. But economics, to the Catholic Church, is distinct from politics. The two do not exist on the same level. Politics should not engulf economic activities (as it does in the Marxist conception), nor should it exclude economics entirely from its interests (the classical liberalist concept).

Special importance is attached by the Catholic Church to the concept of planning. Planning should be pressed into the service of man and aimed at his needs. Plans should encourage, stimulate, coordinate, supplement, and integrate the actions of individuals and intermediate agencies, since the public powers have the duty to choose the objectives which, once selected, must be pursued by common action. Planning now has an established place in Catholic thought, which recognizes the need for it in rationalizing economics, and enabling it to grow and develop in man's service.

The Catholic Church, however, emphasizes the need to avoid "full collectivization and arbitrary planning," which deny "the basic rights of the human person." Hence, centralized planning (socialism) is rejected, as well as the laissez-faire system (capitalism).

Goals Concerning World Peace and Security

The main focus of the Holy See's political endeavors is world peace. The profound hope of John XXIII with regard to the peace mission of the United Nations was echoed in the messages and activities of

Paul VI. While the Holy See, as the historical embodiment of the Catholic Church, considers itself supranational, it has had to recognize that it cannot bear the burden of constant political and diplomatic mediation. Thus it has delegated the moral responsibility for such activities to the United Nations, while retaining the task of "superintending" as the representative of the universal (Catholic) Church.

Nevertheless the Holy See could not turn over to the United Nations all the complex responsibilities it felt proper to the Catholic presence in international affairs. Direct initiatives were taken in some areas where the United Nations was also active, for example in the control of the seas, and in mediation between warring tribes and countries. Its lack of success in such endeavors, however, soon convinced the Holy See that it should restrict its activity to the enunciation of general guidelines such as we review below in connection with Church policies concerned with Latin American, Asian, and African development.

Because of the transcendental and supranational attributes claimed for itself through the Holy See, the Catholic Church successfully avoids alignment with either of the existing power blocs. This has put the Holy See in a new position in relation to communist countries. It now shows the political will to engage in a dialogue. An open-door policy with regard to communist countries was initiated in a series of visits by Msgr. Agostino Casaroli, the Holy See's Secretary of the Council of Public Affairs (a post equivalent to that of foreign minister). In the Holy See's efforts to settle divergencies in these countries, it relies mainly on the indigenous Catholic communities. In this area the Holy See holds itself fully competent, and intends to act directly without delegating the task to anyone.

In taking an increasingly active part in international politics, the Holy See seems to display a more balanced policy toward the Western and Eastern powers, and no longer seems to side unilaterally with the West. The Holy See came out against the arms race at the European Security Conference in Helsinki, and is now promoting an active movement to affirm the rights of all peoples and individuals in Europe. It also continues to affirm such rights for the developing countries. Its role in today's world is thus no longer conservative or partisan, but represents an effort to assume a position *supra partes,* and to act authoritatively as negotiator and arbitrator in questions of dispute and conflict, as they relate to the rights and duties of individuals and nations.

Goals Concerning Developing Peoples

The Catholic Church is making vigorous efforts to remove inequalities among peoples at all levels. As rich countries enjoy rapid economic growth while poor ones develop more slowly, the gap between them widens. In the Church's view, international justice requires that such inequalities be ended.

The task of bringing the Christian doctrine to all peoples is held to be especially urgent today, when new nations are feeling the need for social, political, and religious independence. Even an adaptation of Catholic doctrine to the cultures of these new nations is not felt sufficient. The 1974 synod speaks of the "incarnation of the Gospel in the socio-cultural reality of each country." Christianity is to be made indigenous to each country's own cultural tradition.

The Catholic Church takes account of existing cultural differences of developing areas in discussing their goals, and has held various regional meetings to further this aim. Three broad areas are distinguished: Latin America, Africa, and Asia. With respect to Latin America the emphasis is on the need for liberation, and greater firmness in condemning all forms of injustice. Education must be creative at every level, and keep itself open to its own enrichment. The Medellin Document of 1968, by the bishops of Latin America, condemns investment in arms, excessive bureaucracy, luxuries, and any form of ostentation.

In 1969 Paul VI spoke of a Catholicism appropriate to the African culture. The African contribution to Church doctrine resides in the importance the Africans attach to the concept of the person, which they cannot conceive outside the community. Unlike the stress on liberation for the Latin American Church, the emphasis for the African Church is on development. All people should benefit from technical achievements, but with due respect for the integrity of persons and their living communities. Justice, universal education, and an end to discrimination must be achieved. For this, it is necessary to renew the foundations of development, going beyond the narrower concerns of the economist, the sociologist, and the politician. Development involves progressive humanizing, and freedom from hunger, disease, and ignorance, and from every sort of servitude.

Goals for Asia take into account current misery, malnutrition, disease, and war. The Catholic Church pays attention to the wishes of young Asians, as well as the ancient cultures, religions, and traditions.

The age of passive acceptance of poverty, ignorance, and sickness is over; there are new expectations: "more rice on their tables, knowledge for their sons, yearnings for freedom and unity."

In response to the Catholic Church's analysis of Asian reality, the Asian bishops declared that they wish to be the Church of the poor and of the young, speaking in the name of those in need, concerned with the total development of their peoples, and committed to a true dialogue with indigenous cultures.

Thus the emphasis falls on liberation in Latin America, and development, together with a respect for cultural traditions, in Africa and Asia. The problem of the status of women is mentioned only in documents relating to the Latin American Church.

Goals Concerning Relations with Non-Catholic Peoples

Before the pontificate of John XXIII, more precisely until the encyclical *Mater et Magistra* was issued in 1960, relations prescribed for Catholics toward peoples of other faiths, and atheists, were extremely intransigent. In *Mater et Magistra* there is, for the first time, mention of the principle of collaboration between Catholics and "others who do not share their outlook on life." The new principle is based, among other things, on the pluralistic character of modern international coexistence.

Collaboration with non-Catholics is primarily directed to the economic and social spheres. Catholics are advised to be vigilant, but to be prepared to collaborate in attaining objectives which are good. Yet such collaboration is conditional upon the judgment of the Church; whenever the Church hierarchy has made a ruling on this matter, Catholics are to abide by it.

In the encyclical *Pacem in Terris* Catholics are offered a vast field of encounter and agreement with all human beings in whom natural honesty is present and operative:

> The error must never be confused with the errant, even when it is an error, or inadequate knowledge of the truth, in the field of religion and morality. The errant is always and foremost a human being and at all events retains his dignity as a person; and he must always be considered and treated in a manner in keeping with such dignity. (*Pacem in Terris*, 54)

It is pointed out that, whereas doctrines ". . . once worked out and defined, always remain the same," social movements, acting in concrete historical situations, are "ceaselessly evolving, [and] cannot help being influenced, and therefore cannot but be subject to even profound changes. Moreover who can deny that in said movements, to the extent they are in conformity with the dictates of correct reasoning and interpret the rightful aspirations of the human person, there are positive elements that merit approval?"

If, therefore, historical movements undergo profound changes, "it could happen that an approach or a meeting of a practical order, yesterday considered not appropriate or not fruitful, may become so today or might become so tomorrow." Collaboration becomes possible even in the political field (". . . concordance of activities to achieve honest and useful economic, social, cultural, and political aims for the true good of the community . . .").

To promote communication and dialogue, Paul VI established three secretariats: for the union of Christians, for nonbelievers, and for non-Christians. These secretariats are to carry out dialogue characterized by mildness, trust, and pedagogic prudence, occurring on three distinct levels: the subjective level of simple human relations; the doctrinal level where problems of extreme interest are discussed in the attempt to gain better knowledge through common effort; and the level of action where the task is to establish conditions leading to given ends.

Relations with Non-Catholic Christians

"The separated brethren" are those with whom dialogue is most facilitated. Common aspects are to be underlined; with regard to differences concerning tradition, worship, and canon laws, Catholics should try to meet the exigencies of the other Churches although not compromising "on the integrity of faith and charity."

In the dialogue with non-Catholic Christians a point of particular controversy centers around the notion of the primacy of the pope. Some view it as an obstacle to the unification of the separated churches. But the Catholic Church stresses the pope's function as a unifying center:

> . . . if the Church of Christ lacked the highest, efficacious and decisive pastoral office of Peter, unity would be destroyed. . . . This central hub of the Holy Church is not intended as the supremacy of spiritual pride and of human

dominion, but as the primacy of service, of ministry, of love. (*Ecclesiam Suam,* 113)

Relations with Non-Christians

Dialogue with the faithful of non-Christian religions has become a matter of great interest for the Catholic Church since the time of the Second Vatican Council. Cardinal Franz König said at the International Congress of Missionology (October 1975), "Every religion contains a ray of light, which we must neither despise nor extinguish; especially when this is not enough to give man the light that he needs." However, the first decisive document on this subject was the encyclical *Nostra Aetate* (1965). It opens with the words:

> In our times, when every day men are being drawn closer together and the ties between various peoples are being multiplied, the Church is giving deeper study to her relationship with non-Christian religions. In her task for fostering unity and love among men, and even among nations, she gives primary consideration here to what human beings have in common and to what causes them to live out their destiny together; [for] all peoples comprise a single community, and have a single origin, since God made the whole race of men dwell over the entire face of the earth.

All men look to the various religions for answers to those profound mysteries of the human condition

> which, today even as in olden times, deeply stir the human heart: What is a Man? . . . What gives rise to our sorrows and to what intent? Where lies the path of true happiness? What is the truth about death? . . .

> Other religions to be found everywhere strive variously to answer the restless searchings of the human heart by proposing "ways," which consist of teachings, rules of life, and sacred ceremonies. The Catholic Church rejects nothing which is true and holy in these religions. She looks with sincere respect upon those ways of conduct and of life, those rules and teachings which, though differing in many particulars from what she holds and sets forth, nevertheless often reflect a ray of that Truth which enlightens all men.

The Church therefore invites all Catholics to participate in dialogue and in collaboration with other religions, always in the spirit of Christian faith, in order to promote the "spiritual and moral goods found among these men, as well as the values in their society and culture."

There is explicit mention of the Moslems, regarding whom "this most Sacred Synod urges all to forget the past and to strive sincerely for mutual understanding"; and of the Jews, who "should not be presented as repudiated or cursed by God." A final paragraph is devoted to universal brotherhood and hence to the condemnation of all discrimination, of every theory or practice which "leads to a distinction between men or peoples in the matter of human dignity and the rights which flow from it."

Relations with Atheists

Atheism is condemned as the gravest error of our times. The Church also condemns any ideological system founded on atheism, especially atheist communism. Dialogue with such systems is well-nigh impossible. But this does not mean that the Church is to give up looking into the motives and causes of atheism itself. Atheism sometimes comes into being out of the need for a higher and purer presentation of the divine world than the prevailing one—atheists are filled with anxiety, pervaded by passion and utopian thoughts, and they are frequently generous in their dreams of justice and progress toward social objectives. The hope is held out that one day the moral expressions of atheism will be traced to their sources, which are, it is held, in themselves Christian.

Gaudium et Spes distinguishes various forms of atheism. *Dogmatic atheism:* "God is expressly denied by some"; *agnosticism:* "others believe that man can assert absolutely nothing about Him." Still others "use such a method so to scrutinize the question of God as to make it seem devoid of meaning." Connected with this last type of atheism are the methods of the positive sciences and of certain allied disciplines. "Many, unduly transgressing the limits of the positive sciences, contend that everything can be explained by this kind of scientific reasoning alone, or, by contrast, they altogether disallow that there is any absolute truth." A further form of atheism originates in thought which centers wholly and solely on man, thereby debasing faith in God.

Two forms of "systematic" atheism are distinguished, the one typical of Western secular modes of thought, the other of Marxism. In the first, man is seen as an end in himself, "the sole artisan and creator of his own history," imbued with the sense of power generated by modern technical progress. In the second, man's liberation is anticipated through socio-economic emancipation. Religion is seen as thwarting such liberation by arousing in him a deceptive hope for a future life, and diverting his attention from more concrete this-worldly concerns.

The attitude of the Catholic Church toward both forms of atheism is one of stern reprobation. Nevertheless, rather than condemning atheists, Catholic believers must provide witness of a faith that is alive and mature, trained to see difficulties and to master them. A sincere and prudent relationship with atheists is possible, because the "rightful betterment" of this world requires the collaboration of all people, believers and nonbelievers alike.

(Although this stance is affirmed in principle, the action of particular Church bodies is sometimes inconsistent with it. For example, the Italian Episcopal Conference [CEI] decided at its meeting of December 13, 1975, to squarely forbid Italian Catholics to vote for and support all Marxist political movements.)

Part II:
New Horizons through Global Goals

Perusing the two atlases of national and regional, and international and transnational goals, the reader could form an idea of the nature and the diversity of goals and aspirations in today's world. The reader could also realize that goals and expectations are changing and are becoming more modest and realistic. While the poorest of the poor continue of necessity to demand the fulfillment of basic material needs, and the wealthy and the powerful continue to covet more wealth and power, many people, who are neither starving nor saturated, adapt their sights to changing national and global conditions, while international bodies champion the cause of universal human rights and insist on the greater responsibilities of states, corporations, and social institutions.

But can even the more modest needs and expectations of the world's peoples be fulfilled in coming decades, when populations will be greater and the resources of our planet more depleted? This question has excited the Neo-Malthusian controversies of growth-oriented opti-mists versus finite-world pessimists. The latter have called attention to the existence of "outer limits" constraining the continuation of certain kinds of exponential growth processes. It is clear that these limits can no longer be ignored. But it has also become clear that they must not be regarded as absolute, posed by physical nature. The critical limits confronting mankind are human, not physical. By breaking through the restraining mold of "inner limits" the existing "outer limits" can be stretched—and can in some cases be made to disappear.

Inner limits to global development are inherent in today's short-range and narrowly self-interested goals. The consequences of such goals can activate a whole series of outer limits in the form of deple-tion of natural resources, pollution of the environment, insufficiency of food production, unbalancing of weather patterns, and the destruc-tion of life and habitat through accidents, terrorism and war. Inner limits can, however, be expanded; more long-range and globally re-sponsible goals can be adopted. The pursuit of such goals would push back or eliminate many of the presently constraining outer limits: it would lead to higher levels of global security, safer and more abundant supplies of energy, less depletion of other nonrenewable resources, adequate food production, and the safeguarding of nature and climate.

The achievement of global goals would open new horizons for man-kind. These would be horizons of greater justice and humanism, of development oriented toward the fulfillment of needs and the self-reliance of peoples, nations, and regions. But attaining such horizons calls for reformations in current ways of thinking and planning, key-noted by the growth of world solidarity and the stretching of time horizons. We shall review humanity's moral and intellectual resources for affecting such reformations in Part III. For the present we discuss the global goals themselves—mankind's options for the building of a more just, satisfying, and sustainable world community.

Chapter 12

Global Security Goals

Security for the world community is a precondition of human survival on this planet. Without it life and habitat could be destroyed and civilization as we know it come to an end. Although all nations and peoples desire some form of security—from attack from without and insurgence from within—world security continues to erode. Security is equated with military strength. The build-up of armed forces and sophisticated armaments creates a balance that is precarious at best. Its breakdown would let loose weapons of enormous potency on the human community, and all but annihilate winners and losers alike.

The self-reinforcing logic of mutual distrust and security through arms must be broken if mankind is to live in peace and strive for prosperity. Multilateral, indeed global, negotiations must commence to implement the necessary goals of disarmament and create collective institutional safeguards. The confrontation of the nuclear superpowers needs to be defused, the spread of nuclear weapons in the international community halted, and the burgeoning trade in conventional arms controlled. Achievement of these global security goals would not only remove the lengthening shadow of war from the future of humanity, but free vast sums now spent on arms and the military for purposes of humane growth and development.

Disarmament

Since World War II, nation-states have spent more than $6,000,000 million for military purposes (at 1975 dollar values). This figure is roughly equal to the present annual gross national product of the entire world, and is more than five times the GNP of all the developing countries together. It represents an investment of $1,500 for every man, woman, and child living today. Military costs continue to increase. They were estimated at around $280,000 million in 1975 alone.

As Table 12-1 shows, eleven states spent more than 20 percent of their total budget on defense in 1975, and two were around the 40 percent figure. Money spent on military establishments and weapons of destruction amounted to 20 times the total aid provided to developing countries, and about 3,000 times the funds spent on international peacekeeping.

About 400,000 highly qualified scientists and engineers are today working on the research and development of devices and systems with military applications. In the United States alone 125,000 scientists are so engaged, about one in every four. In the Soviet Union twice as many people may be involved, although at lower per capita productivity than in the U.S. Consequently the arms race escalates both in numbers and in destructive power. The primary goals of world security must be to end the arms race, to reduce military stockpiles, and to bring the proliferation of weapons under control.

The build-up of arms by national military establishments threatens world security in three distinct ways. First, the confrontation of the superpowers keeps the sword of Damocles hanging by a hair over the heads of all mankind. Second, the "horizontal" proliferation of nuclear weapons—there are now dozens of candidates for the "nuclear club" —increases the danger of large-scale destruction in many parts of the world. Third, the immense trade in sophisticated conventional arms to practically all parts of the globe, including the least stable, makes even local conflicts bloody and threatening to world peace. Thus efforts to achieve progressive worldwide disarmament must be aimed primarily at balanced mutual arms reductions on three levels: first, on the level of the superpowers, where the goal is to lessen, if not eliminate, the danger of a holocaust; second, on the level of all would-be members of the "nuclear club," with the containment of horizontal proliferation as the objective; third, on the general level of all states, large and small, in order to reduce the chances of war and violence

Table 12-1
Defense Expenditures of the Top Thirty Nations (1975)

Rank	Country	Defense Expenditure (1975) Million $	Per Capita Defense Expenditure (1974) $	Percentage of GNP on Defense (1974) %	Percentage of Total Budget on Defense (1975) %
1	Soviet Union	103,800	409	10.6	–
2	U.S.A.	92,800	430	6.0	26.6
3	West Germany	16,260	260	3.6	24.7
4	People's Republic of China	4,000– 15,000	4–19	–	–
5	France	12,250	233	3.4	19.1
6	Iran	10,405	314	9.0	28.3
7	England	10,380	184	5.2	10.8
8	Saudi Arabia	6,343	712	15.0	20.0
9	Egypt	6,103	163	22.8	42.0
10	Japan	4,484	41	0.9	6.2
11	Italy	4,220	76	2.8	8.6
12	Israel	3,503	1,043	32.0	37.6
13	Canada	2,960	129	2.0	11.0
14	Netherlands	2,936	215	3.4	11.4
15	India	2,660	4	2.8	21.1
16	Sweden	2,475	298	3.6	10.5
17	East Germany	2,333	137	5.4	7.9
18	Australia	* 2,331	* 179	3.2	* 12.8
19	Turkey	2,200	55	3.7	26.6
20	Poland	2,170	65	3.6	7.0
21	Belgium	1,821	185	2.8	9.5
22	Nigeria	1,786	29	2.9	* 15.2
23	Yugoslavia	1,705	80	5.1	19.9
24	Czechoslovakia	1,542	106	3.8	7.3
25	Spain	* 1,372	* 39	1.9	* 14.3
26	South Africa	1,332	53	3.2	18.5
27	Greece	1,300	144	4.3	28.5
28	Brazil	1,283	12	1.3	9.3
29	Indonesia	1,108	9	** 3.6	** 21.8
30	Switzerland	1,041	125	1.8	19.5

Source: Prepared from "Military Balance (1975–1976)" by International Strategy Institute, England.

The figures for each year in the table are for the fiscal year which starts during the said year. * indicates 1974 and ** indicates 1973.

Defense expenditure of the Soviet Union were obtained by adding 75 percent of its science budget to the published defense budget. Defense expenditure of the NATO countries is based on the "unified concept" as defined by NATO. Defense expenditure of the People's Republic of China indicate the minimum and maximum among the various estimates.

by limiting the amount and destructiveness of arms transferred in
international trade.

Defusing the Potential Holocaust

The destructive potential in the arsenals of the United States and the
Soviet Union staggers the imagination. These two countries now de-
ploy 7,000 times the explosive power used by all parties in the Second
World War. By 1985 the United States, without violating existing
arms control agreements, could have more than 20,000 strategic warheads, each far more powerful than the one which killed 80,000 citizens of Hiroshima in 1945. The Soviet Union could have about
17,000 strategic warheads, with destructive yields even greater than
American weapons. These numbers so far exceed what might be considered strategically important targets—probably 100 to 200 at most
—that general thermonuclear war would not resemble a conventional
war at all, but rather a global inferno.

The likelihood of a general thermonuclear war is, for the moment,
slight. But continued competition in developing more and better strategic arms could undermine the system of accepted mutual deter-
rence, which has until now kept the risk of such a war so low. Many
of the new systems now being developed and deployed at an annual
cost of about $20,000 million pose the danger of destabilizing the
strategic relationship of the superpowers. Multiple independently tar-
getable reentry vehicles (MIRVs) present each power with an opportunity to multiply the number of available warheads, even though the
number of intercontinental missiles may be frozen by agreement. For
example, the Vladivostok Agreements would permit 1,320 of each
side's total of 2,400 strategic weapons to carry multiple warheads. If
each side were to place six warheads on each of those 1,320 vehicles
—which is in fact close to the current U.S. capability—the number of
weapons at their command would be not 2,400 but 9,000. The capability of saturating the adversary's land-based retaliatory forces makes
a first strike less unthinkable, particularly when an escalating "high
stakes" crisis reminds each side that it may be more advantageous to
strike first than to risk being struck.

Improved accuracy and yield-weight ratios, which are being promoted by current research and development in both countries, could
threaten the survivability of retaliatory forces. Intercontinental accuracy of less than 100 meters of error is quite plausible. Moreover,
advances in antisubmarine warfare and, though proscribed by treaty,

antimissile technology, are bound to have an adverse effect on the stability of the strategic relationship between the superpowers. Breakthroughs in underwater acoustic surveillance capabilities would pose a serious threat to submarine-based deterrent forces, while advances in laser technology could lead to missile-defense systems designed to protect a nuclear aggressor from destructive retaliation.

The United States has a significant and potentially expandable lead in weapons sophistication—particularly in missile accuracy, multiple warhead technology, and antisubmarine systems. The Soviet Union has a considerable lead in missile size (or "throw-weight") and in strategic launchers. While these asymmetries now have a compensatory effect, there is no inherent reason why the two leads should continue to offest each other in the future. A critical technological breakthrough by one side or the other could upset this central balance even if quantitative parity were maintained.

The balance of terror could also fail in other ways. The enormous destructive potential of both arsenals could be unleashed through the accidental launch and detonation of a nuclear weapon. Concern is mounting about the capacity of command and control systems to manage tens of thousands of nuclear devices. More likely, collision of political interests, perhaps stemming from a local conflict, could lead to a full-blown confrontation between the superpowers. In such a confrontation, the perceived political costs of backing down might dominate the calculations of each. During the escalating crisis that could ensue, miscalculation, or efforts by either or both to convince the other that it will not back down, could carry the confrontation beyond the nuclear threshold. Whatever the scenario, the consequence could be the release of the very destructive potential that has, to date, rendered stable the strategic relationship between the superpowers.

No nation can safely assume that it could escape unharmed from the consequences of a thermonuclear war. Obviously, it is in the interest of all nations and peoples to defuse the threat of a holocaust from the continued confrontation of the superpowers. This goal must be achieved in two stages: first, by putting a complete end to the quantitative and qualitative strategic arms race; second, by achieving agreements under which nuclear arsenals are drastically reduced, the deployment of the remaining weapons is strictly confined, and the very possibility of using nuclear weapons is proscribed.

An end to the arms race between the superpowers will not be enough to remove the threat of a holocaust until the stockpile of existing nuclear weapons is reduced to a much lower level than at present. To realize the overall goal of nuclear disarmament, seven related subgoals must be achieved. These are:

reduction of major strategic forces to a few hundred warheads at the most;

deployment of smaller-scale tactical nuclear weapons not exceeding a level sufficient to assure security from conventional conflict, i.e., closer to 1,000 than to the present 30,000 such weapons;

removal of nuclear weapons from all territories but those of the nuclear powers themselves (which would clear entire continents of nuclear weapons, and end the nuclear confrontation in Europe);

putting an end to all tests of nuclear warheads and delivery vehicle systems and instituting extensive international verification of arms control agreements to bolster confidence and mutual trust;

obtaining a pledge by all nuclear states not to be the first to use nuclear weapons;

reducing strategic arms expenditures to a fraction of the current thousands of millions of dollars;

commencing an international management of weapons research and development based on the principle that only those developments which strengthen global strategic stability and security are permissible.

As reductions proceed, it will be necessary to involve the other nuclear-weapon states in strategic arms agreements. The Soviet Union, for example, would be unlikely to agree to significant reductions in its forces unless there were some assurances that Chinese, British, and French forces would either be limited or reduced as well.

Containing Nuclear Proliferation
The second threat to global security is posed by the "horizontal" proliferation of nuclear weapons, from the nuclear powers to other nations. The expansion of the "nuclear club" has become a major threat to global security. When India detonated her own nuclear device, she joined six nations that have demonstrated their nuclear arms capacity, and there is a seventh nation, Israel, that may have such capacity but has not demonstrated it. Several other states can now

develop a nuclear capacity within a matter of years. By 1980 Argentina, Brazil, Egypt, Iran, Pakistan, South Africa, South Korea, Spain, and Taiwan are likely to produce plutonium on their own (see Table 12-2). If political and economic advantages continue to be associated

Table 12-2
The Intensity of Nuclear Power Programs in Selected Countries

	I Installed reactor power, 1980 (megawatts)	II Present or Probable NPT * Party	III First indigenous plutonium produced	IV Probable annual rate of plutonium production, 1980 (Ks/year)
Argentina	920	No	1985	340
Brazil	600	No	1985	140
Egypt	no firm plans	No	(1985)	–
Iran	2400 (by mid-1980s)	Yes	1985	–
Pakistan	130	No	1984	46
South Africa	2000	No	1985	230
South Korea	1160	Yes	1985	240
Spain	8550	No	1980s	1950
Taiwan	3110	No	1982	720

The above table illustrates the potential nuclear bomb-making capabilities of key nations during the next five to ten years. The manufacture of a nuclear bomb by fission technology requires roughly ten pounds of plutonium. The likely amounts of this substance produced by each nuclear threshold country by 1980 (last column) will be sufficient to produce small arsenals of nuclear bombs. The critical data are those listed in column III: These indicate when each of the nuclear threshold powers is likely to cross the threshold in its ability to produce on its own the reactor and reprocessing capabilities for weapons-grade plutonium.

* Non-Proliferation Treaty.

with the possession of nuclear arms, many others could join the club before the turn of the century. Nuclear power reactors may spread to as many as twenty-nine countries within the next few years.

The current interest in using nuclear fission technologies to generate power for peaceful purposes creates a major demand for reactors and fuel reprocessing facilities. These multiply and spread abroad the essentials of nuclear arms: plutonium, enriched uranium, nuclear fuel cycle facilities, and technological expertise. Countries that have already acquired nuclear technologies for peaceful purposes jointly produce enough plutonium—a by-product of reactor processes—to permit the manufacture of ten Nagasaki-size A-bombs a week.

If nuclear weapons are acquired by additional states, pressures will be felt by their neighbors to review their own defense situation. With each new acquisition one or more additional states may decide to enter the nuclear club in order to restore regional balance and safeguard national security. Hence proliferation could have a snowballing effect that may be impossible to stop before all but the poorest nations are armed to the teeth with atomic bombs.

The proliferation of nuclear weapons in the international community can be contained by voluntary means only if the advantages at present associated with their possession are removed. Adequate security must be assured for nonnuclear powers, as well as full participation in international decision making. They must suffer no disadvantages in the generation of energy for peaceful purposes and no loss of prestige as "minor" powers.

Hence the major goal of stopping the horizontal proliferation of nuclear arms has the following requirements:

credible assurances by the nuclear states that they will never use, nor threaten to use, their nuclear weapons against nonnuclear states;

phasing out of fission technologies from the world energy system (see Chapter 14);

membership for nonnuclear states in international political decision making bodies and no discrimination against them as minor powers;

removal of nuclear weapons—owned by the nuclear states—from countries and regions which themselves do not possess such weapons.

The achievement of these goals would remove the basic advantages that smaller and less powerful nations now see in the possession of nuclear weapons. Such weapons would no longer be needed as deterrents against aggression by more powerful states, as a means for entering the atomic age with its benefits of peaceful power generation, or as a means for gaining access to major international decision-making bodies. The disadvantages that many states now see in signing the Non-Proliferation Treaty would disappear, as would even the prestige value of membership in the nuclear club. There would, in fact, be suspicion that new countries that seek to join the nuclear club are secretly planning to violate agreements in force. Instead of being acclaimed or admired, they would be greeted with disapproval and subjected to economic and political sanctions. The proliferation of nuclear weapons can be voluntarily contained only if the perceived advantages now associated with their possession come to be outweighed by actual disadvantages.

Curtailing Conventional Arms Transfers

The third major threat to global security is posed by exponential increases in the production and sale of sophisticated conventional arms. According to the calculations of the Stockholm International Peace Research Institute, there were 119 civil and international wars fought between 1945 and 1975, all with conventional but increasingly sophisticated weapons. The combined duration of these wars exceeded 350 years. They involved the territories of sixty-nine countries and the armed forces of eighty-one states, and killed more people than World War II. Since September 1945, there has not been a single day in which some war has not been fought somewhere in the world.

Arms trade is responsible for providing nations and subnational groups with the weapons of destruction. It has grown rapidly and consistently since World War II. In the last few years arms sales have grown exponentially and now appear to be out of control.

In 1975 a total of ninety-five countries imported major weapons, such as missiles, aircraft, ships, and tanks. The actual present value of the global traffic in arms is about $9,000 million a year, but new orders run up to $12,000 million. The most sophisticated conventional weapons are demanded by conflict-prone nations, and are promptly supplied to them. The United States provides Iran with the newest helicopter gunships even as they are introduced into U.S. arsenals. The Soviet Union gives Syria MIG 23 swing-wing fighters even before making them available to Warsaw Pact nations. Arms exporters not only sell weapons; they frequently provide training, technical support, maintenance, and repair facilities. The United States alone had $4,000 million in outstanding contracts in 1975 under the Foreign Military Sales program, much of it from Iran and Saudi Arabia.

The quantity of explosives now stored in national arsenals probably equals the force of about twenty tons of TNT for every man, woman, and child in the world—humanity's "return" on the per capita arms investment of $1,500 during the last twenty years. While most of this megatonnage is in the form of nuclear arms, for now at least these are controlled by the balance of terror. But explosives in the form of conventional weapons encounter no such obstacles and find their way into active use in some of the most unstable regions of the world.

The goal of improved global security demands safeguards to reduce the flow of sophisticated conventional weaponry. Specific steps required for this include the elimination of "imported insecurity" (the deterioration of local or regional security because of imbalances or escalations in the military potential of the local states), and a comprehensive reduction in the level of sophistication of weapons sold internationally.

Areas exhibiting chronic instabilities should receive the least, rather than the most, outside arms. The Middle East, for example, accounts for about 60 percent of all arms imports in the developing world. While per capita GNP for the region as a whole was about $845 during 1974, military expenditure per capita was $135. About 4,100 jet combat aircraft were imported between 1950 and 1975, and about 13,500 medium and light tanks. These included some of the world's most advanced weapons: MIG 23, F-5E, and Mirage III aircraft, and T-62, M-60, AMX-30, and Chieftain tanks.

An effective containment of the perilous trade in world armaments cannot be achieved without international agreements signed by both the arms-producing and the arms-importing nations. Arms production and sales policies in the exporting nations of the developed world are guided by economic as well as political considerations. Even if the superpowers themselves agreed to reduce arms shipments to areas of political and ideological conflict, other arms-exporting nations would probably not be willing to reduce their national revenues by curbing their arms sales. Since the balance of payments of most industrialized countries has worsened recently because of higher oil prices, these nations show less concern with the political effects of their arms exports than with the profits they bring. Governments are thus unlikely to curb the production and export of their armament industries. But these industries, having already grown to giant proportions, need a continuous flow of large and dependable orders to fully utilize their capacities. This, in combination with hands-off state attitudes, causes a vicious circle to develop. The stronger the armament industry of a country, the more it needs to export large quantities of arms to the world's real and potential trouble spots, thus reducing the fluctuation of orders and assuring economies of scale. Thereby it increases instability in the world's trouble spots, which in turn assures larger orders, making for corporate growth and thus for even larger orders to sustain the economies of scale.

As long as the governments of all major arms-exporting countries do not agree jointly to establish limits on the quantity and quality of their exports, and to put a freeze on sales to particularly unstable areas, the armament industry will find ways to circumvent controls in individual nations—for example, by exporting arms through a permissive third country, or producing parts to be assembled in such a country.

Importers themselves could agree on self-imposed limits to their arms acquisitions. Such limits could keep balances of power intact and would not put any country at a disadvantage. In some regions the institutional organization for negotiating such agreements already exists (for example, in Latin America, Africa, and Southeast Asia), but in some of the most sensitive regions (such as the Persian Gulf and South Asia) it does not.

Peacekeeping

Progressive states are unlikely to achieve disarmament by unilateral action. Any state that undertook serious reductions in its defense and strike capabilities would expose itself to aggression by less-conscientious adversaries. Even strategic arms limitations call for bilateral negotiations, which would soon need to be broadened to include all major military powers. The nuclear powers cannot stop the proliferation of nuclear arms unless they guarantee the safety of those who agree not to acquire such weapons. Similarly, the quantitative and qualitative reduction of conventional arms trade cannot be achieved without wide-ranging and enforceable international agreements among both arms-exporting and arms-importing nations.

An effective and authoritative world disarmament supervisory and peacekeeping organization is needed to bring about significant reductions in the levels of arms in national arsenals, and maintain balance in a world that would still be marked by antagonism and distrust, even if it were not so heavily armed.

Arms, after all, aggravate insecurities, but do not usually cause them. The roots of these insecurities lie in colliding national interests in disputed territories, ethnic and religious rivalries and antagonisms, and opposing economic and social policies. These create conflicts both within and among nation-states. The Middle East, Cyprus, Angola, Viet Nam, Lebanon, Northern Ireland, and Bangladesh are recent examples. Ultimately it is not enough to reduce the violence of such conflicts through arms control; the root causes of conflict must be eliminated. While this may be more than any national or international body can quickly achieve, an international peacekeeping body can go far toward increasing levels of trust. It can thereby facilitate arms reductions, and lessen the chances of new upsurges of antagonism.

Apart from the economic interests of large armament industries, the principal factor motivating governments to invest in arms and build up national military establishments is their distrust of potential adversaries. In the absence of international guarantees, such distrust is often well-founded. Since both parties are aware of its root causes, distrust is symmetrical. Accordingly, each country is moved to increase its own military strength to gain an edge over the other.

Mutual distrust escalates arms acquisition and deadlocks arms-limitation negotiations. At least in principle, however, this vicious cycle can be broken unilaterally as well as bilaterally. Japan provides the best example of unilateral action in breaking the cycle of historically rooted distrust leading to a build-up of arms and consequently to more distrust. Following her defeat in World War II, Japan shifted her Asia- and especially China-oriented policy of "rich country, strong army" to one of pacifism, renouncing war as an exercise of sovereign national right (see Chapter 4). Although her Defense Consolidation Plans have built up the National Self-Defense Forces and excite controversy within the country, Japan manages to safeguard her considerable economic prosperity without recourse to large-scale forces and the possession of nuclear weapons.

Japan is not a typical case, however, for her policy was initiated as a result of an unsuccessful war, and was promoted by the rechanneling of national energies into successful economic reconstruction. In the more usual cases, in which mutual distrust has already led to the build-up of national military forces, unilateral reductions could prove ill advised and dangerous.

Bilateral reductions demand not only that both parties to a conflict decide that the other's assertions of peaceful intentions are made in good faith, but that the disadvantages of reduced defensive forces are evenly distributed. If such disadvantages threaten one party more than the other—for instance, when the territorial size and population of one side are disproportionately small—the process of deescalation inevitably comes to a halt. Thus, in the case of bilateral arms reductions by the Arab countries and Israel, Israel would ultimately find herself in a vulnerable position. More success, for example, can be expected in bilateral arms reduction agreements between the United States and the Soviet Union, for here a mutual balance could be maintained with quite low levels of preparedness. In cases of uneven advantage and disadvantage, only third-party guarantees and control offer sufficient protection. The superpowers themselves would probably agree to such roles if their own confrontation were mitigated through mutual arms reductions. But these powers are unlikely to disarm while smaller nations still possess potent weapons and could unbalance regional security.

To break through the circular logic of arms escalation and to create adequate guarantees that no party will take unfair advantage of another when major arms reductions have been effected, international agreements and guarantees are required. Creating a world body to perform these tasks effectively is a major global goal in itself.

Despite the fact that the United Nations was originally conceived as a peacekeeping system and that the principle of interposition by U.N. forces has been generally accepted, the world community does not have an effective peacekeeping body. The efficiency of the Security Council is hampered by the veto power of the major nuclear nations. The office of the Secretary-General, charged with many peacekeeping missions, is not a regularly constituted peacekeeping organization. It has no means of enforcing agreements and bringing conflicting parties to the conference table. Its success has been due more to personal initiatives and behind-the-scenes diplomacy.

Ultimately, an International Disarmament and Peacekeeping Council is necessary—one that is more equitably balanced than the U.N. Security Council and more able to offer rewards and sanctions than the office of the U.N.'s Secretary-General. Such an organization could gradually promote the growth of an atmosphere of trust among member states, coordinate worldwide disarmament processes, offer guarantees against aggression by unconscientious states, impose uniform sanctions on international terrorists, and impel parties torn by antagonisms to come to the conference table and work out their differences without resorting to violence.

Global security through disarmament and collective peacekeeping is vastly preferable to the illusion of national security through a temporary edge over the military forces of potential or real adversaries. The nations of the world will soon have to eliminate the self-escalating cycles of huge arms profits and unstable arms markets, and distrust and arms build-up—this despite the powerful economic interests associated with the armaments industry, the balance-of-payment problems of arms exporting-countries, and the personal and institutional power of arms importers. Those states that can least afford to devote a large proportion of their GNP to military purposes are likely to be the first to take the initiative. But sooner or later the entire international community will have to join in supporting a collectively constituted and mandated disarmament supervisory and peacekeeping body. Unless collective reason prevails over collective madness, a collective catastrophe is certain to result.

Chapter 13

Global Food Goals

As much as 40 percent of the world's population suffers from some form of undernourishment. The lot of millions is downright starvation. As population grows in the poorest parts of the world, always more people will be forced below the subsistence level of food intake. This situation would ultimately lead to catastrophe in a precariously balanced and interdependent world.

Undernourishment and starvation is not the work of fate but of human decisions. World food production has continued to exceed the growth of human population and could provide nourishing food for everyone. But food production is skewed in favor of those who can pay the profit-generating price of luxury foods, locking out of the world market the poor who rely on basic grains for survival. These practices maintain the international market system without regard to its ultimate consequences. Such short-term rationality threatens to transform into long-term cruelty and eventually self-destruction. Long-term rationality demands the creation of a world food system capable of responding to the basic needs of all people, rich or poor. This can be accomplished by improving food production through appropriate agricultural technologies, greater efficiency in production and storage, and more justice in distribution. The relevant goals encompass reform

*of the patterns of land ownership, basic literacy and skill training for
agriculturists, and the creation of appropriate institutional mechanisms
for planning and coordination.*

Famines are familiar features of history, and malnutrition for the
poorest segment of the population appears to be a perennial aspect
of the human condition. Despite unprecedented increases in food
production during the past two decades, famines of enormous scale
threaten in the years ahead, as population continues to grow and the
gap between rich and poor widens. Yet today mankind has the
capacity to wipe out hunger and meet the basic nutritional needs of
everyone.

World agricultural production can still be vastly increased. The
amount of land that could produce food for human consumption is
great, though obviously finite. Only about 10 percent of the earth's
total land surface is at present under cultivation. While much of the
world's land surface has either poor soil, unsuitable climate, inadequate water resources, or is not easily accessible, the potentially
arable land is at least twice, and perhaps four times, the size of the
land now being cultivated.

The amount of water currently available is likewise substantial,
though it, too, is finite. It is estimated at 41 trillion cubic meters annually. But this supply is unevenly distributed, leaving some areas
with untapped water resources and others with shortages. About 40
percent of all the water used by mankind is for irrigation. Water
available for this purpose is running low in many areas, especially
where deforestation and overgrazing have advanced desert areas.
Man-made deserts now claim a land area equal to the size of Brazil.
Yet a new agricultural revolution is under way—the "Blue Revolution"—which permits the more efficient use of existing water supplies
and also opens up new water resources.

The agricultural potential of the earth is constrained by a number
of factors. Some are physical in origin, but many arise from the interventions of man. One physical factor which may pose long-term difficulties is the progressive cooling of the northern hemisphere. This
trend, which began around the middle of the century, has mainly
affected the latitudes above the sixtieth parallel, and thus far has had
no large-scale impact on world food production. Its continuation,
however, could pose a major threat and may even herald the beginning of a new ice age.

Perhaps still more urgent is attention to man-made constraints on the world's food-producing capacity. Ecologically unsound attempts to improve crop yields can erode soils, pollute rivers and lakes, and deplete marine life. If used in increasing amounts over extended time periods, pesticides and chemical fertilizers can cause serious damage. With their use, productivity goes up for a number of years, but then begins to decline. In many areas the fertility of the soil is nearing exhaustion, pollutants are accumulating in the environment, and certain essential species of organism are becoming scarce or extinct.

But neither physical nor manmade constraints on the world's food-producing capacity need prevent vast increases in agricultural productivity. Greater efficiency can halve the amount of land needed to feed people and therewith double the food potential of arable lands. And most importantly, the distribution of food can be greatly improved. The world's food problems can be overcome if feasible and farsighted goals are adopted and pursued in the related areas of food production and distribution.

At current levels, world food yield could nourish every man, woman, and child alive today. The calorie and protein content of today's food production is more than twice the minimum per capita requirement of the world population. But in the developing world demand for food is expected to grow faster than food production. The Food and Agricultural Organization projects a gap of seventy-six million tons of grain by the year 1985. It is assumed that demand in developing countries will grow at the rate of 3.6 percent a year, while food production will grow merely at a 2.6 percent annual rate.

Thus the world food system faces serious problems, despite the fact that the average growth in world food production, at about 3 percent a year, is still outstripping the overall growth of the population—now estimated at 1.8 percent. Yields in developing countries must be increased, total world productivity raised, and adequate buffer stocks created.

There are social as well as environmental problems associated with increasing yields in developing countries. New production methods tend to selectively favor rich landowners, who can afford the chemicals and the equipment, and who own sufficient land to bring about economies of scale. The use of chemical fertilizers and pesticides tends to erode the soil, impair the fertility of the land, and pollute streams and lakes. The improvement of food-producing capacity in the developing world calls for careful social as well as environmental management. That more productivity is not only desirable but also feasible is illustrated by the fact that it takes about 30,000 square feet (2,700 square meters) of land to produce 2,400 calories of plant origin in India, while the same amount can be produced on 10,000 square feet (900 square meters) in the United States. If food self-sufficiency is to be achieved within any reasonable time horizon in the developing world, such productivity gaps must be closed.

An additional challenge facing developing countries is to raise productivity without engaging in highly capital- and energy-intensive methods of farming. Taking the entire food system into account from planting to consumption, it takes six or seven kilocalories of oil in the United States to produce, process, and ship to the consumer one kilocalorie of food. Such energy investment remains unrealistic for the great developing regions of the world, at least until the energy goals discussed in Chapter 14 are far along the road toward implementation. The solution for world agricultural production is not to strike Faustian bargains with dangerous and unclean technologies, or wait idly for clean and cheap energy, but to use the low-energy agricultural methods already available. Many new technologies have been invented in recent years, and some of them are no longer energy- and capital-intensive. They include the recycling of human wastes, zero-tilling, trickle irrigation, fish farming, a variety of mari-cultures, the use of improved nitrogen-fixing legumes, and the innovative use of species which do not presently form a part of human diets. Where capital and energy are sufficiently available, new so-called landless food production methods can also be employed. These include hydroponics (the growing of plants in tanks of water with the addition of proper chemicals), algae farming, synthetic foods, and the growing of single-cell proteins, yeast cells, and similar cultures.

The technological possibilities for increasing world food production are considerable. The realization of such potentials depends mainly on human factors: appropriate research and development budgets, funds for implementation, and the training of farmers in proper application of technology.

The discussion of improved food technologies must not obscure the fact that hunger and malnutrition today stem chiefly from inadequate forms of distribution. In formulating goals of adequate food distribution, human needs must function as the highest criteria. Food must be available to all societies even if, for reasons they cannot control, they are unable to pay the international market price. The notion that feeding poor people only aggravates the world population problem is, as we shall see, severely mistaken. On the contrary, access to the minimum necessities of life on an assured basis mitigates the need to have numerous children, and tends to reduce the average family size.

Hunger among poor people and overeating among the rich are manifestations of the inequality of the present system of food distribution. Even in 1970, when the Green Revolution achieved its greatest successes, U.N. statistics indicated that an estimated 462 million people were undernourished. Yet only 3 percent of the people of the developed world were in this category, compared to 25 percent in the developing world. Almost a third of the entire Far East population was undernourished, a fourth of Africa, 18 percent of the Near East, and 13 percent of Latin America.

Yet the current annual cereal grain production of approximately 1,200 million tons a year, if evenly distributed among four billion people, would provide each person with 300 kilograms. This would be sufficient for the maintenance of life—the subsistence level being approximately 200 kilograms. But the Western European level of grain consumption—including indirect forms, such as through meat— is around 500 kilograms and that in North America is still higher.

Production and distribution are skewed in favor of affluent consumers. Much of the global grain, for example, is produced to feed animals, who in turn feed people. The level of North American grain consumption is seven times higher on the average than that of India, yet Americans eat less grain than Indians—they feed as much as 90 percent of it to animals. In India, on the other hand, about 83 percent of the grain consumed is eaten by people.

But it is inefficient to feed grain to animals since in converting it to meat, considerable calories are wasted. Beef cattle, for example, consume seven times as much calories in fodder as they yield in beef, yet such cattle are raised because of the higher profits associated with meat. Meat is also fed by the affluent to household pets. Because of this, even poor countries produce lower-grade meat for export as pet food, instead of grain for feeding their own populations.

The world food reserves are rapidly being depleted due to ill-advised patterns of production combined with higher prices for energy and fertilizers and unfavorable weather patterns. In 1961 reserves were equivalent to 105 days of consumption, while in 1975 they were equivalent to less than 30 days, the lowest level in twenty-two years. The drop began with a serious shortfall of the Russian wheat crop, continued with the failure of the monsoons to discharge enough water over the fields in India, and was aggravated by the persistent drought in the Sahel region of Africa.

Adequate world food reserves are essential as buffers against large-scale famines and the uncontrolled fluctuation of world food prices. At present the only countries capable of building buffer stocks are the United States, Canada, and Australia. One way to increase such stocks is by adopting agricultural policies that provide incentives to farmers to produce grain for human consumption. Far-sighted international trade policies could also be used to reinforce changes in consumer preference. Poor countries should be motivated to use their precious fertile lands to raise food for local consumption and achieve self-sufficiency, rather than plant cash crops and raise beef cattle for an uncertain export market.

In the long term, it is not enough to have a handful of countries exporting their food surplus to all the rest—even if they were willing and able to do it. An adequate and reliable system of food distribution must be based on the growth of food self-sufficiency in an increasing number of countries and regions. (As the Chinese proverb says, "Do not give a man fish, teach him how to fish.") In order to move toward food self-sufficiency, the nations of the world must achieve the following objectives.

First, they must select the most appropriate of both traditional and modern food-producing technologies. Appropriateness must be measured in terms not only of yield and cost, but also of employment provided to the available agricultural workforce, and of the food produced for local consumption. Often the same or even better results can be attained through labor-intensive methods. Pesticides can be sprayed from inexpensive sprayers, and some species of crop can be hand-pollinated (in India the yield of hybrid cotton has doubled in recent years through hand-pollinating the flowers).

Second, much higher levels of efficiency need to be achieved. This means reducing waste as well as making proper use of seeds, fertilizers, and equipment. In Asia, food losses to rodents, birds, and insects are estimated to be as high as 40 percent of the stored supplies. Throughout the world, rats, insects, and fungi consume as much as 20 percent of all the foodstuffs and destroy some thirty-three million tons in storage. The health level of populations also needs to be improved: Poor public health is one form of food wastage. Intestinal worms, infantile diarrhea, and other diseases of the digestive system prevent up to one-third of the already ingested food from entering the blood stream and providing nourishment for the organism.

Third, farmers in the hinterlands must be educated enough to increase efficiency. Traditional peasant people who cannot read the instructions on a sack of fertilizer can cause much harm through the inadvertent misuse of modern products and equipment. Basic literacy, and beyond that familiarity with the most appropriate agricultural methods, must be imparted to rural people through more attention to and higher funding of village schools, and informative public education programs.

Fourth, productivity needs to be significantly boosted through land reform. Large holdings by absentee landlords usually produce less than small plots farmed by the owners themselves. While large-scale farming has advantages that cannot be matched by private plots and vegetable gardens, if those who work the lands also benefit from its produce, efficiency goes up and waste comes down. The appropriate kinds of land reform will vary with the social order, level of development, and cultural tradition of the country concerned. But improvements on the present system of land ownership and profit distribution can, in most cases, be undertaken. The gap can be reduced between landowners using large-scale modes of production and peasants practicing small-scale subsistence agriculture, and appropriate innovations can penetrate into all sectors of agriculture.

Fifth, buffer stocks need to be built up and made available to needy nations at constant prices. While wealthy countries can normally protect domestic food prices against fluctuations of the international market, poor countries are unable to do so, and are often forced to import food at exorbitant prices. A world food reserve could be created and maintained at a cost of less than $1,000 million a year— a sum jointly manageable without strain by the world's principal food exporters. Such a food bank could be used to stabilize world food prices, and provide emergency relief for famine-stricken areas.

World food production can still be raised considerably. Efficiency and yields can be enhanced, more cultivable land irrigated and farmed. World food distribution and land ownership can likewise be rendered more equitable. Fairer patterns of trade can bring more grains to the table instead of to cattle raising. World food reserves can be built up and made available to areas in urgent need. Self-sufficiency can gradually be improved through labor-intensive technologies, reduced losses, better public health, more adequate rural education and information, and appropriate kinds of land reform.

These tasks call for a wide-scale international coordination of policies and technologies. Food self-reliance is the goal, and the way to it is through cooperation, rather than competition. Matters of food, like matters of security, must be placed beyond the confines of narrow economic rationality. As insecurity can spell destruction, so starvation can spell disease, deprivation, and violence. An interdependent world community cannot allow either phenomenon to affect any nation or people. But to assure a supply of food on the basis of need rather than ability to pay the market price, new international arrangements must be made. The task of coordinating such arrangements and supervising their implementation calls for a more effective World Food Programme, administered by an agency jointly mandated by the world's people. The functions and responsibilities of such an agency would include:

coordination of international food research and development programs, and provision for a continuous flow of up-to-date information on technologies appropriate to different physical, economic, and socio-cultural conditions;

assistance with the implementation of efforts to increase efficiency in food production and distribution through channeling capital toward needed improvements, and making teams of experts available for the initial phases of implementation;

creating educational and informational materials which can update the skill and knowledge of farmers and peasants in different parts and cultures of the world;

monitoring land-use patterns, and advising on efficiency-boosting forms of land reform, consistent with the socio-economic, political, and cultural diversity of contemporary societies;

building buffer stocks for emergency relief programs and for stabilizing the market price of essential foodstuffs in the interest of meeting basic human needs;

regulating access to the food resources of the high seas, and negotiating the settlement of conflicts arising out of contrary short-term production and marketing interests.

Several of these functions are already carried out by international bodies, but they are distributed over many regional and United Nations agencies and are lacking adequate coordination. Other functions still await implementation, and none have as yet a sufficient level of authority and funding to ensure long-term success.

Chapter 14

Global Energy and
Resource Goals

Global consumption and use of energies and nonrenewable raw materials is enormous, and increasing from year to year. Given the underdevelopment of some 70 percent of the human population and the addition of about 2,000 million people in the remaining decades of this century, humanity's need for energy and materials will continue to grow. But the known stocks of currently used fossil fuel and mineral resources do not necessarily grow with the growth of need. Socio-economic development could fail for lack of adequate and economically priced energy and material supplies, while competition for scarce and expensive resources could escalate into violence.

Mankind needs to adopt appropriate energy and resource goals. Wasteful and inefficient patterns of energy use must be reduced to win the time necessary to develop energies that are abundant enough to meet human needs far into the future; that are accessible to all peoples and nations for growth toward energy self-reliance; and that are truly affordable, not only economically, but in terms of social and environmental costs. Mankind's use of materials must likewise respect global prospects for the present as well as coming generations. Nations and corporations must do more with less, rather than engage in hazardous attempts to maximize extraction. Underlying both energy and resource goals is the paramount consideration of satisfying human needs globally and in the long term, under concrete conditions of socio-economic growth and development in a diversified but interdependent world.

Global Energy Goals

Mankind is faced with a difficult dilemma: to attempt to satisfy growing energy demand through presently known technologies and currently available fuels, hazardous and finite as they may be, or to cut back on current demand and develop more appropriate energy sources and technologies for the future.

The problem is further complicated by the emergence of large masses in poor countries for whom energy is not a matter of comfort and luxury but the precondition of survival. At the same time access to new energy sources and technologies promises to be a protracted and expensive process, due to the long lead-times of research, development and application, and the high cost of the alternative energy technologies. Such considerations argue strongly for using whatever energies and technologies are available to assure the needs of basic survival as well as continued economic growth. Yet the opposite side of the coin cannot be neglected either: an unstable world security situation, increasing tensions between industrialized and developing nations, competition for scarce and expensive resources, a deteriorating environment, and persistent rivalries and territorial conflicts. The costs of energy include social, environmental, and political risks in addition to monetary investments.

The way the energy dilemma is resolved today could be decisive for mankind's future. The world community could be saddled with dangerous, costly, depleting, dirty, and unequally available energies. Our children and grandchildren could find themselves with a legacy heavier than one bequeathed to any generation in history.

The dilemma must be properly resolved, for decisions taken now may not be easily reversible in the future. Today's energy policy must be long-term and globally responsible. Long-term global energy goals need to be clearly formulated and continually updated in the light of fresh knowledge and technological innovations. The best global goals need to guide energy policy at any given time, lest short-term thinking lock mankind into a dangerous and possibly irreversible energy option.

Since technologies will no doubt evolve, and will do so in essentially unforeseeable ways, long-term energy planning should not be based on the assumption that currently known "technological fixes" can be applied to mankind's enduring energy problems. Rather, planners should assess existing options in the light of need, and spur research, development, and implementation in the feasible and desirable directions. The only elements of long-term energy plans that can at this time be definitively determined are the basic criteria. These specify what kind of energies would truly solve the long-term energy problem. Rather than discussing the currently known specifics of the various technologies, we will concentrate on basic criteria, and match current technological know-how against them. In this way an element of humanism will be conserved even in the discussion of technologies—a feat all too seldom achieved today.

The basic requirement on world energy use can be clearly stated. It is to serve people. First and foremost, it is to place at the command of all people everywhere safe and clean energies that they can produce and control themselves. Energy must become the servant of people, not people the slaves, and possibly the victims, of the available energies. The production of suitable energy must be sustained far into the future. The best suited source of energy becomes inappropriate if its expected lifetime is short. The present generation would then be enjoying its fruits at the expense of generations to come.

The above requirements can be condensed under the heading of "three A's": *abundance, accessibility,* and *affordability.*

Abundance today and in the foreseeable future means that we must be dealing with an energy source that is either renewable, or has a vast stock. Accessibility means that we must have energy technologies that can be used and controlled by all nations and peoples in the world, rather than being restricted to the few who have the funds and the experts. And affordability means that mankind can genuinely afford researching, developing, and applying the energy technology, not only in terms of capital investment and cost of operations, but also in terms of social and environmental costs. Affordability is a combined index of economic, ecologic, and institutional factors.

There are three "costs" that transcend classical economic calculations of affordability. These are safety, environmental impact, and impact on the global heat balance. An energy technology that can accidentally kill large numbers of people, or be used to do so intentionally, is costly in human terms. One that can despoil the environment is costly in natural terms. And one that could eventually impair the heat balance of this planet may be suicidal for mankind, to say nothing of many other living species.*

Is there a source of energy that can meet all these specifications, and a technology to tap it for human use? Today there is not. But it is virtually certain that tomorrow there can be. This chance cannot be left unexploited. The stakes are too high to settle for second-best solutions, especially since the second-best, failing one or more of these criteria, could prove to be seriously defective.

We shall briefly review how current energy sources and technologies fare in the light of the criteria, and what sources and technologies could eventually satisfy them.

Fossil fuels are still the staple energy source of mankind. Although in some advanced industrial countries electrical power from fission reactors now accounts for up to 9 percent of energy production, as recently as 1970 oil met 36 percent of world energy needs, coal 30 percent, and natural gas 18 percent.

Oil, coal, and natural gas are in finite supply on earth, and coal and oil, when burned, pollute the atmosphere. While the primary reserves of oil would be depleted in thirty to fifty years at currently growing rates of use, the supplies of coal would last for many centuries. But coal mining is dangerous, expensive and, in the form of strip mining, environmentally harmful. Oil, too, is a major pollutant when accidentally released into the environment.

With the exception of coal, fossil fuels are not abundant enough to meet mankind's long-term energy needs, and with the exception of natural gas, they are not clean enough to be truly affordable. While pollutant emissions could be considerably cleaned up, the investment required would pay off only in the near term. Unless the world industrial system can switch back to coal—a remote possibility—cheap oil and natural gas will run out in the coming decades. Secondary sources

---

* The global heat balance is between the energy reaching the planet from the sun and the energy transmitted into space as reflected sunlight and invisible heat radiation. The transmission of energy into space depends on the average world temperature. Excess heat can only be radiated if this temperature rises. A rise in world temperature, however, could have catastrophic results. It could produce major climatic changes, playing havoc with agriculture. Its many side effects may include the immersion of the giant ice sheet of the Antarctic in the seas, causing a rise in water levels sufficient to flood coastal regions the world over. Although nobody knows with certainty how much energy would have to be injected into the atmosphere to upset the present heat balance, the thresholds may lie low enough to be approached within the next century. If so, current energy goals must include the heat balance as one criterion which, though not threatening for our generation, could prove to be a matter of the ultimate importance for those to come.

could then be tapped, but they will be expensive, and likewise constitute but an intermediate solution.

In the absence of a truly acceptable energy alternative, the conservation of fossil fuels is important for the present. Moreover, crude oil has uses other than generating energy, and some of these, for example in medicines and synthetics, are of great value.

Energy conservation today can buy the time needed to research and develop feasible and desirable alternatives to fossil fuels. Many believe that nuclear power is already such an alternative. There are more than 170 nuclear power reactors in operation in nineteen countries, producing a total of about 74,000 million watts of electricity. Another nine countries have their first commercial power plants under construction, and many more have announced their intention to enter the nuclear age. If present plans are implemented, by 1980 there will be twenty-nine countries producing some 220,000 million watts of electric power. This figure may increase by a factor of sixteen by the year 2000.

There is no question that the world is taking the nuclear option seriously. A turn-about is felt only in a few developed countries, especially in Scandinavia and in some parts of the United States and Canada. Here the dangers associated with present nuclear technologies may produce that most remarkable of social phenomena: the willingness to reject an available technology.

But nuclear fission fares poorly when measured against criteria for long-term energy requirements. First, despite popular belief to the contrary, it does not draw on an abundant stock. High-grade uranium of the kind currently used in reactors (U^{235}) is in short supply. While estimates of the reserves vary, and the size of stocks also depends on the amount of capital allowed for extraction and processing, recent calculations show that if all presently constructed and planned reactors were in operation, reserves of economically priced uranium would be depleted even before the reactors reached the end of their expected lifespan. Then ores of low concentration would have to be mined, at rising costs.

Problems associated with the finiteness of natural uranium stocks can be almost entirely overcome, however, by various kinds of so-called breeder technologies. These breed the substance they use, thus cutting down or eliminating the need to supply scarce raw materials. A heavy water reactor developed in Canada uses enriched uranium to which thorium is added to breed the separable isotope U^{233}. With this process one can achieve a near-breeder: The reactor does not actually produce additional fuel but almost holds its own. With the use of enriched uranium-thorium reactors the supply of natural uranium could be extended at least tenfold.

Full breeder reactors are operating on an experimental basis in France, the Soviet Union, the United States, and several other countries. They use the isotope Plutonium^{239} as fuel in conjunction with the relatively abundant isotope U^{238} (in mined uranium 99.3 percent is U^{238} and only .7 percent U^{235}). Plutonium is "burnt" and in the process neutrons are absorbed in the uranium, thereby producing more plutonium. The amount of plutonium in a single large breeder reactor would be on the order of about three tons.

But even if the problem of finite stocks is solved, nuclear fission remains socially and environmentally costly. Reactors capable of generating electrical power for peaceful uses can be converted to produce nuclear bombs. They bring to the user the essential elements: plutonium, enriched uranium, nuclear fuel cycle facilities, and technological know-how. But the military potential, grave as it is, does not exhaust the list of disadvantages associated with fission power. Environmental dangers from accidents and the threat of deliberate international terrorism are yet further dangers of nuclear power plants. Operation of nuclear reactors requires the transport and storing of highly fissionable materials, as well as radioactive wastes. Plutonium^{239} may be the most deadly substance known to man. Ten pounds of it are sufficient to build an atomic bomb capable of devastating major cities, and one milligram of it can cause fatal disease. Yet the substance is practically indestructible: Its half-life is 24,400 years—which means that it will remain hazardous for almost half a million years (about twenty half-lives). Whether the economic cost of nuclear fission power is acceptable or not, its social and environmental costs are surely prohibitive.

There is a new nuclear technology, however, which does away with most of the dangers associated with fission reactors. This is controlled nuclear fusion. While fission is the splitting of the nuclei of heavy elements, such as uranium and plutonium, to form lighter elements and free neutrons, fusion is the combination of two hydrogen nuclei to derive a single helium nucleus, a neutron, and a radiation loss of mass. The latter is converted into usable energy. The fusion process uses deuterium combined with lithium (in a more sophisticated process, deuterium alone), and its by-product is harmless hydrogen. Although lithium is in limited supply, deuterium can be produced from common sea water.

Presently, scientists working on fusion projects are experimenting with two major technologies: magnetic bottles and laser beam implosion. They attempt to go beyond the "break-even point" in the fusion reaction. This is the point at which the output of energy equals the energy required to operate the process. A recent breakthrough (neutral beam injection, which makes it possible to fire a high energy beam into magnetically bottled plasma to heat and enrich it) has assured break-even power production. But how far this point will be surpassed in the future is not known. Let us allow the possibility that the process becomes economically competitive, and also that the more sophisticated deuterium-deuterium reaction becomes operational. We then have a source of abundant energy without dangerous by-products and wastes. But this technology is not free of problems: The reactor structure will become irradiated (because the fast neutrons, which are the main operating ingredient of the fusion reactor, change any element partially into a radioactive species), and the technology itself will remain one of the most complex and capital-intensive operations known to man. Worldwide accessibility to fusion power could only be achieved if the few producing countries distributed their yield to the great majority of nations whose capital and technological capacity fusion clearly exceeds. This would call for a highly centralized world energy system. Making such a system work equitably may be more difficult than making the fusion process work economically.

We turn now to the plethora of so-called renewable energy sources and technologies. These include hydropower, wind, geothermal, tidal, methane, and solar energies. With one exception, these energies fail to meet the criterion of abundance, although they meet the others. Except for the possibilities associated with solar energy, renewable energy sources are too limited to become major energy options for mankind.* But they can become *part* of the energy solution, in locally suitable combinations. Each of these sources can contribute to meeting local energy needs and relieve pressure on the staple source. All

---

* For example, the total annual potential of world tidal power is estimated at around 64,000 megawatts, and that of geothermal power is put at 60,000 megawatts. Hydropower has greater potential—only about 8.5 percent of it is exploited at present—while wind energy is much more limited.

countries can make use of methane, won from the putrification of organic wastes. Almost all can tap the energy of the wind, and many can tap tidal energies as well. Most countries have potentials for hydropower, and many have hot subsurface rocks that could generate usable steam.

But is there a form of energy that satisfies all three A's, abundance, accessibility, and affordability? There is indeed such an energy, although the technology still needs to be rendered economical. It is the most ubiquitous and cleanest of all: direct sunshine.

According to a conservative estimate, solar radiation will continue to pour on the earth's surface for at least another 5,000 million years. Its energy content exceeds the greatest imaginable increases in world energy production. In 1970, for example, world energy production was in the area of .24 Q (where Q equals a thousand million kilowatt-hours of electric power). But the amount of solar radiation reaching the earth above the stratosphere is about 5,300 Q per year, and that reaching only the land areas of the earth, after being filtered by clouds and the atmosphere, is 690 Q per year. Thus the total energy wealth reaching the planet from the sun exceeded recent energy production over 22,000 times, and that reaching the continents alone exceeded it about 2,800 times.

Solar radiation is abundant, but it is also diffuse and intermittent. Economically transforming it into usable power poses severe technological problems. But human ingenuity and technical genius now seems to be committed to finding solutions to them. New production methods are invented every day, and existing ones are refined. Great advances in solar technologies are almost certain to come about in the next few years.

At the present time, solar technologies can be grouped into two broad categories: technologies for solar heating and cooling, and technologies for solar electricity. Solar heating is already used in many parts of the world. Maintenance costs are low—there are no fuel bills to pay—although installation costs can still be considerable. With mass production and use, they could be significantly lowered. The range of simple solar technologies increases exponentially. There are new ideas for collecting solar heat on rooftops, for storing it in tanks of water or beds of crushed rock, for totally insulating houses— building them essentially as thermos bottles—and permitting solar heat to enter through thermopane windows, for pumping water for household as well as agricultural use (exploiting temperature differentials), for using blackened snow surfaces to melt ice layers and win cultivable land, and for obtaining hot water for household use.

Solar electric technologies are more costly. They include two basic approaches: solar-thermal, and solar photoelectric. Solar-thermal systems use mirrors or lenses to concentrate sunshine on receivers, where the energy is absorbed as heat in a working fluid. Steam is generated, which can be used to drive generating turbines in the conventional manner. Photoelectric systems use silicon, germanium, cadmium sulfide, or another photosensitive material in thin sheets to convert some part of the solar spectrum into electricity. Each has further innovative technological solutions. Solar-thermal power can be won not only from sunlight directly, but from sun-warmed ocean water. Floating ocean-thermal generating stations could use warm water from the upper layers of tropical seas to bring liquid ammonia to boil and drive turbine generators, using colder water to reliquefy it and start the cycle anew. Photoelectric cells could be installed in orbiting satellites, where they would tap sunlight before it is filtered by dust and cloud. They could convert the sunlight to microwave energy and beam it to earth, where receiving stations could convert it to electricity.

Solar electric technologies face certain constraints, inherent in the very nature of solar radiation. These are principally the efficiency of systems to convert diffuse radiation inexpensively into power, and the need to store sunlight adequately to make up for its intermittent availability on the earth's surface. Large land or sea areas are required to collect solar radiation due to its low intensity, and areas with a high level of insolation have advantages over relatively cold and overcast regions.* Land area problems could be eliminated through a highly intensive exploitation of the satellite-based solar conversion technology. Yet this would pose problems similar to fusion power: centralization of the world energy system in the hands of those who control the technology (who are likely to be those who can afford to build and operate it), and a risk of purposive misuse or of impairment of the global heat balance.

The most basic problem facing the widespread use of solar electric

---

* For example, to cover the present electric power requirements of the U.S., a "solar farm" roughly one-tenth the size of the state of Arizona would be needed. Yet this estimate is based on a currently achievable efficiency of 10 percent, which is likely to rise considerably in the future.

technologies is economic cost. The generation of electric power using currently priced photoelectric components would cost about ten times as much on the average than generating an equal amount of power through nuclear fission. Thus, if left to market forces alone, the solar options would remain largely unexploited. Yet major cost reductions are foreseen by solar experts if a temporary market can be created to permit mass production. A "bootstrap effect" would then occur, as each reduction in cost would increase the size of the market and eventually permit entry into the international energy market system. Cost calculations based on projections by ERDA (the Energy Research and Development Agency in the United States) show that the total cost of producing one kilowatt of photoelectric power at a sunny location—for example, in New Mexico—would drop from $15,780 in 1976 to $2510 in 1982 and $1400 in 1986. At the same time the cost of generating electric power through nuclear fission reactors could rise in real terms due to escalation of construction costs, the need to install more sophisticated safety features, the rising cost of uranium and of nuclear waste disposal. By 1986, one megawatt-hour of nuclear power may cost more than the same amount of solar photoelectric power. The cumulative cost of the subsidy required to activate solar technology's bootstrap effect may be actually less than the cost of a single nuclear fission generating plant. It takes about ten years to construct a complete nuclear power plant, and ten years to drop the price of the most promising solar electric technologies—at comparable cost. These calculations should provide much food for thought for all people concerned with current energy policies.*

The long-term benefits associated with the various types and forms of solar energy technologies can be summarized under the heading of the three A's.

Abundance. Solar energy is available at an adequate rate for the life of the biosphere.

Accessibility. Solar energy is accessible to all nations and peoples, and in particularly generous and constant quantities to the mainly tropical poor countries. It is adaptable to a great variety of climatic conditions and can furnish different forms of energy (thermal, chemical, electric). The conversion technologies can be built on any scale, from the small rooftop heat collector to the large solar farm. Local

---

* For details see R. H. Murray and P. A. LaViolette, "Assessing the Solar Energy Transition," in the already cited volume, *Goals in a Global Community,* ed. Laszlo and Bierman.

applications allow variations and give scope to personal and social inventiveness. Its use in one village, town, or county does not diminish the resources of others. On the contrary, intensive exploitation of high levels of insolation in poor countries could promote not only economic self-reliance but constitute an important means of generating foreign currency through energy export (through shipment as liquid hydrogen, for example).

Affordability. Solar energy is safe with respect to human lives: It produces no dangerous wastes, does not threaten genetic damage or birth defects. Its by-products do not pollute the environment, and even worldwide use on the surface of the earth would not upset the global heat balance. It cannot be used by terrorists and it is not easy to see how it could be adapted for any kind of warfare. It does not call for rigorous safety measures and the associated secrecy, police forces, and restrictions of civil liberties. Its economic costs are presently high but can come down in a decade or less with more intensive development and mass production.

These are reasons enough to warrant the national and international development of the widest array of solar technologies—not *instead* of other energies, but *jointly* with all harmless intermediate solutions. It should be remembered that the research, development, and implementation of energy technologies is not merely a matter of physical feasibility and price. It is also a social and political matter. It involves choices that cannot be made solely within the perspectives of physics and economics. Just because an energy technology is available is not a good reason to use it. And just because an energy technology is as yet undeveloped with regard to commercial use, is not a good reason to refrain from developing and implementing it.

Mankind's growth toward energy sufficiency and self-reliance requires the international coordination of energy policies. Dangerous alternatives must be discouraged, wasteful duplication of effort eliminated, and the options and possibilities constantly reappraised in the light of criteria based on human need. A better flow of information and a more efficient transfer of technology need to be assured. Funds must be channeled to where they do the most good. If the world energy system is to become safe, decentralized, and capable of satisfying legitimate demands on a sustainable basis, its development needs to be coordinated and supervised by an international body, operating on the basis of clearly defined principles and with enough authority to promote their acceptance. As the International Atomic Energy Agency

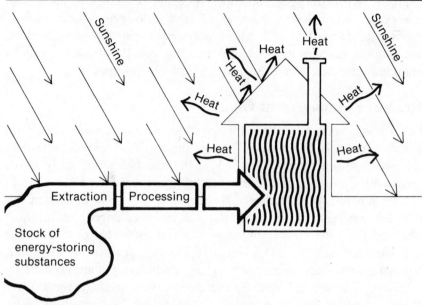

Figure 14.1
Fossil and fissile energy-use pattern. When fossil and fissile energies are used, a finite stock is depleted and heat added to the atmosphere.

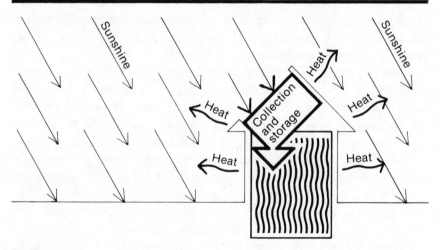

Figure 14.2
Solar energy-use pattern. Through surface-based solar technologies, the heat received from the sun is converted to use, and heat output equals input.

is presently coordinating and supervising the peaceful uses of atomic energy, a more long-term-oriented and universal World Energy Agency needs to coordinate and supervise the research, development, and implementation of all technologies that could ultimately bring to mankind abundant, accessible, and affordable energies.

Resource Management Goals

Great controversy surrounds the question of resource availability on a long-term basis. Whereas in the past the earth's resources were considered to be practically unlimited, in the late 1960s and early 1970s many called attention to the finiteness of nonrenewable resource stocks and the possibility that they would soon be used up. The understanding that has emerged by the mid-1970s is more balanced, however. It distinguishes between *known* reserves of nonrenewable raw materials, and *planetary* reserves. The former are only a fraction of the latter. Known reserves are diminished by the amounts of material actually extracted, and are enlarged by the discovery of fresh reserves. Over the past decades, known reserves have increased, as more stocks were discovered than used up.*

Known reserves are further classified according to whether or not they are economically exploitable with existing technology. The size of reserves that could be exploited at higher cost, or through the development of new extraction technologies, is larger by several factors than the currently economically extractable reserves.

Some resources, such as lead, zinc, mercury, tin, silver, and copper, would be in short supply within a matter of decades—*if* the known reserves continued to be mined at accelerating rates with present technologies. If new discoveries do not continue to add to the size of known reserves, these minerals will eventually become depleted, prices will rise, and further extraction will slow down and come to a stop. Those who warn of impending limits to industrial growth because of the finiteness of natural resources focus exclusively on the time horizons given by known reserves, present technologies, and currently accelerating rates of extraction and use.

On the other hand, there are arguments for the practical inex-

---

* Reserves of iron ore, for example, were put at 19,000 million metric tons in 1950, but known reserves increased to 251,000 million by 1970. In that same time period the known reserves of chromite, copper, lead, zinc, manganese, and others have likewise increased dramatically, partly through discovery of the mineral wealth of the seabed.

haustibility of the planet's natural resources. Planetary reserves are in most cases several million times the annual consumption rates. If all natural resources in the earth's crust could be made available, untold years of industrial consumption would be assured. To expand known reserves toward planetary reserves, more knowledge is needed about the important reserves in the land and under the seabed. And to make more and more of the known planetary reserves economically extractable, great breakthroughs are needed in the technology of extraction, together with enormous inputs of energy. In the final analysis, the question of resource availability is not solely one of natural limitations. It is more a matter of the limitations of technology and energy, together with economic and ecological constraints.

The resource optimists center their attention on the enormous size of planetary reserves, possible creation of new secondary extraction technologies and improved methods of prospecting, and of bringing to bear new sources of cheap and abundant energy. In this perspective limitations of industrial and economic growth due to resource shortages disappear.

However, present reality is neither as somber as those forecasting the imminent depletion of reserves would have it, nor as rosy as the technological optimists paint it. For the present, the extraction of less accessible reserves is prohibitively expensive, and the price will go down only with new technological innovations and the availability of cheap and abundant energy. Neither of these is certain in the short term. Both can be made more probable through greater investment but, in the case of energy, the price may involve grave risks associated with nuclear fission reactors. The environmental costs of secondary reserve extraction are, for the present, exorbitant. Large-scale exploitation would in most cases disrupt ecological cycles, with potentially large and long-term negative consequences.

The world's resource prospects thus depend on a number of factors, in addition to the size of the nonrenewable reserves. These are economic, technological, ecological, and, in the last count, social and political in nature. When all costs are properly taken into account, a period of several decades of relative resource shortage appears inevitable. An appropriate resource goal of mankind is thus not merely to make the most of available natural resources, but to assure an adequate supply without at the same time aggravating related problems in the areas of the economy, the environment, public safety, and health.

In order to have adequate natural resources without resorting to unsafe energies and environmentally and economically unsound practices, better use has to be made of the resources now on hand. This means cutting down on waste, extending the period of use, and recycling scrap. It means doing more with less. This can only be done if there is a reform in the existing manner of economic cost and benefit accounting. Current methods favor high rates of resource extraction, consumption, and discarding, rather than efficient modes of resource utilization.

The pattern of industrial production under the dominant mode of economic assessment is linear. This involves the rapid and large-scale extraction of materials from the ground, and their transfer to processing plants for use in manufactured products. These products are marketed in consumer societies, where large turnover is encouraged, with the consequent scrapping of obsolete products, which reenter the environment as pollutants. By this linear method of production, use, and discarding, high-grade natural resources are rapidly converted into low-grade waste.

Linear production systems can be converted into partially circular systems, which do more with less. The known reserves of usable resources are greatly enlarged by the inclusion of scrap materials found in all industrialized societies which can often be economically recycled, bringing a variety of benefits. First, the total amount of usable materials is vastly increased. Second, the amount of pollutants in the environment is drastically reduced. Third, considerable savings in energy are achieved. Aluminum produced from discarded cans, for instance, conserves 95 percent of the energy otherwise consumed in producing it from bauxite, and steel can be produced from steel scrap with a 75 percent energy saving compared with production from iron ore.

Recycling can be made still more efficient by using standardized and replacable parts in products, and identifying product composition. Material separation, and product repair and replacement, are thus greatly facilitated.

Conversion to such "circular" modes of production requires an appropriate revision of current methods of assessing economic benefits. Products would have to be built for maximum durability and ease of repair and replacement, whereas current calculations of benefit favor the production of goods with "built-in" obsolescence. The fact is that economic progress is still measured in terms of material *throughput,* from extraction to use to discarding, rather than in terms

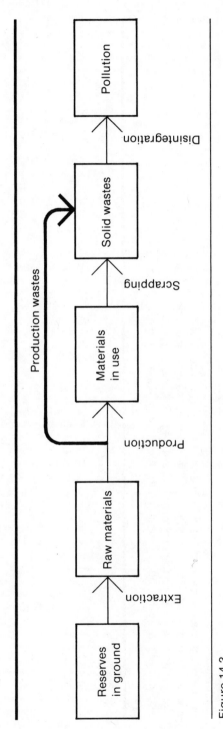

Figure 14.3
Contemporary linear economics. This simple diagram shows how materials flow through the system from the large but finite stock of resources in the ground (left) till they end up as pollution (right)

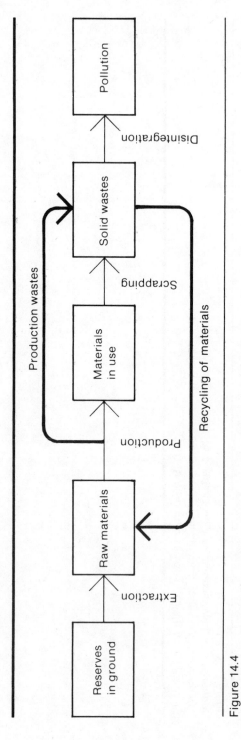

Figure 14.4
Future circular economics. In this system a certain amount of scrapped materials (solid wastes) is recycled back to the stock of raw materials. The two end flows, extraction from reserves and disintegration into pollution, can be reduced drastically without impairing the functioning of the economic system.

of duration of effective use. Indicators such as the GNP reflect the flow of materials through the economic system, not the use human beings are able to make of processed materials. Hence economic growth, measured by standard indicators, has created the "throw-away society," in which products are discarded—often after a single use.

When raw materials and energy were cheap and their sources assumed to be practically unlimited, it was considered appropriate to assess economic benefits in terms of the quantity of material extracted from the ground, processed by manufacturers, and purchased by consumers. But other methods of assessing economic benefits must be found as high rates of use shrink the economically extractable known deposits of raw materials and fossil energy sources despite new discoveries; as prices rise; and as ecological impacts of production processes are worsened. Progress must be measured in terms of the length of time the existing stock of processed materials is in active use; not by speed of product turnover.

Mankind's foreseeable future requirements of raw materials call for a more efficient use of stocks in circulation, and policies which combine conservation and equitable exploitation with regard to the deposits that can be safely and economically worked. To stimulate the economy in this direction, governments need to contemplate taxes proportional to the unrecycled waste contained in products and to the product life expectancy. Related measures could include removing depletion allowances for mining industries, prohibiting the use of throw-away bottles and containers, providing favorable terms of trade for easily repairable products made of clearly identified materials, and encouraging people to create and use local recycling facilities. Such measures would need to be adopted in all industrialized countries, and be included in the development plans of developing nations. In addition, international agreements need to be reached concerning access to natural resources outside national boundaries: the oceans, Arctic regions, and eventually space and the moon.

Implementation of world resource management goals poses the need for a coordinating agency to perform tasks analogous to an international energy body. Uniform standards need to be specified, multilateral trade agreements concluded, and equitable access assured to resources on national territories as well as in the "global commons." The need is for an efficient world agency that can coherently perform all the tasks currently attempted by scores of separate national, regional, and international bodies. Such an agency would not represent a centralization of power any more than its energy counterpart. As long as self-reliance is a major aim, the orchestration of efforts must be left to the main actors, who in turn should be responsible to their peoples. Thus a "planetization" of the earth's natural resources, by means of vesting sovereignty over them in a world body, is no more desirable than it is feasible. This, however, does not obviate the need for responsible and integrated management, on behalf of the nations, regions, corporate entities, and, most important of all, the peoples of the world. If these groups become aware of the need to husband non-renewable resources through appropriate social and technological means, their efforts will need to be translated by state and corporate entities into viable policies, and orchestrated on the global level by a World Nonrenewable Resource Agency. Here, as elsewhere, the task is not to create yet another international body, but to integrate functions now widely diffused, and serve the international community by bringing to fruition the emerging will to join forces in combating problems that threaten all of mankind.

Chapter 15

Global Development Goals

Unless current patterns of socio-economic growth and development are modified, the world may be heading for catastrophe. The gap between rich and poor nations will widen, the poorest will be unable to survive, and mounting pressures will erupt into acts of terrorism and ultimately war. To change current patterns of world development, three major socio-economic goals need to be pursued simultaneously. The developed world must switch from attempting to maximize undifferentiated economic growth to selecting new forms of growth which truly improve the quality of life. The developed world must also work together with the developing to provide the necessary forms of assistance to reduce the development gap and avert major breakdowns. And the developing countries must adopt appropriate strategies of development to overcome internal inequalities, assure the participation of their marginal populations in the process of development, and control the growth of their populations in general and of their cities in particular. A safe and just world socio-economic development can only be assured if all three of these goals are pursued jointly, with equal emphasis and equal dedication.

Socio-Economic Goals for the Developed World

The population of the developed world makes up about 30 percent of the world population, and may shrink to no more than 10 percent in the next century, unless war, famine, and disease slow down the growth of human numbers in developing countries. Less than one-third of the world population controls more than two-thirds of its wealth, possesses 95 percent of existing scientific and technological research and development facilities, consumes some 40 percent of the world's nonrenewable resources, and contributes the lion's share of its pollution.

These conditions impose special responsibilities on the people of the developed world. They must take the initiative in specifying and pursuing global security, food, energy, and resource goals. They must work together with the poor nations to create a more just and sustainable international order. And they must also take care that their own lives are not locked into pathways of alienation, meaninglessness, and stress. There is, we believe, a set of feasible policy alternatives available to developed countries which responds to all these needs. They can improve the national quality of life and at the same time bring about more equity and justice in the world.

The already discussed goals related to security, food, energy, and resources need to be vigorously pursued in the developed world. Combined with them are goals to overcome the worst side effects of technological civilization without demanding unrealistic sacrifices from individuals and leaders.

Present condtions in the developed world arose from historical processes that resulted in significant achievements in the spheres of industry, agriculture, and social organization. These achievements are closely associated with efficient applications of science and technology and the creation of great national and corporate wealth. Discoveries in science led to rapid advances in technology, and these permitted the creation of large-scale production systems with decreasing unit costs. Higher productivity gave rise to increases in real income which, in turn, created a demand for more and more production in an ongoing spiral. The resultant economic process was self-reinforcing, product-proliferating, and energy- and materials-hungry. This pattern continued almost without interruption from the end of World War II to the early 1970s, despite fluctuations of the business cycle.

During the seventies, however, raw materials and energy costs rose, inflation took an upswing, labor became more expensive, demand diminished, and economic growth slowed. The unanticipated anomaly of economic stagnation combined with inflation occurred. The Arab oil embargoes of 1973–74 and the fourfold increase in oil prices led to serious balance-of-payments deficits, and contributed to the instability of the international monetary system. The prices of a number of other industrially important nonrenewable natural resources were also raised by organizations of producing and exporting countries.

During the 1970s many governmental and business leaders began to wonder whether the exponential growth of industries had begun to deplete stocks of nonrenewable natural resources. Since industry depends for continued growth on large stocks of reasonably priced natural resources as well as on cheap and abundant energies, more and more people began to question whether the industrial system would undermine itself by depleting its essential stocks.

The growth–no growth debates, triggered by *Limits to Growth,* the famous first report to the Club of Rome, are now history. Without rehashing well-worn arguments, it is enough to say that the issue for the economy is not whether to grow or not to grow; it is *how* to grow, and for what *purpose.* Growth for its own sake often proves to be contrary to human interests—it can depress, rather than enhance, the quality of life. Economic growth should serve human ends—and should occur only when it can fulfill this function. Further growth in pollution, traffic jams, urban conglomerations, mindless automation, and impersonal bureaucracy is contrary to human interests, although it might register as a contribution to economic growth when measured by such overall quantitative indicators as gross national product, national income, and international trade. But growth can occur in many areas where human needs are truly served—where the quality of life within developed countries is enhanced, and where world development and justice are promoted. Such growth is not undifferentiated but selective, and responds to social and cultural needs. The fact is that notwithstanding pockets of poverty, the basic material needs of people in affluent countries can already be fully met; the problem is better distribution, not more material growth. Further material growth would merely create increasing gaps between rich and poor. Hence rather than emphasizing overall growth, problems of distribution and injustice need to be addressed, and ways and means found to reduce, and eventually eliminate, the alienation, isolation, and impersonal tenor of life in affluent urban environments.

Socio-economic progress is not necessarily geared to overall economic growth. Public and business policies should calculate human, social, and environmental, in addition to purely economic, costs and benefits. Those in charge of policy decisions must take two types of factor into account: first, the classical quantifiable ones, such as profitability, cost/benefit, and growing market share for expansion; second, the new qualitative factors, such as social responsibility, environmental impact of production methods and development projects, and the personal safety and job security of employees. The concept of economic growth as a panacea for the human condition needs to be replaced by the more far-reaching and humane concept of socio-economic progress measured in terms of the quality of life.

To improve the quality of life in developed countries, policies must be geared to reducing the undesirable side effects of economic growth —such as unemployment and inflation—and promoting the satisfaction of material, social, and cultural needs. Major goals must be to place less emphasis on material- and energy-wasteful modes of production and more on conservation and recycling; less emphasis on automated machines and more on human services. Industrialized societies can progress by improving education, health and social services, cultural activities, and recreational opportunities.

There is a great need to improve educational systems. More, and more relevant, knowledge is needed for living and working in advanced industrial societies. Access to professional education for all strata of the population could bring about a better distribution of income and opportunities. Access to a liberal education would permit the public to develop a well-balanced view of national and international processes, problems, and prospects.

Communication in the political sphere needs to be expanded. People should become better informed about current public policies and feasible alternatives. They should have the freedom to choose appropriate lifestyles and to express new consumer preferences.

In most of the free market economies, health and social services are insufficiently funded. Hospitals are overcrowded and their staffs overburdened. The aged, the poor, and the mentally ill are given inferior treatment. As urban crime rates rise, public security decreases.

While there is much room for progress in such services areas, a linear increase in materials- and energy-wasteful production systems would worsen rather than improve the overall quality of life. The artificial inculcation of demand for certain types of products is a disservice to the public, as illustrated by advertising designed to sell gas-guzzling private automobiles. Continued increase in the number of such automobiles would produce serious health hazards, create transportation breakdowns, and increase energy and raw material costs.

Cars, like all products of technology, should be viewed as devices to perform services for human beings. Their energy efficiency could be increased and reliance on them could be moderated by wider and more efficient public transportation systems. Many tasks that now require physical transportation could be better accomplished with the aid of electronic communication systems. These could increase contact among individuals and eliminate some of the wasteful uses of private cars—for trips to outlying shopping centers, for example. Consumers could select purchases through videophones and deliveries could be made by small, efficiently operating trucks. A great deal of movement from one part of a city to another could be replaced by electronic teleconferencing, with a consequent decrease in traffic jams and air pollution, and a saving on fuel.

A trend toward the standard concept of a "postindustrial" society, however, is not without its grave dangers.* Technologies should not be put in use simply because they are available—not even automated production systems or electronic communication technologies. Employment could be much reduced, and there could be a decline in face-to-face communication. Privacy could be invaded, and extensive data files used to control behavior. People could be exposed to information overload. Indeed, wide use of electronic communication systems could be a bane as well as a blessing. On the one hand people could be freed from many manual chores, could have much leisure time, and could have the cultural and environmental facilities to fill such time with enjoyment; on the other hand such societies could become impersonal technocracies, subject to a high degree of surveillance, saturated with services, and plagued by unsolved problems of unemployment and alienation.

The use of centralized data banks could make life especially difficult. Much like nuclear reactors, such data banks could have "leaks,"

---

* Postindustrial society is usually conceived as affluent, automated, and service-oriented. As computerized automation takes over the tasks of production, workers gravitate into the service sector. The society is managed by hard-working intellectuals, who apply their theoretical knowledge to practical problems. The production, collection, storage, and dissemination of knowledge acquires the greatest importance. Intellectual institutions become the centers of innovation, which they transmit by electronic technologies. Postindustrial society as a whole depends crucially on such technologies, especially on computers linked with communications networks.

could be misused, could trigger social "chain reactions," and could serve as instruments of blackmail in the hands of national and international terrorists. At present their diseconomies and the relative uselessness of much of their contents outweigh their unpleasant side effects. There is a 10–90 rule that says that 90 percent of the stored data will be used less than 10 percent of the time.

Responsible socio-economic progress in the developed world requires careful assessment of the available technologies—even those in the information sciences—and a major emphasis on meaningful and socially useful employment. Every person who can work should be able to find useful and satisfying forms of employment. It must be recognized that much of the existing workforce will be displaced when automated production and management systems become widely substituted for human labor, when energy- and materials-efficient methods cut down on the workforce required for extracting and processing of raw materials, and when production quotas are reduced because of quality goods that last longer and need less servicing. Instead of condemning many people to unemployment, and burdening the state with their support, the required workload could be more evenly distributed, with shorter working hours and fewer workdays for everyone. As more and higher-quality social, cultural, and recreational services are made available, a larger percentage of the working population could find satisfying forms of employment, and better ways to spend the increased leisure time.

Responsible socio-economic progress in the developed world thus calls for selectivity among policies and technologies. These must be oriented to human benefit, rather than serving abstract ideals of economic growth. The great discovery that awaits the industrialized world is that it has the power to say no to a technology that is feasible, and could even bring short-term economic benefits. This power needs to be exercised in the areas of energy research and development, in agriculture, in the armaments and defense industries, in resource-intensive production processes, and even in the application of electronic communication technologies. Goals for a better quality of life must be pursued together with the long-term goals of security, food production and distribution, energy production, and resource use. They jointly constitute a set of objectives which could reorient social and economic patterns in the affluent world, and make them not only serve the well-being of its own people, but also assist in the survival and development of the rest of the world.

World Development Assistance Goals

The current responsibilities of developed peoples and nations embrace the responsibility to promote a more equitable and sustainable world economic system. The affluent people of the world cannot be assured of serving the best interests of the entire human community—and therewith also their own long-term self-interest—merely by taking care to become still richer. The "trickle-down" theory of wealth has failed both nationally and internationally. While the rich get richer, the poor get children. Pockets of poverty persist and even grow amidst the greatest affluence. And the wealth transferred through charitable channels often flows into the pockets of a numerically small elite, leaving the poor as poorly off as before.

The notion that an invisible hand is sure to distribute the benefits if all do as well for themselves as they know how, has proven an illusion. Increasing gaps between rich and poor people and nations are the mark of today's reality. There is little that the poor can do about changing things on their own—short of dying quietly of starvation and disease, or committing noisy acts of terrorism. The initiative must come from the developed world. This fact does not absolve poor nations, nor the rich elites of poor nations, from corresponding responsibilities. We review first the required long-term development assistance goals of developed countries, and then the parallel responsibilities of the decision-makers of developing nations.

1. Assistance by Governments

At present, aid is given by the rich countries mainly to further their own short-term economic, political, and military advantage. Even with such strings attached, aid levels have failed to reach the minimum recommended by the United Nations. Initially only Sweden filled—and recently even exceeded—its quota of .7 percent of GNP, but the Netherlands has now followed Sweden's example. Although affluent countries could well afford such aid levels by a moderate rearrangement of their priorities, the flow of official development aid from them to the poor countries amounted only to .3 percent of their combined GNP in 1975. At $11,000 million—equal to but $6,000 million in 1970 prices—this assistance constituted the lowest level of real aid so far in the decade. Despite the noteworthy efforts of some medium and small developed countries, the average aid level is not expected to rise and, according to a World Bank estimate, may dip to .28 of the combined GNP by 1980.

The terms of aid also need to be revised. Payments of interest on aid previously received are actually higher for many developing countries than the value of the aid they are currently receiving. India is thus an exporter of capital, despite the country's desperate need to finance her own development. The fact is that many forms of aid, such as direct provision of food, do not generate further economic growth and fail to add to the recipient country's reserves of foreign exchange. Yet much aid is in the form of long-term loans, which have to be repaid with interest (though the rates are often low).

In order to promote the growth of the economies of developing countries, and open the road to their eventual self-reliance, new international aid and assistance policies are required. In the RIO Report to the Club of Rome (*Reshaping the International Order*), Jan Tinbergen and his associates recommend an international redistribution of incomes through such means as an international income tax, a tax on luxury consumer durables, an armament tax, and taxes on the use of natural resources. Sales taxes in industrialized regions could be progressive, ranging from exemptions on the basic necessities of life to luxury rates imposed on the predilections of the rich. Land taxes of various kinds could be imposed. The export position of industries located in the developing world could be enhanced by more advantageous trade policies. Preferential quotas and prices as well as new commodity agreements are required.

Funds for developmental aid could also be raised by the international community through collective agreement on the use and exploitation of the "global commons." The increasing use by national agencies and multinational corporations of space and the oceans beyond the boundaries of sovereign territories could be taxed and internationally administered for development. The autonomy of the governments of wealthy nations in deciding when and where to give assistance must be tempered with responsibility for promoting world development, just as the autonomy of the governments of poor countries in deciding on the model of development to follow must likewise be tempered with accountability to the international community for the soundness of their strategy.

2. Assistance by the Public

The developed world overconsumes in several of the areas in which the greatest lack occurs in the developing world. Many in affluent countries eat too much meat for their own good, use unnecessarily large amounts of fertilizer for decorative plants and shrubs, grow physically less fit by engaging in motorized sports and pastimes, waste energy, pollute the air, and worsen traffic conditions by driving oversized cars, and add to general pollution of the environment by an advertising-stimulated preference for throw-away products and containers and for newer, bigger, "improved" models of appliances. Yet food, fertilizer, energy, and raw materials are badly needed in many parts of the world just to satisfy the most basic human needs. More thoughtfulness in these areas must be part and parcel of the responsible socio-economic growth of the developed world.

Reduction in meat consumption through one meatless day a week, for example, would free grain fed to large herds of beef cattle for export or for a world food bank to stabilize prices and offset famines. Less use of fertilizers for decorative landscaping could put more of this precious commodity on the international market for agricultural use, and contribute to reducing its cost. Cutting back on pleasure driving, using more energy-efficient cars, and favoring nonmotorized sports and pastimes could relieve the pressure on energy demand. Preference for long-lasting consumer products and insistence on recycling could conserve precious raw materials.

These changes in lifestyles and consumer preferences constitute sacrifices only in the light of a now obsolete value system. More of everything is not necessarily better—people are learning to distinguish between *maximum* and *optimum*. And when the optimum serves people's physical and mental health, as well as the material interests of the world's poor, it constitutes a desirable alternative, not a sacrifice.

All such choices on the part of the people of the developed world become futile, however, in the absence of a new international framework for the effective transfer and utilization of resources. Such a framework must rest on a compact of solidarity and a perception of shared interest between developed and developing countries, and between rich and poor strata within the countries.

The public of affluent countries can not only conserve precious resources and commodities in the interest of world development, it can also take an active part in promoting such development. People can assist with ideas, information, and with voluntary service abroad. Young people are already responding to calls by organizations such as the Peace Corps, for a period of voluntary service in some needy area, and they submit ideas and information when organizations such as VITA (Volunteers for International Technical Assistance) call for them. These trends, and the emerging public attitudes toward global problems, augur well for the future of public developmental assistance. With more information programs on world problems and alternatives, and more opportunities for people to participate in the shaping of the future, voluntary public assistance could become a major factor in international development.

3. Assistance by Scientific Communities

Science and technology are crucial to development. Even more than capital and resources, the intellectual wealth of modern know-how is essential. The equitable production, transfer, and utilization of scientific and technological knowledge is a key issue in the evolution of a just and sustainable international order.

But scientific and technological knowledge is concentrated in the developed world. Some 95 percent of the world's research and development facilities are in developed countries, along with the funds needed to pursue many necessary types of project. In view of the universal need for science and technology, and its current concentration in a few countries, a reform of the world's science and technology transfer and information mechanisms is badly needed. In attempting such reform, whether through bilateral arrangements and contracts or through the United Nations (where attention will focus on this problem at the 1979 Conference on Science and Technology), the initiative clearly must come from the developed world.

What can the scientists and science policy bodies of rich countries do to live up to such responsibilities? First and foremost, they need to reorient the focus of scientific and technical research from its present concentration on military applications—which serve no human need and represent the greatest waste of human and natural resources in the contemporary world—toward research on the manifold aspects of human and social life. The problems of industrialized countries must continue to receive attention, but responding to such problems should not exclude attention from the grave problems encountered by poor people living in different climatic, economic, and cultural milieus. At present problems that are not of direct interest to the rich countries receive disproportionately small funding. For example, of the $5,000 million spent each year on medical research, only about $30 million goes to support work on communicable tropical diseases. Such funding patterns disclose a dangerously short time horizon on the part of science policy makers and scientific communities.

A more informed science policy would encourage basic as well as applied research on topics such as the following:

developing high-yield grains, low-cost methods of food production, and labor-intensive farming techniques to produce foodstuffs acceptable to indigenous cultures

improving the use of indigenous water resources with labor-intensive and low capital-cost methods

creating an early warning system with respect to natural disasters (volcanic eruptions, earthquakes, hurricanes, cyclones, typhoons, floods, and tidal bores) together with emergency relief procedures drawing on available human and natural resources

evolving local cottage industries by improving on traditional techniques of tanning, weaving, carpetmaking, pottery, ceramics, carpentry, and food processing, and finding novel uses for the local products

developing additional uses for products based on locally abundant materials, such as mineral ores, industrial chemicals, natural fibers, wood, and stone

inventing birth control techniques and devices that are safe, inexpensive, simple to use, and acceptable to the local cultures

developing small-scale energy technologies that use nonpolluting and renewable sources (windmills, watermills, organic waste conversion, solar panels for cooking, hot water, and space heating, etc.)

discovering effective methods of preventing and treating schistosomiasis, trypanosomiasis, smallpox, leprosy, cholera, malaria, and trachoma.

The transfer of ready-made scientific and technological information is not the full answer to the problem of reducing the knowledge gap between the developed and the developing worlds. Ultimately, self-reliance in science and technology becomes as desirable and necessary as self-reliance in food production and energy. To this end the scientific communities of the world need to help developing countries to build local research and development facilities. By doing so they will also help to put a stop to the brain drain which currently robs developing nations of many of their best qualified scientists and technicians.

4. Assistance by the Business Community

The world's great businesses are still, by and large, run from the developed world. Although multinational corporations engage in all activities of international business, including trade, portfolio, and direct foreign investments and operations, and often have affiliates in many other countries, they are controlled by the financial interests of their home offices in the developed world.

Yet, in spite of the business community's close affiliation with the countries of the developed world, its long-term interests are increasingly tied in with the progress and well-being of the developing countries. Raw materials, energy sources, favorable labor markets, and a growing consumer market attract multinationals to developing lands, and make their continued growth conditional on local development. These opportunities and constraints are already recognized by an increasing number of multinationals (see Chapter 10). To promote the continued and rapid adaptation of the entire international business community to the new realities of today's world, a few overarching goals need to be specified, related to investment policy, choice of production technology, choice of location, and strategy of ownership and management.

The decision on where to invest is usually guided by the relative returns expected on the investment. Regions and nations that offer high rates of return receive the lion's share of direct foreign investment, while others are selectively bypassed. But multinationals would also do well to consider the long-term development needs of various countries. Even a lower rate of return proves a good long-term investment if it contributes to the host country's economic development. Orientation toward local markets is good policy. In a world where the affluent minority is approaching a point of saturation with many kinds of material goods, and where the great minority is in process of development, orientation toward their development opens new markets. Corporations that evolve symbiotic relations with their host country can look forward to a long period of gradual growth, whereas those that look only to rapid returns on current investments may oversaturate markets and, failing to harmonize with the host country's interests, become subject to restrictive measures.

Similar considerations apply to the choice of production technologies. The latest technology is not necessarily the best choice, even if it brings highest returns in the home country, and even if it promises for a time to do the same in the host country. Multinationals that create employment opportunities in the host country also create future clients and customers. Lesser efficiency in per capita production quotas may mean more efficiency in creating a growth-promoting environment for corporate activities.

The selection of sites for future facilities is also important. A site that offers immediate benefits will not necessarily prove best in the long run. Almost all developing countries now recognize the need to overcome their urban-rural gap by decentralizing the major cities and upgrading rural areas. Instead of running counter to such policies by locating in already overcrowded urban regions, multinationals could expand into rural areas with products and services needed by farming communities. Through policies of participatory management and co-ownership they would avoid antagonizing tradition-oriented regions and would be welcomed as partners in development. In the long run both the corporations and the host countries would benefit.

Relations between multinationals and host countries can be markedly improved by informed ownership and management practices. Many multinationals are already abandoning the once-preferred strategy of 100 percent ownership of foreign branches. But joint ownership with local nationals is often limited to the local elites. These constitute but a small segment of the host country's population, and their allegiances are subject to change. To overcome the danger of alienating the enterprise from the local milieu and ensure that it responds to widespread needs and perceptions, new plans, such as employee coownership, need to be much more widely implemented. Such innovative strategies of ownership can help spread the wealth instead of restricting it to a small elite.

Multinationals can also play unconventional roles in the host country's economy, acting as management consultants and suppliers of technology and capital. Such strategies make possible substantial savings in the importation of human resources, and they bring new opportunities to local businesses. Most of the large corporations are now supplementing imported executives with trained local personnel. They realize that discrimination against local talent is no longer desirable —nor indeed feasible, since many nations may emulate Canada's requirement that the top executive of a multinational subsidiary be a local national.

Development Goals for the Developing World

The responsibilities of the developing world are no less crucial for the future of humanity than those of the developed world. Developing nations must ensure that assistance reaching them is put to humane and farsighted use; that indigenous poverty is relieved; that self-reliance is actively striven for; and that the evolving international order becomes balanced and secure.

Specific goals related to security, food, and energy, as well as natural resources, have already been outlined. While the brunt of the responsibility for implementing such goals rests with the developed countries, developing nations cannot abrogate their responsibilities to carry out their part of the compact. Without their active and conscious participation, no world order can become just, sustainable, and safe for all.

Special responsibilities rest with developing countries to meet the basic material needs of their people, to satisfy their fundamental requirements for education, and to guide the growth and distribution of their population.

Concerning material needs, there is much room for improvement. There must be considerable increases in industrialization to produce the things that can assure a life of basic dignity to marginal populations. While industrial development must follow globally responsible patterns, it must use locally appropriate technologies including labor-intensive methods, and must respect local cultural values and traditions. The economic development of a country cannot be divorced from its socio-cultural evolution—a typically Western pattern of development tends to Westernize the people. This can put stresses on the social fabric. Even if its succeeds, it leads to a loss of cultural identity and the disruption of any sense of historical continuity and national unity.

Rather than imitating past patterns of Western industrialization, henceforth industrial development in the Third World must follow locally appropriate pathways. This means a careful selection of the types of industry to be developed and the kinds of technology to be used. It is no longer true that the value of a technology is proportional to its "altitude"—that the higher and more sophisticated a method is, the better it is. Alternative technologies are beginning to be valued, independently of whether they occupy "high" or "intermediate" levels. This change is due to the realization that the use of an automated technological process in a country that has neither the capital nor an adequately trained labor force can be more a bane than a blessing. While modern large-scale production facilities turning out computers and TV sets have prestige value, they do little to satisfy the most urgent human needs. The rank and file of the people cannot afford the products, and cannot even find employment at the automated production lines. High technology often produces something that should not be produced at all, and does so with minimal use of manpower and vast consumption of energy and raw materials.

A technology is appropriate if it employs the available labor force, produces goods and services required for the satisfaction of human need, respects local values and lifeways, and does not demand more capital than is available. Although appropriateness remains relative to concrete socio-economic and cultural conditions, some of the basic features of appropriate technologies can be stated in general terms:

> They aid in the production of staple foods, essential medicaments, and basic consumer goods and services in quantities and forms suited to the local population and its culture;

> they require low capital investment to install and operate, and can employ unskilled or semiskilled labor;

> they use locally available low-cost raw materials;

> they do not pollute the environment, or change it contrary to the basic conceptions of the local culture.

In sum, appropriate technologies respond to local basic needs without playing havoc with social and cultural requirements. They promote an organic development of the entire economic, social, and cultural system, instead of creating rich-poor, urban-rural, and modern-traditional gaps.

One of the most pernicious of these gaps is that between Westernized urban elites and marginal rural and urban populations. In many of the developing countries the new intellectuals recognize the threat produced by this gap and demand a recovery of cultural values together with a reeducation of the most Westernized groups. As our world atlas of goals has shown, a large number of recent national development plans now reflect this emerging concern.

Basic needs encompass not only food, shelter, clothing, and hygiene, but also the irreducible minimum of knowledge that all people must possess to participate in world development. Developing countries must concern themselves not only with keeping their populations alive, but with constantly increasing the quality of their peoples' lives—as well as guiding the evolution of their numbers.

It is people themselves that are the greatest asset of developing countries. Developing peoples are in social and cultural transition, from a past dominated by tradition and foreign colonial powers, to a future in which modernism looms as a promise. This can make for a loss of perspective. Modernism at all costs may provide much less than was bargained for. It can mean loss of ethnic and cultural heritage, and a sense of disorientation through erosion of basic values and codes. Appropriate forms of education must respond to this challenge. The future for developing countries need not be totally divorced from the past. A path must be judiciously chosen between rootless modernism on the one hand, and hidebound conservatism on the other. Every culture can evolve if the feelings and creativity of its members are called into play. Education must call attention to the need to combine the best of traditional wisdom and ingenuity with the most appropriate elements of modern life, and to create a pattern where it is the culture of the people themselves that guides development.

The basic skills of reading and writing must come first, followed by general knowledge and appreciation of the history of the local people, and the value of their customs and beliefs. This should not blind people, however, to the need to learn from other cultures what is useful and feasible. There is no need to take over total patterns of production and consumption, but people could learn to select what they need and can properly use. Building the new and unfamiliar into the context of the old and familiar governs all processes of learning. It needs to be especially operative in the educational systems of developing countries.

The governments of developing nations are making significant efforts to enlarge their educational systems. Countries where the per capita GNP is between $120 and $1,500—the resource-rich developing countries—now show an enrollment of 80 percent or more in primary schools. It is only in the poorest countries where enrollments drop under 50 percent, and even here there are exceptions: India, Pakistan, and Bangladesh, among others. But the dropout rates tend to be staggering. This is due in part to the prevalent system of education, which educates for the higher academic levels, rather than for life and work in modest economic circumstances. Secondary school enrollments barely reach 50 percent even in the relatively affluent among the developing countries—such as Argentina, Venezuela,

Singapore, and Cyprus—and they drop to about 5 percent in countries like Afghanistan, Chad, Upper Volta, and Zaire. In these countries university enrollments stand at about .4 percent, though they have increased in recent years.

These countries invest around $20 per student per year. If they are to break the vicious circle of poverty breeding ignorance, and ignorance breeding more poverty, they clearly must increase their investment in education.

More and better education is part and parcel of responsible patterns of development. Schools must educate all the people, and educate them for life in an evolving socio-cultural context, not for getting diplomas by repeating information from another time and another culture.

The problems posed by population growth are inseparable from those of education and development. Although world population is not increasing by more than 1.8 percent on the average, it is growing by around 2.7 percent in the poorest regions. Because in those regions almost half the population is under sixteen years of age, population size cannot be stabilized earlier than the next century.

Developing countries are now aware of the great difficulties caused by their rapid population growth. As their population doubles, their work force trebles. Unless development is geared to the entry of these many young people to the workforce, the growing masses of unemployed and disease-ridden populations will create insoluble problems for them—and for the world community in general.

Yet people must be credited with enough sense to respond to problems when they become aware of them. Although cultural traditions in most parts of the developing world encourage large families, most populations show a surprising willingness to use family planning methods. Those who can extricate themselves from the bondage of absolute poverty do not want to fall back again by having to support large families. Development is the best pill, as spokesmen for developing countries point out. But the pill needs to be made more potent by education, and by enlightened family planning programs.

It is noteworthy that fertility tends to be lowest when the average per capita income in a population reaches the equivalent of about $1,000 a year. There is nothing magic about this number; in countries with a highly developed welfare system (socialist countries for the most part) fertility rates drop well before this income level is reached. Guarantees of minimum living standards appear to be the best pill of all. Yet a balanced approach to the population problem must include employment and education, together with assured access to food and shelter. The fundamentals are appropriate modes of economic development, guaranteed minimum living standards, and at least the minimum necessary forms of learning. From these foundations more employment can result, together with better health and more adequate skill levels. A better employed, better fed, and better educated population has a greater sense of security and a desire for smaller families. If it has access to birth control devices, it will have fewer children.

A drop in average fertility rates does not solve all population problems, for it leaves the *distribution* of population unaccounted for. As long as people converge on cities, a reduced population growth rate merely succeeds in leaving the country underpopulated, doing nothing to mitigate the staggering growth of metropolitan areas.

Urbanization is a worldwide phenomenon. Like the growth of population in absolute numbers, it will create essentially intractable problems unless it is slowed. Projections indicate that the population of dozens of developing-world cities could soar above ten, and indeed twenty million by the year 2000. (Mexico City, for example, is expected to count twenty-eight to thirty million inhabitants by the turn of the century.) Since cities seem unable to provide for the needs of even a few million people, it is difficult to see how they would cope with such rates of growth in the future.

Even high-income developing countries cannot tolerate urban populations growing in excess of 7 percent per year and hence doubling in ten years. The necessary infrastructure for such an increase cannot be built fast enough even with large-scale investments and heavy reliance on imported planners and experts nor, indeed, can employment opportunities increase to keep pace. Poor developing countries are in an even worse predicament. Many shantytowns near large cities are without food and water, without sewers, medical and health services, shops, schools, and garbage collections. People flocking from poor rural areas frequently find that their condition of life, instead of improving, has worsened. If shantytowns and urban ghettoes continue to grow, unemployment, undernourishment, and disease will become widespread. Depressed urban areas, often growing in the shadow of modern apartment complexes and within sight of luxurious villas, could become the breeding grounds of economic and political unrest. The development of many countries could be interrupted, and perhaps seriously set back, by the eruption of urban chaos and violence.

Figure 15.1
Relationship of fertility levels to appropriate strategies of development

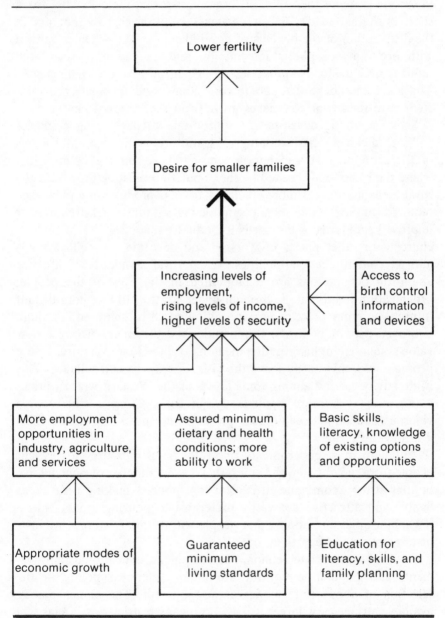

The problems of urbanization, like those of population growth itself, are closely tied in with levels and forms of socio-economic development. Developmental patterns that concentrate wealth and power in the cities invite the influx of large masses of people looking for a share in the better life. A better balance between city and country in the distribution of the benefits of development could, when combined with programs of public information and education, reduce such influxes and make the processes of urbanization more manageable. The goals should be to upgrade rural areas, and to create self-sufficient agro-industrial complexes away from the major urban centers.

Socio-economic development appropriate to developing countries will include an emphasis on progress toward self-reliance in all spheres of the economy. This means greater emphasis on the countryside, where the basic foods needed by the population must be grown. In the rural areas not only is more efficiency in food production and storage required, but the whole socio-economic and cultural infrastructure for improved standards of life needs to be built: schools, cultural centers, churches or other places of worship and devotion, as well as roads and telecommunication facilities. When rural standards of life rise and rural occupations are rehabilitated in the eyes of the people, urbanization trends can be brought under control. In the more distant future even a moderate reverse migration could be achieved. Through improved conditions in the countryside, and the emergence of a new value system reemphasizing the meaning of life close to nature, young people could voluntarily leave the cities for towns and villages. This is already occurring among some layers of the Western world's urban youth and, even more significantly, in some Chinese cities where vigorous educational campaigns promote the move "up to the hills, down to the villages."

Although most governments rightfully resist measures to prevent people from moving into the cities, they have a number of noncoercive options at their command. It is clear that policies making rural areas livable and attractive are vastly preferable to pouring money into a few major cities and hoping that people will refrain from moving in— or attempting to keep them out.

Goals of appropriate economic development, educational improvement, and population control are major reference points in the selection of appropriate modes of development. The choice among available strategies is large; it is by no means restricted to a classical capitalist, or a classical socialist, model.

The standard Western model. This strategy relies on laissez-faire practices and the free market mechanism to promote rapid and generally unselective economic growth, with highest emphasis on the industries. The ratio of capital to labor rises as science and technology are rapidly and intensively applied to all phases of production, marketing, and consumption.

The Marxist communist model. This entails the nationalization of the means of production and the central planification of the economic life of the country, traditionally with emphasis on quantitative growth and heavy industry.

The Euro-Communist model. A newly evolved strategy, it gathers all the progressive forces of society for the specification and pursuit of a national path to socialism without a dictatorship of the proletariat, and with adequate state control of a mixed private and public economy.

The Scandinavian socialist model likewise does not nationalize the means of production, but production and distribution patterns are determined by the people of the entire nation on a basis of equality and solidarity. The aim is planned management in a welfare state, where security is provided to all against old age, illness, and unemployment.

The Yugoslav socialist model. Here the distinctive feature is worker participation in the management of state-owned enterprises. Through such participation worker alienation is reduced, decision-making power is widely distributed, and the economy is made more responsive to the needs of the people.

The Chinese communist model. A locally most successful strategy, where the equality of benefits, self-reliance, collective interests, and appropriate technologies are stressed, with full state control of all aspects of life and minimal reliance on outside trade and support.

"Another development." A development model proposed by the 1975 Dag Hammarskjöld Report and promoted by Sweden's Dag Hammarskjöld Foundation, geared to the satisfaction of needs, and aiming at the eradication of poverty in the Third World through reliance on indigenous human and natural resources.

Until recently, the choice among developmental strategies was thought to be restricted to the early Western and the Marxist communist models. Then Sweden, Yugoslavia, and the People's Republic of China made their own paths of development known to the international community, and the ideas of Euro-Communism became more widely discussed. At the same time, various alternative models came to be debated in international development circles.

The range of options is not restricted to the above—it is still growing. The standard choices are rendered obsolete by changing circumstances and more innovative ideas. Past patterns of highly centralized and relatively undifferentiated industrialization, incorporated in classical applications of Western, and Marxist communist models, are less appropriate than concentration on labor-intensive, decentralized, and environmentally sound alternative technologies which can safeguard nature, protect the culture, and ensure broad popular participation in the development process. The good points of various models and strategies can be creatively combined, while the inappropriate aspects are eliminated. Each developing nation can make its own path of development, custom-tailoring it to its needs, capacities, and opportunities.

As we have seen, the goals of appropriate development encompass a wide variety of factors and objectives. But the principles underlying the selection of strategies can be clearly stated. A basic principle is that development must serve people, rather than people serve a preconceived plan of development. Making development serve people means using industrial growth to create employment and produce the necessities of life, rather than pursuing abstract ideals of efficiency and prestige. For the roughly 750 million of the absolute poor of this earth—whose income is less than $50 per year or less than one-third of their country's average—food, shelter, and hygiene are of more importance than cars, planes, and sophisticated household appliances. Employment and the distribution of the fruits of development, rather than imported methods of efficiency and classical growth indicators, deserve primary attention. Gross economic indicators do not measure social and economic injustice, the depths of deprivation, and the degrees of relative backwardness. Several developing countries, most notably the People's Republic of China, have learned the importance of putting the culturally harmonized satisfaction of basic human needs first. In industrial production, no less than in food and in energy, socially acceptable self-reliance is the ultimate goal. Without it humane and culturally sound development, and a safe and sustainable world order, will be all but impossible to achieve. The new horizons of world development are horizons of collective self-reliance, through international cooperation, and the autonomous but responsible choice of appropriate strategies and technologies.

Chapter 16

The Current Goals Gap

Global goals could open up new horizons for the world community, provided they are pursued with dedication and in cooperation. Nations, institutions, corporations, and people would have to factor in global objectives, as they now factor in more local concerns. How far are current goal settings from this ideal? To answer this question, we present here illustrative charts on the current goals of some nineteen nations representing a broad geographic, social, economic, and political spectrum.

The national goals charts locate the current goals of various segments of a nation's population on a scale, of which the lower end represents goals and aspirations uninformed by global and long-term considerations, and the upper end signifies globally responsible goals. Each chart offers a general—and necessarily approximate—measure of current national goals in relation to global goals in various relevant areas of social and public policy.

A horizontal bar indicates the average of current goals on a scale where 0 indicates self-centered and short-term goals and 10 means a full consideration of global goals. Averages for each nation are likewise on this scale.

Collaborators in various parts of the world scored the charts on

Figure 16.1
Key to National Goals Charts

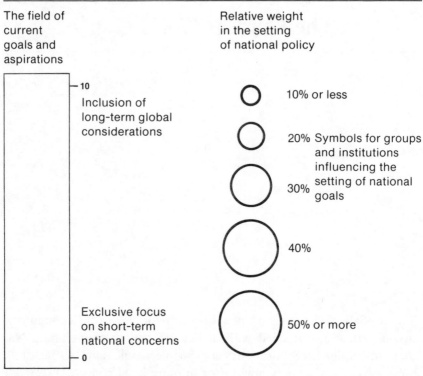

The field of
current
goals and
aspirations

Relative weight
in the setting
of national policy

10 — Inclusion of long-term global considerations

10% or less

20% Symbols for groups and institutions influencing the setting of national goals

30%

40%

Exclusive focus on short-term national concerns

0 —

50% or more

In the field of current goals and aspirations, groups and institutions influence the setting of national goals in the various areas of social and public policy. These groups and institutions have different weights in the goal-setting process, depending on their influence with respect to a given policy area.

The groups and institutions represented on the charts are the following:

GOV the political leadership and hierarchy

PEO the broad masses of people: workers, farmers, peasants, migrants, etc.

BUS private and public decision makers in the business sphere: owners, managers, officials, etc.

REL the religious and spiritual leadership and hierarchy

INT the intellectual groups: writers, journalists, scientists, artists, non-governmental public opinion-makers.

the basis of field work, available survey data, and personal knowledge of people and conditions. The results were subsequently drawn on a standard scale, tabulated, and analyzed. Although all investigators acted in good faith, subjective value judgments are unlikely to be entirely absent. Elements of the charts influenced by them will, we hope, be corrected by subsequent comments and criticism.

Charts were not available from all nations, partly because time and resources did not permit the research and preparation of individual charts on the world's almost 150 nation-states, and partly because in some areas, such as the Soviet Union and communist Eastern Europe, they proved to be inappropriate for international project team members at local research institutes. (This was due mainly to the plurality of goals recognized by the charts and the possibility that even the leadership could fail to be fully informed by global concerns.) But our sample of nations selected for review nevertheless represents all four of the contemporary "worlds": the Western-style developed, the communist (through China and Viet Nam), the resource-rich developing, and the resource-poor developing.

National Goals Gaps in the Developed World

The United States

The United States still exhibits a relatively wide goals gap in all major policy areas. While religious groups and the intellectual community evolves aspirations similar to the global goals outlined here, the weight of these groups and communities in national decision making is not great. Since business goals, though changing, are still predominantly short-term ones, considerable gaps result in most areas between these and globally informed goals. The government itself tends to emphasize overall economic growth without major concern for long-term consequences, and thus lends support to business objectives. Aside from citizen activist groups, consumer movements, and the alternative cultures—which are significant but involve a numerically small part of the population—the American people allow major national goals to be set by government and business.

Policies in the area of resource and environmental conservation are changing and progressively moving toward global goals. The Energy Research and Development Agency has recently shifted emphasis from the development of nuclear power to energy conservation, and a similar (but slow) shift in public attitude seems to be occurring.

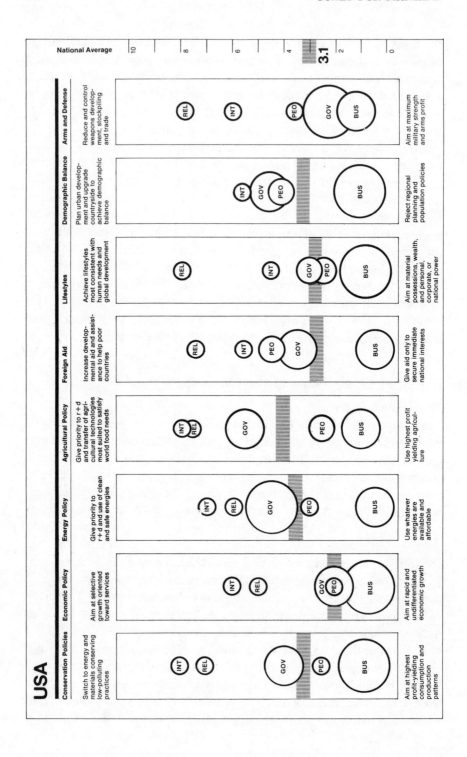

While the economic system itself is not particularly oriented toward conservation, in energy policy the government has taken the lead in reducing the goals gap. This may be a breakthrough, since the federal government has been traditionally reluctant to set and enforce formal economic goals.

The smallest gap for the U.S. occurs in the area of agricultural policy. This is significant, since the country is the world's largest food exporter. But powerful interests representing farmers and the food processing and marketing business are often pulling in the opposite direction, motivated by short-term considerations of economic interest. Governmental emphasis on food exports is sometimes associated with the "food as weapon" strategy, which perceives an advantage in having other nations depend on the U.S. for vital food supplies.

Foreign aid policy has been traditionally defined in terms of the country's own short-term economic and military interests, rather than in terms of the recipient's developmental needs. This is not likely to change in the immediate future, but voluntary assistance continues to pour from the American people to the rest of the world through a wide variety of channels.

Patterns in popular lifestyles are to a high degree artificially created by powerful business interests. But recent poll data indicate a new public awareness of world issues and a new willingness to adopt more appropriate lifestyles (see Chapter 1).

A crucial and still large goals gap for the U.S. occurs in the area of arms and defense. Here, too, policies are highly influenced by economic interests. The country is at present the leading arms exporter in the world, and opposes controls and reductions in arms trade. The government sees the U.S. as responsible for preserving world peace by countering aggression wherever it occurs, and thus seeks to maintain a high level of U.S. military capability. While these ideals have become somewhat tarnished since the long struggle in Viet Nam, defense spending remains high. Concurrently with arms exports, the government pursues strategic arms limitation talks with the Soviet Union, and favors the limitation of nuclear weapons to countries already possessing them. At the same time it continues to permit the export of civilian nuclear technology, in full knowledge of its potential for military applications, and permits the development of new weaponry which makes international arms control difficult to achieve.

Canada

Goals are changing in all segments of Canadian society and are generally moving to close existing goals gaps. Some important gaps, however, remain.

The positive trends are attributable to religious groups, scientists, and intellectuals, as well as to the government itself. Canadian business lags furthest behind (partly because its interests are so closely tied in with the U.S.A. and international business), but some far-sighted corporations are moving up. Typically for Canada, the gap is smallest in agriculture, foreign aid, demographic balance, and arms and defense—all issues on which the government has significant influence.

Government still has a low weight and only a moderately progressive posture in relation to policies dealing with economic issues. In conservation, economic, energy, and lifestyle policies and issues, the widest gap is attributable to business. The market-based economic system is still the major determining factor in Canada, and it suffers at present from a cutback on services as it attempts to encourage general material growth. The Department of Energy, Mines, and Resources, however, has begun a campaign to encourage energy conservation. The Science Council of Canada is cooperating with several universities in promoting the idea of a "Conserver Society," where emphasis will be on service and quality, rather than on production and quantity. In energy policy the rather poor showing of the government is due to its nuclear policy and its lack of a strong domestic fossil fuel policy.

Lifestyles show the largest gap because of a heavy emphasis on material goods and possessions. These trends also appear to be influenced by business policies but here, too, the weight of the government and the general public may be increasing.

The government (including provincial governments) scores remarkably high in a number of areas. These include promoting appropriate agricultural research and development, provision of relatively high levels of official foreign aid, and attempts to achieve a better demographic balance between cities and rural areas.

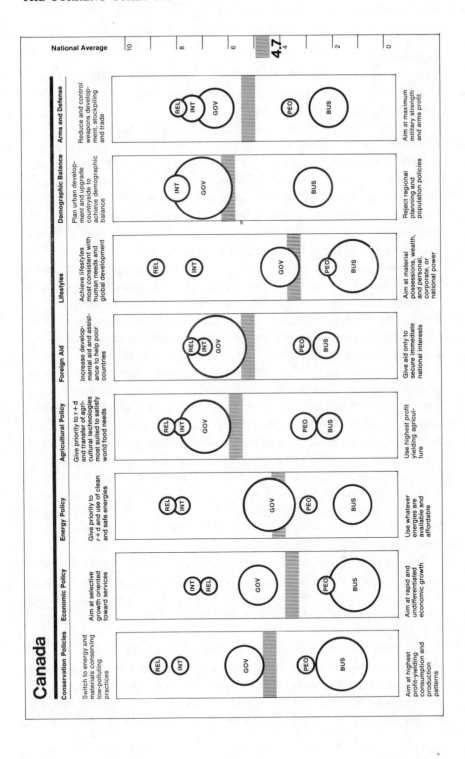

Belgium

Belgium provides a fairly typical example of goals in the European Community nations. While changes are occurring on several fronts, many wide goals gaps still remain.

Belgian business shows small concern for environmental issues. Domestic groups have small influence on basic economic policy, mainly because the major corporations—steel mills, chemical industries, textile mills, machine industries, and the armament industry—are foreign-trade oriented. Yet the government is attempting to institute conservation policies through a secretary of state for the environment, established in 1973, and through the Foundation for the Improvement of the Environment, set up in 1976.

Natural gas and oil have recently ended Belgium's primary reliance on abundant coal resources. Three nuclear power plants are in operation, but the opening of a fourth was delayed because of public opposition. The energy sector is privately controlled, and remains in favor of producing abundant energy to meet demands without much apparent concern for side effects and long-range outcomes.

The government is the most important influence in agricultural policy, which is clearly directed toward a common European Community policy. But the government is under pressure from farmers and the food processing industry, both of which aim at high and immediate profits. Religious groups are exerting a counterinfluence, pressing for more global considerations. Movements for assistance to developing countries, such as that of Father Pire, have begun in Belgium, but the government remains the main force in determining levels of foreign aid. It is supported by many segments of the people. Belgian business, however, is less enthusiastic in the aftermath of its experience in the Congo.

Except for significant achievements in the area of urban renewal, the government has not heeded advice from intellectual circles concerning the need to create better demographic balances. Its "laisser aller—laissez faire" policy has exacerbated difficulties in this densely populated nation.

Defense policy is keynoted by membership in NATO. Belgian arms manufacturers are heavy exporters to the world's trouble spots, despite attempts at government control spurred by some degree of public pressure. The churches oppose arms production and trade, and in this they are joined by a moderately active academic community.

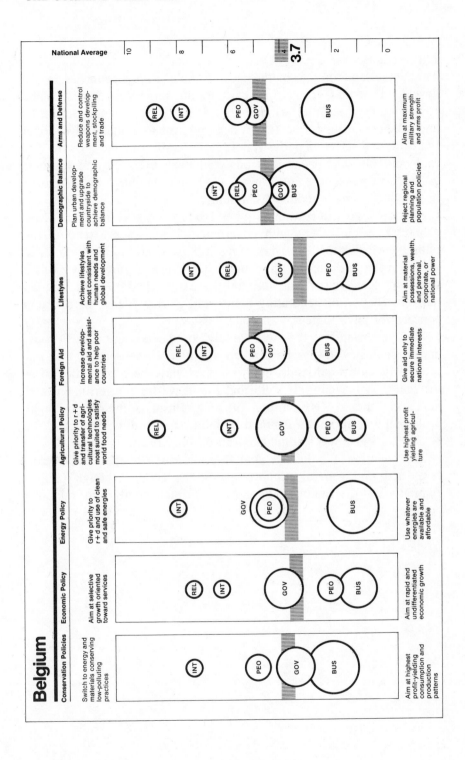

The Netherlands

The Netherlands is one of the most globally aware countries in the developed world. Current goals gaps are due largely to internationally connected business interests, and are offset by governmental, scientific, and religious groups, who take a keen interest in global and national limits to, and selective pathways of, social and economic growth. The rank and file of citizens is strongly influenced by current business goals. Most people are enthusiastic about their country's participation in the European Economic Community.

Economic growth continues to be urged by business interests. These conflict to some extent with governmental goals for extending the public service sector. Recovery of natural gas from the North Sea will provide more income for the country in the near future, as well as a source of clean energy. Massive opposition to nuclear power has halted the construction of generating plants and gives evidence of a strong concern for environmental and safety issues.

The Netherlands is the most densely populated country in Europe, and as such has always paid much attention to conserving and improving its cultivated lands, many of which have been reclaimed from the sea. The recycling of solid and liquid wastes for fertilizing and improving the soil is common practice. Business interest in high-profit-yielding agricultural practices influences land-use patterns; the Netherlands is now a leading exporter of dairy products.

The government's defense goals are aligned with the NATO concepts and find general support among the people, though greater emphasis on disarmament is shown by intellectuals and religious groups.

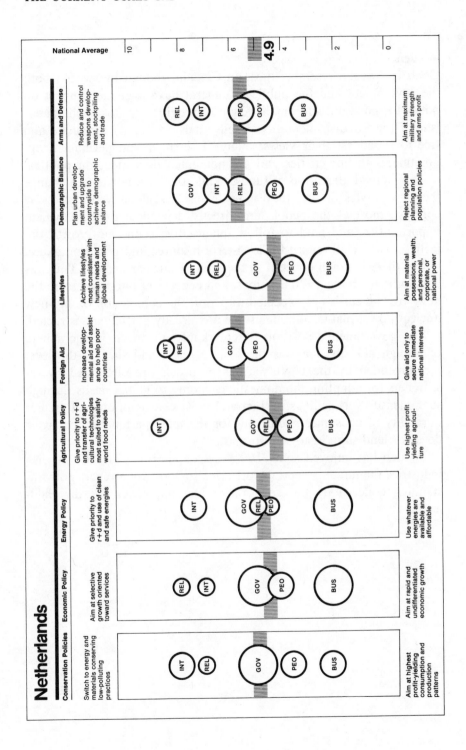

Netherlands

Sweden

Goals in Sweden resemble those in Canada, though in Sweden both the government and the public in general have a greater impact on policy formulation. The small weight of religious groups is characteristic of the Swedish mentality. Intellectuals are highly articulate and free to broadcast their views; many of them are on permanent appointments in universities and are not much dependent on political or commercial allocation of funds. While they are not apt to change their own styles of life, they show themselves globally oriented. By contrast, most of the people are directly dependent on employment opportunities, and tend to follow quantitative economic growth objectives with small regard for long-term resource and pollution issues.

Yet there is much concern in the area of nuclear energy. This was a major issue in the 1976 elections, and because of public pressure the new government is not expected to permit the completion of any new nuclear power plants, although some are already partially constructed.

The government's position is remarkably advanced in the sphere of foreign aid. Sweden was the first to reach and surpass the level recommended by the U.N. Various proposals are circulated by researchers for adapting the domestic economy to global needs through such measures as ceilings on fuel and meat consumption and greater durability of consumer goods, but for the most part public behavior does not lend support to such proposals.

Sweden has enjoyed some 160 years of unbroken peace. Swedish industries manufacture and export arms for profit, however, notwithstanding concern by the government and opposition by the intellectuals.

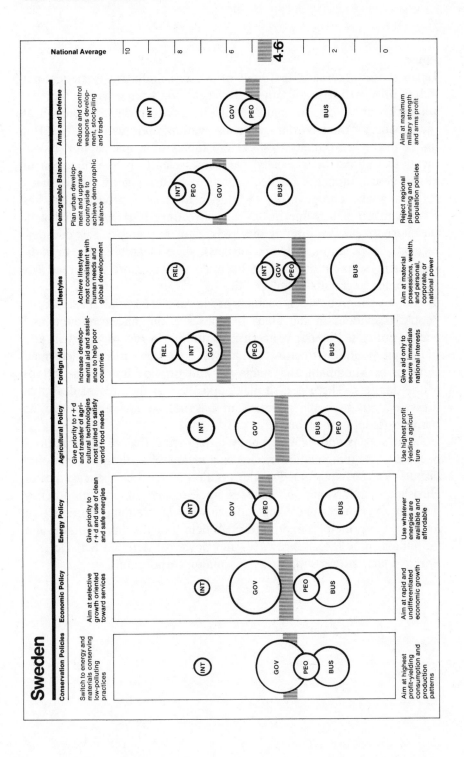

Japan

Japan shares several of the goals of Western industrial societies, but differs in regard to some others. Business goals tend, as in other developed countries, to be mainly concerned with profit and growth at the expense of the environment, conservation, and quality of life. But unlike in the West, many strata of the Japanese people support movements to redirect their society, sometimes clearly in the direction of global goals. Japanese intellectuals also discuss vigorously the need for new goals. The government is open to fresh approaches but has not yet taken a firm line in any one direction. It is confronted with the alternatives of continuing the "rich country" policy of past decades, in close cooperation with big business, or of searching for new directions in cooperation with intellectuals and the more concerned (or traditional) segments of the public.

A polarization between business groups and the broad masses of the people is evident in the areas of conservation, and economic and energy policies. Popular concern is mounting in regard to urban and industrial pollution; deaths, sicknesses, and the birth of deformed children in Minamata and Ashio-Do-Zan provide harsh illustrations of the dangers. There is a similar opposition in the area of desirable lifestyles, but here the government has not so far relinquished its position in support of business.

Japan's arms and defense policy differs from that of other nations because of its renunciation of war as a means of settling international disputes (see Chapter 4). Popular opinion, shaped by the tragedies of Hiroshima and Nagasaki, opposes nuclear and other high-potency weapons. Yet there is growing concern with the seeming contradiction between the principles expressed in Article 9 of the Constitution, and the increasingly large, expensive, and powerful national Self-Defense Force, which enjoys support by the major corporations.

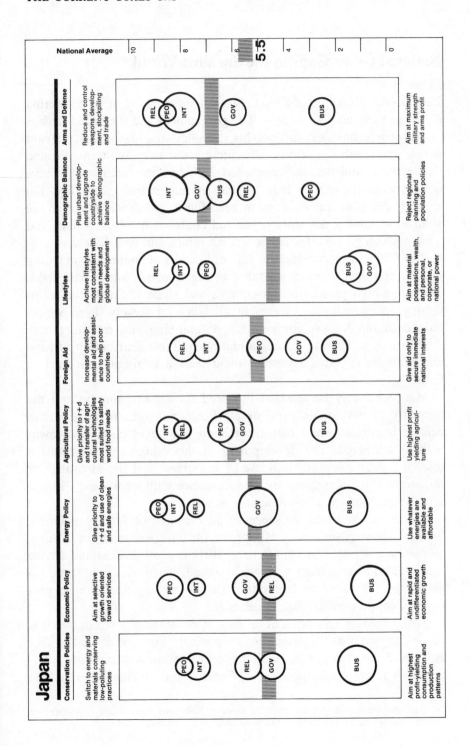

National Goals Gaps in the Socialist World *

China

The People's Republic of China comes significantly close to respecting global goals in all policy areas. The government and the broad masses of the people have similar weights in policy making on the relevant issues, and similar positions. Dissenters are mainly Western-educated intellectuals, and persons concerned with business affairs who have not divorced themselves from an earlier materialistic mentality. Essentially religious influences have been felt in the development of the villages, stemming not from organized churches but from values and beliefs which go back to the Confucian ethics and world view.

The Chinese emphasize the full utilization of materials including wastes, and devote much attention to maintenance and repair tasks. They give high priority to agriculture, and stress the need for maintaining adequate food reserves at all levels of society, even within individual families. A combination of planning and rationing with the ideology of sharing assures a highly equitable distribution of food and provides effective assurance of at least a minimum standard of living.

Mao constantly emphasized the need for urban planning and the necessity of developing rural areas. Further growth of large urban centers is opposed, and industrialization in smaller cities and towns actively furthered. The development of the villages, the orientation toward conservation and full use of resources, and the assurance of minimum living standards are in accordance with traditional Chinese social aspirations and reverence for nature.

China had had relative successes in the area of family planning, brought about by the spread of literacy, the improved status of women, and welfare services and guarantees. Birth control devices and advice are free, and antifertility pills widely used. These developments, together with a stress on late rather than early marriages, have produced a drop in the average family size.

In the field of security China aims at developing a strong nuclear capability and missile system, but supports the concept of nuclear-free zones and the principle of no first use against nonnuclear states. The country's international posture continues to reflect Mao's saying, "dig

---

* Charts on the Soviet Union and the Eastern European communist countries are omitted for reasons mentioned in the beginning of the chapter.

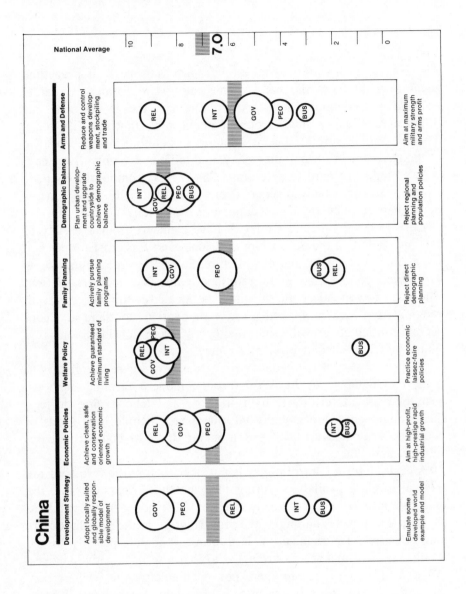

tunnels deep, store grain everywhere, and never seek hegemony." In her foreign policy China has supported wars of national liberation and in some cases provided materials and training to revolutionary groups. China, however, does not engage in arms trade on a commercial basis.

Viet Nam

Viet Nam is in a state of transition from a wartime to a peacetime
economy, and faces the task of integrating two formerly separate
political and economic areas. At present it is the government, the
broad masses, and a small group of intellectuals that set Viet goals.
There are no discernible business interests operating in independence
of the government's economic policy, and religion is highly diversified,
with an influence hard to determine. Since it is a communist country,
its goals are not highly diverse. There is an especially close concordance between government and popular aspirations.

Current developmental strategies have elements from a variety of
sources, including the Soviet Union, China, and Eastern Europe, and
are applied in a locally adapted mixture. Some Viet intellectuals show
preference, however, for more traditional patterns of industrialization.
The aim of economic policies cannot be located within the spectrum
ranging from high profit and prestige motivations to clean and con-
servation-oriented growth, since neither of these considerations is a
major factor in current economic policy.

The key sector of the economy is agriculture, where the goal is to
achieve self-sufficiency by 1980 through modern farming methods,
increased use of fertilizers, hybridization, and labor-saving devices.
The welfare goals are globally informed, and include high levels of
social security and services and a major drive to combat disease,
hunger, and illiteracy.

A decisive birth control policy is not likely before the results of the
next census are available. During the past thirty years of war, the
population increased at a steady rate notwithstanding high casualties.
By contrast, policies aiming at the redistribution of the population are
most decisive. Deurbanization is a primary goal, especially in the
south; the government urges refugees to return to their native villages.
There is also an attempt to open "new economic regions," where people from cities and towns can move and reclaim fallow lands, forests,
or swamps. These areas are now being cleared by about one million
of the former South Vietnamese troops.

Viet Nam scores low on arms and defense policy. It continues to
maintain combined air and land forces ranking in strike capacity immediately behind those of the U.S., the Soviet Union, and China. With
the long struggle clearly in mind, all major population strata support
such high levels of military preparedness. Some military hardware is

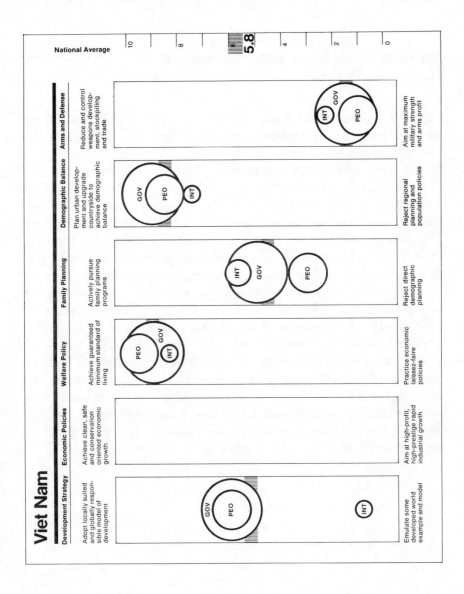

expected to be converted to peaceful uses, but the country's naval forces are to be further strengthened to protect the shoreline and the offshore islands, especially in view of China's territorial claims.

National Goals Gaps in the Resource-Rich Developing World

Algeria

Algeria has considered oil income, and like other oil-rich North African countries, the government controls the revenues. In Algeria the government uses such income to pursue strong ideological goals which are, on most policy issues, remarkably aligned with global goals.

Algeria favors a form of socialism adapted to the Moslem culture. Two characteristics of this form of socialism are a greatly limited impact of profit-motivated business goals on public policies, and a strong commitment to guarantee minimum standards of living. Other aspects of welfare, such as education, medical care, housing, and transportation, also enjoy high priority. The government has support among business, religious, and intellectual groups, but in issues concerned with population growth and distribution it faces a lag in popular perceptions. The broad masses of the Algerian people hold views similar to those in more conservative North African and Mid-East nations.

Algeria's international stance is highlighted by a leadership position among the Group of 77 developing nations, and the country has advocated, among other things, the creation of a new international economic order. The government scores low on arms and defense policy, however, since it aims at a heavy arms build-up. The other strata of the population tend to adopt a more moderate stance.

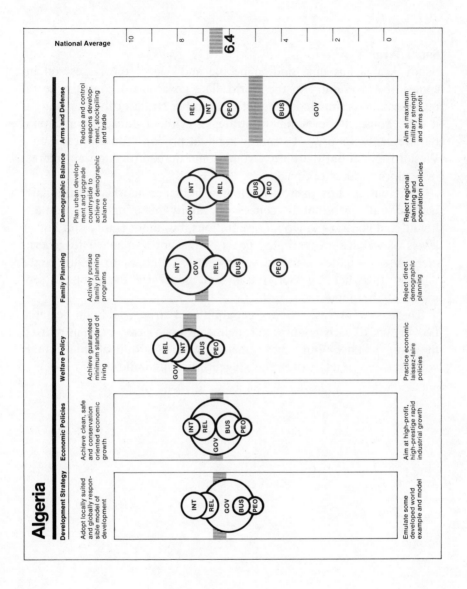

Algeria

Saudi Arabia

Saudi Arabia has nine million people and one of the largest oil incomes of any country in the world. The government controls the oil revenues and is thus independent of all other strata of the population; it can choose its development strategies without concern for capital requirements. Its present strategy is based primarily on the traditional Western model but there are strong domestic controls and an interest in exploring other options.

Religious groups exercise a major influence in this traditionally Islamic state. Moslem influences on family planning are tradition-bound and contrary to global orientations, but more equity and higher levels of welfare are accepted goals of the government. The government also promotes urban development, and hopes to create larger villages to gather together, settle, and modernize the nomadic segments of the population.

The desire for vast military capabilities is strong, and can be satisfied in this oil-rich country through enormous arms purchases from the United States. Only the numerically small group of intellectuals voice serious concern over the staggering arms build-up.

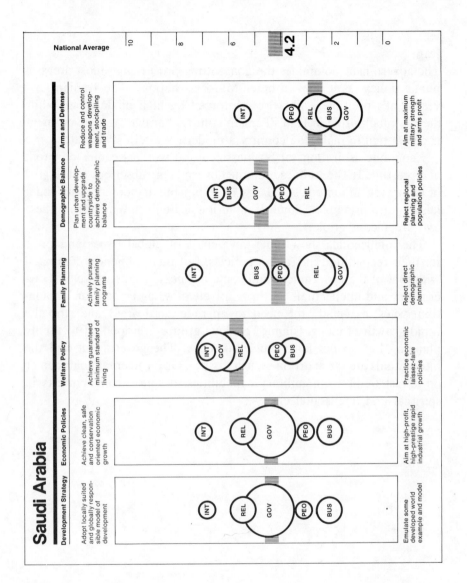

Iran

The government dominates the goal-setting processes in most areas of public policy, as it does in other Mid-East nations. The Iranian government's position is likewise reinforced by high oil income. While there is much pride in Iran's Persian cultural heritage, the government is committed to make the country a modern Western-style state.

Economic aspirations of businessmen and workers center on profit and prestige. In the welfare area the government subscribes to the goal of achieving minimum standards of living but it does not surrender laissez-faire principles. Some Iranian intellectuals now hold that these two are incompatible.

The intellectuals show much awareness of global issues and press for their recognition in Iranian policies. But their influence, compared with that of the government and some business groups, is weak. Government and intellectuals are in relatively close agreement on population issues, especially the need to upgrade rural areas and stop the rapid growth of cities. Islamic religious groups are opposed to family planning but do not have much influence. The government and the intellectuals are far apart on security issues. Governmental goals center on a vast build-up of military capabilities, despite strong protests in spiritual and intellectual circles.

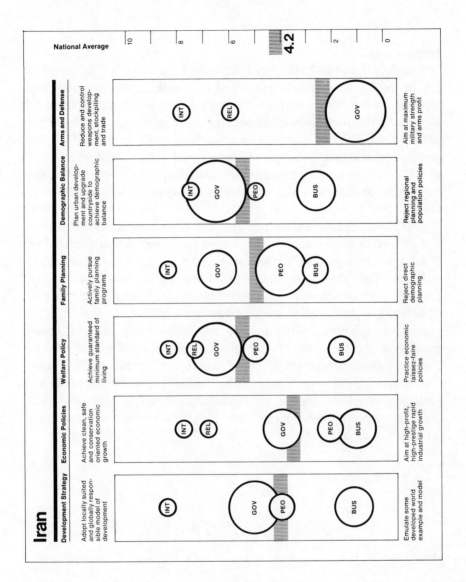

Brazil

In Brazil, as in other Latin American countries, there is a major goals gap in the areas of development and industrialization. Corporations are supported by the government in their efforts to emulate traditional Western patterns of growth. However, many segments of the people divorce themselves from such ambitions. The goals of intellectuals are especially advanced. Since a long-term development strategy has not so far crystallized, the commitment of the various segments of the population to the goals as indicated on the chart is fragile and transitory.

Brazil's insistence on economic growth has also influenced local population and environment policies. Goals for development center, first of all, on creating more employment and securing a higher standard of living. This gives a relatively advanced stance in welfare policy. There is, however, a more short-sighted attitude toward direct family planning, the environment, and the gap between cities and rural areas.

Arms and defense policy focuses on national and regional issues and leaves the responsibility for global security to the superpowers. Current governmental goals reflect the view that Brazil, like other Latin American nations, is responsible neither for global resource and ecological problems nor for world insecurity and can, therefore, concentrate on promoting her own economic development without great concern for global goals.

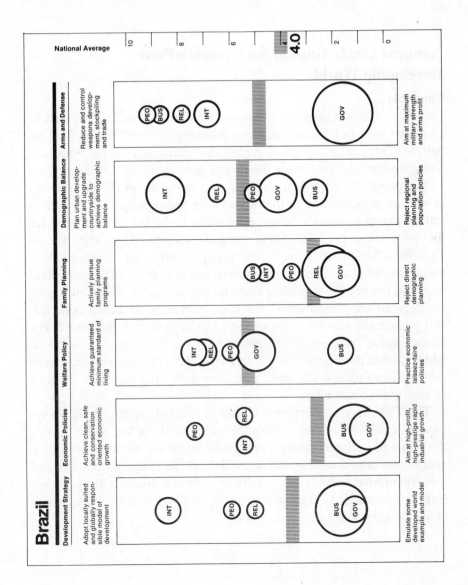

National Goals Gaps in the Resource-Poor Developing World

Colombia

Like most Latin American countries, Colombia is still committed to an active policy of industrialization following the traditional Western pattern. This goal is expressed in most economic areas by both business and government, and causes the largest goals gaps in the country.

The people themselves have somewhat more say in the formulation of welfare policies than in the direction of the economy. Better material standards of life are believed by many to be the best solution for the population problem. Birth control is opposed by the Roman Catholic Church, extreme leftist groups, and some intellectuals—mainly economists. The entrepreneurial upper class favors family planning and the people in general show no aversion to it, although it goes contrary to the "machismo" tradition prevalent in Latin America. But population growth is not expected to drop before the year 2000. Demographic balances are threatened by the rapid growth of cities, which double their populations every ten years. The government insists that it wishes to upgrade rural areas but does little to check the flow of migrants to the cities.

The Colombian government's attitude toward security is fairly typical of Latin American nations. World security is felt to be outside the scope of national control, and goals center on building up a conventionally armed military force, to defend the country's borders and achieve internal stability (especially to counter extreme leftist groups). But most people in Colombia oppose the build-up of arms, being aware of its dangers and costs.

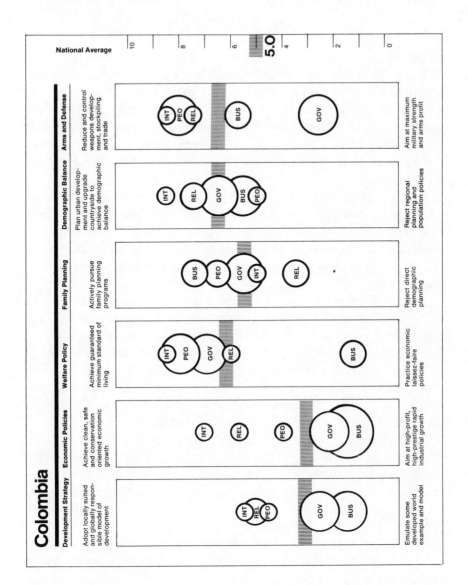

Colombia

Egypt

In Egypt, as in Algeria, the government has a decisive influence in the setting and execution of all major policy goals, although in Egypt the domain of family planning constitutes an exception. The political leadership wishes to combine the advantages of central planning with the efficiency of private enterprise. Economic incentives are provided, but business corporations are not allowed to determine the goals for the economy.

Heavy population growth tends to drive development strategies to whatever channels are immediately available. Corporations seek private capital from oil-rich Arab nations and expertise from developed countries. Developmental models tend to emulate the traditional Western pattern, and show little concern for the environment, conservation, and recycling.

The government would like to provide a reasonable standard of living for all people through assuring minimum wages, old-age security, health services, and free education. It wishes, at the same time, to provide enough incentives to encourage private enterprise, and thus is forced to practice a certain amount of economic laissez-faire. The state's limited resources also constrain its attempts to cope with the population growth rate. Here the activities of nongovernmental (often volunteer) groups are of increasing importance.

Egypt scores highest in the area of demographic balance. Current plans include several large-scale programs to upgrade rural areas and provide water and electricity to all villages. There are many new schools, hospitals, and rural development centers. Nevertheless, the urban populations continue to increase, both in absolute numbers and in relative share of the population.

A national goal of overriding importance is national security. A maximum build-up of Egyptian armed forces is thought necessary to counter the threat of Israeli aggression. Since 1948, expenditure on the military has been the principal constraint on economic development, and is not likely to be significantly reduced in the absence of a lasting settlement of the Arab-Israeli conflict. In this area the government is the sole institution that determines the nation's goals.

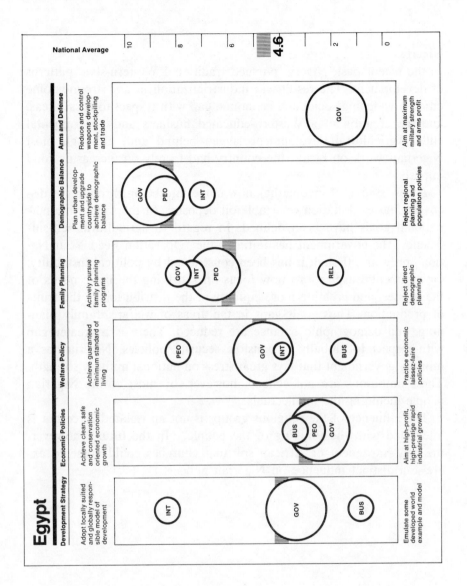

Egypt

	Development Strategy	Economic Policies	Welfare Policy	Family Planning	Demographic Balance	Arms and Defense
	Adopt locally suited and globally responsible model of development	Achieve clean, safe and conservation oriented economic growth	Achieve guaranteed minimum standard of living	Actively pursue family planning programs	Plan urban development and upgrade countryside to achieve demographic balance	Reduce and control weapons development, stockpiling and trade
	Emulate some developed world example and model	Aim at high-profit, high-prestige rapid industrial growth	Practice economic laissez-faire policies	Reject direct demographic planning	Reject regional planning and population policies	Aim at maximum military strength and arms profit

National Average: 4.6

Nigeria

In the recent past, Nigeria pursued traditional Western-style patterns of development. The result was industrialization in and around some cities, a widening social and economic gap with respect to rural areas, and the creation of a Western-educated business and governmental elite. Agricultural development lagged behind and, although most Nigerians work on farms, the country had to rely on increasing food imports.

A new source of income has now come into being through the discovery and exploitation of sizable oil deposits. At the same time new national goals have been defined. In regard to agricultural self-sufficiency, the government has initiated the "Operation Feed Your Nation" program, though it has been constrained by political instability. Governmental aspirations now focus on satisfying the basic needs of the masses, and creating more equality in the distribution of the fruits of production. Thus goals gaps in the areas of welfare, family planning, and demographic balance are reduced. There is a greater gap with respect to globally responsible security policies. Nigeria has a military government that lays great stress on national military strength. These ambitions are not echoed, however, by most of the Nigerian people including the intellectuals.

The influence of the religious groups is not an isolated force but is integrated with the thinking of the people. (In the future, however, the new movement of African spiritual churches could come to exercise a distinct influence on Nigerian policies.)

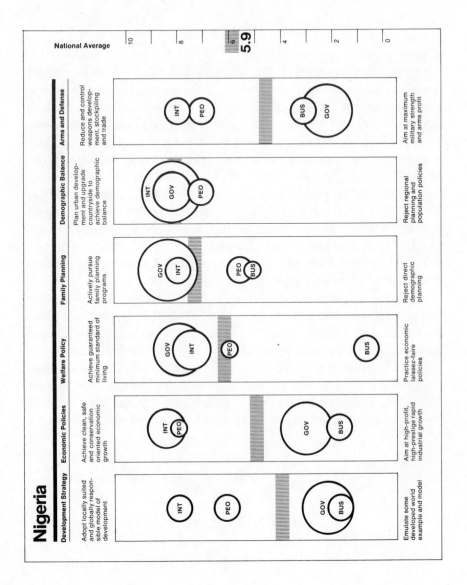

Ghana

The government dominates the setting of Ghana's goals in all relevant areas, although the country's intellectuals have a say in the area of demographic balance, and business corporations influence goals in economic and welfare areas. The government takes an advanced position on all issues, except arms and defense. Development policy, as in many other African nations, is now centered more on equality and self-sufficiency than on overall economic growth. Since Ghana is heavily dependent on the export of a cash crop—cocoa—diversification of agriculture and food self-reliance are major goals. Industries are to reorient their methods to employ more people and provide basic goods, rather than cater to the demands of the small elite. The latter is felt to have been alienated from the country's traditions and culture, and in need of reeducation.

Pollution and resource concerns are outweighed by the demand for industrial goods. But soil and water conservation are recognized goals, as well as reforestation; the drought in the Sahel region has created a new concern for environmental issues. The government is now vigorously promoting family planning programs, which provide education and advice. The government still favors building up the national military forces, but both the broad masses of the people and the intellectuals perceive a greater need to spend money on development.

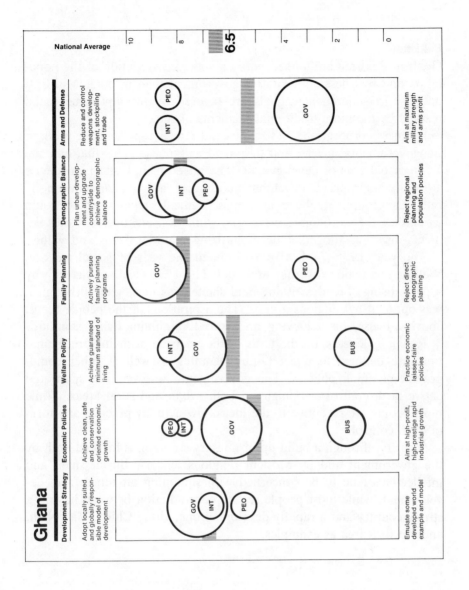

Ghana

	Development Strategy	Economic Policies	Welfare Policy	Family Planning	Demographic Balance	Arms and Defense
	Adopt locally suited and globally responsible model of development	Achieve clean, safe and conservation oriented economic growth	Achieve guaranteed minimum standard of living	Actively pursue family planning programs	Plan urban development and upgrade countryside to achieve demographic balance	Reduce and control weapons development, stockpiling and trade
	Emulate some developed world example and model	Aim at high-profit, high-prestige rapid industrial growth	Practice economic laissez-faire policies	Reject direct demographic planning	Reject regional planning and population policies	Aim at maximum military strength and arms profit

National Average 6.5

Pakistan

Goals in Pakistan are influenced by a wider cross-section of the population and by a less authoritative government than in other Mid-East nations. In general, new goals are favored by the government and resisted by the more traditional segments of society.

Business corporations and intellectual circles represent the modern nongovernmental layers, and they tend to espouse goals that emulate Western patterns of development. The government's efforts to devise a locally appropriate developmental model are hampered even by religious groups. Intellectuals oppose radical changes which could jeopardize their economic privileges, while conservative religious elements insist on altogether deemphasizing material needs and values.

The year 1976–77 has been declared the year of social welfare. Welfare is a major governmental goal. The 1970 election was won by a party using "bread, clothing, and shelter" as its slogan, although it was opposed by religious groups. The aspirations of the people focus, above all else, on achieving an assured minimum living standard.

Religious leaders, on the basis of the doctrine of divine predestination, are inclined to reject family planning as well as other demographic-planning policies. The government, however, has sponsored active birth control campaigns in both urban and rural areas. While most people are receptive to the ideas, few actually practice any form of birth control.

Security, through a build-up of military strength, is favored both by the government and by Moslem religious leaders. Businessmen and intellectuals tend to be concerned with siphoning off funds from development, while most people see no contradiction between having a strong country and a rapidly developing one, citing China, Viet Nam, and North Korea as examples.

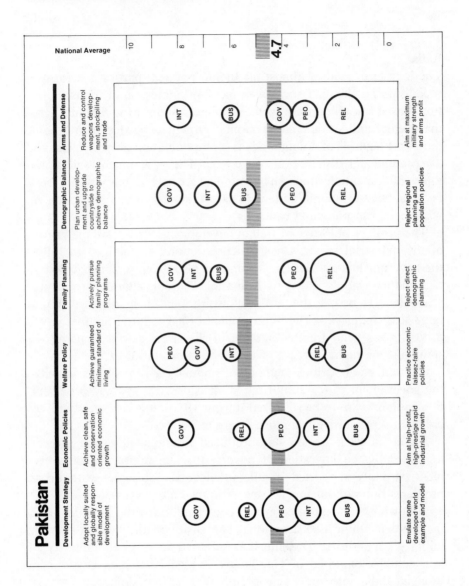

Pakistan

National Average 4.7

India

The long-term goal of almost all Indian political parties is a form of socialism. To this end the government promotes rapid industrialization, based initially on a mixed economic system. Most Indians agree that steady and sustainable economic growth is needed to overcome the worst legacies of colonial days: high population growth rates, and a most unequal distribution of income. The government and a majority of the intellectuals share similar goals, but business interests favor a freer economic system, while religious groups are taken up with their own parochial concerns.

The primary objective of Indian development strategy is the growth of the industrial sector. Business corporations are obliged to follow the government's policies. Importance is also given to small-scale cottage industries, advocated by Mahatma Gandhi, although rural programs tend to be overshadowed by aspirations for highly mechanized large-scale industries. The improvement of agricultural productivity is a continuing goal. Limited success in this area is wiped out by the simultaneous rapid increase of the population, however.

The failure of various methods of population control has impelled the government to try authoritative measures. From four to ten million Indians were to be sterilized during 1976 alone. A variety of coercive and persuasive techniques were to be used.

Rapid industrialization has produced unregulated urban growth, increased by the migration of poverty-stricken masses. The government, strongly supported by the intellectuals, struggles with urban problems but without much hope of immediate success.

Following an unexpected armed confrontation with China in 1962, there is something like a national consensus on the need for strong military capabilities. Dissenters are limited to a small minority of intellectuals composed of Gandhians and pacifists. The government brought India into the nuclear club with strong domestic support, arguing that it is unsafe for the country to be militarily weak as long as her neighbors are highly armed.

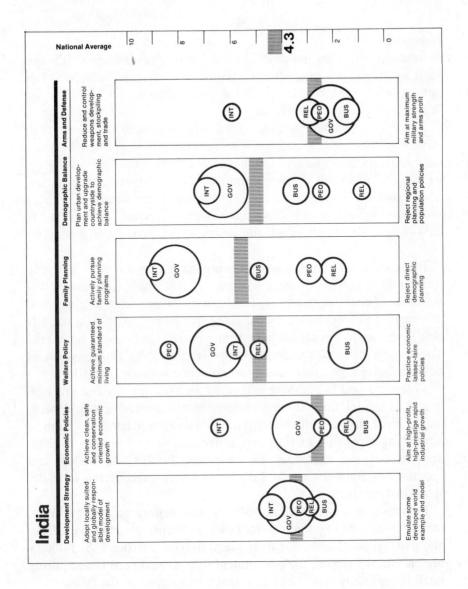

Indonesia

Indonesian goals are mainly dictated by the government, although local scientists and intellectuals exercise considerable influence. The latter, however, are often U.S.-trained technocrats who insist on Western modes of development.

There are considerable goals gaps with respect to developmental, economic, and welfare policies. The government, supported by business interests, strives for capital-intensive high-technology industry, with capital and skills training imported from the developed countries. The export of oil, minerals, and the produce of plantations is to finance such development. More forward-looking policies are adopted in the field of agriculture, where self-sufficiency in rice production is a major goal.

Environmental considerations do not have a major role in policy formulation. The government recognizes great inequalities in the distribution of income, but policies to combat them tend to consist of presidential exhortations for officials to live more simply, and for foreign investors to engage in joint ventures with Indonesian nationals. The leaders of local religious groups (mainly Moslem) have more advanced views, but their ability to influence policies is small.

Voluntary family planning programs are widespread, and are supported by the intellectuals and tolerated by the government. Indonesia makes great efforts to distribute the population over her many islands, attempting especially to shift people from Java to Sumatra, Borneo, and Celebes. But the programs are poorly funded and staffed, and spontaneous immigration to Java most likely exceeds the officially sponsored emigration.

Indonesia is a member of ASEAN and maintains a large army, mainly to control regional revolts (such as occurred in the West Irian and Portuguese Timor, for example). Relying on the U.S. military presence in the region, the government sees no real need for acquiring nuclear capability now, but keeps that option open in the future.

The Current Goals Gap: A Brief Diagnosis of the Root Causes

In every country in the world, people expect more from the future than the past has accorded them. While they are skeptical about the future of the world as a whole, they are confident that their own personal futures will be brighter. Popular expectations within the international

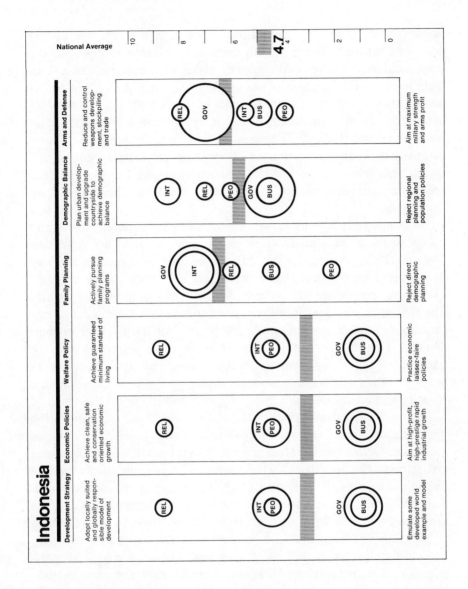

community, while more moderate and selective than in past decades, are still high.

In the affluent countries of North America, Western Europe, and Japan, most people are worried about inflation, unemployment, and the high cost of living. They want to improve further their material standard of life. In the developing countries of Latin America, Africa, and Asia, the majority worries about survival itself: The greatest single concern is getting enough food. Nowhere, it seems, are people poor and satisfied. While wealth does not guarantee happiness, the typical citizens of developed countries claim to be better satisfied with their lives than the people of developing regions. (According to the first Gallup world survey, those most satisfied with their quality of life are the North Americans, followed by Western Europeans, Latin Americans, and Africans. The least satisfied are the people of Southeast Asia.) At the same time the poorer people expect more of the future than those who are better off; Africans and Latin Americans are more optimistic about great improvements in their lives than Europeans.

Economic security and growth, steady and gainful employment, and access to the goods and services required for survival are dominant and universally shared concerns. In the eyes of most people, the way to achieve them is to have more and bigger industries in their country. The poorer people are, the more they want national industrial growth. The richest do not want it in their home communities and want it only moderately in their nation, while the poor want it anywhere in their country. The affluent young oppose further industrialization, but the underprivileged young favor it. To the affluent industrial smokestacks mean pollution and inhumane work; to the poor they mean economic security and access to highly desired goods and living conditions.

Few still value traditional patterns of rural living—although the youth cultures and the technology-saturated citizens of rich countries are rediscovering such values as alternatives to those of industrial civilization. But in Africa, where almost 80 percent of the people live in rural areas, 70 percent would like to live in the city. Also, in Asia and Latin America the poorer and younger people are, the more they want to break from their rural roots and settle in a metropolis.

Normally, governments and businesses attempt to satisfy people's expectations by promoting rapid economic growth through industrialization, and the creation of bigger and better cities. But governments, businessmen, and the more informed segments of the general public now recognize that there are limits to rapid economic development, as well as to the size and livability of cities. Since it would be inhumane and impractical to attempt to depress people's expectations, public policies vacillate uneasily between trying to promote further economic growth through more investment in bigger industries and larger cities, and pursuing alternative goals. But only a few governments, businesses, intellectual and religious groups, and popular forces have hit upon and adopted goals that correspond to the long-term requirements of the global community. The difference between today's goals and the globally required alternatives is what constitutes the current goals gap.

The root causes of this gap are mistaken expectations and beliefs that traditional policies can produce conditions that will fulfill today's basic hopes and needs. For example, people want rapid economic growth through overall industrialization in the expectation that this will improve their lot; governments want it in the expectation that it will raise the overall standard of living in their country. People want many children—the desired number is still six in Africa and more than four in Latin America—in the expectation that their numerous offspring will relieve their burdens and assist them in old age, and the remaining pronatalist governments want a larger population in the expectation that this will contribute to national wealth and power. People consent to have their hard-earned tax monies spent on expensive military hardware, believing that this will contribute to their personal safety, and governments invest in arms and the military on the assumption that they thereby strengthen national security and assure the grandeur of their country. The desire for urban living, for profits, for material goods, and for "modernism" in general is similarly motivated. Environmental, resource, long-term, and global issues are discounted, or postponed to some later time, in the belief that this will not really prejudice the attainment of such basic goals as economic security, employment, and a rising material standard of living.

Mistaken goals spurred by legitimate expectations need to be changed; the chances of fulfilling such expectations need to be increased. This does not call for "changing human nature," for destroying public institutions and private national and multinational corporations, and for overthrowing governments. It calls first of all for a recognition, by people, businesses, and governments, that their expectations are not likely to be fulfilled through the policies they currently adopt, but that there are other strategies which have far greater chances of success.

Alternative strategies include greater concern with the quality of life than with quantitative material-economic growth in the rich world; more attention to appropriate modes of development in the poor world; and a better-functioning international economic order to assist in creating a more equitable pattern of development. Such strategies call for the conservation of finite sources and stocks of energy and other natural resources, for developing safe and economical alternatives, and not being seduced into Faustian bargains with dangerous technologies. Alternative strategies require more efficient food production, storage, and distribution systems, and replacing reliance on arms for national security with reliance on trustworthy international institutions. The legitimate expectations of the world's people could be fulfilled through such alternative strategies, but not through a blind pursuit of traditional methods.

But the specification, adoption, and achievement of globally responsible long-term alternative strategies presuppose a much wider basis of international cooperation than we have at present. It is not enough that people realize that their current goals are not likely to satisfy their expectations; they need also to recognize that the feasible alternatives call for a new sense of mutual trust and solidarity in the global community. People and governments must dare to venture together on the new roads which none could travel alone. For the international community as a whole, the old saying has acquired the force of a categorical imperative: We either hang together, or hang separately.

A new world order will come about when the people of all nations demand of their leaders that they be given a constructive role in building the shared human future; when a new global ethos emerges based on trust and solidarity; when a new standard of humanism crystallizes as the norm of conduct in all major areas of public policy.

Many doubt today that mankind is capable of breaking through the current inner limits inherent in short-term and narrowly self-interested goals. Many are skeptical that egoism, chauvinism, and short-term thinking can be cast aside. We do not share this view. We have examined the major value and belief systems of mankind and found that they contain the seeds of the needed humanism—that they are capable of overcoming humanity's current inner limits and inspiring the growth of world solidarity. But we shall let the reader judge for himself. Here follow our studies of the world order potentials of the great religions, and of the major modern ethics, world views, and alternative cultures.

Part III: Breaking through the Inner Limits

Global goals, as we have seen, are intrinsically achievable. They would push back or eliminate many of the outer limits presently constraining human growth and development, and open new horizons for the world community. But wide goals gaps persist, and it is not clear whether global goals will be actually achieved. Mankind could remain constrained by the current limits inherent in today's short-range and narrowly self-interested goals. These inner limits are critical; they need to be overcome. Perspectives of thinking and action must be enlarged to take in the global and the long-term dimension. To this end the rapid growth of solidarity among diffferent peoples and with coming generations is imperative.

In the third and final part of this Report we review mankind's moral and intellectual resources with respect to the growth of world solidarity. We then consider possible "scenarios" of a world solidarity revolution, and the kind of world that could result. By this method we will have complemented our descriptive survey of current goals, and our normative assessment of desirable goals, with an evaluation of the ways and means of transforming the former in the direction of the latter: the strategy for breaking through mankind's current inner limits and opening up new horizons for the global community.

Chapter 17

The Great Religions and
World Solidarity

In this chapter we assess the potential role of the great religions in breaking through mankind's constraining inner limits and inspiring the birth of higher levels of solidarity. We recognize the great influence of the religions in the contemporary world. In spite of the erosive effects of modern science and lifestyles, and despite the spread of atheistic ideologies and the secular ethics and principles of business and government, the great majority of the people in every nation outside the Communist bloc and Japan appears to believe in God or a universal spirit, and claims to belong to a church, religious group, or faith.* Hence apart even from the complex theologies of the world religions, the forms of allegiance and value they inspire constitute a major force in the world. This force cannot be neglected when assessing the future, even if it is difficult to express quantitatively and with precision.

In the studies to follow we analyze only the religions which influence vast numbers of people though we recognize, at the same time, that several smaller religious groups exercise important and relevant forms of influence (the principal aim of the Baha'i faith, for example,

---

* This was a conclusion derived from the results of the first Gallup world opinion survey, conducted in 1976.

369

is precisely world unification). We review in turn Judaism, Christianity, Islam, Hinduism, Buddhism, the Chinese tradition (Confucianism and Taoism), and the African tribal religions.

Judaism and the Growth of World Solidarity

Although contemporary Jews are few in number compared with the followers of the other great religions, they occupy an important position in the management of issues of international scope. Jews participate in business, civic, and governmental leadership in several major countries. They also have their own state, Israel, which plays a crucial role in the balance of power in the Middle East and, as a result, in the world.

At the time of Christ an estimated six million Jews lived in the Roman Empire. By the beginning of the nineteenth century the world's Jewish population had shrunk to perhaps three million. By 1939, however, it had grown to eighteen million. Six million Jews were killed in the Nazi holocoust and today there are a few more than fourteen million Jews in the world. Nearly six million live in the United States, three million in Israel, and more than two and a half million in the Soviet Union. The rest are widely scattered (Britain, France, Canada, South America, South Africa).

The religion of this relatively small but influential group of people is Judaism. It is not religion of abstract theology, but a concrete guide to action which even nonpracticing Jews find compelling.

For Judaism it is in history that man experiences God. Jewish history, as the model for all human history, is seen as an ongoing series of revelatory experiences in which the deity reveals to his people the various aspects of his relationship to all his creatures. The Hebrew scriptures contain what Judaism considers the "revelation-history" of the continuing relationship between God and man. Beginning with the divine creation, God's plan unfolds year after year, steadily progressing, despite repeated resistance on man's part, toward the final fulfillment of the divine purpose. Man's proper role on earth is the advancement of God's purposes in history. Judaism sees man as a partner with God in the ongoing work of creation. The exalted Jewish conception of man as "the image of God" calls man to the creative human tasks which reflect the labors of the Divine Creator himself. This "creation theology" is central to the Jewish world view. One cannot speak of the God of Israel apart from the history of Israel, since it is through the experiences which make up that history that the Jew comes to know his God.

Jewish tradition is traced to Abraham who, according to the Bible, was commissioned by God to be, together with his descendants, God's chosen witnesses.

> Now the Lord had said unto Abram, Get thee out of thy country, and from thy kindred, and from thy father's house, unto a land that I will shew thee: And I will make of thee a great nation . . . and in thee shall all families of the earth be blessed. (Genesis 12:1–3, King James Version)

This passage reveals the two sides of an oft-misunderstood conception that goes to the heart of Judaism: the "chosenness" of Israel. Here God is seen as the founder of the Jewish people and as their guide to a new land which he will bestow upon them. Later in the Scriptures, God is seen as enjoining upon his people a system of special regulations designed to maintain their religious separation from other nations. But here, in God's call to Abraham, we find the total conception of the election of Israel, including both the particularistic and universal aspects without which the idea is incomplete. It is clearly stated that the particular aspects of the commission (separate peoplehood, separate land) exist for the sake of the universal witness to all mankind ("in thee shall all the families of the earth be blessed"). Israel must remain "a peculiar people" so as to remember its worldwide redemptive task. Israel is not called out of all relationship to humankind in general, but into a new relationship in which Israelites must be "a light to the nations," moral teachers of all mankind. There is no assumption anywhere in the Bible or in Judaism that this exalted task implies any superiority on the part of individual Jews. The commission comes from God and does not depend on human talents or abilities. The people of Israel are no better than any other people and, in fact, must be constantly trained for and reminded of the enormity of their mission. All Jewish history is viewed by Jews as an ongoing series of God-inspired events in which God refines his people for their sacred task.

In the 1930s and 1940s, Hitler brought Jews into agonizing confrontation with radical evil of a kind they had tried to forget had ever existed. The immediate result was the widespread acceptance of Zionism by almost all Jews, the vast majority of whom had rejected it as pessimistic and parochial prior to the holocaust in which six million Jews died. One-third of the world's Jews, all but a mere handful of Europe's Jewish population, had been wiped out in less than three years. Only the Zionists had spoken of such a possibility, and even they had failed to envisage the enormity of the catastrophe. Now they were proven to have been tragically right. All debate over their program of Jewish nationalism ceased. There was no longer time to discuss the political versus the religious interpretation of Judaism. The acceptance of Zionism by world Jewry did not indicate a general adoption of the Zionists' secularized and politicized view of Jewish existence; it simply meant that Jews now almost unanimously recognized the need for a refuge, a place of safety, a true home for the pitiful remnants of European Jewry. The holocaust gave the descendants of the eighteenth- and nineteenth-century universalist Jews a new ethnic self-consciousness and a new emphasis on Jewish self-help. Universalist sentiment was still central in the Jewish world view, but it was now combined with an acute concern for Jewish survival—for the continuity of the particular community which bore the universal message.

Today, as in Abraham's day, Jews combine concern for the general (the world community) and the particular (the Jewish people). The optimism of the past two centuries is generally viewed by postholocaust Jews as touchingly naive. A new sense of the fragility of life, and the transiency of all temporal conditions regardless of how secure and permanent they may seem, today reflects the ancient prophetic view. The messianic spirit still motivates Jews to take leading roles in the ongoing struggle for justice and for a more humane society, but both the prophetic view and the holocaust are seen as warnings concerning the illusory nature of the belief in easy and inevitable progress. Science and technology continue to attract leading Jews, but many of them are the first to speak of the dangers of a science without humane ideals, and a technology not directed to the task of building a just society. Judaism continues to teach the universal brotherhood of man and the infinite value of every human life in the eyes of God, but it demands the respect of mankind for the right of the Jewish people to life, and respect for their integrity as a religious and cultural community. The Jewish emphasis on the life of the mind and spirit continues to shape contemporary Judaism and to lead large numbers of Jews into the study of the arts and humanities. But there is no longer the bland assumption that such studies will always be humane; constant vigilance is required in the academic as well as the general community, together with a firm commitment to law and civilized restraint.

There is no call anywhere in Jewish tradition to convert the world to Judaism. Many of the laws of Sinai are for Jews and Jews alone. Sabbath observance, abstention from forbidden foods, laws of family purity, these are spiritual disciplines enjoined upon the Jewish people as constant reminders of their mission to the world, and of the special nature of Israel as a holy nation, sanctified to God's eternal purposes. The Jewish "mission" to mankind is strictly ethical in nature. Since the face of God is hidden from all men, no religious system can embody all truth. There is no *true* faith or theology. Therefore respect for other religious systems is essential to the Jewish world view. However, Judaism is insistent on the universal application of moral principles of social justice and human dignity, and on the fulfillment of the divine commission to bring the knowledge of these ideals to all men. What is always recognized is that different societies can realize these ideals in different ways, in accordance with their own traditions and history.

Christianity and the Growth of World Solidarity

Christianity evolved from Judaism in the teachings of Jesus of Nazareth, and in the beliefs which sprang up concerning his personal significance in and beyond history. After an initial period of persecution by the Romans, the Emperor Constantine made Christianity the official religion of the Roman Empire, and it became the established religion of Western and Eastern Europe. It spread with the extension of European civilization to North and South America, Asia, Africa, and Australia. Its current influence, direct and indirect, is extremely widespread. It underlies the morals and world views of statesmen, businessmen, artists, and scientists, and influences their decisions. The policies of organized Christian Churches have worldwide impact (see Chapter 11). Current emphases in Christian thought thus have a crucial influence on the hearts and minds of many whose words and actions help decide the fate of mankind.

There is continuity of history and belief between Judaism and Christianity. Both are monotheistic, and Christians see themselves as fulfilling the Jewish people's historic mission to the world. Jesus did not think of himself as founding a new religion. He did, however, think of himself as "the Anointed One" (the Christ) of God, the Messiah who would usher in the Kingdom of God. To his contemporaries this event would mean the rule of God over the whole earth. It would also mean the freeing of the Jewish people from Roman domination.

In the ferment of the times many others had put themselves forward as the Messiah and had been crucified by the Romans, a fate reserved for slaves, political offenders, and insurrectionists. Jesus, who left no written records and no organization but a small and dismayed band of nonmilitary followers, might have been forgotten as were these others had it not been for the quality of his life and the conception he preached and demonstrated of the marks of the Kingdom of God.

The heart of Jesus' preaching was the oft-reiterated but sometimes forgotten message of the prophets that laid stress not on the tribal Lord of Israel, but on a universal God of one relationship to all men. Jesus' theology was not cosmology or metaphysics. It was ethical throughout. He set forth God as the most certain fact of man's experience, as simple reality accessible to everyone. The universality of his message did not have to be proclaimed as a dogma. God was continually present to all men. His fatherly love, his transcendent righteousness, his mercy, and his goodness shone like the sun on the just and the unjust.

Jesus summed up his teaching in a call for supreme love to God, and for the same kind of love for our fellow beings as we have for ourselves. He was known as a friend of outcasts. Oneness with God, he taught, is service to fellowman. The marks of the Messianic kingdom were not rank and glory, but helping roles and self-sacrifice for the good of others. What was more, the citizens of the Kingdom of God were those who did the will of the Father, whether their theology was correct or not. Thus, according to Jesus, the ethical thrust of the Jewish tradition found its highest expression in self-sacrificing love.

Jesus knew himself to be utterly in tune with the mind of God as he conceived it. His utter trust in God, even in the face of the crucifixion which he knew to be the fate of all who proclaimed themselves as the Messiah, was awesome.

Although stress is laid on the divinity of the Christ, the general consensus among Christians has always been that Jesus, the man, was also fully and truly human. This means that he was a man of his times, sharing the political and social perceptions, hopes and expectations of his people. He expected that the Kingdom of God would be ushered in through himself, as the Messiah. But it was not to be by leading an army, rather by offering himself as the suffering servant spoken of by the prophet Isaiah (Chapter 53), and the first to die in the confrontation between the Kingdom of God and the kingdom of the world—symbolized at that time by Rome. The crucifixion of Jesus ended, however, as other crucifixions had before his—except for the claim that began to be made shortly afterward, that Jesus was seen alive by many on various occasions after his death.

It is entirely in keeping with the Messianic climate of Jesus' times to maintain, as many do, that Jesus himself, as well as his followers both before and after the crucifixion, expected the immanent, direct intervention of God on the contemporary political scene. The resurrection experiences convinced the disciples, and through them a fast-growing number of others, that God had indeed intervened significantly in history through the person and the work of Jesus, that he was indeed the living Christ, that they could still be in communion with him, and that they must spread the good news about him as widely as possible. They were to do so quickly, for the end of the age was thought to be close at hand. Jesus would then return to become in fact what he was already in spirit, savior and king of all.

Christians began calling themselves the New Israel, and claimed to be in a new covenant relationship with God. As time went on, and the physical return of Jesus was less emphasized, his teachings and the events of his life were committed to writing. The most authoritative among these accounts, together with the most valued letters and historical writings of the early Christians, became the books of the New Testament (new covenant), as distinguished from the ancient Hebrew writings, which Christians called the Old Testament. The Old and New Testaments together comprise the Christian Bible.

Whatever non-Christians are to make of the many and varied interpretations of Jesus' life and work that have been made by theologians and philosophers from the beginning of the Christian era to the present day, there are two things worth noting in connection with the universality of the Christian message and its relationship to the growth of world solidarity.

First, there is the staying power of Christianity as a universal religion, relevant to all men without distinction of nation, race, or caste. Christianity, although it has mainly flourished in Europe and in those nations founded by Europeans, has been widely accepted by varied races in very different stages of culture, and has maintained itself through many centuries in lands where transformations in political structure, social conditions, science, and philosophy have been numerous and extreme. There is no inherent obstacle to it in the Asian mind. Its founders were Hebrew. Its original writings were in the common international language of that time, Greek. But its current influence has extended far beyond those who have formally embraced the faith. Gandhi was a notable example. If the Christian Churches begin to stress world solidarity as an essential element of the Christian world view, the impact could be very great. They need not hold world solidarity to be conditional upon the conversion of all men to formal adherence to the Christian faith. In the Gospel according to St. Matthew (Chapter 8) Jesus is reported as saying, "Not every one that saith unto me, Lord, Lord, shall enter into the kingdom of heaven, but he that doeth the will of my Father which is in heaven."

This leads to the second point worth noting, the persistence of the ethical emphasis in all forms of Christianity. To be at one with God is to have the mind of Christ, who went about doing good. The marks of the Kingdom of God are justice and mercy, forgiveness, sharing, self-sacrifice on behalf of all who are in physical or spiritual need, and brotherhood with no distinctions of class or race. "By this shall all men know that ye are my disciples, if ye have love, one to another." (John 8:35)

Christianity has great potentiality for extending its community of brotherhood to all people, regardless of their formal adherence to any given religion, or to none. As we have seen in Chapter 11, the Christian Churches are making remarkable progress in overcoming ancient feuds among themselves as well as with non-Christians and even atheists, and encouraging the growth of a new humanism which embraces all people. The World Council of Churches, with its 285 member churches in all parts of the world, examines issues of global relevance, and has come out with recommendations for creating a just and sustainable world society. It has set itself the task of encouraging the promotion of world peace with justice and freedom; the development of international law and effective international institutions; respect for the observance of human rights and fundamental freedoms; the international control and reduction of armaments; the furtherance of economic justice through international economic cooperation; acceptance by all nations of the obligation to promote to the utmost the welfare of all peoples and the development of free political institutions; participation in the struggle against all forms of racism; the advance toward self-government in still-dependent territories; and the promotion of social, cultural, educational, and humanitarian enterprises internationally.

The similar humanitarian world concerns of the Roman Catholic Church, and the individual initiatives of particular Christian Churches are moving Christians everywhere toward global consciousness and world solidarity. There are also individual Christians, such as Martin Luther King, Jr., the Berrigan brothers, and Father Drinan in the United States, and Dom Helder Camera and Father Camillo Torres in Latin America, who have worked inside or outside the mainstream of society, and have become leaders and—in some cases—martyrs to the cause of great social movements.

Islam and the Growth of World Solidarity

Islam, as a "positive" or historical religion, began in Arabia in the seventh century. Subsequently it spread across three continents, extending from the Arabian Peninsula and northeastern Africa all the way to Iran and the valley of the Indus in the east, and even beyond into Indonesia and China. In the west it reached into Spain, Morocco, and western Africa. Islam is the dominant religion in most countries of the Middle East and North Africa. There are perhaps 600 million Moslems in the world. They include some of the wealthiest people in the world, as well as vast poverty-stricken masses.

"Islam," in an empirical sense, is a noun that denotes the totality of religious, juridical, political, economic, social, and cultural experiences, expressions, and conceptualizations which have developed through the centuries where the doctrines of Islam have held sway. Any theological or sociological definition of Islam should keep the door open for an almost limitless variety of expressions.

Islam as an empirical or positive religion is as broad and many-faceted as any other human phenomenon. If one focuses, however, on the classical sources, one finds a dominant affirmation in the Qur'an (Koran), which provides a normative concept of Islam as religion. This affirmation is, "There is no God but He, the Powerful, the Wise." The Qur'an also states, "Religion with God is Islam [submission to the divine will]." Allah is the primary symbol of the Ultimate, the One, indissoluble and absolute. Allah is reality itself—that which matters, and has consequences in any and every situation.

Yet the symbol expressing the Absolute is relative, i.e., Allah is an Arabic name which has had specific associations outside the Arabic context. The name Allah is an example of the historically conditioned status of every revelation and every symbol.

This is to say that Islam, like all the great religious traditions, expresses itself simultaneously as *the* religion and as *a* religion. As *a* religion it makes specific historical claims: the holy language for Moslems is the Arabic of the Qur'an; Mohammed is the last of the prophets; to become a Moslem one must sincerely recite the *shahada* (testimony), "There is no god but Allah, and Mohammed is his apostle." These are examples of the concrete historical expression of religious experience and revelation.

The Qur'an itself, however, provides the basis for understanding Islam as religion in a generic sense. Islam means devotion as well as submission; it is the affirmation that there is finally only One, beside whom there is no other.

Islam, as religion in a generic sense, is based on the fundamental principle of *tawhid,* which means "unity, affirmation of unity." Unity, as theological doctrine, involves the religious witness, "There is no god but Allah." As a theological and metaphysical principle it proposes that reality is one and that man and world are only provisionally real in relation to it.

Tawhid is also a method of integrating human existence. The dominant form of *tawhid* in Islam is law, or *shari'a* (also "way," or "path"). This is the outward or exoteric form of devotion. The form that complements the legal way is Sufism (*tasawwuf*). This is the inward or esoteric form.

Shari'a, as the law of Islam, has an inevitably exclusivist tendency: It emphasizes the identity, special role, and prerogatives of the Moslem historical tradition. The *shari'a* attests that all human beings are sacred in the sense of being creatures of God, and that all were made to live in harmonious relationships. On the other hand, as the law of an historical religion, *shari'a* has justified various sorts of discrimination. Only Moslems may play a full political role in an Islamic state. "Scriptuaries," however, are allowed many privileges. Scriptuaries, or "people of the book," are Jews, Christians, and all those who are viewed as fulfilling two basic religious requirements: affirming that God or reality is one; and having a sacred scripture.

While *shari'a* represents an exclusivist tendency in Islam, this tendency is moderated by the spiritual way of the Sufis, or *tasawwuf.* The relation and tension between *shari'a* and *tasawwuf* originate in the

Qur'an and the experiences of Mohammed. Mohammed was both a legislator and a mystical prophet. It is recounted of Mohammed that he did not "begrudge the Unseen," and that "Surely he saw of the signs of his Lord the greatest!" (Qur'an)

Sufism, although historically afflicted with occasional charlatans, and often riddled with superstition in some of its later forms, expresses the universal, generic basis of Islam that connects with the quest for meaning in other religions, East and West. The Sufi journey is a search for perfection of soul, for the coincidence of opposites, for rest in God and completeness—all universals in the history of religion.

The tension in Islam between the universal and the particular, the inclusivist and the exclusivist, is also exemplified in relation to the Qur'an. The Qur'an is considered by Moslems to be the last of God's scriptures, just as Mohammed is the seal of the prophets. It is said to be incomparable, superb, majestic. One must read it or hear it in Arabic to be an authentic Moslem (whether one understands the Arabic is secondary). In these and other respects, the Moslem doctrine of scripture is exoteric and exclusivist. There is, however, a fundamental and universalist religious affirmation at the base of the Moslem idea of scripture: that the Qur'an, along with all sacred writings, comes from the Heavenly Book.

The Heavenly Book (literally, "mother of the book"—*umm al-kitab*) is a metaphor of the wisdom of God from which revelations were granted to Mohammed. This Heavenly Book functions not only as a validation of the Qur'an as sacred scripture, but also as an indication of how Islam is related to other traditions. All true or prophetic religion is based on disclosures from the Heavenly Book.

As a metaphor of divine wisdom and providence, the Heavenly Book is rooted in ancient Near Eastern religious traditions. It stems from the context of the ancient Babylonian Book of Destinies, which established decrees of fate for each coming year in the Babylonian New Year Festival. This Book of Destinies is reflected in many Old Testament references to a Book of Life, in which all human deeds and world events are written. The mythical idea of a celestial archetype is also found in religious movements preceding Islam in the Middle East, such as Manichaeism and Elkesaitism. (It is a mistaken notion that Judaism and Christianity were originally the sole, or even the dominant, religious influences upon Islam.)

The Qur'an incorporates the archetypal figure of the Heavenly Book as a way of expressing the relation of the Qur'an to other scriptures, and of Islam to other religions. All true religion is disclosure of the divine wisdom, and the human response of submission and devotion to God.

Islam, like other monotheistic religions, is informed by a message of the end, of God's judgment, of "the Day." Eschatology is mythology that speaks of the end of history. Islamic eschatology offers a vision of an ultimate community of being. The images of this ideal community are those of a garden (commonly called Paradise), abundant fruit, wine mixed with camphor and ginger, and the light of God shed over all the righteous. God, man, nature, and society constitute a quaternity of being, reconciled in perfect harmony.

This ultimate community of being is a vision of divine transformation of the world; it denies that men, by any means whatever, can bring about a perfect world society by themselves. Such a belief would be idolatry, man's worship of himself. Human institutions are always under divine judgment.

Islam does not deny that human beings should seek to establish the finest moral communities they can. For Islam, the model for human society is that of Medina under the Prophet. The Covenant of Medina provided a just coordination of different tribes and interests, and offered protection to Jews and pagans as well as Moslems. Treaties with nonbelievers are to be fulfilled in all circumstances except those of outright betrayal and hostility—"for God loves the righteous." (Qur'an)

Islam possesses rich moral and spiritual resources for the future of mankind. The emphasis of Islam on human fraternity, its articulation of the universal dimension of what it means to be human, its conviction that man is always *homo religiosus* and that, by God's grace, he can make the earth his provisional home—these are recurring themes in the history and thought of Islam, and they could inspire greater solidarity between Moslems and the rest of the world community.

But there are obvious problems within Islam itself. The Islamic peoples have emerged in this century from colonial rule into independence and self-determination. Faced with a host of problems within and without their own countries, Moslems are divided in their prescriptions for recovery. Three groups offer three different prescriptions.

First the traditionalists, or conservatives, believe that the *shari'a* is the foundation of Islam, yet not as it has been developed by the classical jurists. The definitive *shari'a*, they maintain, is the Qur'an, the example of the Prophet (called the *sunna*), and the precedents of the first four caliphs. The second group, composed of reformists, point out that the *shari'a* has always been interpreted and developed in a manner to meet particular historical conditions. But its older interpretations are now dated. It must be renewed in the light of present-day problems.

The third group consists of the secularists, who have been most influenced by Western ideas and values. They believe that it is impossible to reverse the historical process that launched Moslem states on a course of Westernization with respect to administration, representation, adoption of penal codes, and systems of education and defense. The secularists espouse separation of state and religion, holding the latter to be a personal matter.

Islamic states themselves are making varied efforts at coping with their own traditions in the context of the modern world. Saudi Arabia has launched an experiment to live by the *shari'a* as the sole criterion; it attempts to reestablish the ideal Moslem state which flowered under the Prophet Mohammed and his immediate followers. At the opposite end of the scale, Turkey replaced the *shari'a* with Swiss and Italian legal codes when it established a secular state in 1926. Pakistan experimented with the conception of an Islamic state based on the *shari'a,* but her conservatives, reformists, and secularists have not been able to agree on the best formulation and have wasted much energy in internal struggles.

In its own way each state and people of Moslem tradition struggles to resolve what appears to be a conflict, or contradiction, between Islam and the modern world. Yet the history of Moslem and Christian cultures expresses no irreconcilable conflict, and shows many elements of harmony. They were close to a common experience during the late Middle Ages, which was also the period of flowering of Islam. Their meeting grounds included the arts and crafts of Spain and their joint legacy of Hellenic culture. Islam did not suppress its share of classical civilization, but went on to perfect it. In the universities of Baghdad during the tenth to thirteenth centuries many scholars devoted themselves to the translation of Greek literature and philosophy. Arabs developed inductive reasoning, conducted experiments in chemistry, and evolved geography, botany, and the physical sciences. They did so following the Qur'an's injunction to study the stars and the earth and the mountains and rivers, "for here indeed are signs for men of understanding."

The values instilled by Islam have positive relevance to the present world. Islamic society discourages waste and display of worldly goods; it stresses the need for people to accept their role in the community and live in accordance with an ancient but flexible code of law and morality. Its mystic tradition, transmitted by the Sufi culture, substitutes spiritual concerns for the material values of consumption and possession.

If the Islamic culture is permitted to flower again in the countries of the Middle East and North Africa—a process which is actively promoted by many but, as we have seen in Chapter 6, encounters great difficulties—it could be a source of needed values and ethics, bringing Moslems into closer community with other cultures. As it is said in the Qur'an "O Mankind! We created you into nations and tribes that you may know each other."

Hinduism and the Growth of World Solidarity

Hinduism is the dominant religion of India. Its influence also extends into neighboring Pakistan. With 600 million people, the giant Indian state is a critical element in the balances that will determine the future of mankind. Although India strives toward modernism and emancipation from tradition (see Chapter 7), Hindu ideals have a strong hold on the mind of the majority of the population. These ideals could have harmful as well as beneficial effects, depending on which elements in Hindu thought gain predominance.

Hinduism is unique among the higher religions in that it has no individual founder. It began with a class of people called *rishis* (Sanskrit for "seers"), who lived between 2000 and 1000 B.C. They included blacks and whites, high- and low-born, men and women, Aryans and non-Aryans. They lived with their disciples in *ashrams* (hermitages) in the mountains and forests. A holy man radiated *darshan* (spiritual magnetism, blessing, charisma), stimulating a spiritual awakening in the disciple. This master-disciple (*guru-chela*) relationship was fundamental in Hindu mysticism (as also in Mahayana Buddhism and Islamic Sufism), and has enabled the mystical tradition to be handed down intact for three to four thousand years.

The *rishis* saw, with the eyes of spiritual vision, the poems which comprise the basic Hindu scriptures, the Vedas (derived from the Sanskrit *vid,* "to know"). Developed from 1500 to 800 B.C., the vast compendium of the Vedas took written form in Sanskrit after 150 B.C.

They range from hymns of praise and magical formulas to philosophical poems (*Upanishads*), which must rank among the highest religious expressions of the human race. (*Upanishad* means "a session at the feet of a guru.") Two other important scriptures are the Bhagavad Gita and the Code of Manu. The former, a poem, has been called "the Sermon on the Mount of Hinduism," and forms part of a long epic, the *Mahabharata* (400–200 B.C.). Manu was a legendary lawgiver (about 200 B.C.) who defined and gave religious sanction to the social institutions of Hinduism—the caste system, the joint family system, the position of women. The Code of Manu constituted, until modern times, the "canon law" of Hinduism.

Shining forth from the myths and poems, underlying all the verbiage of the theology as the boughs of a tree underlie its foliage, there is a simple and comprehensive Hindu concept of reality: The universe is a cosmos, an ordered spiritual harmony; matter is a form or precipitation of spirit; consciousness in some sense pervades everything, from the rocks to the gods. The term *maya* (illusion) is used by Hindu philosophers to denote matter. "Not this, not that," say the Hindu scriptures. But in the "his-her" personal aspect of matter, he-she may be worshiped as Brahma (creator), Vishnu (preserver), Siva (destroyer), Krishna (God in the Bhagavad Gita), and many other forms. Since the Hindus affirm that the essential nature of the universe is the blending of the myriad diversities of God's creation in one grand unity which enhances rather than destroys their diversity, they see no problem in attuning to this unity through any expression of the diversity. Hence it is said that Hinduism postulates one God and 330 million gods. By the same token the worship of the God or gods of any other religion is equally respected.

Central to Hinduism is the cosmic principle that the unity of the Creator's marvelous phenomena is expressed through diversity, as the different instruments and harmonies blend in an orchestra. Any man can develop his *atman* (soul) and attain the cosmic consciousness by his own efforts. He does not need to believe in anything, even in God, in order to set out on this path. He simply has to tread the path, for when he gets to his destination, he will "know."

Hinduism, like most of the great religions, affirms that man has free will. He can attune himself to the cosmic harmony, thus expressing creativity (goodness); he can remain inert; or he can behave in a destructive way, thus expressing evil. But since *atman* is indestructible, sooner or later he will wake up, desire to go forward on the path, and put right what he has done wrong. Justice is built into the very nature of the universe. For the ordinary person, one lifetime in the physical body is far too short a period in which to put right the results of past misdeeds and attain cosmic consciousness. Hinduism developed the doctrine that each person has his or her *karma* (fate, destiny, accumulation of past acts, good and bad), which he or she works out through a series of incarnations. Only when people have completed their *karma* are they free from the "wheel of rebirth" and able to soar off permanently to higher spiritual realms.

Some schools of Hinduism teach that *karma* can be transferred— one can bear another's burden. And Hinduism also contains the doctrine that God reincarnates from time to time as an *avatar* (redeemer). Hindus recognize as *avatars* Krishna (the form in which God revealed himself in the story of the Bhagavad Gita), the Buddha, Moses, and Christ. They believe that a final *avatar* will eventually appear to redeem the world completely from evil.

Hinduism emphasizes a holistic world view. At the philosophical level this is expressed in the idea that when a certain level of consciousness has been reached, the universe is experienced as one, and all opposites (good and evil, right and wrong) are transcended.

Hindu holistic philosophy embraces not only gods and men and women, but all created things. God, or consciousness, resides in everything, including rocks and plants. If men fail to live in empathy with nature, and seek only to dominate and exploit it, they are violating the cosmic harmony. The main reason why most Hindus do not eat meat is that their religion requires them to practice harmlessness (*ahimsa*) toward all things. Although Hinduism as a religion is less focused on nature than Chinese Taoism or African religion, its philosophy is fully in line with modern ecological concerns.

Hinduism opens up paths of self-realization. Through the centuries it has developed various methods for discovering and following these paths. They are known as *yoga,* which means both "yoke" and "self-realization."

Integrated in an all-encompassing spiritual unity, the diverse elements of Hindu society each had their allotted functions. Thus battle was the concern of the *kshatriya* (warrior), and in times of conflict battles took place between troops of the fighting classes without affecting the rest of society. No matter who won, social life continued on its defined course. The stream of life was not diverted, and the goal of the collectivity unthreatened.

Society comprised a fourfold order, originally based upon temperament and choice of work. There were the *brahmana* (devoted to the pursuit of knowledge), the *kshatriya* (devoted to the acquisition and exercise of strength and power), the *vaishya* (devoted to the organization of production and distribution), and the *shudra* (devoted to service). There was natural mobility within the system till the curve of Indian civilization reached a period of decline, and the habit of determining caste by birth set in.

The individual also had four well-marked stages in life: student, with the discipline of celibacy; householder, participating in the life of the community in full exercise of his rights and fulfillment of his duties; elder, with an advisory role; and pilgrim, in quest of God. The aim of society was to ensure the freedom of the individual to grow along lines congenial to his nature. Society was to provide the opportunity. Yet society drew upon the individual for its own progress. There was a general acceptance of a benign power (God) as the ruler and dispenser of justice in the universe. Man was expected to use his life to elevate his consciousness toward the divine. This gave him a purpose in life. He was the architect of his own destiny.

The entire scheme of Hindu life was geared to the evolution of man, individually and collectively, toward fulfillment—harmony, perfection, liberation from the limitations of nature, discovery of the truth.

Great Hindu leaders have emphasized the universal humanism of their traditions and have attempted to bring this humanism to bear on the life of their country as well as on the rest of the world. Sri Aurobindo, who died in 1950, believed that the human species is evolving toward a higher level of consciousness capable of producing a world union on which a fairer, brighter, and nobler life for all mankind can be based. Mahatma Gandhi initiated the concept of "spiritualizing politics." He believed that nonviolence and love can provide the energy to transform political, social, and economic conditions. Beginning in 1915, he spent thirty-eight years transforming the country by preparing it for independence from British rule, abolishing the caste system, bringing women into political life, achieving harmony between Hindus and Moslems, and regenerating Indian village life through the creation of cottage industries.

Buddhism and the Growth of World Solidarity

Buddhism grew out of Hindu traditions when Gautama Siddharta (known as the Buddha), a historical person of the sixth century B.C.,

achieved enlightenment and taught his disciples the Buddhist sense of
the *dharma*. The *dharma* is, for Buddhists, the universal law (the
way things work), taught "for the welfare of the many." Although in
some forms of Buddhism the figure of the Buddha is clothed with
divine attributes, the faith of Buddhists resides fundamentally in the
rightness and inexorability of the *dharma*.

Buddhism is the main religion and dominant influence in a number
of Asian countries including Sri Lanka, Burma, Thailand, Cambodia,
and many areas of Viet Nam. There are pronounced Buddhist influences also in India, Japan, Tibet, Mongolia, and Malaysia. Even in
the communist and socialist regimes of Asia the Buddhist concept of
the world exerts its influence. Today there is a surge of interest in
Buddhism also in the West, especially among American and European
youth.

The Buddhist *dharma* was first taught in a period of social, economic, and political crisis. Under pressures of rapid population
growth, political centralization, and the rise of a money economy,
people crowded into cities in great numbers. There, uprooted from
ancient tribal patterns, they experienced the psychic and economic
dislocations of unchecked urbanization: economic and social disparities, loss of identity, and helplessness. The situation was made worse
by the growing power of the new monarchies and the *brahmana*. The
latter were ritual technocrats with a monopoly on the knowledge and
techniques requisite to a good life now and hereafter. Increasing numbers of people questioned the assumptions upon which this concentration of power was based, and dropped out of conventional society.
Roving bands of seekers and teachers became common. Gautama was
one of these teachers, but instead of withdrawing to the forest as
others did, he directed the preponderance of his teaching to an urban
audience, including members of the power elite.

Gautama's teachings were presented as the fruit not of divine
revelation, but of mental and psychological exploration which began
with an overwhelming vision of human suffering, and culminated in
an experience of enlightenment. This enlightenment was an insight
into the way things are, and came after a period of intense attention
to the processes of mind. He saw such enlightenment and the transformation it produced as open to all, and called upon his followers
not to rely upon his authority but to make this discovery for themselves.

His vision was primarily an insight into the interrelatedness of reality, and he gave expression to this insight in his teachings. Central to his vision is the notion of "dependent coorigination," which holds that all reality is a fluid network of causes and effects. Within its processes man, once awakened to the realization that he is not in essence a separate entity, can discover and school himself in harmony and liberation.

Gautama's teachings were given capsule formulation in the Four Noble Truths: Since all phenomena are impermanent and interdependent, no lasting satisfaction can be achieved through acquiring or manipulating the things commonly sought after. Indeed, efforts in that direction subject man to restlessness and pain, a gnawing discontent that burns like a fever. The recognition of the suffering that characterizes this existence (*samsara*) is the first noble truth. The second is the Buddha's teaching that the root cause of this universal suffering is man's craving to satisfy that which cannot be satisfied—the desires of the separated ego, the yearning for private fulfillment. The declaration that this suffering can be made to cease, and that man is not doomed to perpetual pain, constitutes the third noble truth. The fourth presents the training in conduct and consciousness (the Eightfold Path) that makes release from suffering possible.

Because cravings perpetuate the fiction of a permanent ego, and that fiction in turn both fuels the cravings and renders them unquenchable, release is possible only through a schooling in mental alertness that removes the illusion of the separate ego. The passions are thus cooled and ultimately extinguished, which leads to the state of *nirvana,* variously understood as cool passionlessness, extinction, ultimate bliss. The Indian belief in a round of rebirth, under the conditions that reigned in the Buddha's time, had become a cause of despair. The ritual sacrifices of brahmanism and the austerities of *yoga* had come to be understood as means of escaping the remorseless cycle of incarnations. The Buddha taught that such liberation came not from ritual, nor from self-mortification, but from the extinction of the desiring ego, in *nirvana.*

What the Buddha preached was not a philosophic system, but a path, a way. Those of his followers who could cut loose from temporal tasks entered the *sangha,* an alternative community, and were called by Buddha the order of *bhikkus* and *bhikkunis*—terms which originally meant "sharers" rather than monks or nuns. Ideally, the *sangha* was more than a monastic retreat from the world. It was a vehicle for the Buddha's teaching, and a locus for the restructuring of consciousness through meditation. It also served as a model of economic sharing, social equality, and democratic process. The *sangha*'s interaction with lay society, based on the reciprocal giving of religious guidance and accepting of material support (*dana*), symbolized for both parties the basically symbiotic nature of the world.

Identification with others is cultivated by Buddhists in meditations specifically devoted to the heightening of capacity for loving-kindness and the corollary virtues, compassion, joy in the joy of others, and impartiality. Compassion is particularly stressed, and finds its epitome in the ideal figure of the *bodhisattva,* the enlightened being who forgoes the bliss of ultimate *nirvana* to return repeatedly to earth for the sake of those still caught in the round of suffering. Mythic portrayals of the *bodhisattva* convey an acute awareness of the needs of other beings and the sensory endowment such awareness would require: hearing sharp enough to register the cries of torment from the greatest distance; a multitude of eyes to discern the pain; many hands to reach out in succor. The ideal of compassion is fostered also by the Jatakas, canonical stories of the Buddha's past incarnations in animal and human form, which feature the countless ways he has offered himself to relieve the sufferings of others. As popular tales heard since childhood, they condition the believer toward a posture of caring, an attitude further strengthened by the thought that any form of life could be a loved one from a previous existence.

To Buddhists their future lives are as real as tomorrow. The assumption of rebirth brings goals for future generations within the scope of personal concern; future conditions will be experienced firsthand by oneself or, since one may enter *nirvana* or one of the heavens, at least by loved ones. Belief in *karma* gives added motivation to take the future seriously; the task left undone now will have to be faced again, under more difficult circumstances. Such an outlook across vistas of hundreds of thousands of years is nurtured by scripture and meditation; it accustoms the mind to vast temporal expanses, collapsing time and bringing close distant centuries.

This century has witnessed a revitalization of the Buddhist tradition and a renewed consciousness of its social dimensions. For many Buddhists the colonial experience in South and Southeast Asia served to heighten an awareness of their own religious heritage and identity. In reaction to Western economic values and colonial policies, they perceived the accumulation of capital as theft, and saw competition as aggravating the disease of self. The two world wars dramatized to them the sickness and greed of imperialism. In their subsequent struggle for independence in Burma, Ceylon, and Indochina, Buddhists turned to their scripture and history for the ideals of the proper distribution of wealth and the practice of nonviolence and democracy. Asian Buddhists formed lay groups which studied Buddhist sources and discussed their contemporary relevance, while broader-based movements, like the Young Men's Buddhist Association, modeled after its Christian counterpart, broadened awareness of Buddhist values and expressed them in social service activities.

These developments, along with the pressures of rapid political and economic change, have stimulated in some circles a rearticulation of the social message of the *dharma*. Countering the otherworldliness of previous generations, its central doctrines are given fresh formulation: dependent coorigination is reevaluated as interdependence and as a mandate for change; the *bodhisattva* vow is reemphasized; and *karma* reinterpreted to promote a greater awareness of human responsibility.

The Chinese Tradition and the Growth of World Solidarity

The ancient Chinese cultural tradition lives on through contemporary forms of, and interest in, Confucianism and Taoism. Confucianism still exerts an influence in China, although many of its elements are rejected by Maoists. Taoism is being rediscovered by intellectuals and youth groups all over the world. Thus the combined influence of these Chinese systems of thought on today's world is by no means negligible.

To label Confucianism the "orthodoxy" and Taoism the "heterodoxy" of Chinese tradition is to miss the characteristic unity of the Chinese way of viewing the place of man in the universe. To use the metaphor of the *I Ching* (the *Book of Changes* whose oracles predate both Confucius and Lao-tzu), Confucianism is the *yin* in the Chinese tradition and Taoism the *yang*. Yet the tradition itself fuses the two polarities. Lao-tzu's *Tao Te Ching* expresses the Chinese world view just as much as does Confucius's *Analects*. Confucius himself, while he formalized the everyday conduct of Chinese life, admired the venerable ancient tradition. Reverence for nature characterizes the Taoist view, which links together the cyclical rhythm of nature and human events. In the long history of the Chinese people, these systems of belief have served as the catalysts of foreign ideas.

They enabled Indian Buddhism to be modified and assimilated in ancient China. They are having a similar effect on Marxism in the twentieth century.

Confucianism and Taoism guide people's conduct in their relationship with society and nature. The guidance is concrete and practical. As the Chinese say, "One picture is worth a thousand words." The ideographic or pictorial character of the Chinese language itself points up the concrete and practical way of Chinese life. The ideogram "man," for example, depicts the upright human posture, and the ideogram "humanity" (*jen*) is composed of "man" (also *jen*) and "two." Together these symbolize the quality of being wholly human within the whole of human society. Again, the unity of knowledge and action (*chih hsing ho yi*) has been a central and perennial theme within Chinese thought. The primacy of action is stressed; knowledge is the beginning of action, action the completion of knowledge. This concept lies at the heart of contemporary Chinese political thought.

Confucius insisted that *jen* must be applied to everybody if it is to have any meaning. To understand man we must first understand the power of his words. The "rectification of names" (*cheng ming*) means that to be meaningful, words must be translated into action. The *Analects,* no less than the *Tao Te Ching,* contain many aphorisms to this effect. The sage, or virtuous man, is one who translates his thoughts and words into behavior and performance.

The harmony of human relations is the focus of Confucianism, while esthetic sensibility lies at the heart of Taoism. *Tzu-jan* (self-thusness) is the natural way of things, the recognition that each thing has its own way (*li*). In Chinese, *tzu-jan* means both external nature (*wan wu* or ten thousand things) and the intrinsic and inherent quality of each thing. In virtue of *tzu-jan* man can attune himself to nature. This attunement is the meaning of the oft-quoted saying of a Zen master, "When I began to study Zen, mountains were mountains; when I thought I understood Zen, mountains were not mountains; but when I came to full knowledge of Zen, mountains were again mountains." *Tzu-jan* represents our trust in things as themselves. The beauty of nature lies in its being exactly what it is in and by itself. To revere things is to leave them natural. In the principle of *tzu-jan* the earth stands for the poetry of space; its soul, nature, stands for the eternal music of time. It is the intrinsic beauty of nature that captures the reverential gaze of man, whether in a blade of grass, a butterfly with dancing wings, a restful dragonfly on a leaf floating in a pond, a spider's web sprinkled with dew in the early summer morning, a cricket singing in the evening, or the majestic beauty of a soaring mountaintop.

In the *Tao Te Ching*, Tao is the "nameless one" in which everything in nature originates. For lack of a better term, it is called "great." But the other three powers of the universe—heaven, earth, and the king—are also great. The sovereign is deeply esteemed. His ideogram is *wang*, which stands for political authority. It is composed of three parallel horizontal strokes joined together by one vertical stroke. The three horizontal strokes stand for the three spheres of heaven, man, and earth; the vertical stroke connects and unifies them. The sovereign symbolizes the great cosmic unity.

Chinese thought is humanistic without being egocentric or even anthropocentric. Harmony is the principle that governs man's conduct in society and his relationship with the rest of nature. The harmony is both ethical and esthetic. The ethical in Confucianism deals with human relationships, and the esthetic in Taoism with the relationship between man and nature. However, there is an affinity between the ethical and the esthetic. The good and the beautiful are synonymous. As the good is the harmony between man and man, so the esthetic is the harmony between man and nature. By virtue of harmony, all things are both good and beautiful.

The Chinese tradition embodied in Confucianism and Taoism holds a unified concept of man in relation to other men in society, and to other things in nature. There is an interdependence among all things and all acts, both psychological and physical (all in each, each in all). Man himself is a mortal and earthly being. Because he is the only being who is aware of his own mortality, he is the most mortal of all mortals. He dwells on earth with other mortal beings and nonliving things. In Chinese cosmology man, heaven, and earth symbolize the triadic unity of the universe. As the Taoist Chuang Tzu said, "Heaven and earth were born at the same time I was, and the thousand things are one with me." The rhythmic cycle of interrelatedness is expressed in the *Tao Te Ching:* "Man follows the earth. Earth follows heaven. Heaven follows the Tao. Tao follows what is natural" (*tzu-jan*).

The inextricable relationship between man and man on the one hand, and between man and nature on the other, is the foundation of Chinese thought. If in thought and concept all may be said to stand together, and the virtuous man is one who translates his ideas into active behavior, those who share the Chinese tradition today will strive to bring about greater harmony in man-man, as well as man-nature, relationships.

African Traditions and the Growth of World Solidarity

Black Africans share a common basic cultural tradition which appears in countless variations. In its richness, this tradition defies description. It has no universally acknowledged sacred texts, and no common prophets. Yet its common elements pervade the thinking and feeling of the majority of black Africans, and influence the goals and expectations of that continent's newly liberated countries.

The Africans have a mythical view of the world. Their view is dynamic and pluralistic, and is concerned with concepts of order and disorder. In the African cosmology the universe is not a fixed reality with laws that human beings can discover and must obey. Rather, the mythic reality of Africans is living and evolving. It is a process of becoming, which allows human action to be creative and spontaneous.

The entire universe, including the earth and the phenomenon of life, appears as a stupendous process of creation initiated by a Supreme Being. It is to this Supreme Being that the many forces at work in the universe owe their existence. Having initiated creation, the Supreme Being has closed himself in, withdrawn, and merely observes the consequences of his work with goodness, mercy, and understanding. He is not, however, totally closed off from man. Human beings can make him face the consequences of what man has done on his own initiative.

In this dynamic universe, the African himself exists in a state of dynamic tension. He is continually uniting, coordinating, and harmonizing the many spiritual entities that are sheltered in various parts of his body, and answering for the results of the creative actions performed by the union of all his forces.

The spiritual entities that make up the African personality have different origins and are acquired by the individual at different times. One may come from an ancestor; another from a divinity; a third from the Supreme Being himself. A person also adds new spiritual entities to different parts of his body at each of the rites and initiations of growth and maturation. On the other hand, when someone is afflicted with a spiritual imbalance, these entities may be replaced or renewed by appropriate rites and magical acts.

Spiritual entities can be located in the forehead or elsewhere in the head, in the stomach or abdomen, and even in a big toe. To give them safe shelter, secret altars are erected, sometimes in the immediate surroundings of the person, in a place known only to himself, or at most to a few initiates. The same altar can shelter several different spiritual entities. It can even be reduced to a small size so that it can be carried wherever the person goes.

The African personality is dominated by a continuing effort to bring all these constitutive entities together, so that they may cooperate in the execution of purposeful and creative actions. These entities have no less reality for Africans than the physical parts of the body.

The coordination of the multiple components of the African personality has, as its ultimate goal, admittance into the community of the souls of the ancestors. Each person feels he must share his life and achievements with his ancestors in a community composed jointly of the dead and the living. This goal is so fundamental that if it is not achieved the African feels himself excluded from the community of living and ancestral souls, and he becomes afflicted with madness and may die as a consequence. The only real hell conceivable by Africans is a state of rejection from this community. African communities grow as agreements among the living are ratified by the dead. A basic element in African community life is the resonance of feeling between two beings who come together after separation. This resonance is variously called "understanding," "contract," and "love."

This African sense of community could be instrumental in extending the solidarity of Africans from the local village and tribe not only to their newly independent nations, but to the African continent and beyond that to mankind as a whole. The fact that they see the world as always in process of creation, never fully completed, enables Africans to accept and welcome positive developments. The present incompleteness of the human orders is not an imperfection but a basis for creative action.

Africans know, from cultural heritage and current experience, that freedom has no meaning if the individual is separated from society. Africans feel themselves interdependent with the human community, and also with generations yet to come. Freedom means ceaseless creative struggle, first of all within oneself (coordinating one's diverse spiritual and physical powers), and secondly within the community of living and ancestral souls.

Dialogue, which implies nonviolence, is of paramount importance for the African mentality in the formation of human community. It is through dialogue that different aspects of the issues to be confronted are patiently and methodically examined, stakes defined, and collective agreements reached. The power of the word for Africans is a tangible phenomenon, manifesting one of the major aspects of the creative powers of man. The use of dialogue constitutes the best apprenticeship for the responsible exercise of freedom.

African traditions include both a deistic element, which recognizes the Supreme Being as the creator of the world, and an anthropocentric core, which sees man as truly in the center of the world of the living. Its mythical tradition provides the African personality with suppleness, realism, and creativity, as well as a sense of responsibility. But the future can never be presented as known and thereby closed to creative action. And the possibility of constructive dialogue must never be ruled out. It is through the exercise of such dialogue that the scope of African communal commitment can grow to embrace all nations on the African continent, and ultimately all nations of the human family.

The Influence of the Great Religions on the Growth of World Solidarity: Pros and Cons

The religions of mankind influence the minds and behavior of the majority of the people living today. This influence could promote the growth of world solidarity, or it could increase ethnic and cultural separateness, depending on whether the particularist or the universalist elements of the teachings gained dominance.

The religions of the world need to overcome the divisiveness, exclusiveness, and intolerance that have marked much of religious history. Those who do not belong to the inner circle, the recognized fold, of a religion, but profess some other religious or secular view, need nevertheless to be recognized as fully human and deserving of all the care and concern accorded to members of the most immediate human family. The rights of man include the right to freedom of belief without diminution of esteem or weakening of the bonds of solidarity. It is not likely, nor is it desirable, that differences of religious and philosophical views will disappear from the world scene. But the different religions and philosophies must learn to live and work together on this small and interdependent planet. Religions in the past have shown considerable flexibility when the problem of living together had to be solved. In today's world there are many signs that this spirit of accommodation can grow much more rapidly than ever before, as common global dangers kindle a fresh appreciation of the universalist elements in all the major cultural and religious traditions of man.

Religion was once the essential agent of socialization, and it remains that for traditional cultural regions. In the past, societies and the predominant religious systems of each society tended to be highly conservative. Whether it was religion that made society conservative or vice versa could be long debated. In general, however, those who questioned the existing order or tried to change it were exposed to both societal and religious sanctions. In Japan, for example, a person who behaved in a way "other than expected" could be executed by his social superior. In Africa anyone with exceptional talents and learnings was suspected of being bewitched, and could be ostracized from the tribe—the greatest punishment known to the African mentality. In medieval Europe and in early modern America, many nonconformists were branded as heretics or witches, and were treated accordingly.

Deeply religious societies also had a high degree of fanaticism. They generated conflicts which often issued in bloody wars. When each side believes itself in full possession of the truth, and thinks of its actions as having received the stamp of a higher authority, it feels less compunction about shedding blood and creating upheavals than is felt within ordinary secular contexts. Although religious conflicts also have social and economic dimensions, the fanaticism of the faithful often spurs feelings of intolerance and fans the flames of aggression. Such is the case today in Northern Ireland, Lebanon, the Philippines, and India, and wherever fanatical religious sects come into conflict.

The orientation of religions toward the past needs to be combined with greater emphasis on an orientation toward the future. In place of reliance on received dogma, on revelation to chosen individuals, religions need to look to the needs and desires both of those living today and those to be born tomorrow. All the great religions possess concepts and teachings which encourage concern for the future. The eschatology of the monotheistic religions, and the reincarnation doctrines of Oriental thought are examples. The golden age of the past will be matched by a still more glorious age in the future. A redeemer has come before, and will come again. Man and man, and man and nature are evolving together. Creation is an ongoing process, not a finished act of the far distant past. Elements such as these are basic in the great religions of mankind. They need to become uppermost in their current teachings, counteracting the age-old leanings toward intolerance and sectarianism.

Many forward-looking religious groups and institutions perceive the challenge to religion in today's world and are acting to face it. They recognize the need to put the survival and harmonious development of mankind above the sacredness of unchanging traditions. Today's religions have begun to evolve new forms of humanism, maintaining their own values and beliefs, but encompassing within their sphere of concern and solidarity all human beings, believers and nonbelievers, as well as the faithful of other religions.

The coming together of the great religious movements in today's world is a sign of greater unity within their diversity, not of syncretism and uniformity. A single world religion is as unlikely, and as undesirable, as a single philosophy, a single social order, and a single set of values. But unity within current diversity is possible, and it is necessary if some of the deepest thoughts and experiences of mankind are not to give rise to the exclusiveness and intolerance that breeds inhumanity and violence. Such unity is beginning to arise today. Promoting it is one of the major tasks and responsibilities of all people who cherish their religious heritage and believe that it has a constructive role to play in the coming age.

Chapter 18

The Modern World Views
and World Solidarity

Although religions dominate the minds of a majority of the world population, decisions crucially affecting the fate of humanity are now mostly taken in the light of predominantly secular modern views and assessments of the world. Modern nation-states embrace primarily secular ethics and principles, much as major corporations and institutions do. Among members of the young generation new "alternative" cultures are spreading which combine religious views and beliefs with contemporary motivations and convictions. They, too, depart from the classical faiths of the great religions.

We examine here the three great streams of thought and value that permeate the thinking and behavior of modern societies. Although they often intermingle in reality, they are identifiable by the familiar tenets of liberal democracy and Marxist communism, and by the less clearly but no less insistently voiced claims of the alternative cultures. Their impact on the modern mind is great, and may be crucial in promoting the expansion or transcendence of inner limits in the growth of the human spirit toward world solidarity.

Liberal Democracy and the Growth of World Solidarity

Liberalism, which has been a dominant social theory for three centuries, has bred widely divergent political movements. Yet despite the different directions liberalism has taken in public affairs, there remains a hard core that has withstood modification. Liberalism has survived the excesses of capitalism (which it generated and legitimized) and the challenge of socialism.

John Locke was the first great proponent of liberal theory. The list of his intellectual descendants is long: Voltaire, Montesquieu, de Tocqueville, Mandeville, Rousseau, Jefferson, Dewey, and Keynes. His *Treatise on Government* helped inspire both the American and French Revolutions. The stimulus for his theory was the English development of common law and the events of 1688, when William of Orange landed in England. The "Glorious Revolution" of that year divested the monarchy of its ultimate political power, conferred supreme authority on the people through Parliament, and guaranteed protection from governmental tyranny by the establishment of basic civil rights.

Individualism had been on the rise in Europe since the Renaissance. The latter restored to man a sense of individual worth and dignity. The Protestant Reformation added the belief that the individual was his own authority, since he was capable of perceiving truth by himself. The Enlightenment asserted that man was a rational being who could determine for himself what is good. These three belief systems centered authority previously vested in Church and state on the individual.

Locke's liberal theory made the role of government one of service to the individual. People have a natural desire to be free. Unrestrained governmental power threatens individual liberty and may degenerate into tyranny. The desire for freedom from governmental tyranny is as natural for man as an animal's desire for release from captivity.

Liberals sought to limit govermental power by prescribing rules to protect the basic rights of individuals. The spirit of liberalism is expressed in the phrase, "The government which governs best, governs least."

Liberalism thus became naturally allied with the concept of democracy. Democracy—from the Greek words *demos* (people) and *kratos* (authority)—is a classical Greek concept of rule by the people rather than by tyrants. (The Greeks themselves found fault with it as the ultimate form of political organization, and sometimes reverted to oligarchies and even tyrannies.)

The confluence of the great thought streams of the Renaissance, the Protestant Reformation, and the Enlightenment gave rise to theories of society as based on a "social contract" of free and autonomous individuals. The concept of democracy was thus resuscitated: It expressed the central concern of liberals for the freedom of the individual. Liberal democrats hold that social and political order is established through the free consent of individuals in order to serve their interest. Individuals are free to accept, modify, or reject any social or political system. They are also entitled to own property as the fruit of their labor; the liberal doctrine of natural law recognizes the right of individuals to private property and forbids governments to limit or expropriate it. The primary function of government is to regulate the distribution, use, and transfer of property. Bills of rights in modern constitutions offer protection for individuals against violation of their rights to life, liberty, and property.

Transferred to the sphere of the economy, liberal democracy paved the way for classical capitalism. Its theory was worked out in detail by Adam Smith. Capitalism relies on the free market mechanism of supply and demand to satisfy the needs and wants of people. Governmental interference with the equilibrating mechanisms of the free enterprise system are considered illegitimate; they are forms of tyranny. In this tradition such otherwise outstanding political thinkers as Bentham, Paley, James Mill, and Malthus found it necessary to oppose governmental interference even when it was designed to regulate the working conditions of women and children and offer relief to the poor.

Since the late eighteenth century, liberal democracy has created powerful social and political systems in Europe and America. Government, in the words of the American statesman Daniel Webster, is "made for the people, made by the people, and answerable to the people."

The great achievements of the liberal democratic tradition need no separate eulogy here. The suitability of some of its operative premises with respect to contemporary and future world conditions does, however, need analysis. The questionable premises of liberal democracy may be summed up in these three propositions:

That *people are essentially separate,* so that little intrinsic responsibility is felt for the effect of present actions on individuals who are far away or on generations to come.

That both social growth and the protection of one's own interests are best served by *competitive aggressive behavior.*

That the individual should be free to make his own choice of "the good," and that the choices he makes in pursuit of *self-interest will somehow add up to desirable overall societal choices.*

These premises of liberal democracy have given rise to attitudes and assumptions which are no longer well adapted to the management of global problems. The separateness of individuals is transferred to groups, states, and nations. Competitive aggressiveness is likewise transferred to the sphere of international politics. The choices of individuals, groups, states, and nations, as they pursue their perceived self-interest, tends to be thought of as necessarily adding up to desirable national and global choices.

The above premises are not essential features of liberal philosophy, but instrumental appendages which were found valid in a period of rapid and relatively unconstrained economic growth. The basic moral premise of liberalism is its commitment to the greatest good of the greatest number of individuals. Its ethic is basically utilitarian; it judges an action or a policy right and proper if its consequences increase the happiness and well-being of people. That in the nineteenth century, and until recently in the twentieth, liberal democrats adopted a policy of minimum interference with the actions of individuals was due to the fact that rapid economic growth was fueled by free competition, and such growth was equated with human happiness. When unrestrained competition no longer promotes rapid overall growth, and when economic growth is no longer the sole criterion of progress and happiness, liberal democracy could bring its moral concerns to bear on the new situation of the global community, and shift its instrumental objectives accordingly. This would mean an important change of emphasis. The concept of the total freedom of individuals to pursue whatever goals they wish (as long as they do not overtly break the system of liberal laws) would give way to an emphasis on the freedom *and responsibility* of individuals to pursue those goals of enlightened self-interest which result in benefit both to themselves and to their society.

Indeed, sophisticated philosophical theories of utilitarian ethics have never advocated self-interest as the basis of moral behavior without qualification. Utilitarians have gone beyond concepts of "the good" as immediate pleasure or profit. "The greatest good of the greatest number" requires the achievement of goals that are compatible with the goals of others in society. J. S. Mill himself, the nineteenth-century philosopher whose name is most commonly associated with utilitarianism, distinguished between lower and higher pleasures, and rated the latter as constituting a greater good than the former. But the higher pleasures, such as those derived from virtue and knowledge, are obviously far more compatible with the pleasures of others, especially in a finite and interdependent world, than the lower pleasures of miserliness and greed.

Liberal democrats could achieve world solidarity without in any way running counter to the individualistic core of their values and beliefs. They would need to recognize that the sustainability of the system in which individuals find themselves—a system made up of economic, social, cultural, and political as well as ecological elements—is a precondition of the fulfillment of individuals. No person can absent or abstract himself from this system of relations. No one can meet his needs and pursue those higher pleasures of which great liberal thinkers spoke, unless society affords him (or her) equal and sufficient opportunity. To assure this, liberal democrats must concern themselves not only with the affairs of individuals, but also with the growth and evolution of the social, economic, cultural, political, and ecological system. This system is not necessarily best served when individuals are given maximum freedom to do whatever they wish. Such would be the case only if all individuals were fully aware of all constraints on their society, and fully committed not to transgress the thresholds of sound development. As long as such knowledge and commitment is not encultured in all the people, the human community will have to exercise collective vigilance to avoid pushing their societies irreversibly toward collapse. This danger was not evident in the eighteenth and nineteenth centuries, and the great liberal thinkers could not have readily foreseen it. Such dangers arise now in the late twentieth century not only because of the growth of human numbers (a threat foreseen by many, including Thomas Malthus) but also because of the enormous and unforeseen increases in energy and raw material use and pollution generation, and because of the revolutions in transportation and communication, and the development of terrifying capabilities for mutual destruction.

Individuals now have the power to throw the global system in which they live out of balance, and even to destroy it. Unrestrained competition could have such outcomes. These must, at any cost, be prevented.

Although individuals can no longer allow themselves the luxury of maximum unqualified freedom to pursue their interests in any way they think best, they can and should make use of the possibilities for *optimum freedom*. This still means freedom to exploit new opportunities conferred by human ingenuity and power, and enjoy the benefits of a richer and more diverse web of social, economic, cultural, and political relationships, but only within the bounds of sustainable growth in the global system. Human groups, be they business corporations, social, political, or cultural organizations, or nation-states, can no longer allow themselves the corresponding luxury of maximum freedom to act as they wish in pursuit of their own short-term perceived interests, but they, too, can seize the chances of optimum freedom to choose their own pathways of growth and development within the bounds of the sustainable evolution of the entire system of global relations. Individuals and organized groups must recognize that they are not abstract and separate from one another. Their actions mutually influence one another, and the sum of their actions determines the future of their overall system of relations—their collective destiny.

Liberal democracy grew from a core of genuine humanism at a time when coercive power by sovereign kings and princes was abusing human freedom, and reducing the options for the fulfillment of human need, and for growth and development. At the dawn of the modern age its emphasis was, properly and understandably, on the maximization of the freedom of individuals and minimization of state interference in their endeavors. In today's world of precarious balances, global stresses, and increasing interdependencies, the same humanism which inspired insistence on *maximum* freedom for individuals must extend the concept of *optimum* freedom to persons, as well as to organizations, corporations, and nation-states. This need not mean restriction on freedom, but a call for moral responsibility for the consequences to others of one's actions. Rather than contemplate the creation of coercive institutions to exercise surveillance and control over the behavior of individuals and groups, liberal democrats could strive to instill a sense of responsibility in individuals and groups for the exercise of self-restraint and self-discipline.

For institutions of democracy to adapt to the new age of global community, certain necessary conditions must be met: The spirit of unqualified laissez-faire must be replaced by the spirit of joint responsibility; the pure and simple principle of noninterference in the affairs of citizens, organizations, and corporations must be replaced by joint participatory planning by private and public bodies; and the humanistic concern with the welfare of individuals must expand to concern with the safe and selective development of all systems of relations in which individuals participate and on which they depend—including not only corporations and nation-states, but the economic, social, political, and ecological system of the world community itself.

Indeed, if liberal democrats were to adjust their thinking to the new conditions of life on this planet, they would doubtless perceive world solidarity as a necessary condition for achieving their time-honored and perenially valid goal: contributing to the greatest good of the greatest number through voluntary self-restraint and a sense of moral responsibility.

Marxist Communism and the Growth of World Solidarity

Forms of Marxist socialism and communism dominate the economic, social, and political behavior of as much as a third of mankind. Socialist thoughts had been voiced before Marx, and came to be clearly expressed in the writings of the utopian socialists of seventeenth-century Europe. These writers called for man's liberation from the yoke of economic and social exploitation, and for the creation of a classless and just socialist society. Marx, together with Engels, gave a basic philosophical structure to such aspirations, and also formulated a program for the advancement of history to socialism and communism through conscious human action. Libraries are now teeming with the writings of Marx, Engels, Lenin, Mao, and their collaborators and followers. This study will not add to that body of literature but merely note the potential contribution of Marxist communism to the transcendence of inner limits and the growth of world solidarity.

The first factor to take into account is the basic humanism which inspired Marx's thinking, and came to be expressed most clearly in his early writings. Marx stood for the equality of all people regardless of nationality, race, or sex. He wished to eliminate all factors which pit one human being against another in competition and exploitation. He believed, however, that progress comes about through conflict. Humanity progresses dialectically, as one class struggles with another, gains in strength and overthrows the existing order, establishing a new stage in history. This stage, too, develops its own internal contradictions and works dialectically toward the next. These processes mark mankind's advance from the earliest forms of tribal communism to communism in its final, mature form. The intervening stages are marked by various forms of alienation and injustice, due mainly to the introduction of private property as a social and economic force.

Marx foresaw the necessity of a socialist revolution against the background of nineteenth-century European society. The emerging working masses were denied the full value of their labor, and the social product, owned by others, became a power used against the workers. Control and ownership of the means of production had to be returned to the workers themselves, said Marx, in order to restore the dignity of work and liberate the working classes from social and economic injustice.

Marx perceived the socialist revolution as a necessary means of achieving dignity and fulfillment for human beings. Rising against the existing exploitative system of production, the workers would establish the dictatorship of the proletariat. When socialist society had been established worldwide, and the remnants of bourgeois forces liquidated, state functions would wither away. All people would enjoy the benefits of social production, which they would direct toward the fulfillment of genuine human needs.

Marxist humanism, combined with the dialectical view of history, throws a distinctive light on the issue of contemporary world solidarity. The following attempt to reconstruct some features of the Marxist view of history may illuminate this issue, and provide food for thought to modern Marxists as they endeavor to assume a responsible and valid role in confronting global problems, and seizing global opportunities, through cooperation with societies based on different social and economic principles.

In the Marxist concept of historical evolution, separation and unification, differentiation and integration, individualization and socialization, autonomy and heteronomy constitute fundamental features of social existence. Many centuries prior to the development of capitalist society, with its commodity-based economy and large-scale production processes, social existence was characterized by communities based on personal or blood relationships. Each member shared in the community and identified himself with it. These naturally formed communities were necessarily of a narrow scope, embracing first only the tribe, then the larger village community. Even in the Middle Ages, consciousness of being part of a larger socio-economic unit was blurred for most people. Communities were largely integrated inward, and differentiated outward with respect to other communities.

The development of civilization introduced into such naturally formed communities a relationship not derived from nature but from the self-regulation of the societies themselves. This new relationship consisted of the division of labor, which gave rise to class relations. Comprehensive communal units became polarized, and built intricate systems of loyalty and antagonism between individuals and the community, and among the communities themselves.

These processes culminated in capitalism, which cuts off the individual from the "umbilical cord" of the community, to use a phrase of Marx. Although some naturally formed social units, such as the family, persist, their force in society has declined. They no longer determine the individual's sphere of activity. Now there are wider opportunities for choosing a profession or employment, a wife or husband, an ideology, a lifestyle, and even a community.

Such mobility transforms the nature of social relations. Whereas in naturally formed communities individuals belonged to the same group all their lives, and normally belonged to only one communal group, under modern capitalism man participates in many different communities. But this participation does not involve his entire personality, merely his socio-economic role in the system of commodity relations.

The new pattern of many-tiered relations opens up tremendous possibilities. It can extend the individual's relationships beyond the community to the nation, and beyond the nation to the whole of mankind. His consciousness could, likewise, extend from his family, tribe, and community to the entire species. In principle, new organizations, institutions, and production systems could emerge to connect small and large communities, nations, and regions, and integrate them in a vast system of socio-economic patterns.

In the Marxist view the relationships among individuals and the relationships among communities (including nations and states) do not constitute two different categories but merely two aspects of the same thing. If mankind is to achieve a condition in which states and nations exist harmoniously as members of an all-embracing world community, the internal structure of the member societies must be based on the same principle of community, that is, on the elimination of the private exploitation of social labor. In genuine Marxist thought, the achievement of such a society on a world scale is the great historical task of humanity.

Marxist thinking measures the short- and long-term goals of societies by this basic aim. This is how progress can be made beyond the unsolved contradictions in the ethical thought of past centuries. From this perspective the phenomenon of the individual detaching himself from the preestablished and naturally formed communities to accomplish his autonomy may be seen in a different light. Social development has now reached a stage where autonomy is jeopardized, not so much by the remnants of the old feudal society as by those who would make autonomy an end in itself. In the socialist interpretation the autonomy of the individual is no longer a goal, but rather a condition. The goal is to find or establish a community capable of providing autonomy. Socialist ethics is built on the concept of harmony between the individual and the community through praxis, that is through working together for a specific purpose. It is not based on the priority of the community over the individual (as in Asiatic and feudal societies), nor on the priority of the individual over the community (as in capitalism).

The achievement of a single all-embracing human community is as yet a relatively remote goal. In the meanwhile, communists recognize the emerging conditions of an interdependent planetary system composed of societies of widely differing social, economic, and political orders. In this system communist countries have attained a major status. Most of them have embarked on the road to industrialization, and now face problems that are in many respects similar to those of industrialized capitalist societies: resource scarcity, urbanization, lagging agricultural productivity, high costs of energy, and the need to protect progressive human interests in a world under the shadow of nuclear terror and made precarious by the shifting allegiances of new nations.

In such a situation the means for achieving a peaceful and harmonious world society cannot be violent confrontations of raw power, but rather the harmonious development of all societies, guided by a new ethic of humanism and mutual solidarity. As the Soviet leadership, among others, recognizes, peace and cooperation can lead to a world community of unalienated and unoppressed people far more surely than the politics of confrontation and terror.

The Alternative Cultures and the Growth of World Solidarity

Alternative cultures emerge in many parts of the world as a response —often a radical one—to the problems of life and the alienation experienced in modern "establishment" society. Where dissatisfaction focuses not on underdevelopment but on the ills of development (or, as some would have it, *over*development), rebellion centers not on tradition and backwardness as ills to be overcome, nor on modernization as the positive state of affairs to be achieved, but rather on dehumanizing forms of mechanization, and on the division of life into meaningless fragments in terms of roles and specialties.

In developed countries fragmentation occurs both with respect to the social and personal aspects of life, and within the many social roles themselves. In most industrialized countries residential areas are removed from the working areas. Also the physical and cultural characteristics of residential suburbs and downtown office or peripheral industrial centers are strikingly different. The attitudes expected of people in these environments is likewise dissimilar. As residents, persons are treated by developed industrial society as consumers, and are encouraged to be free, impulsive, and ready to take advantage of the myriad opportunities open to them. But as workers, whether blue or white collar, the same people are admonished to be conscientious, reliable, and stable.

Specialization within the working sphere adds to the ill effects of the working-living split. In order to be successful (to make money to become a "good" consumer), individuals are forced into narrow specialty niches. Within them they know much about few things, but at the cost of knowing little or nothing about most other things. This state of affairs has a twofold disadvantage. First, if the market changes, as it increasingly has in recent years, certain specialties may become much less in demand, or may be entirely displaced by automation. Yet the specialist is not qualified for anything other than his own specialty, and must be retrained or face the disagreeable alternative of a less interesting kind of work, perhaps at a lower salary. Second, specialization can narrow people's horizons, causing them to pay attention only to things that are related to their area of specialization. Life loses its integral wholeness, and becomes a semiautomatic discharging of expected functions. Persons who spend the greater part of their waking hours in such a restricted milieu have difficulty in maintaining a sense of meaning in life during their leisure time.

The fragmentation of life, its mechanization and resulting meaninglessness force many young people to question the career choices offered by their elders, and prompt many sensitive older persons to wonder about the worth of continuing with their established patterns of life. Those that "opt out" tend to come together and share their grievances, desires, and experiences. They evolve into an almost invisible "society within society" as a culturally, rather than merely politically, dissident group. They search for alternative styles of life and work. Their activities embrace public service and educational organizations, citizen activist groups, and nature and consumer protection movements within mainstream society, and the varied tasks connected with running more or less self-sufficient and independent urban and rural communes. (See Chapter 2.)

The mentality of persons who have opted out of mainstream society to search for more desirable alternatives shows some striking common features, especially when contrasted with the typical mind set of advanced industrial societies. Their emphasis is on service rather than achievement, communication rather than prestige, fulfillment of social tasks rather than career-making, and life in the here-and-now rather than preoccupation with the future.

Members of these cultures tend to be honest and blunt. They are sensitive to the plight of others, whether in their own nation or elsewhere, and sympathize with the underprivileged. They protest against the unfeeling exploitation of man by man, and of nature by man. They seek to uncover the inner reality of human beings, their feelings and experiences. They want to penetrate beneath the surface of manners and forms imposed by society. They also seek a new lifestyle that expresses their concerns. Living quarters, food, clothing must be authentic and expressive of their sincerity as feeling individuals. Personal relations are direct, aspiring to love, but often unconstrained to the point of rudeness. There is no discrimination between races or sexes.

Self-discipline is imposed, conspicuous consumption despised, wastefulness condemned. Members of alternative cultures seek a return to a modest, self-disciplined, and responsible lifestyle, even in the midst of affluent industrial societies. Their actions are not seen as a sacrifice for some ulterior cause, but as a means of liberation from the curse of possessive materialism and immorality in a world that distributes unequally its finite resources.

The alternative cultures recognize the finiteness and vulnerability of Earth (which they capitalize as the planet's proper name). They are rediscovering a consciousness that mankind has all but lost in its obsession with material-technological progress: the consciousness of being one with nature. Paradoxically, the most recent explosion of this consciousness was triggered by one of the greatest technological achievements of modern industrial society: the Apollo space missions. Photographs of Earth from outer space brought a visual confirmation of what in primitive societies was grasped intuitively, and in modern societies at best intellectually: the seamless oneness of our life-giving environment. Planet Earth appears small, lonely, unitary, finite, and vulnerable. It provides one integral life-support system for the human species. The thin envelope of air is indivisible; the seas are one; the land is limited. The alternative cultures perceive the tribes of man to be in one and the same spaceship together, facing a common destiny.

Yet these cultures, especially the youth factions, do not take a deadly serious attitude toward life and its problems; they show a spirit of adventure, almost of playfulness. This is entirely in keeping with their emphasis on honesty and sincerity, but it is in sharp contrast with the career-and-achievement-oriented earnestness of established cultures. Life is for living today, without concern for achievement tomorrow.

Related to the diminished concern for personal achievement is a blurring of the distinction between working for others and working for oneself. People are not conceived as isolated from one another, but as forming a community in which the work of one becomes a service to the whole. Performing tasks for the community, rather than accumulating career points for oneself, is what matters.

Most members of the youth cultures reject the idea of long years of preparation at the expense of society before embarking on socially productive work. Schooling for a career in a profession is seen as a mark of the establishment, where the individual's many years of education are seen to be no more than a stepping stone to a position of high income and prestige. In contrast, members of the youth cultures wish to begin contributing to the human community as soon as they reach physical maturity, and to go on learning as they live and work. There is no separation for them between working and leisure-time enjoyment. Constructive, task-oriented service to the community is pleasurable, and usually continues beyond the hours conventionally allotted to gainful employment.

The alternative cultures are mistrustful of plans created by specialists for implementation by others. Their members want to be planners and implementors in one. Yet they wish only to set broad directions in which to proceed, rather than specific ends to be attained. They oppose any centralized system of power and authority, where those who make plans give directions to others. Their ideal is a decentralized community where planning is interactive and responsibilities are shared.

The communities of the alternative cultures thus strive to be self-organizing rather than controlled from the outside. Their members are bound together by a sense of solidarity, expressed in the highest instance as love. The major determinants of personal relations, and hence of communal organization, are emotive. Reasoning without feeling is rejected; negative emotions, such as aggressiveness and violence, are abhorred, as is also the absence of emotion shown in indifference. Members of these cultures perceive one another as friends and partners, rather than opponents, competitors, or enemies.

The complementary side of loving relations to others is a loving relation to oneself. Individuals in search of alternatives express a great concern for their own inner life, the quality of their experience. They believe that man's potential for self-actualization has been thwarted by establishment society, where achievement and prestige are measured by external norms. Society has condemned man's inner reality as irrational, unscientific, and unworthy of concern. But the alternative cultures no longer view the material sphere as the locus of all value; the inner world takes primacy over possessions and external achievements.

Self-actualization becomes a major goal. It is marked by both relatively transient peak experiences, and sustained plateau experiences. Such experiences resemble those of yogis and religious mystics. A peak experience has been described as a sudden expansion of consciousness, an obliteration of familiar thoughts and perceptions, ecstasy and bliss, and a sense of wonder, oneness, and totality. Plateau experiences are more serene, transcendent, calm, filled with quiet joy, unifying awareness, and an enduring state of mystical illumination.

Psychedelic drugs produce similar experiences and sometimes visions of striking beauty and significance. They can also prompt mystical and religious experiences. There is a heightening of the feeling of existing in the present; sense impressions become more vivid. Time appears to stand still, and sights, sounds, smells, tastes, and tactile impressions can be savored in a way almost forgotten in the hurried pace of industrial society.

In the majority of experiences in such altered states of consciousness a new meaning infuses all that is perceived. Interconnections are noticed and hidden meanings emerge. The universe as a whole begins to make sense, lessening the feeling of meaninglessness, suspicion, and chaos that marks persons fragmented by modern institutions and habits of life. Language, however, is inadequate to describe the full flavor of such experiences. Verbal description is like "looking through a glass darkly" or, as Zen masters have said, it is the finger pointing at the moon—which is not the moon itself.

The alternative cultures grow and spread with great rapidity, principally but not exclusively in the developed societies of the First World. They establish networks of communication among themselves through newsletters, journals, leaflets, magazines, as well as small radio and television stations, exchanges of sound and video tapes, rock festivals, traveling singers and bands, and street festivals. There are centers of contact for them in most major cities, often bookstores, or places of exchange and gathering.

The alternative cultures evolve their own lifestyles and modes of existence. They form relatively independent communes. While urban communes are more dependent for jobs and services on outside society, rural communes strive to be self-sufficient by growing and marketing their own produce and also living off it.

The commune experiments have great promise and attraction for members of the alternative cultures, but they are not without problems and difficulties. Observers note that a year or more after a commune is established, members often hit a crisis, when they must decide whether to commit themselves further or move out. This point is usually reached after the creative excitement of working together to build the commune abates. The original enthusiasm needs to be replaced by a more lasting bond. There cannot be a continued quantitative growth of the commune without reverting to the very practices of fragmentation, specialization, and market-orientation that the commune was created to avoid. Hence the new bond usually proves to be spiritual. In at least two-thirds of the American communes, and a smaller proportion of those in Europe, some form of Eastern or Western religion constitutes the new and more enduring cement that holds the members together.

Urban communes face additional difficulties through exposure via the public media to the values of mainstream society, through daily contact with "straight" individuals on the streets and in outside places of work, and through the educational system. Hence many communes lose members or dissolve altogether. Individuals reassimilate into establishment society when they reach middle age, obtain a position that challenges their interest, or simply fail to overcome the letdown in commitment after the first period of excitement. Communes also disperse when they fail to make it financially. Yet many people continue to adhere to the values acquired during their active participation after they are once more leading a conventional life.

The Influence of Modern World Views and the Growth of World Solidarity: Pros and Cons

The influence of modern world views on the minds of contemporary people, especially in the developed world, is considerable. This influence could do much to further the transcendence of inner limits in the form of short-term and narrowly self-interested goals, by raising the level of mutual solidarity among the world's people. Liberal democracy, Marxist communism, as well as the new alternative cultures are fundamentally concerned with human life and well-being. They are committed to improving the quality of life for all. But they diverge in their views about how best to translate these concerns into positive action, and their mutual distrust breeds antagonism and intolerance among their adherents.

The most open and historically crucial conflict arose between the two "establishment" ideologies: the liberal democracy of the West and the Marxist communism of the Soviet bloc. Liberal democrats show a deep faith in human nature but also a deep skepticism about the possibility of humane social orders. Their foremost concern is to liberate the individual from the yoke of public authority, protect him from exploitation by public power, and guarantee his individual human rights in a free society. Socialists and communists, notwithstanding divergences among themselves, share a deep-seated mistrust of individuals left to their own devices without adequate social supervision. They champion first and foremost the social rights of man, and attempt to build social, economic, and political structures to limit the excesses of egoism and human shortsightedness, and to bring the development of living societies into line with the evolutionary dialectics of history.

The positive potentials of liberal democracy and of Marxism in its many forms can be overshadowed by the negative consequences of conflict between the chosen strategies of each, and by the excesses of both systems in practice. Laissez-faire liberalism gave rise to the social and economic inequities of early forms of capitalism. In today's world laissez-faire practices lead to a widening gulf between rich and poor nations and mounting tensions in an uncoordinated, anarchic international system. Socialism and communism, on the other hand, have given rise to arbitrary forms of dictatorship, based on the whims and power-thirst of unscrupulous leaders. They have constrained individual enterprise to the extent of reducing incentives and strangling personal creativity.

The "childhood sicknesses" of these modes of thought have now been largely cured. But they need to continue growing toward full maturity. Liberal democracy's respect for social rights needs to evolve further, so as to curb the excesses of individuals bent on maximizing their own wealth and power. And Marxist communism's appreciation of individual human rights needs to develop further so as to preserve and enhance the freedom and creativity of persons.

There are many progressive elements among the champions of both world views. But many others are lagging behind present realities, still arguing the doctrines advanced in the past. Yet all liberal democrats could now recognize that hunger, disease, squalor, unemployment, and illiteracy are as great restrictions on human freedom as any imposed by a willful dictatorship. All communists could realize that an equitable world society can only be reached rapidly and humanely through international cooperation in pursuit of goals to eliminate some of the worst threats facing mankind. The greatest good of the greatest number, and the freeing of oppressed people and their development to full humanity, requires the cooperation of peoples and societies of different world views and diverging principles of social and economic organization.

The positive aspects of liberal democracy and Marxism are their shared humanitarian concerns, directed to all the peoples of the world. Their negative aspects are tendencies to excesses at home and intolerance in confrontation with each other. At present the negative aspects are being played down in a new mood of international cooperation in a few selected areas. These trends could grow in the future, but they could also be reversed. A growth of the positive potential is needed on both sides to reinforce their own brands of humanism and to guard against narrow concerns and short-range policies.

A fruitful meeting ground for these great ideological currents of modern times would be the arena of international cooperation with respect to global problems and opportunities. Liberal democrats could perceive international collaboration as a means to assure the greatest good for the greatest number, in accordance with their pragmatic utilitarian ethics. Communists could perceive collaboration with societies of different social and economic order as a means to liberate mankind from the oppression of poverty, hunger, and disease, and open the way to the all-round development of all human beings. Promoting the nascent trends in these directions now constitutes a moral obligation for all liberals and communists who are truly committed to the basic humanism of their respective world views.

The alternative cultures differ from both liberal democracy and Marxist communism in not being "institutionalized," and refusing to become so. They mistrust establishment doctrines whether on the left or on the right of the political spectrum. Yet they, too, could promote the expansion of the horizons of cooperation in the pursuit of global goals by realizing their own positive potentials. The outstanding potential of the alternative cultures resides in their commitment to finding new and harmonious ways of living, without demanding large quantities of material goods or living wasteful modes of life. Their sensitivity to human deprivation could influence other strata in relatively affluent societies to cooperate in the creation of a more equitable world economic order. Their awareness of one Earth, and their condemnation of war and violence, are further factors in their favor.

Among the negative characteristics of the alternative cultures we find an often excessive sense of grievance against society, which leads many vigorous young people to totally reject working with or "within" the system and to seek, instead, the isolation of rural communes. There is also a tendency to withdraw through the use of psychedelic drugs and excessive preoccupation with inner experiences at the expense of individually and socially healthy activity. Many members of such groups develop a dependence on mystical leaders or disciplines as a compensation for their perceived failure in the "straight" world. Little is done to integrate their new patterns of work and new approaches to education in society, though there is a tendency to be serious to the point of dogmatic fanaticism about new endeavors and ideas. Concentration on the present can also lead to the lack of any serious sense of responsibility for the future.

A strong potential for furthering global solidarity lies in the alternative cultures' world concept. This is basically holistic, and embraces the whole human and natural realm. Their thinking has a strong affinity with the holism of oriental religions, as well as with some of the newer concepts of the ecological and social sciences. Indeed, the alternative cultures may effect a new synthesis between some of the traditional religions and the newest developments in the contemporary sciences, and translate this synthesis to the level of everyday experience and behavior.

Chapter 19

A World Solidarity Revolution

The achievement of world solidarity is the great imperative of our era. It is needed to expand mankind's current inner limits and prompt the espousal of global goals, bringing long-term benefit. Religions as well as secular modes of thought could promote its emergence.

Could world solidarity come about in time, and in all major parts of the world? This question cannot be answered with certainty. Yet the possibility of an almost universal and rapid growth of world solidarity can be demonstrated. We do so by outlining a few basic "scenarios" whereby adequate levels of solidarity spread among people in their own nation as well as in different nations. These are scenarios of an epochal advance in human concern and consciousness. We call this advance the world solidarity revolution.

Revolutions in ideas and commitment to action have occurred in the past and have had great impact on human affairs. Indeed, since the French Revolution of the eighteenth century, most of the great social transformations, including the revolutions in Russia and China, have had an "ideological" background and motivation. We are in the midst of another revolution in consciousness today, activated by the spread of communications and technology. It is a "revolution of rising expectations." As formerly backward and isolated masses of humanity enter into the interdependent global community, they recognize the universality of human rights, and compare their lot with that of more advanced peoples. Understandably, their demands and expectations rise dramatically. This rise in expectations has resulted in the formation of the Organization of Petroleum Exporting Countries (OPEC) and the developing nations' Group of 77; in demands for a new international economic order; and in shifting balances of power.

There are other shockwaves of worldwide consciousness which have traversed the international community—ecological consciousness, population consciousness, exhaustible-resources consciousness, all coming together in a new awareness of our planet as a fragile spaceship. These developments help prepare the way for a truly species-level humanism which may prove to be the indispensable means of achieving a sustainable, just, and humanly satisfying future.

There are people and groups in almost every society who are aware of the interaction and interdependence of the principal elements of today's global society, and wish to promote the development of collaborative world-level actions and policies. These people and groups form the advance guard of the next revolutionary advance in human thinking and commitment. How such an advance might unfold in reality can be illustrated by different "scenarios."

A Religion- and Science-led Scenario

In principle, any segment of a national population could take the lead in achieving a global level of consciousness and solidarity (although the most deprived and isolated segments are unlikely to do so). There are positive elements in the systems of value and belief held by political and religious leaders, business executives, scientists, and intellectuals. Indeed, as the charts of contemporary goals in Chapter 16 show, varying strata in different societies lead or lag with respect to global goals.

The initial distribution of goals depicted in Figure 19-1.A is inherently plausible, though somewhat optimistic. Many religious (REL) and intellectual (INT) (including scientific) communities are highly conscious of global problems and promote global solidarity for resolving them. We assume here that such communities have significant weight in the formulation of policies in the areas of security, population, conservation, lifestyles, etc. The question is, how does the globally conscious religious and intellectual community communicate its

Figure 19.1

Policies informed by long-range, global goals

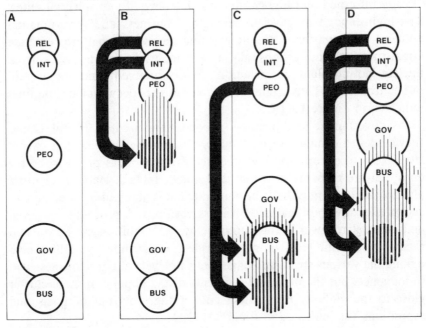

Policies motivated by short-range, provincial goals

insights to the people (PEO), the government (GOV), and business (BUS)?

It is possible that some scientific and religious leaders have direct access to political decision makers. Functioning as formal and informal advisors, they may directly influence the formulation of policies. But let us take a more difficult case, where the influence of scientists and religious leaders on policy formulation is not through direct channels, but through their prestige in the eyes of the people. In this scenario large middle-class urban groups look upon their leading scientists and intellectuals as possessed of superior wisdom, and broad rural masses attribute to their religious leaders the insight of prophets. Churches, temples, and religious gatherings serve as channels for the spread of global solidarity from religious leaders to the people; universities, popular scientific literature, and various scientific discussion forums serve in an analogous capacity for scientists.

Let us assume that such channels of communication are properly used; that the people's level of solidarity shows a rapid rise. (Figure 19-1.B) Even if this rise does not reach the levels of solidarity of the already informed and highly educated intellectual and spiritual elites, it is high enough to have an impact on business and governmental policies. New consumer preferences and new voting patterns emerge. Grass-roots pressure groups take up a number of relevant issues, from nuclear power plant construction, to disarmament and the use of public transport. Thus a change in goal settings occurs along the lines indicated in Figure 19-1.C.

As government and business become sensitized to global issues, they undergo changes in leadership. Progressive leaders and executives come to occupy the higher echelons; their ideas prove to be the ones that are responsive to public demand. Indeed, leading scientists and intellectuals may become motivated to enter public life, and to accept executive political and business positions. A process of national and cultural renewal is thus initiated which mobilizes all strata and raises the overall level of consciousness and solidarity. Differences among the various strata still exist, both in levels of consciousness and in influence, but the principal segments of the population now cluster close to the globally responsible end of the spectrum of goals and aspirations (as indicated in Figure 19-1.D).

A Government-led Scenario

The globally thinking segments of populations are not always confined solely to the religious and intellectual communities; some societies are fortunate enough to have a farsighted political leadership. Let us assume in this scenario that the government is both farsighted and powerful, and that the religious and intellectual communities, while informed and committed, have considerably less influence. We further assume that the masses of the people do not possess much feeling of solidarity beyond their own group, and that business interests exploit public shortsightedness and thus lag still further behind (Figure 19-2.A).

The task of the government in this case is clearly to raise the average level of consciousness and solidarity in the country. Its first move may be to enlist the help of the intellectual and religious communities. To do this the government organizes forums for discussion and debate, and stimulates many forms of scientific, cultural, and spiritual participation in public affairs. It thereby increases the influence of the local intellectual and spiritual communities and gains added pres-

Figure 19.2

Policies informed by long-range, global goals

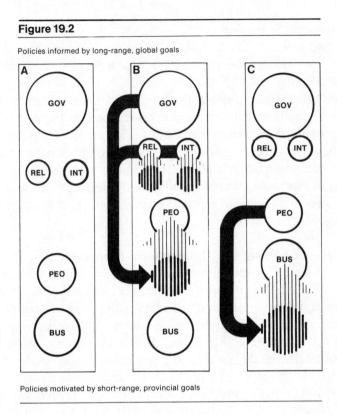

Policies motivated by short-range, provincial goals

tige through their support. The public media pay more attention to innovative ideas since they are now voiced not only by politicians, but also by scientists, humanists, and spiritual leaders. The joint impact on public opinion of organized religion, established science and art, and the political regime is becoming strong. Broad segments of the public are mobilized and come to espouse more appropriate aspirations. (Figure 19-2.B) Changes in consumer preferences affect the business community. Thus, if the first phase of the world solidarity revolution succeeds in raising the sights of the people, the second phase succeeds in bringing about adaptive changes in free-enterprise business practices (Figure 19-2.C). (In centrally planned economies the second phase of this scenario is folded into the first, since the business community is under government control.)

Other Domestic Scenarios

This second scenario can be further varied by assuming that the government has the confidence of the business leadership and can influence its thinking through debates, seminars, and workshops. This variation gains added plausibility if the committed leaders of the religious and intellectual communities participate in the events.

Other national scenarios might start with an informed and committed business elite, or without an organized religious community, or with only a minuscule scientific and intellectual group. The same principle of "spreading waves" applies in all instances, but with variations related to changes in the initial conditions, and to the specifics of the evolving situation.

A Business- and Science-led International Scenario

Since local nuclei of global awareness may not be present in every country, we need to contemplate scenarios in which a sense of mutual solidarity could be transferred internationally. Such a transfer need not follow the classical pattern in which one culture or ideology is imposed upon another. Every country possesses religions, world views, and cultures that could promote the growth of world solidarity. The need is merely to activate them. Through their international contacts scientists, intellectuals, and business and religious leaders can stimulate the growth of global thinking and commitment by calling attention to world problems and opportunities, and to the need for responsible action with respect to them on the part of all nations.

We present in Figure 19-3.A a scenario in which the world solidarity revolution spreads from country to country through business and scientific modes of communication, which operate quickly and efficiently. Both science and business are global in outreach, and their members have little difficulty in communicating with one another. Contacts are highly evolved and frequent; travel for meetings and consultations is worldwide. Cross-catalysis could occur easily and rapidly.

Businessmen and scientists are in contact with other strata of their society, including the political leadership and the public at large. Their own level of solidarity, heightened by their international professional contacts, can become a focal point for the domestic rise of global consciousness. Thus the international scenario relies on foreign contacts only in its initial stages; it becomes national as it progresses (Figure 19-3.B).

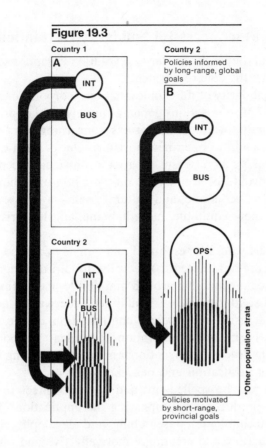

Figure 19.3

Country 1

A

INT

BUS

Country 2

Policies informed by long-range, global goals

B

INT

BUS

Country 2

INT

BUS

OPS*

*Other population strata

Policies motivated by short-range, provincial goals

Ideally, growth in commitment and solidarity needs to occur simultaneously both within and among the nations. Since global goals cannot be achieved unless most societies cooperate in their pursuit, the revolution in world solidarity can succeed anywhere only if it succeeds almost everywhere. Fortunately, the cultural and moral resources of all peoples and nations can be drawn upon, and neither the spread of a uniform system of values nor the imposition of foreign ideas is necessary. With the aid of modern communication channels, the revolution of world solidarity can spread at least as quickly as the present revolution of rising expectations. Indeed, unless this revolution does spread wide and fast, the new expectations are slated for early disappointment.

The Fruits of a Successful Solidarity Revolution

Assuming that the world solidarity revolution is rapid and widespread, what would be the concrete benefits?

The new solidarity of all peoples, nations, corporations, and organizations would prompt serious debates in many public, private, governmental, and nongovernmental forums concerning joint endeavors to head off crises and to open new horizons. Out of such debates would eventually emerge a consensus on a set of universally beneficial global goals. These would be seen as the *sine qua non* of achieving all other social, political, economic, and cultural goals—as the way to a future that is safer, more equitable, more humane, and less crisis-prone than the present.

Global goals would be espoused and actively pursued in areas that include (but are not limited to) security, food production, population trends, and socio-economic growth and development. Impelled by the rise of world solidarity, efforts would get underway to achieve global security by defusing the nuclear confrontation of the superpowers, stopping the horizontal proliferation of nuclear weapons, curtailing the burgeoning trade in conventional arms, and creating a more effective system of arbitration and peacekeeping.

Policies would be spelled out and put into effect to increase the world's food production by improving the application of appropriate agricultural technologies, researching and developing new methods of food production, and creating a more effective and just world food distribution system.

National policies would be coordinated to reduce high fertility rates by guaranteeing minimum living standards to the poorest populations, launching effective family planning programs, and making birth control devices widely available. Problems of urbanization would be handled through mutual aid, assistance programs, and exchange of information concerning ways to upgrade rural areas and check migration to the cities.

A new world economic order would be not merely discussed but actually implemented by switching to production methods that conserve resources and energy, and protect the environment; by selectively promoting the growth of services in industrialized countries and of basic industries in the developing world; and by coordinating the research, development, and worldwide application of safe and economical alternative energy and resource-use technologies.

Developmental assistance would be transformed from sporadic charity giving, and aid-with-strings, to an enduring compact between rich and poor nations. The affluent would provide loans, outright aid, and other forms of asistance through international channels, would provide indirect help by voluntarily reducing consumption of scarce and expensive resources, and would facilitate the transfer of appropriate science and technology. The international business community would help create a basis for economic self-reliance in developing countries through enlightened corporate policies. International financial bodies would attempt to make hard currencies accessible to rich and poor nations alike. Developing countries would, in turn, carefully select their strategies of development to make optimum use of the various forms of assistance made available to them, and create a sound basis for increasingly self-reliant development.

To implement such global goals, existing institutions would be reformed and adapted, and new institutions would be set up. Present institutions are "vertically" oriented, whereas global issues are "horizontal." Institutional reform would enable decision-making and implementation capabilities, appropriate for the specification and achievement of global goals, to be extended in the horizontal dimension. This process would start with the better coordination of existing institutions which have capabilities in the the areas of the global goals, and would continue with the creation of a few special horizontal agencies. Coordination would be assured first of all by the agencies of the United Nations. An enhanced role would be played by such U.N. bodies as the Security Council and the associated disarmament and peacekeeping agencies; the Food and Agriculture Organization and the World Food Council; the United Nations Fund for Population Activities, the Population Division of the Department of Economic and Social Affairs, and associated agencies; the various offices and centers of the Department of Economic and Social Affairs; and the U.N. Development Programme, Conference on Trade and Development, and Industrial Development Organization.

New horizontal institutions would grow on various levels, including the national, regional, and the corporate. Their creation would follow a pattern established in the past decade, when international bodies were established to meet specific emerging problems and needs (for example, in the area of the environment, space, the oceans, habitat, and so on). The new institutions would be specifically designed to monitor and assess the setting of goals at each major societal level.

They could be called GARDs: Goals Advisory and Research Departments (or Divisions). They would be consultative and advisory organs attached to national governments, regional organizations, and multinational corporations. Their overall coordination would be assured through a world-level GARD created as a specialized agency of the United Nations.

GARDs at ministries and departments of nation-states would be in regular contact with GARDs attached to the forecasting offices of major corporations, and with those operating within the framework of such regional bodies as the European Community, the Organization of African Union, the Association of Southeast Asian Nations, the Andes Pact countries, the CMEA, and so forth. The U.N. GARD would assemble and integrate the corporate, regional, and national goals reported by its worldwide counterparts, and conduct regular meetings of national, regional, and corporate GARD representatives to eliminate conflicts and inconsistencies. Its reports would be circulated to all member governments and furnish a matrix for the work of the United Nations system itself.

As national, regional, and corporate goals become better orchestrated, the implementation of global goals could be placed on the active agenda. This would necessitate the creation of the special-purpose international agencies suggested in Part II. These agencies would include a body capable of ensuring equitable access to and the necessary conservation of the natural resources of the "global commons"; a world energy organization, modeled after the present International Atomic Energy Agency, but entrusted with the multifold tasks of coordination and supervision of appropriate energy technologies; an international food agency, incorporating the functions of a world food bank along with related tasks currently shouldered by FAO, UNESCO, WHO, the World Food Council, and the Agricultural Development Fund; and an international disarmament supervision and peacekeeping body better balanced than the current Security Council, and more authoritative than the good-offices missions of the U.N. Secretary-General.

Through the birth of a spirit of world solidarity, the cooperative projects envisaged by the international community could be implemented. The world would change from an arena of marginal security and economic and political conflict, to a global society of undiminished diversity but firm collective self-reliance, greater security, and more equity.

Acknowledgments

The project director wishes to express special thanks and appreciation to the following groups of persons and institutions.

The Club of Rome. Beginning with informal exploratory discussions in the summer of 1974, Aurelio Peccei and Alexander King, dynamic and dedicated leaders of the Club, and later an ever-increasing number of members, have provided encouragement and inspiration, as well as incisive assessment and constructive criticism. Without these discussions this project could neither have begun nor have reached completion. Nobody associated with the Club of Rome is, however, responsible for the opinions expressed in this report, which is made *to* the Club and not *by* it.

The International Project Team. This team, composed of individual researchers and regional *ad hoc* research teams, incorporates persons of widely different backgrounds: from academic fields, from business, from government, as well as from the youth and alternative cultures. Unknown to each other with but few exceptions, they have shown a commitment to the joint task and an expertise and efficiency in carrying it out that went beyond all expectations. They provided the flesh to clothe the bare skeleton of the project concept and have done so at great investments of time and energy—and often also of personal and local funds, as expenses exceeded the relatively modest project budgets.

The Project Consultants. Consultants worked both with the project offices and directly with the members of the international project team. People of considerable accomplishment and often of leading position, they gave unstintingly of their busy time. Their comments and suggestions were at all times gratefully received and seriously considered. If they could not always be fully incorporated in the final text it was because of restrictions of space and the need to choose between divergent, and in some cases even conflicting, viewpoints and positions. Thus they bear no direct responsibility for the final shape of the diverse sections of this report.

The Panel of Distinguished Advisors. The advice of these internationally renowned individuals has been particularly valued, even if opportunities to work closely together have been less frequent than with the consultants. Their interest and encouragement have been important factors in the implementation of the complex tasks of this project. That they should agree with its conclusions in all respects may be too much to ask, but that they may feel that their confidence was not misplaced is sincerely hoped.

The Project Staff. Coordination of the work of over a hundred individuals in all corners of the world poses formidable problems of logistics. The project staff at both the Geneseo and the UNITAR locations performed on the whole admirably, and provided important back-up with the research itself. A core project group of mostly young and enthusiastic investigators should be remembered in this context. Although by the end of the summer of 1975 the need to assemble an international project team was evident, many of the initial core group remained with the project and provided valuable inputs.

The Aspen Institute for Humanistic Studies. On the invitation of Joseph Slater, its president, the project director and the majority of the initial core group spent over a month at the Institute's beautiful Colorado location. Informal discussions during that time with many eminent persons, including Harlan Cleveland, Douglass Cater, George W. Ball, Thomas W. Wilson, Jr., and others have aided immeasurably in crystallizing the basic concept of the research tasks and in deciding upon the ways and means of carrying them out.

The International Institute of Applied Systems Analysis (IIASA). A similar period of in-house research was conducted at IIASA's sumptuous headquarters in Schloss Laxenburg, near Vienna. There many opportunities presented themselves for formal and informal discussions with experts from both Western and communist nations, and these have further helped clarify the nature and the magnitude of the research tasks.

The United Nations Institute for Training and Research (UNITAR). At the invitation of Davidson Nicol, UNITAR's distinguished director, and on the initiative of Philippe De Seynes, former U.N. Under-Secretary-General and leader of the Project on the Future, a project office was established at the United Nations in October of 1975. This office, which functioned for the remainder of the project life span, proved to be invaluable both for handling the complex logistics of research coordination and in providing access to experts and leaders from all parts of the world. It made it possible to realize many of the plans and ideas which multiplied constantly and often terrifyingly throughout the period of work.

Thanks and appreciation are due also to the National Science Foundation, Washington, which provided the greater part of the project funds, and to a few individual contributors who prefer to remain unnamed. The funds were ably administered by the Research Foundation of the State University of New York.

It is impossible to acknowledge here by name all the individuals and institutions who expressed interest in our work and provided advice and information on matters of relevance. We hope that their interest and assistance will continue in the future, as we confront new tasks in carrying forth the work which here was merely begun.

E. L.
November 1976

References

A Note to the Reader
This report is addressed to the general public, and consequently the heavy use of footnotes and references is avoided. Directly quoted source materials are usually identified in the text; where the identification is not sufficient or the reference is indirect, the sources are listed below.

Not listed here (unless directly quoted in the text) are the following types of materials:

National and international documents from official sources (government white or green papers, Party Programs, national development or five-year plans, documents of the U.N. and other international organizations, and so on)

Standard writings on world religions, liberal democracy, and Marxism

Standard writings on world security, food, energy, resource, population, and development issues

Published works in these areas are public knowledge, and a detailed bibliography would demand a separate volume in itself. Like-

428

wise omitted are the sources of confidential surveys and personal interviews by members of the international project team.

Readers interested in more detailed documentation may consult *Goals in a Global Community: Original Studies of the Goals for Mankind Report to the Club of Rome* (edited by Ervin Laszlo and Judah Bierman) of which Volume I contains studies on the conceptual foundations, and Volume II, the international values and goals studies.

Ali, A. Yusuf, *The Holy Qur-an.* Dar al-Arabia 1968 (*Islam and World Solidarity*)

Berlinguer, Enrico, *Unità del popolo per salvare l'Italia* (Unity of the People to Save Italy). Speech at the 14th National Congress of the PCI, March 1974. Editori Riuniti, Rome 1975. (*Goals of the Community Party of Italy*)

Blainey, Geoffrey, *The Tyranny of Distance.* Sun Books, Melbourne 1966. (*Goals in Australia*)

Boulding, Kenneth, The Economics of the Coming Spaceship Earth, in *Environmental Quality in a Growing Economy.* Johns Hopkins Press, Baltimore 1966. (*Resource and Development Goals*)

Brown, Lester, An Overview of World Trends, *The Futurist,* December 1972 (*Food Goals*)

Cleveland, Harlan, *The Planetary Bargain.* Aspen Institute for Humanistic Studies, New York 1975 (*Development Goals*)

Collectif, *Manuel de la vie pauvre* (Handbook of the Poor Life), Paris 1974; and *le Catalogue des resources* (The Catalogue of Resources), Paris 1975. (*Goals of European Alternative Cultures*)

Colloques Internationaux du Centre National de la Recherche Scientifique, *La notion de personne en Afrique Noire* (The Concept of the Person in Black Africa). Editions du CNRS, Paris 1973. (*African Traditions and World Solidarity*)

Commission of the Churches on International Affairs, *Human Rights Basic Programme Paper.* World Council of Churches, Geneva, February 1974. (*Goals of the World Council of Churches*)

Dahl, Robert A., *Democracy in the United States.* Rand McNally, Chicago 1972. (*Liberal Democracy and World Solidarity*)

Documenti CEI (Documents of CEI, the Italian Episcopate). CEI, Rome 1974, 1975. (*Goals of the Roman Catholic Church*)

Dutt, Sukumar, *The Buddha and the Five After-Centuries.* Luzac, London 1957. (*Buddhism and World Solidarity*)

Enayat, Hamid, The Interrelation of Cultural Disputes with International Conflicts. *Inter-National Relations Quarterly,* 1974.3. Tehran. (*Goals in the Middle East*)

Feinberg, Gerald, Some Hopes and Doubts About Technological Answers to Future Materials Problems, in *Political Economy of International Resource Flows,* G. Garvey, ed., forthcoming. (*Resource Goals*)

Feld, N. T., et al. (eds.), *The Impact of New Technologies in the Arms Race.* Proceedings of the Pugwash Conference. M.I.T. Press, Cambridge, Mass. 1970. (*Security Goals*)

Ford Motor Company, *Ford: A Catalyst for Economic Progress.* Dearborn 1974. (*Goals of Multinationals*)

Fraser, Hon. Malcolm, *National Objectives—Social, Economic and Political Goals.* 46th ANZAAS Congress, November 1975. (*Goals in Australia*)

Girvetz, Harry T., *The Evolution of Liberalism.* Collier, New York 1963. (*Liberal Democracy and World Solidarity*)

Greenwood, T., et al. (ed.), *Nuclear Proliferation: Motivations, Capabilities, and Strategies of Control. 1980s Project.* McGraw-Hill, New York 1977. (*Security Goals*)

Hankiss, Elemér, Változások a társadalom értéktudatában (Changes in Society's Value Consciousness). *Kultúra és Közösség* 1974.4. Budapest. (*Goals in Hungary*)

Harrington, R. E., *Deere Activities in Connection with Agriculture in Developing Countries.* Deere and Co., Product Planning Department, April 1976. (*Goals of Multinationals*)

Harris, Louis, The Emerging Shape of Politics for the Rest of the 1970s. Remarks to the National Conference of State Legislators, Philadelphia, October 7, 1975; and unpublished poll data, September 16, 1975. (*Goals in the United States*)

Hubbard, M. King, The Energy Resources of the Earth, in *Energy and Power,* The Scientific American, W. H. Freeman and Company, San Francisco 1971. (*Energy Goals*)

Huddle, F. P., *The Evolution and Dynamics of National Goals in the United States.* Study prepared for the Committee on Interior and Insular Affairs, U.S. Senate, March 1974. (*Goals in the United States*)

International Management and Development Institute, *Top Management Report on Corporate Citizenship in the Global Community,* Washington, D.C., January, 1976. (*Goals of Multinationals*)

Johnson, D. E. (ed.), *Uppsala to Nairobi, 1968–1975.* Report of the Central Committee of the Fifth Assembly of the World Council of Churches. Friendship Press Spak, New York and London 1975. (*Goals of the World Council of Churches*)

Kanyechamba, G. W., *Constitutional Law and Government in Uganda.* E.A.L.B., Nairobi 1975. (*Goals in East and Central Arfica*)

Kaunda, K., *National Council of United National Independence Party.* Zambia 1967. (*Goals in East and Central Africa*)

King, Alexander, *Report on the State of the Planet* (forthcoming). (*Global Goals*)

Kühl, P. H. and Koch-Nielsen, I., *Fritid 1975* (Leisure-time 1975). Danish National Institute for Social Research, Copenhagen 1976. (*Goals in Scandinavia*)

Lalèyê, I.-P., La Conception de la personne dans la pensée traditionelle Yoruba, "approche phénoménologique" (The Conception of the Person in Traditional Yoruba Thought, a Phenomenological Approach). Publications universitaires Européennes XX/3, Berne 1970; and *La Palabre Africaine, école de liberté* (African Discourse, School of Liberty), Presses Universitaires du Zaire, Kinshasa 1977. (*African Traditions and World Solidarity*)

Lecht, L. A., *Changes in National Priorities During the 1960s.* National Planning Association, Washington, D.C. 1972. (*Goals in the United States*)

Liu Ta-nien, *Chung-Kuo Chin-tai Shih Chu Wen-ti* (Problems in Modern Chinese History). Peking 1965. (*Goals in China*)

Lov om arbeidervaern og arbeidsmiljø, Saertrykk (Law for Workers' Protection and the Work Environment, a Special Print). Kommunal og arbeids-dept., Oslo 1976. (*Goals in Scandinavia*)

Maisonrouge, J. G., Summary Statement. Hearing before the group of eminent persons. United Nations Economic and Social Council, United Nations 1973. (*Goals of Multinationals*)

Making Work More Human: Working Conditions and Environment. Report of the Director-General to the International Labour Conference. International Labour Office, Geneva, June 1976. (*Goals of the I.L.O.*)

Mates, Leo, Personal Communications. (*Goals in Yugoslavia*)

McHale, J., and McHale, M. C., *Human Requirements, Supply Levels and Outer Bounds.* The Aspen Institute for Humanistic Studies, New York 1975. (*Food and Resource Goals*)

Meadows, D. L., et al., *Dynamics of Growth in a Finite World,* Wright-Allen Press, Cambridge, Mass. 1974. (*Resource Goals*)

Morse, David A., *Origin and Evolution of the ILO and Its Role in the World Community.* Cornell University Press, Ithaca 1969. (*Goals of the I.L.O.*)

Murphy, T. A., The Impact of Multinational Corporations on the Development Process. Statement on behalf of General Motors to the group of eminent persons. United Nations Economic and Social Council, United Nations 1973. (*Goals of Multinationals*)

Nasr, S. H., *Ideals and Realities of Islam.* Beacon Press, Boston 1972. (*Islam and World Solidarity*)

National Goals Research Staff, *Toward Balanced Growth: Quantity with Quality.* U.S. Government Printing Office, Washington, D.C. 1970. (*Goals in the United States*)

Nyerere, J., *Man and Development,* Tanzania Publishing House, Tanzania 1974; and *Freedom and Development,* Tanzania Publishing House, Tanzania 1974. (*Goals in East and Central Africa*)

Ogot, B. A., ed. Zamani, *A Survey of East African History,* E.A.P.H., Nairobi 1928. (*Goals in East and Central Africa*)

Pardue, Peter, *Buddhism: A Historical Introduction to Buddhist Values and the Social and Political Form They Have Assumed in Asia.* Macmillan, New York 1968. (*Buddhism and World Solidarity*)

Philips in the Developing Countries. N. V. Philips Gloeilampenfabrieken, Eindhoven 1974. (*Goals of Multinationals*)

Piekarski, A., *Szkice o kosciele w Polsce: Fakty, liczby, informacje* (Briefs on the Church in Poland: Facts, Numbers, Information). Interpress, Warsaw 1974. (*Goals in Poland*)

President's Commission on National Goals, *Goals for Americans.* Prentice-Hall, New York 1960. (*Goals in the United States*)

Proceedings, Man and Resources Conference. Canadian Council of Resource and Environment Ministers. Montreal, 1973. (*Goals in Canada*)

Prokol-Gruppe, *Der Sanfte Weg* (Prokol Group, *The Smooth Way*), Stuttgart 1976. (*Goals of European Alternative Cultures*)

Rabier, J. R., *Satisfaction et insatisfaction quant aux conditions de vie* (Satisfaction and dissatisfaction concerning conditions of life). Brussels, June 1976; and *l'Europe vue par les Européens* (Europe Seen by Europeans). Brussels, August 1976. (*Goals in the European Community*)

Ruggiero, Guido de, *The History of European Liberalism.* Oxford University Press, London 1927. (*Liberal Democracy and World Solidarity*)

Science and Technology for Canada's Energy Needs. Report of the Task Force on Energy Research and Development to the Minister of Energy, Mines and Resources. Ottawa, 1975. (*Goals in Canada*)

Science Council of Canada, *Towards a National Science Policy for Canada.* Report No. 4. Ottawa 1968. (*Goals in Canada*)

Seaborg, Glenn T., 1994: The Recycle Society, in *Energy: Today's Choices Tomorrow's Opportunities.* Anton B. Schmalz, ed., The World Future Society, Washington, D.C. 1974. (*Resource Goals*)

Seers, Dudley, New Approaches Suggested by the Colombian Employment Programme. *International Labour Review,* 102.4. October 1970. (*Goals of the I.L.O.*)

Siçinski, A., Prognozowanie a planowanie spokeczne w systemie gospodarki socjalistycznej (Forecasting and Social Planning in the Socialist Economic System), in *Polityka gospodarcza a polityka społeczna.* KiW, Warsaw 1976. (*Goals in Poland*)

Situationist International, *Leaving the 20th Century*. London 1974. (*Goals of European Alternative Cultures*)

SODEPAX, *The Churches and the Search for a Just and Sustainable World Society*, Discussion Paper. December 1975. (*Goals of the World Council of Churches and of the Roman Catholic Church*)

Spekke, Andrew A. (ed.), *The Next 25 Years: Crisis and Opportunity*. The World Future Society, Washington, D.C. 1975. (*Food, Energy, Resource, and Development Goals*)

Stockholm International Peace Research Institute, *World Armaments—Abundance Amid Scarcity*. SIPRI, Stockholm 1976. (*Security Goals*)
Strategy for International Development Cooperation, 1975–1980. Canadian International Development Agency, Secretary of State for External Affairs, Ottawa 1975. (*Goals in Canada*)

Tévoèdjré, Albert, *For a Contract of Solidarity*. Report of the Secretary-General to the World Symposium on the Social Implications of a New International Economic Order. Geneva, January 1976. (*Goals of the I.L.O.*)

The Gallup-Kettering Global Survey on Human Needs and Satisfactions. Selected Documents, The Kettering Foundation, Dayton, Ohio 1976. (*Causes of the Goals Gap*)

Tinbergen, Jan, et al., *Reshaping the International Order;* a Report to the Club of Rome. Dutton, New York 1976. (*Development Goals*)

Unilever's Role as a Multinational Business; and *Unilever and World Development*. Unilever Ltd., Rotterdam and London 1973. (*Goals of Multinationals*)

Vitányi, Iván, Etikai világkép, etikai magatartás (Ethical World View and Ethical Behavior). *Valóság,* 1976.7. Budapest; and Összefoglaló a müvelödésszociológiai kutatások eddigi eredményeiröl (Summary of So-far Achieved Results of Investigations in Sociology of Culture). *Collection of Selected Documents*. OKT, Budapest 1976. (*Goals in Hungary*)

Wagner, G. A., The Impact of Multinational Corporations on Development and on International Relations. Statement on behalf the Royal Dutch Company to the group of eminent persons. United Nations Economic and Social Council, United Nations 1973. (*Goals of Multinationals*)

Watts, W. and Free, L., *The State of the Nation, 1972*. Potomac Associates, Washington, D.C. 1973; and *The State of the Nation, 1974*. Potomac Associates, Washington, D.C. 1976; and Hopes and Fears of the American People. *Potomac Associates Policy Perspectives,* Washington, D.C., 1977. (*Goals in the United States*)

Willrich, M. and Taylor, T. B., *Nuclear Theft: Risks and Safeguards*. Ballinger, Cambridge, Mass. 1974. (*Security and Energy Goals*)

Wilson, Thomas W. Jr., *World Food: The Political Dimension.* Aspen Institute for Humanistic Studies, New York 1974. (*Food Goals*)

Wittwer, S. W., Priorities and Needed Outputs in Food Production, *Food Technology,* September 1975; and Maximum Production Capacity of Food Crops, *Bioscience,* 24.4., April 1974. (*Food Goals*)

Working Group on Church and Society, *Energy for a Just and Sustainable Society.* World Council of Churches, Geneva, July 1976; and *Report on Social Responsibility in a Technological Age,* Reports from the Nairobi Assembly. World Council of Churches, Geneva, January 1976. (*Goals of the World Council of Churches*)

Zulu, J. B., *Zambian Humanism.* Lusaka 1970. (*Goals in East and Central Africa*)